HEART OF AMERICAN DARKNESS

ALSO BY ROBERT G. PARKINSON

The Common Cause:
Creating Race and Nation in the American Revolution

Thirteen Clocks:
How Race United the Colonies and
Made the Declaration of Independence

HEART OF AMERICAN DARKNESS

BEWILDERMENT AND HORROR ON THE EARLY FRONTIER

ROBERT G. PARKINSON

W. W. NORTON & COMPANY

Independent Publishers Since 1923

For information about permission to reproduce selections from this book, write to
Permissions, W. W. Norton & Company, Inc., 500 Fifth Avenue,
New York, NY 10110

For information about special discounts for bulk purchases, please contact
W. W. Norton Special Sales at specialsales@wwnorton.com or 800-233-4830

Manufacturing by Lakeside Book Company
Book design by Daniel Lagin
Production manager: Anna Oler

Library of Congress Cataloging-in-Publicaton Data Available

ISBN 978-1-324-09177-6

W. W. Norton & Company, Inc.
500 Fifth Avenue, New York, N.Y. 10110
www.wwnorton.com

W. W. Norton & Company Ltd.
15 Carlisle Street, London W1D 3BS

1 2 3 4 5 6 7 8 9 0

For Julia

CONTENTS

DRAMATIS PERSONAE

Adlum, John (1759–1836) Revolutionary War soldier from Pennsylvania captured by the British in New York City in 1776, later started a surveying business, which brought him to northeastern Pennsylvania where he met Cornplanter and Tod-kah-dos in 1794.

Bouquet, Colonel Henry (1719–1765) British officer who fought in Seven Years' War and Pontiac's War. Commander at Fort Pitt in 1760s.

Braddock, General Edward (1695–1755) British commander sent to eject French in 1755, killed at Battle of the Monongahela.

Carleton, Sir Guy (1724–1808) British Army officer and governor of Canada in 1770s. Becomes principal villain of patriots during Revolutionary War.

Clark, George Rogers (1752–1818) Business associate of Michael Cresap in 1770s, military leader in Dunmore's War. His exploits in the Revolutionary War earned him the nickname Conqueror of the Illinois.

Connolly, Dr. John (c.1745–c.1798) Dunmore's representative for Virginia at Pittsburgh in 1770s border dispute; leader during Dunmore's War, and plotted during the Revolution. He was a correspondent and associate of Washington, and was rumored to be George Croghan's nephew.

Cornplanter (?–1836) Seneca leader who fought with Iroquois and British in Revolutionary War. Advised neutrality in 1790s and would receive the first reservation in US history, known as the Cornplanter Tract, in 1796, where Tachnedorus and Tod-kah-dos came to live. His daughter married Tod-kah-dos.

Cornstalk (1720?–1777) Shawnee leader and commander of Native forces at the Battle of Point Pleasant (1774). Negotiated end of Dunmore's War, and attempted to maintain neutrality with patriots during Revolutionary War. Murdered by settlers at Fort Randolph in 1777.

Crawford, William (1722–1782) Virginian and officer in Washington's Virginia Regiment during Seven Years' War. Later moved to Pennsylvania and became Washington's land agent and a Pennsylvania county officer. Switches sides during Pennsylvania–Virginia border dispute. Active officer during Revolutionary War. Captured and ritually murdered by Ohio Natives at end of Revolutionary War.

Cresap, Daniel (1728–1798) Eldest son of Thomas Cresap. Bought and lived at an estate in the Conococheague settlement (Williamsport, Maryland). Original partner in the Ohio Company. Sons Michael, Daniel Jr., and Joseph served with Captain Michael Cresap in Dunmore's War and Revolutionary War.

Cresap, Captain Michael (1742–1775) Youngest son of Thomas Cresap. Born in Oldtown, operated stores in Redstone and Wheeling and became land scout, partnering with George Rogers Clark. Fought in Dunmore's War and commanded a rifle company in their march to Massachusetts in 1775. Married to Mary Whitehead; they had five children, three daughters and two sons.

Cresap, Colonel Thomas (c. 1700–1787) Patriarch of Cresap family and allegedly the first to use the word "frontiersman." Gained fame in border dispute between Pennsylvania and Maryland in 1730s; founder of Oldtown, Maryland; original partner in Ohio Company. He was a trader, speculator, surveyor, justice of the peace, assemblyman, and militia officer.

Cresap, Thomas, Jr. (1734–1756) Middle son of Cresap family; killed in combat during the Seven Years' War.

Croghan, George (c.1718–1782) Rival and nemesis of Thomas Cresap. The leading Pennsylvania trader in goods with Natives, British Indian superintendent deputy 1756–1771; involved in many land deals. Had own claim to two hundred thousand acres just to west of Pittsburgh; also partner in "Suffering Traders" scheme and Vandalia colony project. Active negotiator with Natives during Dunmore's War.

Draper, Lyman Copeland (1815–1891) Starting in the 1830s, became one of the leading historians and archivists of the late eighteenth-century Ohio, collecting many documents and conducting many interviews. He would become the leading force behind the State Historical Society of Wisconsin, depositing his trove of papers there.

Dunmore, Lord (1730–1809) Royal governor of New York (1770–71) and Virginia (1771–76). Instigated and perpetuated Virginia–Pennsylvania border dispute that led to Dunmore's War; personally negotiated end at Treaty of Camp Charlotte. When Revolutionary War began, he fought against Virginia patriots and issued an emancipation proclamation offering freedom to enslaved people who fought for the Crown.

Gage, General Thomas (1718/19–787) With Braddock at Battle of the Monongahela; became commander-in-chief of British Army after Seven Years' War throughout late 1760s–70s. Sent to Boston in 1774 to put down rebellion.

Gibson, Colonel George Jr. (1775–1861) Son of George Gibson who was a Virginia partisan in 1774 at Pittsburgh. Nephew of John Gibson. He joined the U.S. Army, served in the War of 1812, and became commissary general until the Civil War, where he supervised the logistics of Indian Removal.

Gibson, John (1740–1822) Indian trader; taken captive in Pontiac's War. He married Koonay and their child survived the Yellow Creek massacre. He was the translator and transcriber of Logan's Lament. Sided with patriots in 1775, helped expose the Connolly/Dunmore plot, became a general in the Continental Army, and an early territorial governor of Indiana.

Gist, Christopher (1706–1759) Scout and colleague of Thomas Cresap, especially active in 1740s–early 1750s with Ohio Company.

Greathouse, Daniel (c.1752–1778) Colonial settler in 1770s on Ohio River in what is now West Virginia. Ringleader of Yellow Creek massacre.

Guyasuta (1725–1794) Seneca leader of Ohio Natives in 1770s, involved in Pontiac's War. Lead negotiator in Ohio in 1770s; met Washington several times. Instrumental diplomat during Dunmore's War. Was hostile to United States during Revolutionary War.

Hamilton, Colonel Henry (c. 1734–1796) Lieutenant governor of Canada during Revolutionary War, stationed at Detroit. Patriots called him the Hair Buyer because of his reputation for encouraging Natives to scalp Americans during the Revolution. Captured at Vincennes in 1778, and put on trial in Williamsburg for encouraging Native resistance.

Hillsborough, Earl of (1718–1793) President of the Board of Trade and first American secretary of state. Was in and out of power in the 1760s–70s. Hardliner against Americans in imperial crisis; hostile to all western development; enemy of Vandalia colony project.

Jefferson, Thomas (1743–1826) Author of *Notes on the State of Virginia*, which features Logan's Lament and established Logan's fame. Subsequent controversy over its inclusion led him to investigate the Yellow Creek massacre in 1797–99.

Johnson, Guy (c. 1740–1788) Nephew of Sir William Johnson, assumed his position as Indian superintendent after his death in 1774. Became principal villain of patriots during Revolutionary War.

Johnson, Sir William (c.1715–1774) British Indian superintendent, 1755–1774. Lived at Johnson Hall in Johnstown, New York. Had significant political influence with the Iroquois/Six Nations.

Killbuck, John (1737–1811) Leader of Delaware Natives in Ohio, grandson of Neawatwees. Challenged Thomas Cresap to a duel in 1760s; became lead negotiator in Ohio in 1770s. Maintained friendship with patriots during Revolutionary War.

Lee, Thomas (c.1690–1750) Virginia Northern Neck planter who, with Fairfaxes and Washingtons, created the Ohio Company. Land manager for Fairfax Grant. Became interim Virginia governor and member of Governor's Council.

Logan, James (1674–1751) Famous, controversial Pennsylvania Indian agent; secretary to William Penn. With Shickellamy, was a chief architect of the Walking Purchase (1737). Their relationship was so strong that Shickellamy named two sons after him.

Logan, Jesse (1809–1916) Grandson of Tachnedorus, son of Tod-kah-dos, father of James Logan. Lived at Cornplanter Reservation throughout nineteenth century.

Martin, Luther (1748–1826) Attorney who became Maryland's first attorney general after independence, and held the job for decades. Married Michael Cresap's daughter Maria in 1783. Initially an anti-Federalist, became a Federalist and launched a campaign against Jefferson in 1797 for getting his facts wrong in *Notes*.

Mayer, Brantz (1809–1879) Founder of the Maryland Historical Society in 1844, gave a lecture called "Tah-Gah-Jute: Or Cresap and Logan" in 1851 and developed it into a popular 1867 book.

Scarouyady (?–1758) Oneida; Six Nations' agent to Ohio Natives in 1750s; colleague of Tanaghrisson. Ally of Pennsylvania early in Seven Years' War, worked with Sir William Johnson.

Shickellamy (c.1700–1748) Oneida; patriarch of Shickellamy clan. Agent of Iroquois/Six Nations at Shamokin; close ally of Pennsylvania Indian agent James Logan, named two sons after him. Lead Native orchestrator of Walking Purchase.

Shickellamy, John Petty (?–1774) Cayuga; youngest son of Shickellamy.

Shickellamy, Koonay (1741–1774) Cayuga; daughter of Shickellamy. Married John Gibson in 1770s; their young child survived the Yellow Creek massacre.

Shickellamy, Neanoma (?–1774) Cayuga, married to Shickellamy. Mother of two daughters (Cajadis and Koonay) and five sons. Three of them (Tachnedorus, Soyechtowa, John Petty Shickellamy) would go on to be important political figures in backcountry. Another died in infancy, and a fifth, "Unhappy Jake," died fighting the Catawbas.

Shingas (?–1764?) Delaware; leader of devastating raids on Pennsylvania and Maryland in 1755–56.

Soyechtowa (James Logan Shickellamy) (1725–1780) Cayuga; second son of Shickellamy; becomes known in 1770s as the "famous Mingo chief" Logan. Perhaps also known as Tah-gah-jute.

St. Clair, Arthur (1737–1818) Soldier in Seven Years' War, farmer in Pennsylvania in 1760s. Became leader for Pennsylvania in Virginia–Pennsylvania border dispute. General in Continental Army during Revolutionary War, but often in disgrace. Later governor-general of Northwest Territory in 1788 and was responsible for one of the worst defeats in American military history in 1791.

Tachnedorus (John Logan Shickellamy) (1718–1820?) Cayuga; oldest son of Shickellamy; also known as Captain John Logan. Iroquois ambassador in 1750s–60s; father of Tod-kah-dos; lived in Juniata valley from late 1760s until moving with his son to Cornplanter's tract in the early 1800s.

Tanaghrisson (c.1700–1754) Seneca; Six Nations' agent for Ohio Natives in 1750s. With Washington at Jumonville's Glen in 1754. Also known as Half King.

Tod-kah-dos (?–1844) Son of Tachnedorus, father of Jesse Logan; lived with his father Tachnedorus in the Juniata River valley region, later on the Cornplanter reservation in early 1800s. Married Cornplanter's daughter, Annie.

Walpole, Thomas (1727–1803) British banker and member of Parliament, nephew to Sir Robert Walpole, prime minister of England from 1721–42. He was the lead investor of the Vandalia colony project.

Washington, George (1732–1799) Inherited Ohio Company stock; had extensive land claims in Ohio Valley as a result of his military service to Virginia in Seven Years' War; went to Pittsburgh and down Ohio River in 1770 to investigate claims where he met John Connolly, Guyasuta. Had land disputes with Michael Cresap over Ohio River bottomlands, which would be in courts throughout his time as Continental Army commander and president of the United States.

Weiser, Conrad (1696–1760) The most important Pennsylvania Indian agent of the early eighteenth century. Close associate and friend of Shickellamy family.

Wharton, Samuel (1732–1800) One of the heads of the important Philadelphia merchant firm Baynton, Wharton, and Morgan, and associate of George Croghan and William Trent. Became lobbyist and leader of "Suffering Traders" and Vandalia colony project.

White Eyes, Captain (c. 1730–1778) Delaware leader who rose to prominence in the Ohio Valley in the 1770s, died under mysterious conditions in 1778, at the hands of colonial settlers.

IN THE MIDST OF THE
INCOMPREHENSIBLE

"There is no initiation either into such mysteries. He has to live
in the midst of the incomprehensible, which is also detestable.
And it has a fascination, too, that goes to work upon him."

—*Heart of Darkness*

On the final day of April 1774, the *Minerva* was plying the waters
of the Atlantic Ocean, headed for Boston. On board were London newspapers bearing the first news of England's response to the Tea
Party. Bostonians would soon learn that, as punishment, the Crown had
decided to close the port, a step that would spark a civil war in the British empire. Hours before the *Minerva*'s lookout spied Boston Harbor,
seven Native people crossed a smaller body of water as they traveled to
a meeting that they hoped would prevent a similar breakdown in relations with colonial settlers. The party knew the trip put them in mortal
danger and yet they went anyway; it's what their family had done for
more than four decades.[1]

That family had negotiated relationships between Natives and colonists since the 1730s. So despite whatever apprehensions they might have
had, they climbed into their canoes and let a tributary called Yellow Creek
carry them about a mile down to the Ohio River. Today, they would
have passed under Ohio Route 7 and a graffiti-covered railroad trestle
right as they caught the big river's course. Paddling against the current,

Figure 1. The mouth of Yellow Creek as it joins the Ohio River. On the opposite shore is Baker's Bottom, now the site of the Mountaineer Casino and Racetrack.

they soon reached their destination, a small log cabin that sat just up from the eastern shore on a piece of ground known as Baker's Bottom.

The seven Natives—four men, two women, and a baby—were invited into the cabin's front room, where a few colonists poured them drinks and allegedly launched into a conventional ceremony of keeping peace. Things were tense, but the alcohol helped. The two groups joked with one another. One of the colonial hosts had a British regimental uniform. As they all got a little tipsy, a Native man put on the red coat and paraded around the room. Someone proposed a shooting contest as a diversion and perhaps to further clear the air. Several went outside and identified a target. You go first, the white men told the Natives, and the latter fired, leaving themselves disarmed. The trap was sprung.

There were more than a dozen colonists hiding in the back room of the cabin. When the shooting started, the crouching, silent men leapt into action, running out into the yard, advancing on the unsuspecting Natives, who turned and sprinted for their canoes. Bullets took down one man, then another and another, spilling blood over the ground as acrid gunsmoke rose into the air. An elderly woman also fell. A second Native woman clutched her baby and ran for the water's edge. When she realized escape was impossible, she turned and begged the men to spare the child's life. She's the daughter of a white man, the mother pleaded about her child, hoping that might convince them. They paused and allowed her to hand over the baby before shooting her in the face.

Three more Natives, worried about what might be happening across the way, had come looking for their relations. They were caught in the middle of the river when the colonists fired away, killing two of them, too. One, a woman, survived, but was gravely wounded and barely made it to the other side.

In all, eight Native people would perish in the horror at Yellow Creek on April 30, 1774. In contrast to many stories from America's history about Native-European encounters, where we know little about the lives of half of the participants, in this case we know several of the victims well. We know their family biography. They were the family of Shickellamy, one of the most significant Iroquois leaders of the mid-eighteenth century. His importance lay in the role he had played as an ambassador for his people: decades before, the Six Nations tasked him with checking white colonists' desires for more and more land along a different river, the Susquehanna, east of the Ohio Valley. He befriended the man who was in many respects his opposite, James Logan, Pennsylvania's agent tasked with satiating colonists' thirst for land. Shickellamy honored his friend and colleague by giving two of his sons the name Logan. Those boys would become Native negotiators in their own right. The Shickellamys were one of the most prominent political families in North America in the middle of the eighteenth century. They had tried for a generation to forge deals between colonists and Natives. They had participated in and shaped many of the most consequential events in the history of colonial America. Despite their efforts, they had largely failed and now nearly all of them were dead. Shickellamy's wife, youngest son, and a daughter were among the slain at Yellow Creek.

The interpretative paths we have constructed to help guide us through the baffling, bewildering forests of early America struggle with horrific scenes like these. One of the most prominent of these paths was blazed by a thirty-two-year-old historian named Frederick Jackson Turner. Delivered as an address in 1893 at an exposition commemorating the four hundredth anniversary of Columbus's voyage to the New World, Turner's "The Significance of the Frontier to American History" is widely considered to be among the most influential pieces of writing about American history.[2]

How Turner reached his conclusions has become its own legend. As the story goes, Turner gathered the ideas that would become his "frontier thesis" after reading the results of the 1890 census. The bureaucrats in the Census Office proclaimed that the frontier, a line of "settlement" that had steadily advanced across the continent throughout the eighteenth and nineteenth centuries, was now closed; it was a relic of the past. Turner read this report with alarm. It compelled him to investigate what effect

Figure 2. Frederick Jackson Turner, 1902.

the frontier had had on the United States. In "The Significance of the Frontier," Turner declared that the process of "perennial rebirth, this fluidity of American life, this expansion westward with its new opportunities . . . furnish the forces dominating American character." It was the secret to what made the United States different from and better than every other nation. For Turner, incidents like Yellow Creek were aberrations perpetrated by a "line of scum that the waves of advancing civilization bore before them." Unfortunate episodes such as these were merely a small part of a larger glory, of a world-historical dynamic that had made America—and Americans—great.[3]

Since the 1940s, scholars have challenged Turner's thesis. They have pointed out all of the men and women whom Turner left out of his fabulous tale. Critics have especially taken issue with his notion of an advancing frontier line, using other words that emphasized space over time, place over process. Focusing on regional differences, historians have presented evocative and powerful accounts of how colonists and Natives encountered one another on middle grounds, native grounds, borderlands, and bordered lands. Each of these terms offered a new analysis of Native-colonial encounter, focusing on who dictated political, economic, and cultural terms and how power ebbed and flowed. They contend that geography matters: what happened in the region they are studying could only have done so in that specific spot. This is by design; a rejection of Turnerian meta-narratives.[4]

More recently, scholars looking to interpret encounter between Native peoples and colonists have relied on the concept of "settler colonialism." Developed largely by Australian scholars writing about what happened to Indigenous peoples there, the concept of settler colonialism has been used to argue that European settlers in the Americas did not simply take land and resources from Indigenous peoples but *eliminated* them after the fact by destroying their history and discrediting their way of life. Settler colonialism posits a "double dispossession": Europeans did more than invade Native lands—they occupied them. For theorists of settler colonialism, incidents like Yellow Creek are all too easy to understand; what happened to the eight Natives at Baker's Bottom was not only predictable, but an inevitable and unsurprising part of the conquest of North America.[5]

At its core, settler colonialism represents a reversion back to a focus on time. It is another process argument, one that has an oddly Turnerian quality to it. Although its claims come from precisely the opposite track than Turner's celebration of pioneers, settler colonialism has a logic, a thrust, a teleology, too. Just as Turner's tale had frontiersmen laying the foundation of American greatness through the trials of taming the West, historians who subscribe to settler colonialism tell us the double dispossession—the destruction of Native America—was also inescapable. "Invasion is a structure not an event," Australian historian Patrick Wolfe, the leading theorist of settler colonialism, has argued. It is a process that "pursues a specific end point," another has written. Advocates of settler colonialism look back from the perspective of the modern world and interpret the past nearly as confidently as Turner did.[6]

The confidence that comes from knowing how things actually *did* turn out is an inherent hazard on all these interpretive paths. While we can acknowledge that white colonists possessed enormous power, not least in their sheer numbers, that alone does not explain imperial encounter. Either dismissing the horror of Yellow Creek or expecting it doesn't tell us how that particular event happened, why it mattered, or what legacies it left. Interpretations that leave little room for contingency, choice, biography, and even irrationality and misperception ultimately do a disservice to all the people who lived through imperial encounter, and to ourselves as we try to make sense of its consequences. Anishinaabe historian Michael Witgen has argued that, even in the twenty-first century, "the settler colonial project of the United States is not complete but remains an ongoing process." That such uncertainties remain today only underscores the ambiguous nature of power in the bewildering Ohio Valley two hundred fifty years ago.[7]

━━━

Perhaps the problem is we are "seeing" things wrong. Maybe it would help if we went back to the 1890s and started over again. In that decade there was another writer of Turner's generation who developed his own vision of imperial encounter. The path he laid might lead toward a better understanding of what happened in the early American backcountry.

Józef Teodor Konrad Korzeniowski was born in 1857, four years before Turner, in what is now Ukraine, to a family of Polish nationalists who had also lived through an imperial conquest. After Russian officials exiled his father for plotting against the czar, the young family fell apart. Both parents died of tuberculosis before Józef was eleven. He eventually fled to the sea, where he signed on with the merchant marine at age sixteen, and began to call himself Joseph Konrad.

Konrad's years afloat coincided almost exactly with the "scramble for Africa" in the final quarter of the nineteenth century, which saw European powers race to colonize that continent. At age thirty-two, with "large black eyes," "a determined chin," and a "thick, well-trimmed, dark brown mustache," Konrad spent part of 1890 in central Africa, on the Congo River, witnessing imperialism. What he encountered led him to see the process of taming the wilderness vastly different from Turner.[8]

When he escaped from the Congo—he almost didn't survive, he was so ill—he decided to give up his career as a sailor and become a writer. Anglicizing his last name to Conrad, his first novel, *Almayer's Folly*, would appear two years after Turner's address to the Columbian Exposition. In 1899, *Blackwood's Magazine* serialized a story Conrad had written about his harrowing months in central Africa. Three years later, that novella would be published as *Heart of Darkness*. It would come to be regarded as an essential book about European imperialism and what the exploitation of Africa revealed about human nature.

Conrad's vision of imperial encounter, on its face, would seem to please a theorist of settler colonialism. There is, after all, no heroic mission in *Heart of Darkness*; there is no triumph. "The conquest of the earth," Conrad's narrator says, "which mostly means the taking it away from those who have a different complexion or slightly flatter noses than ourselves, is not a pretty thing when you look into it too much." Imperialism is not an intrepid adventure that brings out humanity's best. It is

Figure 3. Joseph Conrad, 1904.

a horror. In *Heart of Darkness*, the reader doesn't find sturdy Turnerian pioneers but rather haunted white men surrounded by severed heads on pikes. But stopping there would miss much of Conrad's point. It is not enough to simply describe the violence and exploitation of imperialism. The achievement of Conrad's novella is not a "thesis" about imperialism but a description of how people caught up in it encountered and experienced the chaos it produced.[9]

It is antithetical to the historian's job—if not simply a heresy—to say that we sometimes cannot confidently sort out what happened in the past. Although it is the historian's remit to make sense of the people and events that came before, to delineate causes, explain origins, and measure consequences, there are instances when our imposition of order on the past misleads. Not only that, but historians' sweeping interpretations can become forces in their own right.

Turner's thesis is perhaps the best American example of how a proposition about the past can shape the future. "No myth has become more powerful, more invoked by more presidents, than that of pioneers advancing across an endless meridian," one scholar has recently written. "Onward and then onward again." Those who came after Turner transformed his thesis into an "ideology of limitlessness," and used it to justify American power all over the world. Settler colonialism, by contrast, suggests that the United States should reconsider its global ambitions and come to terms with how it became a superpower in the first place: via the conquest of a continent and the people who lived in North America. Turner's interpretation celebrates; settler colonialism condemns.[10]

Heart of Darkness is useful because it undermines the historians' project of confidently knowing or being able to account for what happened in confusing places like the ones Conrad saw in the Congo. When he reflected on the consequences of empire, Conrad saw no logic or teleology. He saw mayhem. There is no surety in *Heart of Darkness*; everything that happens in the novella suggests absurdity and bewilderment. Upon arriving in the Congo, the book's narrator, Charles Marlow, finds mountains being blasted apart to make room for railroads that go nowhere. He watches "incomprehensible" European gunships lobbing shells at "enemies" who cannot be seen or even identified. He recoils as he stumbles upon a "grove of death," an idyllic place right next to the deafening Congo rapids where Native people are worked to the edge of life because they have been judged "criminals," though they have committed no offense. A Belgian trading company has sent Marlow to find and bring home a man named Kurtz, and he scoffs when he first sees that Kurtz, the German word for "short," is tall and lanky. Nothing is what it seems in this bizarre world. Marlow's perception is marred by fog or smoke or flickering shadows, and he can't believe the things his eyes see. As one literary scholar has stated, "moments of intense bewilderment occur so frequently in Conrad's fiction that they seem less unusual than customary." This is especially true of *Heart of Darkness*.[11]

Marlow becomes an observer of this bewilderment, registering the strangeness around him. His purpose, as a character, is to document and explicate for the reader the senselessness of empire. We are supposed to be put ill at ease by the absurdity and cruelty of the imperial Congo. Bewilderment, for Marlow, is a state of mind; it is a way of existing in this upside-down world.

But imperialism has even more insidious effects on those who fully engaged in it. The man Marlow has been sent to the Congo to find operates on a deeper level of bewilderment. Kurtz is a veteran of empire, and it has turned him into a chaos agent. Marlow is sent to retrieve Kurtz because the latter no longer seems to work for anyone except himself. Kurtz has grasped the power of bewilderment and is now exploiting it to his own benefit. In Kurtz's hands, it is no longer just a description of what imperial encounter does to the world but rather a weapon to be brandished. Bewilderment, for Kurtz, is a state of play; it is a way of making this upside-down world work to one's advantage.

In the 1890s, Conrad faced imperialism's bewildering effects. He watched how some Europeans tried to sow even more confusion to maximize their own rewards, a strategy that further compounded the violence. He tried to render it the best way he knew, through fiction, and the resulting sentences evoked the incomprehension that is inherent to imperial encounter.

What does this have to do with America? What can a novella about the "scramble for Africa" teach us about this nation's history? Indeed, *Heart of Darkness* does seem quite alien. To this day, publishers reinforce this sense of foreignness with cover art depicting impenetrable, foreboding jungles, or out-of-place steamships puffing their way through spooky mists and low-hanging vines, or firing cannonballs at elephants. Sometimes the publisher wants to emphasize depravity, perhaps with a skeleton staring back at us with haunted, red eyes, or a half-naked man crawling around on the ground as if gasping for breath. Whatever the case, the reader is meant to feel that the world they are about to enter into is a foreign one, with strange, lethal hazards around every turn.

Americans are probably more familiar with Francis Ford Coppola's famous adaptation of *Heart of Darkness* in his epic 1979 film *Apocalypse Now* than they are with the novella itself. And Coppola's film similarly provides audiences with another utterly foreign setting. For Coppola, the brutality and irrationality of the Vietnam War stood in for the "scramble for Africa," with little adjustment needed to characters or plot. The distance, the detachment abides: these are strange, terrible things that happen *out there*. It certainly isn't us. And it certainly didn't happen here in the United States.

But consider what might result from bringing Conrad's vision of empire to the early American backcountry. The contention of this book is that Conrad's account does offer something essential to "seeing" what empire did to people in that particular time and place. His rendering of the "scramble for Africa" in the Congo can be applied to the woodlands of eastern North America in the eighteenth century. Set aside the interpretations that project inevitability, and one can perceive mayhem and bewilderment.

Drawing inspiration from a piece of fiction set in a far different time and place as a means of taking a fresh look at the American past may strike the reader as an unusual exercise. It surely is that. But as the acclaimed novelist Charles Johnson writes, "Real fiction makes the familiar *un*familiar. It shakes up calcified ways of seeing." Novels have a way of getting to the truth of situations that is complementary to research-driven history writing. Writers of fiction can connect us to the past by capturing things that often elude scrupulous, source-bound historians. The totality of all the pain Kurtz has inflicted is evident more in his whispering of two ghastly words—"the horror"—than would be a list of all of his colonial crimes.[12]

Conrad himself would approve of this act of transposition. After all, that is precisely how *Heart of Darkness* begins. The first lines spoken aloud in the novella interrupt the silence as four men, stuck on the deck of a boat in the Thames River, wait for the tide to rise. "'And this also,'" said Marlow "suddenly, 'has been one of the dark places of the earth.'" Marlow wasn't talking about the Congo. He meant the dirty waters that swirled around them; he meant the Thames. Marlow proclaimed that now, at the end of Britain's glorious nineteenth century, the waterway nurtured "the dreams of men, the seeds of commonwealths, the germs of empires." But, he declared, it hadn't always been so. The Thames was once considered a dark place. "'I was thinking of very old times, when the Romans first came here, nineteen hundred years ago,'" Marlow said, after his abrupt remark. He then asked his audience, the group of stranded mariners drawn up around him, to see this river from the perspective of a terrified Roman soldier. "'Imagine him here—the very end of the world, the sea the colour of lead, a sky the colour of smoke . . . and going up this river with stores, or orders, or what you like. Sandbanks, marshes, forests, savages—preciously little to eat fit for a civilized man, nothing but Thames water to drink." Conrad is signaling to the reader that the story Marlow was about to tell had little to do with the jungles of central Africa. The bewilderment he experienced there was not endemic to the Congo in the late nineteenth century. Conrad's vision of encounter was (and is) transferable.[13]

Heart of Darkness is a novella about empire in the making, about exploitation and cruelty, about death and derangement, about not being able to grasp what is really going on, about a strange river that winds through lands of potential and desire, and about reputations made, lost, and redeemed. Key elements of that story can be detected in eastern North America during its "colonial period," too. Setting it there would be to make the familiar unfamiliar. It would be to turn what many think is a predictable story into one that is bewildering.

Heart of American Darkness is an attempt to recover the *feeling* of contingency, to get comfortable with and accept bewilderment, confusion, and mystery as causative historical forces. It is a way, as Conrad put it, to "live in the midst of the incomprehensible." It helps us come closer to capturing what living through imperial encounter was like, how it evolved, and why it matters. Hopefully, by the end of this book, the reader will experience what Marlow comes to understand about bewilderment and incomprehensibility: "it has a fascination, too, that goes to work upon" them. This interpretation is not really bound to a specific place, and is an alternative kind of process, one that does not assume an end point or a conclusion that fits with what the contemporary world looks like.[14]

With *Heart of Darkness* as inspiration, it becomes possible to better appreciate the human tragedy of what happened at Yellow Creek: how these colonists and Natives were bewildered by—and themselves bewildered—the experience of imperialism all around them. This book is not a work of fiction, and I am not suggesting a one-to-one correlation between Conrad's fictional Congo and Ohio in the late eighteenth century. I am not in search of an American Kurtz, although we will meet a man who arguably fits his description. Rather, *Heart of Darkness* offers, I hope to demonstrate, a set of claims about imperialism that can inspire and encourage a fresh and revealing approach to the American past.

What follows is a story about how the experience of empire-making affected particular people. It traces the history of not only the Shickellamys but of a colonial family, the Cresaps, as they wound their way through the river valleys of the mid-Atlantic, from the Susquehanna to the Potomac and Monongahela, and eventually to the waters of Ohio—and Yellow Creek.

Thomas and Hannah Cresap, their children, and their extended kin, were indispensable actors in colonial expansion that spilled into the Upper Ohio Valley by the 1750s. Their family found themselves at the center of several border controversies, were original partners in the Ohio Company, defied King George III's Proclamation Line, and were in large part responsible for starting two wars. From their outpost along a bucolic, rippling branch of the Potomac River, the Cresaps initiated diplomatic expeditions, supplied military campaigns, and organized economic adventures in land and trade. Their house was a launching pad for colonizing the Ohio country. In fact, Thomas Cresap coined the word *frontiersman*. His family was one of the most prominent colonial families in North America in the middle of the eighteenth century. They are essential to telling any story of how European colonialism arrived in the Upper Ohio Valley.

This is not, however, a one-way story of western expansion. When both Turner and Conrad wrote about imperial encounter, they focused their attention solely on the so-called pioneers—on the white people. If they were writing this story, it would only be about the Cresaps. To state the obvious, there is another side. This book brings Indigenous people into view.

Joseph Conrad's refusal to depict any Congolese as true human beings in *Heart of Darkness* has rightfully become the focus of stringent criticism. Nigerian novelist Chinua Achebe published a scathing attack on Conrad in 1977 entitled "An Image of Africa." He was "a bloody racist," Achebe concluded, condemning generations of readers for blithely accepting and implicitly endorsing how Conrad portrayed Africa and Africans throughout *Heart of Darkness*. "White racism against Africa is such a normal way of thinking," Achebe wrote, "its manifestations go completely undetected." It took three generations for critics to make their voices heard in denouncing Conrad's racism. Until Achebe, no one had really pointed out that Africans in *Heart of Darkness* were not individuals who possess the same feelings as the white men who bedevil and torment them. They don't even have names. One Congolese man helped Marlow navigate his rickety steamship past treacherous snags on the Congo River. "For months I had him at my back—a help—and instrument. It was a kind of partnership," Marlow allows. When he is mortally wounded, the dying man gives him a look that Marlow says is "like a claim of distant kinship." But never once in those months does Marlow bother to ask his name. Conrad only refers to him as "the helmsman." He doesn't have a personhood or an identity of his own. Wherever Marlow sees suffering Natives, he's "horror-struck" by the sight of their agony, but to him they are just "phantoms," "creatures," or "bundles of acute angles." Throughout, the Congolese are only described by parts of their bodies.[15]

This book confronts Conrad's colossal blindness by doing its best to make Indigenous people visible. It traces the history of the Shickellamys, too, documenting how they also wound their way through the river valleys of the mid-Atlantic, from the Susquehanna to the Juniata and Alleghany, and eventually to the Ohio. Very little happened in the Susquehanna River Valley in the mid-eighteenth century without the Shickellamys' approval. In the face of colonialism, war, and economic pressures, they too made excruciating, dangerous choices that pushed several members of the family to the west to settle in the Upper Ohio Valley by the early 1770s.

However, even concerning the Shickellamys themselves, bewilderment, not confident facts, is the theme. Shickellamy's sons were famous in the mid-eighteenth-century American backcountry. One of them would become "Logan, the Great Mingo Chief," one of *the* most celebrated Indians in the history of America. This person captured the admiration of Thomas Jefferson, James Madison, and generations of writers who found his speech, the famous Logan's Lament, among the most significant ever delivered in American history. But we really don't know *which* brother Logan was. Controversy has raged since the late eighteenth century about whether the man who became the famous Logan was Shickellamy's first-born son or the second. The question persists to this day, a consequence of imperial bewilderment and a glaring example of the double dispossession.

Eventually the Cresap and Shickellamy families collided near the place where Yellow Creek empties into the Ohio River. Although none of the Cresaps actually pulled any triggers at Baker's Bottom that morning in April 1774, the event became news all over the continent, and most people in America—including Thomas Jefferson—asserted that a Cresap had murdered Shickellamy's kin. After the horror of Yellow Creek, the two families would be forever intertwined, occupying a central place in American folklore. For generations, American politicians, historians, writers, poets, and orators would wrangle over what happened along the Ohio on that spring morning. Legends about Logan and Cresap would be told and retold even into the time when Turner was growing up.

Americans in the eighteenth and nineteenth centuries knew a great deal about the Cresaps and the Shickellamys. But telling their story also features many people more familiar to American readers today. George Washington and Thomas Jefferson play essential roles, as do many other power brokers in the British Atlantic world on the eve of the Revolution, including Lord Dunmore, George Croghan, General Thomas Gage,

Sir William Johnson, Luther Martin, and the surveyors Mason and Dixon. This book recounts famous events from that century, including the race to the Forks of the Ohio, Braddock's rout at the Monongahela that touched off the Seven Years' War, Pontiac's War, protests over the Stamp Act, the news of Lexington and Concord, the beginning of the Revolutionary War, and American Independence. But if I have succeeded, the book will show, through Conrad's vision of imperial encounter, how these familiar people and events can be made *un*familiar.

That vision revolves around the utter absurdity, violence, treachery, greed—and, above all, bewilderment—of empire-makers. The actual plot of *Heart of Darkness* doesn't concern me. It is not important to what follows; you don't have to have read *Heart of Darkness* to understand this book. What I am interested in is how Conrad articulates empire. The images Conrad conjured to show us imperialism—groves of death, ships firing blindly, severed heads on pikes—are immediately recognizable in eighteenth-century America.

There are passages in what follow that may seem bewildering at times. People will shed their names, switch sides, fall from grace, and experience the most unlikely redemption. Throughout several bloody border conflicts, "savages" become patriots and vice versa. They will encounter bewilderment—and some of them will encourage it, employing it as a strategy to resolve the inherent confusion of imperial encounter in their favor. If you yourself are bewildered at times, you are reading the book as it is meant to be read. You are understanding empire as it existed, day to day and on the ground.

This feeling of bewilderment was especially the case in 1775–1776. For most people in North America, the civil war between Britain and the thirteen colonies was likely the strangest experience they ever lived through. Its result—an extended republic based on citizenship that was itself an empire—was also something new, another peculiar development that required getting adjusted to. The republicanized American empire after 1776 would be a place where some, but not all, would belong. The resolution of that particular instance of bewilderment would have drastic consequences for millions. Living through the Revolution was arguably the greatest American example of bewilderment as a state of mind. Revolutionary leaders, moreover, realized the potential of the upheaval and readily embraced bewilderment as a state of play.

How the Cresaps and the Shickellamys influenced the Revolution is critical to trying to understand the mysteries of the American founding. As I strive to show, the blood shed at Yellow Creek—why it happened, who was held responsible, and what the lessons were—would become embedded in the very meaning of American independence and patriotism. Yellow Creek, the Cresaps, and the Shickellamys would continue to fascinate Americans long into the nineteenth century. But their influence was more profound than that suggests. Turner was correct, at least in one sense: the frontier helped make America. Just not in the ways he described.

⸻

One thing everyone—Turner, Conrad, and the settler colonial theorists of recent vintage—might agree on is that the experience of imperial encounter must be reckoned with by those living in its long historical shadow. Turner thought that anything that happened in or to the United States was only significant when it related to "western expansion." Even his sharpest critics would largely approve of this claim.[16]

Conrad confessed something quite similar in *Heart of Darkness*. When he began recounting what his confrontation with empire in the Congo meant, Marlow reflected that it "seemed somehow to throw a kind of light on everything about me." It was essential for Marlow to relate this "sombre," "pitiful" tale of what he witnessed in the Congo, even though it was still "not very clear" in his mind. He knew people needed to listen to, to wrestle with, the confounding nature and effects of imperial encounter. Here, then, is another penetrating—and adaptable—observation from Conrad. Colonialism still throws a kind of light on everything about the United States. Americans today need to tell and listen to these stories, sombre and pitiful, bewildering and unclear as they may be.[17]

PART 1

THE DREAMS OF MEN

The Dreams of Men, 1730–1763

Ottawa

Michilimackinac

Lake Michigan

Lake Huron

Au Sable

Muskegon

Lake Ontario

A N I S H I N A A B E

Grand

Grand

Genesee

Thames

Detroit

Lake Erie

Allegheny

Maumee

W. Branch Susquehanna

Wabash

D E L A W A R E

Logstown   see inset at left

ALBANY PIKE

Battle of
Forks of the Ohio   Monongahela

Pickawillany

Scioto

M I N G O

OHIO COMPANY
GRANT

Forbes Rd.

Muskingum

Redstone

Wills Creek   Great C

Braddock Rd.

Ohio

S H A W N E E

Ohio Company
Storehouse

Monongahela

Opessa's
Town/
Oldtown

Winchester

Kanawha

Great Warrior Path

Shenandoah

Greenbrier

VIRGIN

Inset map:

Logstown

Ohio   Allegheny

Forks of
the Ohio/
Fort Duquesne   Battle of
Monongahela

Monongahela   Forbes Rd.

OHIO COMPANY
GRANT   Braddock Rd.

Kentucky

Redstone   Redstone
Creek

James

Cumberland

Holston   New   Roanoke

NOR'

CHAPTER 1

A SCRAMBLE FOR OHIO, 1730–1753

"At that time there were many blank spaces on the earth, and when I saw one that looked particularly inviting on a map (but they all look like that) I would put my finger on it and say, When I grow up I will go there."

—*Heart of Darkness*

European mapmakers early in the eighteenth century left much of North America west of the Appalachian Mountains blank. For the most part, these gaps merely reflected their imperfect and unreliable knowledge of the interior and whoever might reside there. In the Upper Ohio Valley at the start of the 1700s, however, blankness wasn't just an expression of the ignorance of mapmakers working in European capitals. For a short period of time, this part of the Ohio Valley was nearly devoid of permanent inhabitants. It *was*, in fact, blank.[1]

According to archaeologists, bands of Natives that would later be referred to as Shawnees had lived nearby continuously from at least 1000 CE until the late 1600s. But over the course of the seventeenth century, a combination of forces—climate change, the prospect of better trade networks, and military threats from Iroquois raiders—convinced them to leave these settlements. Some went southeast toward Carolina, others to the Susquehanna River basin. Eventually, Shawnees would be known as one of the most migratory people in North America, but during this period, they all came from Ohio.[2]

One group of Shawnees, led by a man colonists referred to as King Opessa, had relocated to the lower Susquehanna River region around the turn of the eighteenth century. Opessa (or Opessah) participated in several negotiations between Pennsylvania authorities and the Iroquois in the century's first decade, including a significant deal made with William Penn in 1701 that secured a permanent residence on Conestoga Creek for an embattled group of Natives, who would henceforth be known as the Conestogas. Not all relations with Pennsylvania were positive, however. Within a few years, Opessa and his small band of Shawnees went west to the Potomac River, where they founded a village in the Appalachian foothills around 1711.[3]

The village, which became known to colonists as King Opessa's Town, was strategically situated: it was easily accessible by water, located at a ford just past where the North and South Branches of the Potomac merged, as well as by land, next to a trail Iroquois warriors followed to raid their enemies in the south. Its place on the Potomac sat right outside the southern fringe of Iroquois influence, and it was far to the back of colonial settlements. In the 1720s, Opessa's town symbolized Native autonomy in the mid-Atlantic.[4]

Then, around 1727, Opessa and his Shawnees packed up and left, continuing their western sojourn back to Ohio. The "Shuano Town on Potomac (commonly called Oppessa's Town)," as Maryland's council referred to it, would lay abandoned throughout the 1730s.[5]

Opessa's group was on the leading edge of what would become an unprecedented, large-scale migration. Over the next fifteen years, several Shawnee, Delaware, and other groups would leave Pennsylvania, New Jersey, and Maryland in ever greater numbers to establish significant new settlements near where the Alleghany and Monongahela Rivers converged to form the Ohio River. Although Shawnees had been returning to the Ohio Valley for several years in a "steady" but "slow" migration, the pace accelerated significantly in the 1730s. Many of them had their eyes on the soon-to-be infamous confluence which was known as the Forks of the Ohio.[6]

The Shawnees' desertion of their village along the Potomac concerned the Iroquois. Even before the mass migration began, the Six Nations of the Iroquois worried about what might happen if they lost control over the many Native peoples who lived in the mid-Atlantic. The secret to Iroquois power had been their dominance over "lesser" Native groups (like Opessa's Shawnees), peoples who had been either subjugated or who voluntarily sought their protection after disease and colonial violence reduced their population. If these groups were able to survive independently, the mystique of Iroquois political and military power could dissolve, and their ability to control events in the eastern American woodlands might be at an end.

To prevent this loss of political prestige and to stem the tide of migration, the Six Nations dispatched Shickellamy to the region. Shickellamy was, and remains, a somewhat mysterious figure. At times he was called Ungquaterughiathe, Takashwangaroras, and Swateney or Swatana. Shick-

Figure 4. "Portrait of the Oneida Chieftain Shikellamy," artist unknown, c. 1820.

ellamy is probably an Anglicized form of an Oneida name meaning The Enlightener. We don't know where he was born. He seems to have had a European (French) father, leading some to believe he was raised as a Frenchman and perhaps had a Catholic baptism. Others refer to him as a Cayuga. He claimed he was adopted into the Oneida at an early age, but why this came about is unknown. Nor do we know exactly what his official capacity was when his people, the Iroquois, sent him to the Susquehanna in 1727. Contemporaries and historians have marshaled a battalion of labels to depict what the Six Nations empowered him to do there: "deputy," "ombudsman," "viceroy," "overseer," "ambassador," and more.[7]

We do know that Shickellamy apparently made a good impression when he first exercised his diplomatic skills in 1728, travelling to Philadelphia to observe a treaty with Pennsylvania and the Delaware Indians. While he was in the city he befriended perhaps the most important person in Pennsylvania, James Logan. If you were a settler seeking land in the Quaker colony, Logan, William Penn's secretary, was the man to see. James Logan and Shickellamy developed a mutually beneficial relationship, the importance of which is indicated by the fact that Shickellamy gave two of his sons second, alternate names that honored this powerful friend in Philadelphia: his oldest son Tachnedorus would also be known as John Logan Shickellamy; the second born, Soyechtowa, was called James Logan Shickellamy.

By the end of the 1720s, Shickellamy settled his family at Shamokin, a new village at the confluence of the North and West branches of the Susquehanna (today Sunbury, Pennsylvania). Here Shickellamy lived with his wife, a Cayuga named Neanoma. The two sons would be followed by a third, known as Sagogechyta, but more commonly called John Petty Shickellamy. Neanoma bore several more children, including a son known as "Unhappy Jake" who would die fighting the Catawba, another who did not survive infancy, and two daughters named Cajadis and Koonay.[8]

The merging of the two Susquehanna branches made the river valley at Shamokin broad and impressive, a commanding spot for someone tasked with keeping order throughout the mid-Atlantic. The Iroquois intended it to be a new gathering place for Natives of many affiliations and allegiances, as well as Pennsylvania's leaders. Shickellamy's job at Shamokin was to prevent Native peoples from following Opessa's example and going west to slip free from Iroquois authority in Ohio.

The centerpiece of Shickellamy's diplomatic career—and his friend-ship with James Logan—lay in the central role the duo played in the infamous "Walking Purchase" of 1737. He and Logan crafted and rati-fied a fraudulent land deal that ceded more than a million acres of what is today northeastern Pennsylvania to the Penns. The notorious Walking Purchase was a total conquest of the Delaware Indians who lived there. The Iroquois hoped Shickellamy could convince the now-landless Dela-wares to resettle near him in the central Pennsylvania highlands around Shamokin, but most refused. Native groups displaced by the Walking Purchase would join the Shawnee migrants headed for the Ohio Valley. As they walked past Shamokin, they nursed bitter and hostile feelings for the Iroquois—and specifically for Shickellamy, the man who orches-trated their betrayal.[9]

That bitterness would explode in an eruption of violence in the mid-1750s, but, for now, the Walking Purchase served to bolster Iroquois authority in Pennsylvania and cemented Shickellamy's reputation with the Six Nations and his new allies in Philadelphia. It came at an espe-cially opportune time for the latter, as James Logan and the Penn family had other problems along the Susquehanna in the 1730s. Sixty miles downriver from Shamokin, Pennsylvania teetered on the edge of war with Maryland.

Like Shickellamy, little is known of the early life of the man who would later be nicknamed the Maryland Monster. Thomas Cresap was born sometime between 1694 and 1701 in the village of Skipton, in York-shire, England. He came to America in his youth, either as a teenager or in his early twenties. We do know that, in April 1727, right around the time Shickellamy arrived at Shamokin and Opessa's Shawnees left the Potomac, Thomas married Hannah Johnson of Baltimore County, Maryland. Cresap and his new bride lived briefly near Havre de Grace, by the mouth of the Susquehanna, but the threat of debtors' prison caused him to flee Maryland for Virginia. In Virginia he met several important men who would later become business partners, including Thomas Lee and Augustine Washington, George's father. He rented a house from the latter and sought to establish his new family. After a few months, he returned to collect Hannah, but instead found her pregnant with their first son, Daniel, and in no mood to leave. Unable to convince her to move, he stayed in Maryland and took up a license to operate a ferry across the Susquehanna.[10]

Sometime around 1730, Cresap received a patent for a tract of land on the western bank of the Susquehanna, halfway between what would become the towns of Lancaster and York, and started his ferry business. Two centuries later, a New Deal dam project would turn this part of the Susquehanna into Lake Clarke, now a twelve-mile-long paradise for Pennsylvania boaters. In 1730, however, this was Maryland. Or at least that's what Thomas Cresap thought.

The charters of both Pennsylvania and Maryland were rather vague about where one stopped and the other began. Both documents made reference to the fortieth parallel as a boundary, but given the poor geographic knowledge of America at the time, if the fortieth were truly the colonial border, Philadelphia would be in Maryland! With more people coming to Penn's Woods and heading west, Pennsylvania colonial officials underscored their claim to the area on the Susquehanna by establishing Lancaster County in 1729. According to Maryland's maps, however, Lancaster County was theirs.

In June 1731, Maryland granted Thomas Cresap a patent for a 150-acre plot on the west bank. He called this spot Pleasant Garden, and opened up Blue Rock Ferry to shuttle settlers across the river from an outcropping of blue limestone on the eastern shore. In earlier decades, this idyllic spot had been known by a different and more sinister name:

Fort Demolished. In the middle of the 1600s, the Susquehannock Indians had built an outpost in a clearing a few hundred feet up the ridge above where Cresap sited Pleasant Garden. Seneca-led Iroquois warriors attacked and destroyed it in the 1670s, leaving the ruins of the wrecked palisade. Sixty years later, the same spot along the nearly two-mile-wide Susquehanna was to witness further bloodshed, this time between colonies, in what would be known as Cresap's War.[11]

To contest Maryland's claim on the territory, Shickellamy's friend James Logan quietly told the new Lancaster justice of the peace to eject Cresap from Pleasant Garden. On October 31, 1731, three men boarded Cresap's ferry and, when they were about halfway across the widest part of the river, pulled their guns and told him that he was under arrest for trespass in Pennsylvania. A fight broke out on the raft, and Cresap ended up in the river. He managed to swim to an island and escaped. As soon as he dried out he promptly informed Maryland authorities what had happened.[12]

Figure 5. This view is taken from the spot of Fort Demolished on the ridge above where Thomas Cresap built Pleasant Garden, looking across the Susquehanna River where the Blue Rock Ferry operated.

Maryland's governor escalated matters. He deputized Cresap as a justice of the peace for this region west of the Susquehanna. The Penn family responded by issuing a warrant for Cresap's arrest and told the Lancaster sheriff to grab him if he ever got the chance. The sheriff put together a posse, and they watched and waited. When a party from the property was spotted leaving to cut firewood, the posse thought they had the drop on Cresap; however, someone had informed them, and Thomas sent Hannah out with a saw in his place. Frustrated, the posse rushed to attack Cresap's house. When the Pennsylvanians tried to force their way through the bolted door, Cresap opened it slightly to fire a warning shot. The enraged Pennsylvanians broke in and a brawl ensued inside the house. But outside, shouts and cries stopped the fight. Cresap's warning shot had struck a servant named Knowles Daunt in the leg, smashing his bone. The sheriff's men panicked and took off, callously leaving the bleeding man behind on the riverbank. Daunt died a few days later.[13]

Cresap rushed to Maryland for reinforcements and returned with twenty gunmen. They menaced the houses of Pennsylvania settlers on the west side of the river, arrested them, and hauled the "trespassers" to Annapolis. The Susquehanna was now the central front in a simmering colonial civil war, and Pleasant Garden became an armed compound. Throughout the fall of 1735, the two colonies continued to threaten one another. While there were few incidents, the festering conflict made it difficult for the Penn family to sell tracts of land to immigrants. Western land sales in Lancaster County began to dry up, a concerning prospect to the deeply indebted and overleveraged Penn family. Something had to be done about Thomas Cresap, and in the last days of 1736, the Penns decided to put an end to five years of troubles with the disruptive Marylander.

Late in December, a party of more than three dozen Pennsylvanians warily approached Pleasant Garden in possession of a warrant the Penn family had sworn out for the murder of Knowles Daunt, dead now for more than two years. Cresap refused to go along quietly. According to one Philadelphia newspaper, Thomas, a very pregnant Hannah, his sons Daniel (six) and Thomas Jr. (three), and a half dozen neighbors responded by "vilifying our Proprietors and People by the Appellations of *Damn'd*

Quaker Sons of Bitches," and asking the Sheriff why he would "fight for such *Quaking Dogs.*" They proceeded to open fire on the arresting party, and volleys of musket fire went back and forth.[14]

When the sheriff ordered the house torched, the defenders decided to make a break for it. According to the paper, "*Creasap* with his Gang ran out" into a hail of gunfire. More than one bullet struck Cresap, though his wounds would not be serious. The Pennsylvanians won the day, and several in Cresap's party were soon headed to the Lancaster jail.[15]

Cresap, deemed too valuable to be held in a county stockade, was put on a cart headed to Philadelphia. Upon entering the city, people lined the streets to hurl taunts at the prisoner, allegedly calling him a monster. Those shouts and that infamous ride through Philadelphia created a nickname that historians and biographers ever since have taken to be true. Pennsylvanians forever after, so the story goes, derisively referred to Cresap as the Maryland Monster. They didn't; that sobriquet wouldn't be coined for more than a hundred years.[16]

Cresap's response to his reception in the Quaker City, on the other hand, was better documented. According to a deposition filed by a Pennsylvania justice of the peace, George Aston, at some point during his rough ride through Philadelphia, Cresap turned to him and said, "Damn it, Aston, this is one of the prettyest towns in Maryland."[17]

While Cresap sat in the Philadelphia jail, news of the prolonged violence along the Susquehanna finally captured the attention of imperial officials across the Atlantic. When King George II learned of the skirmishes, he issued a series of cease-and-desist orders and demanded all prisoners released. The king also identified a temporary boundary line. Both the Penn and the Calvert families lodged complaints about its location, however, and the subsequent court case would take decades to wind toward a conclusion. Finally, in 1760, the court decided in Penn's favor and ordered surveyors be dispatched from England. In 1763, Charles Mason and Jeremiah Dixon crossed the Atlantic to draw an official boundary between the two colonies.[18]

In the meantime, James Logan needed to find a secure place of settlement for the increasing crush of immigrants flooding into Philadelphia. The west was in turmoil, so he turned his attention north to the Delawares' land. Soon, as Cresap shivered through the winter and spring of 1737 in a Philadelphia jail waiting for his release, Logan and Shickellamy sketched their plans that resulted in the Walking Purchase. Cresap's War had a direct effect on that infamous land deal; in fact, one of the runners Logan employed to maximize Pennsylvania's claim had gotten into peak physical form by fighting the Marylanders. Thomas Cresap and Shickellamy would never meet, but already their lives and families had started to become entangled.[19]

Upon the king's order for his discharge, Thomas Cresap decided that he was finished with the Susquehanna River. He returned to the charred ruins of his house—a second home demolished on that particular riverbank—collected his wife, two young sons, and a new baby he hadn't yet seen (Hannah had given birth to a daughter, Elizabeth, while he was incarcerated) and headed west. His exploits had made him a hero in Maryland and had earned him enough standing to borrow £500 from a wealthy lawyer, planter, and land speculator named Daniel Dulany Sr., whom Maryland's governor had dispatched to Philadelphia to negotiate Cresap's release. Dulany, a principal proprietor of the newly founded Conococheague Manor on the Potomac, thought a man with Cresap's experience might prove essential to the success of this ambitious land venture.[20]

Cresap put his borrowed £500 to good use in Conococheague. Within two years he purchased a five hundred-acre farm on Antietam Creek, about two miles from present-day Hagerstown, Maryland. Along with a friend from his days on the Susquehanna, he built a new house there. Cresap set out on another career change, this time becoming an Indian trader. He established a small store in Hagerstown and began collecting furs.[21]

Thomas found his new life in the west didn't free him from old problems. He had more legal troubles with his neighbors (including nearly being convicted of the felony of horse theft), and he faced bankruptcy yet again when a large consignment of furs he was shipping to England got caught up in the wars between European nations that raged on the Atlantic in the 1740s. A French warship captured the English merchant vessel on the Atlantic and seized its cargo. Thomas's loss was total. Despite these serious setbacks, Cresap's fortunes steadily improved and he proceeded to buy up more land around Conococheague.[22]

Over the first few years of the 1740s, he bought seven tracts totaling nearly 1,500 acres in various spots. His favorite was a place then called Indian Seat, which he bought in 1740 for £100. He also bought four hundred acres of the adjacent Indian Fields that sat at the confluence of the North and South Branches of the Potomac. Indian Seat was, by all accounts, an idyllic spot. Several years later, a British officer described the beautiful setting as "a piece of low ground entirely surrounded by the mountains, the prospect romantic, high rocks on the sides of the mountains some hundred feet perpendicular to the river Potomac." It charmed Thomas Cresap as it had Shawnees a generation before. "Indian Seat" was King Opessa's Town. In going from the Susquehanna to this spot on the Potomac, Cresap had walked almost precisely in Opessa's footsteps.[23]

In 1741, Cresap resettled his family there, changed the area's name to Oldtown, and began building another house on a hill gently rising a hundred yards or so above the Potomac. As he had a decade earlier on the Susquehanna—establishing Pleasant Garden where Fort Demolished had already been—Cresap had "founded" Oldtown where Opessa's village had previously existed.

Oldtown was indeed as perfectly situated for Cresap as it had been for the Shawnees. It was near foot traffic on a well-traveled north-south trail, and easily approachable by calm, shallow water on both branches of the Potomac. Cresap's Indian trade could flourish at a place like this. His family could, too: on June 29, 1742, Thomas and Hannah welcomed their third son, Michael. He would be the Cresap's fifth and final child, and the only one born at Oldtown.

Thus far, this telling of the scramble for Ohio hasn't been about Ohio at all. It's been about people negotiating for, arranging for rights to, or fighting one another for control of valuable lands along the Potomac

Figure 6. This photo is taken at Indian Seat, where Thomas Cresap would build his home and town, Oldtown, and it faces Indian Fields. The hill slopes gently down to the North Branch of the Potomac, just past the line of trees on the far right. In the center of the picture, in the distance, is the confluence of the North and South Branches of the Potomac.

and Susquehanna Rivers. Like Thomas Cresap and Shickellamy, many nurtured dreams of life along the Susquehanna before they even heard of Ohio. Bewilderment, both as a matter of confused misunderstandings and as a strategy for human scheming, defined the people who clung to those dreams, as they fought over hazy boundaries and provincial loyalties. Soon enough, greed and desire encouraged colonial speculators and settlers to fantasize about what potential riches lay farther to the west.

On the day Michael Cresap was born, the region around the Ohio River was no longer a blank spot on the earth. The mass migration of Native peoples to the area, which had accelerated a dozen years before his birth, continued to gain force during his early childhood. While many of these new arrivals had come from the east, others arrived from the northwest, an area whose center of political power could be found at the straits of Mackinac, where Lakes Michigan and Huron converged.

A group of Algonquian-speaking Natives who called themselves the Anishinaabeg dominated this region from Hudson's Bay to the Ohio Valley, a homeland they named Anishinaabewaki. They included Natives Europeans referred to as Odawas, Chippewas, Ojibwes, Potawatomis, and others. The French had established a trading post in the center of Anishinaabewaki at the Mackinac Straits, called Michilimackinac, in the 1680s, but in 1710 colonial authorities in Quebec made a critical mistake. To bolster trade farther south, the French closed their post there and transferred their trading energies to Detroit. The Anishinaabeg, worried that Detroit might embolden their rivals, chose to make war on anyone who traded with the French there, especially Natives known as the Fox. The conflict that emerged in 1712, called the Fox Wars, devastated the Great Lakes region for a quarter century.[24]

The Fox Wars accomplished a great deal for the Anishinaabeg, most importantly by forcing the French to reverse course and reestablish their post at Michilimackinac. By the middle of the 1730s, just as things were looking precarious for the Iroquois, the Anishinaabeg had seemingly achieved unchallenged authority in the region. Their alliance with the French was strong, and they dictated the terms of diplomacy. French traders loaded their canoes with goods to float west toward Anishinaabewaki.

But appearances deceived. Many survivors of the Fox Wars did not return to the fold but instead headed south toward Ohio. Natives known as Wyandot broke away from Detroit and resettled on the southern edge of Lake Erie at Sandusky. Groups of Miami also left Michigan for the Wabash River in southern Ohio. These Algonquian-speaking peoples heading south joined Shawnees and Delawares coming west. Ohio's emptiness was a thing of the past. Thousands of Natives—like their European counterparts—looked to fill in blank spots they thought would be inviting. And just like the leaders of Pennsylvania, Virginia, and Maryland, Native peoples sought to control these new Ohio settlers. Both the Iroquois and the Anishinaabeg insisted their authority extended into Ohio.[25]

In the 1730s, Shawnee, Delaware, and some Iroquois migrants established villages and trading centers a few miles downstream from the Forks of the Ohio. The Iroquois, having been unable to block western migration, pivoted to a new position: if their people went there, Iroquois sovereignty would go right along with them. Since the Iroquois claimed sponsorship over Shawnees and Delawares, their migration, they argued, meant an automatic transfer of their authority to Ohio. Shawnees and Delawares couldn't escape their grasp simply by walking away. Anyone who wanted to live on this emerging Native frontier there had to seek their permission—or so the Iroquois proclaimed.[26]

Despite his inability to stop western movement, the Iroquois were pleased with Shickellamy's accomplishments. Since it looked like their creation of an ambassador in Pennsylvania had reaped great success, they repeated the gambit in the Ohio Valley. The Six Nations deputized two more ambassadors, known as half-kings, and sent them to the new settlements near the Forks. One, Tanaghrisson, a Seneca, had responsibility over some Iroquois-speaking people who went west and called themselves Mingos. The other representative, an Oneida named Scarouyady, lived with Shawnees in Ohio. Together, they were, like Shickellamy, to monitor and manage Shawnee and Delaware migrations into the Ohio country on the Iroquois' behalf.

Iroquois claims of authority also depended on recognition by colonial leaders. They needed the validation of colonial speculators who cast their hungry eyes on lands over the mountains. If wealthy, well-connected Virginians respected the Iroquois' claim to Ohio sovereignty, others would also recognize them as gatekeepers; the only ones who could grant permission as to who was to potentially purchase those lands.

A planter from one of the richest, most influential families in Virginia, Colonel Thomas Lee, understood this game and played right along. Lee had inherited thousands of acres of land and enslaved people, was the longest-standing member of the Governor's Council, and was also the manager for Lord Fairfax's massive land grant that stretched from the Chesapeake Bay to the headwaters of the Potomac River, somewhere deep in the Appalachian mountains. In the summer of 1744, however, the fifty-four-year-old grandee had his sights set farther west. Colonial authorities from Virginia, Maryland, and Pennsylvania met with Iroquois leaders at a landmark treaty conference held at Lancaster, Pennsylvania. Shickellamy was there, although he kept in the background. While the meeting was nominally concerned with clashes in the Shenandoah Valley, Lee wasn't interested in that place. Lee had come to Lancaster with his eyes on a much bigger prize: Ohio. He would leave town two weeks later with glee, getting far more than he could have expected.[27]

The 1744 Lancaster conference was a farcical bit of theater. The participants all spoke very seriously about lands over which they had no control. No Shawnees or Delawares were present. Worse, everyone talked past one another, reading from different fictional scripts. As a result, the treaty agreed to by Iroquois representatives and delegates from Maryland, Pennsylvania, and Virginia only created more confusion because it contained a fatal flaw. The Lancaster treaty stipulated the Iroquois had renounced their rights to "all Lands within the said Colony" of Virginia. By this, the Iroquois meant to cede the lands in the Shenandoah Valley up to the Ohio watershed, but no farther. They were willing to give away that valley but not the Ohio one. They didn't know, however, that a century and a half earlier an English king had written in a charter that Virginia had the right to all lands from sea to sea. Lee and other planter-speculators rushed to exploit the "mistake." In their next session, the Virginia House of Burgesses, assuming the Iroquois had ceded *everything* west of the Blue Ridge, approved grants totaling three hundred thousand acres of lands to the west of Lord Fairfax's Potomac grant. Maryland's assembly also began handing out claims to these lands. The bewilderment at Lancaster—and Thomas Lee's exploitation of the confusion—set the colonial scramble for Ohio in motion.[28]

Despite the fact that the agreement would soon unleash mayhem throughout the heart of North America, the Iroquois were satisfied with the outcome at Lancaster. When Shickellamy returned home, Pennsylvania's venerable Indian trader Conrad Weiser (who had served as translator at Lancaster) spent two weeks helping the Oneida ambassador build himself a new log house at Shamokin. Weiser reported back to the Pennsylvania government that it was a house fit for such an important person: "49 ½ foot long, and 17 ½ wide, and covered with shingles." The new dwelling reflected, in part, the expansion of Shickellamy's trade into a family enterprise; over the preceding few years, he had involved his two eldest sons in his ambassador business, sending the oldest, Tachnedorus (John Logan Shickellamy), on a potentially hazardous job to collect goods a Shawnee raiding party had stolen from a Pennsylvania trader. He also brought Soyechtowa (James Logan Shickellamy) along when he trekked north on one of his last diplomatic trips to Iroquoia. Even though everyone's attention was shifting to the west in the mid-1740s, both colonial governments and the Iroquois still depended on the negotiating skills of the successful firm of Weiser, Shickellamy, and Sons.[29]

The ultimate effect of the agreement at Lancaster would be profoundly shaped by the outbreak of war between England and France, known in the colonies as King George's War (1744–48). This was the conflict that nearly broke Thomas Cresap when a French frigate impounded his fur shipment. English victories curtailed France's ability to provide trade goods to Natives throughout Canada. Even before the scarcity hit, however, the war caused Native leaders around the Great Lakes to reconsider their connection to New France. The French had not been solid partners. They had only recently made amends for the Detroit fiasco in the 1720s, and Anishinaabeg leaders worried that perhaps their French allies were weak and vulnerable.[30]

The most visible example of a growing disaffection among Ohio Natives was Pickawillany, a new settlement 350 miles downriver from the Forks. During King George's War, Memeskia, a Miami leader, sought to escape the control of both the French in Quebec and the Anishinaabeg, and led four hundred families south to found Pickawillany. Nearly overnight, it became the greatest threat to the French alliance in the Great Lakes and attracted the attention of English traders hungry to secure new customers.

George Croghan, a recent emigrant from Ireland who was quickly becoming Pennsylvania's preeminent Native trader, sensed this discontent with the French in the Great Lakes. This opened up a "fair opertunity," Croghan wrote to a Pennsylvania council member in the spring of 1747, for the Natives were (like the letter's author) "very much led by Any Thing that will tend to their own self-interest." Over the next few years, Croghan made steady progress developing trade relations with these "rebel" Indians at Pickawillany whom the English sometimes referred to as the Twightwees.[31]

Meanwhile, in Virginia, speculation-minded Chesapeake elites who dreamed about Ohio—especially Thomas Lee—cultivated their political networks. They fostered relationships in three directions: in London, with the powers-that-be in colonial capitals (Williamsburg, Philadelphia, and Annapolis), and also with prominent frontier traders who had emerged as point men in the woods of the mid-Atlantic. Whoever was going to take charge of the Ohio Valley would not only need impeccable political connections in England but also the expertise of at least a few of these woodsmen, like Shickellamy's partner Conrad Weiser or other emerging traders and go-betweens, such as William Trent, Christopher Gist, George Croghan—and Thomas Cresap.[32]

As King George's War was drawing to a close, Lee started to put his plans into motion. He began piecing together a syndicate to be known as the Ohio Company.

It started out largely as a family affair. The Lees (via the Fairfaxes) were close friends with the Washingtons, so Augustine Jr. and Lawrence, half-brothers to the then-teenaged George Washington, both signed on as original Ohio Company partners. Others who were invited to participate were either already married to a Lee or a Washington or soon would be. Fathers acquired shares for their sons. Colonel Francis Thornton, for instance, needed something for his second-born, five-year-old son William to inherit, and so hoped the company profits would do the job. Thomas Lee did the same for his second-born, Philip Ludwell Lee. One of the only families who were outside the Lee-Washington network who were extended an invitation to become a partner in the

Ohio Company was the Cresaps. Thomas and his first-born son, then twelve-year-old Daniel, both signed Lee's petition.[33]

Thomas Cresap recognized the Ohio Company might be his family's ticket to a prodigious fortune, and he therefore had no plans of being a passive partner. He was going to see to its success personally, taking on the task of traveling to Williamsburg, paying the fee, and filing the Ohio Company's petition with the colonial clerk on October 24, 1747. The Ohio Company requested a grant for a half million acres around the Forks of the Ohio—two hundred thousand immediately and three hundred thousand to follow once the company's success was assured. While Cresap hoped that this journey to get the company in motion would help secure a financial windfall for his family, the more immediate consequences turned his private life upside-down.[34]

To help its standing with the Crown, the Ohio Company attempted to recruit John Hanbury, a prominent merchant and preeminent importer of Chesapeake tobacco, to serve as their lobbyist in London. At some point before 1747, Cresap was connected with William Manduit, a Chesapeake planter and one of Hanbury's agents. We know, at least, that he had already crossed paths with William's twenty-year-old daughter Elizabeth. Perhaps, as Cresap travelled to Williamsburg to file the Ohio Company's petition, he also paid a visit to Mauduit's home to discuss the possibility of how to approach Hanbury.

Elizabeth Mauduit was already married to a man named Lamy (or Lamme) when she met Thomas, who was more than twice her age. What happened to Lamy is unknown; however, by 1749, Thomas Cresap and Elizabeth were living together in Frederick, Maryland, while Hannah and their children were presumably in Oldtown. We don't exactly know the nature of their relationship, but enough people were upset by it that the vestry and churchwardens of the Anglican church Cresap attended in Frederick, All Saints Parish, brought a suit against Thomas in November 1749 for "cohabitating with" Elizabeth Lamy. The charge was dismissed two years later when Thomas, then a magistrate for Frederick County, did not appear. It is clear, however, that the relationship continued. What

Thomas's public affair meant for Hannah and their eight-year-old son Michael, we cannot know.[35]

In addition to personal scandal, Cresap's involvement with the Ohio Company also engendered suspicion among other colonists who dreamt about Ohio at that moment. One member of the Pennsylvania council wrung his hands that the Virginians would sink his colony's claims. He worried about the loyalty of Croghan and Weiser—Pennsylvania's most important trading agents—and how Lee's proposal might affect other unsavory sorts out on the frontier, perhaps emboldening people with whom his government had clashed in previous years. At the top of that list was Thomas Cresap.[36]

A decade after locking him in a Philadelphia jail, the governors of Pennsylvania and Maryland exchanged another round of correspondence about the "monster." "Mr. Cressap's schemes or views are quite unknown to me," the acting governor of Maryland confessed, "but I believe it very possible he may have his own Interest chiefly at heart." He assured Pennsylvanians that whatever Cresap was doing, it had not come from Maryland. Thomas had received "no encouragement from me to do anything unfair or unreasonable," he wrote. This apparently didn't fully put the Pennsylvanians at ease. They suspected Cresap was behind the whole Ohio Company scheme. "That vile fellow Cressap has proposed a scheme to Col[onel Thomas] Lee and some other great men in Virginia to make trading Houses" in Ohio, a Pennsylvania council member wrote to Thomas Penn. They suspected that, just as he had done on the Susquehanna, Cresap planned "to rob [Pennsylvania] of advantages" and the company would "not stick to settle lands that may be within [our] limits & so create new Squabbles." He admitted Lee had "a plotting head," but his disgust with Cresap blurred his vision of who was the prime mover.[37]

With the petition filed and plans for expansion into the Ohio Valley coming into focus, there remained one crucial yet unanswered question: Would the king approve of any of this? Would the Royal government want to encourage a steady stream of colonists moving farther and farther away from provincial capitals—and therefore imperial authority? It was not a foregone conclusion the Crown would endorse a colonial scramble for Ohio.

Luckily for Thomas Lee, Thomas Cresap, and the Ohio Company, recent political changes across the Atlantic Ocean played right into their hands. In London, the winds of strategic planning had begun to shift. A faction of politicians in opposition to government began to see land war in Europe, like the one they just fought from 1744 to 1748, as detrimental to Great Britain. Wars were increasingly expensive and did little to advance Britain's interests. This faction, which styled themselves as "Patriots," insisted that, rather than focus on protecting British interests in Europe, the government put commerce—and colonies—first. The interior of North America, in their eyes, thus became essential to England's national security. The men surrounding King George were suddenly enthusiastic about British flags waving and snapping all over the American backcountry. They now encouraged their sovereign to support plans just like the one Thomas Lee had proposed. By winter's end of 1748, the King's Privy Council took Lee's Ohio Company proposal under consideration.[38]

Meanwhile, the men surrounding the French king, Louis XV, reached similar conclusions. When strategists in France spread out their maps of North America, their stomachs churned with anxiety. French colonial ventures in Louisiana and Canada struggled and yet were exorbitantly expensive. From 1731 to 1744, the Crown spent more than 10 million livres, a staggering sum, mostly on defense, yet there were only a few thousand more colonists in all of Canada than in Rhode Island. The French could not project power, and English traders were showing up in ever-increasing numbers of Native settlements.[39]

Policy makers in Paris knew that it was only a matter of time before English settlers followed the traders over the mountains. French planners worried that if the British gained control of the Ohio, they could dominate the entire Mississippi Valley, "and then to the river's mouth on the Gulf of Mexico, and from there to the possession of Spain." To prevent such a nightmare from becoming reality, the governor-general at

Quebec made plans for French soldiers to occupy the Ohio Valley. The French, like their rival, suddenly began to view British expansion into Ohio as a matter of the highest national security. Though expensive and risky, occupying the Ohio Valley could reap enormous benefits: not the least, it could help secure their shaky alliance with the Anishinaabeg. If they could pull it off, France would have the upper hand throughout North America.[40]

The other great power in the area also sensed the possibility of conflict on the horizon. The Six Nations, worried about the loyalty of the Great Lakes Natives who had relocated to the lower Ohio, invited several leaders from those new villages to a meeting in the summer of 1748 to engage in negotiations with them and Pennsylvania leaders. If all went well, the Iroquois—and Pennsylvanians—hoped to solidify formal trade arrangements with the Pickawillany "rebels." When the parties arrived, Scarouyady, the Iroquois' half-king representative, spoke on behalf of the Twightwees, though they refused to recognize his attempt to bring them under Iroquois control.[41]

It's possible that this Native delegation stopped at Cresap's house along the Potomac on the way home from the conference, as it was becoming a popular spot for traders, surveyors, explorers, and Natives on the move. Earlier that spring sixteen-year-old George Washington, laboring through what would be his first of several trips up the Potomac, noted the commotion at Oldtown. After spending a few March nights out in the rain, he was probably happy to see Cresap's house, especially since he had to endure "the worst road that ever was trod by Man or Beast" to get there. Washington spent four nights at Oldtown in 1748 in the company of one of the Fairfax sons. The young squires witnessed something far different from the tidewater society to which they were accustomed. "We were agreeably surpris'd at the sight of thirty odd Indians coming from War with only one scalp," Washington wrote in his diary. After sharing some of the liquor they had brought along, the Natives cleared a large circle, made a bonfire, and began to dance. Washington transcribed what happened next: "the best Dauncer Jumps up as one awaked out of a sleep & Runs & Jumps about the Ring in a most comicle Manner[.] He is followd by the Rest and begins there Musicians to Play." Apart from this recitation of the ritual, Washington did not offer much commentary in his description.[42]

One wonders, however, what the teenager from tidewater thought about this scene around the fire in front of Cresap's house. Washington observed this Native dance one year after he had painstakingly transcribed 110 "rules of civility" into his commonplace book, a list cobbled from European advice texts about how to conduct oneself properly in all social situations. But that self-help guide was of little use around the Oldtown bonfire. Washington portrayed himself as above it all; dismissive, just documenting the facts as a detached observer. In the next diary entry he sniffed, "nothing Remarkable on Thursday, but only being with the Indians all day so shall slip [skip] it."[43]

The diary doesn't tell us what Washington thought of the Cresaps, though these frontier folks were important to his family and connections. In fact, the four spring days he spent in Oldtown were virtually a rump meeting of the Ohio Company, with three current members (Thomas and Daniel Cresap, George Fairfax) and a future one (George Washington) present. What did Washington think of the hybrid culture that his family's business partners cultivated? A week later he would uncharacteristically break his detachment, admitting to his diary he found a group of Cresap's neighbors "as Ignorant a Set of People as the Indians." What were his first impressions of the youngest child who ran around the Oldtown compound, six-year-old Michael? Washington would get to know father and son well in the decades to come, but at this age, he probably longed to be surrounded by Lord Fairfax and his servants rather than Thomas Cresap and his frontier children.[44]

Six months later, it was the Washingtons' turn to host. On October 20, 1748, the Ohio Company's first birthday, the members gathered at Lawrence Washington's place on the Potomac bluffs named Mount Vernon. The house was not yet the Palladian mansion his younger brother would build there, but it certainly dwarfed the Cresap's rough-hewn home nearly two hundred miles upriver. Even though it would be another month before the Privy Council approved the Ohio Company's plan, the group was optimistic and ready to get a head start. And from the very first agenda item—reimbursing him £12 for the costs of filing the original petition with the council clerk at Williamsburg—to the pooling of funds for him to purchase a cargo of goods to make a good first impression with the Ohio Indians, all of the Company's plans revolved around Thomas Cresap.[45]

The waning rays of bright autumn dusk helped Thomas and his son Daniel paddle home from Mount Vernon. Those same sunsets would be among the last Shickellamy would see. Things had been falling apart for Shickellamy at Shamokin, his headquarters at the confluence of the North and West Branches of the Susquehanna. Three years before, the Oneida ambassador had made some new friends. In 1745, Moravian missionaries asked permission to establish a church there. Shickellamy, not given to distrust colonists, welcomed these unusual Christians who did not command or scold Native people. But other Natives in Shamokin didn't see these German settlers the same way, and they abused and threatened them. Their experience in Shamokin was so disturbing that Moravians later labelled Shickellamy's village "the very seat of the Prince of Darkness."[46]

Then, in 1747, smallpox struck. The "feaver" swept away eleven members of Shickellamy's family. His oldest son Tachnedorus (John Logan Shickellamy) lost five children and his wife, Vastina. Only one of their children, a son named Tod-kah-dos, survived. The middle son, Soyechtowa (James Logan Shickellamy), likewise mourned the loss of three of his children. Conrad Weiser informed the Pennsylvania council that Shickellamy was "a proper object of Charity; he is extreamly poor . . . and I cannot see how the poor old Man can live." Weiser suggested the council should send him some goods to aid this "true Servant to the Government," and they agreed. Shickellamy managed to make the sixty-mile journey to Weiser's to collect Pennsylvania's gift, but while there heard surprising news of the Ohio Indian "rebels" meeting with the Iroquois. He had been cut out of this loop. This was the clearest evidence that the

Six Nations had turned their attention west, and away from Shickellamy and Shamokin. Making matters worse, his old friend Weiser had helped orchestrate the Iroquois' strategic shift to the Ohio. He tried to stop this threat to his power and place in the Iroquois diplomatic apparatus, but to no avail. The 1748 conference with the Twightwees signaled the decline of Shickellamy's influence.[47]

After he returned home from his journey, Shickellamy sought comfort with his last friends, the Moravians. His bitterness toward Weiser over his Ohio betrayal only grew (they would never reconcile), but Moravian ministers came and cared for the all-but-broken Iroquois ambassador. In November 1748, he took the final step, traveling to the Moravian settlement at Bethlehem to practice as a Christian. A few weeks later, in December, as he attempted to hike the hundred miles home across rugged terrain, illness struck him on the road. Wind gusts that week were so strong they capsized a boat in New York harbor. At the top of one of Pennsylvania's steep ridges, their biting force must have been overwhelming. While Shickellamy managed to make it back to Shamokin, he died shortly after his return, on December 6, 1748.[48]

Shickellamy's sons grieved yet again. They had lost a brother in the Iroquois' wars with the Catawba. Smallpox had destroyed their households, and now they had lost their father. With attention moving west to the Ohio country, Shamokin no longer commanded the attention it had only a decade ago. Its power wasn't completely gone, however. Shickellamy's sons, who had been trained by their father in the diplomatic arts, would continue the family legacy as important Native brokers.

The following summer, the Ohio Company convened again, this time near Fredericksburg, halfway between the Lees and Washingtons. Although the Company still hadn't received approval, the members moved ahead with their plans anyway, authorizing Thomas Cresap to start surveying, laying out roads, and plotting for trading stations into the Ohio country.[49]

By mid-summer, George Croghan had heard disturbing rumors in the backcountry. He sent riders east over the mountains with letters warning Pennsylvania's leaders about "an alarm that Mr. Cresap . . . spread amongst the Indians last fall that ye Virginians was going to settle a Branch of Ohio called Yougagain," and thus disrupt their trade networks. This information prompted one Pennsylvania leader to contact Thomas Penn about the threat posed by "that vile fellow." Croghan responded a bit differently to this news: he set off on his own, negotiating with some Ohio Natives to buy an enormous tract of two hundred thousand acres for himself between the Monongahela and Ohio Rivers.[50]

Unbeknownst to the Penns, at the moment they were fuming about Croghan's information, Thomas Lee received the news that the king had indeed ratified the Ohio Company's plan. They had permission to take up two hundred thousand acres on the south side of the Ohio River west of the Forks up to a place called Yellow Creek. There was, however, one catch. Since the Crown wanted to encourage western settlement, rather than merely land speculation, they put in a condition: if Lee's organization wanted the additional three hundred thousand acres they had requested, they were going to have to prove themselves first. They needed to sponsor families to go west, and the Ohio Company was to provide protection by building and garrisoning a fort—all at their own expense. England's expansion into the Ohio was going to be largely a private concern. It was to be the Ohio Company's responsibility to govern and protect this huge territory, and all the people therein.[51]

Pennsylvania (or George Croghan) wouldn't be the Ohio Company's only competition. In Paris, the Ministry of Marine agreed with the assessment that New France's survival depended on its expansion into Ohio. In June 1749, just as the Ohio Company met in Fredericksburg, the governor dispatched a small force of two hundred soldiers under the command of Captain Pierre-Joseph de Céloron de Blainville into the Ohio Valley. Their task was the same as that given to Cresap that month: to survey Ohio and lay down markers establishing new boundaries. Céloron's baggage was loaded down with small lead plates bearing the French royal seal. He was to bury these at strategic places along what would be a three-thousand-mile canoe trip from Montreal down the Alleghany, turning west with the Ohio, and finally circling back to Detroit and up the lakes to return home.[52]

The report Céloron filed upon his return was anything but sunny. Things were worse than the French had feared: enthusiastic English traders had made promises everywhere, and Ohio Indians were gravitating into their orbit. He, too, heard rumors that colonial authorities in Virginia, Maryland, and Pennsylvania were not far behind. If they were going to extend New France and trap the English against the mountains, they needed to hurry.

⸻

The summer of 1749 was a glorious one for Thomas Lee. In July he received word that his company had been granted the rights to annex Ohio. A month later, he became Virginia's acting governor. Then, in September, he chaired the third meeting of the Ohio Company, at which they approved the purchase of a small spot of land where Wills Creek flowed into the Potomac, fourteen miles to the west of Oldtown. In the years to come, English forces would build Fort Cumberland on the spot, and around it would grow a settlement that would eventually become the second largest city in Maryland. But in 1749 the clearing Thomas Cresap and his team hacked out just above the riverbank was to feature a single building: the Ohio Company's storehouse for Indian goods going over the mountains to Ohio.

Cresap and his men finished building the fortified storehouse at Wills Creek by late summer 1750. Stocking it became another family affair. The shipment of goods the Company had ordered the year before—£4,000 sterling worth—had safely crossed the Atlantic and travelled up the Potomac to Daniel Cresap's place on his father's land at Conococheague. When the Wills Creek warehouse was complete, they brought the cargo up and stacked it inside, ready for further transport to Native country. The storehouse was the Ohio Company's foothold in the west and, in many ways, an extension of the Cresaps' own estate. What's more, in an incident that sheds light on Thomas's private life at this moment, one of the contracts he took out on the Company's behalf for purchasing cattle to stock the warehouse had two witnesses—an Oldtown neighbor and Elizabeth Lamy. It was an act she could not have performed as his wife. Thomas had not only continued his extramarital affair, but Elizabeth had also moved from Frederick to Oldtown.[53]

Just as he relished these achievements in the west, Thomas Lee's fortunes cruelly turned against him. In February 1750, his wife died at age forty-nine, and before the year was over, he would join her. The company's political connections evaporated with Lee's death. In fact, the new leaders of the Virginia Council were now hostile to the Ohio Company, having their own competing land interests at heart. Lawrence Washington took over as head of the Company, and the group began looking for new friends in Williamsburg. When they heard Robert Dinwiddie was to be Virginia's new lieutenant governor, the Company astutely cut him in by voting the fifty-eight-year-old Scot a share. Given the potential riches that the Ohio Company promised, Dinwiddie was happy to accept membership. Soon, he had struck up a correspondence with Cresap, who kept him apprised of Native activities on the frontier. "As you are a member of the Ohio Company," Dinwiddie wrote, "I think your good offices will be very necessary, and . . . I shall be glad to hear frequently from you."[54]

With political favor reestablished in Williamsburg, the Company made plans to extend their claims over the mountains. Now that the storehouse was ready, they pushed to scout the entire grant and began clearing a road to the rivers south of the Forks, the Monongahela and Youghiogheny. Cresap's scouting partner had died in the spring of 1751, and the Company replaced his services with Christopher Gist. As mentioned earlier, Gist was a rising trader and a go-between in the area. At the Company's request, he set off from Cresap's house for a prolonged journey to the Ohio Valley, visiting the new Native villages along the Ohio River and documenting the best lands as far south as Kentucky.[55]

Cresap soon followed in his steps, cutting a path from Wills Creek to the Monongahela. By 1752 the road was shoddy but complete, and Thomas began construction of the Company's second outpost, a fort where Red Stone Creek dumped into the Monongahela (now Brownsville, Pennsylvania).[56]

For two decades, a storm had been slowly gathering over the Ohio Valley. In June 1752, the first drops began to fall. That month, Gist and Croghan escorted a delegation of Virginia commissioners to Logstown, a Native village fifteen miles down the Ohio from the Forks, to meet with Tanaghrisson, the Mingo's half-king. They wanted to gain permission to build a third Ohio Company installation, this one at the Ohio Forks.

Aware that the suggestion would likely prove controversial, the Virginians came prepared, carrying the 1744 Lancaster treaty with them to prove their "right" to the Ohio Valley. If that didn't work, they also brought £1,000 worth of goods from the Wills Creek warehouse. They were unprepared, however, for the hostility they encountered from Shawnees and Delawares, who were unmoved by claims about what the Iroquois had done at Lancaster. Tanaghrisson, however, listened. In addition to being an agent for the Iroquois, his eyes dazzled at the mound of gifts that Gist "heaped on the ground before him." Tanaghrisson decided to play for time, agreeing to allow the Ohio Company to build a strong house at the Forks, but deferring the truth of the Virginians' claims about Lancaster until he could check with his superiors in Iroquoia. Not wanting to displease the Ohio Indians, the English, or the Six Nations, Tanaghrisson was between several fires.[57]

A week after the conference broke up at Logstown, a group of 270 Anishinaabeg warriors and 30 French soldiers stealthily took up positions surrounding the Pickawillany settlement. On June 21, 1752, they launched a surprise attack on Memeskia's "rebel" settlement. As most of the Twightwee men were away on a hunt, the village fell without much difficulty. The Anishinaabeg-French force took Memeskia captive and marched him out of the village. In full view of the people he had led to the Miami River, the Anishinaabeg killed, boiled, and ate him.[58]

The Pickawillany raid and Memeskia's fate dramatically shifted the balance of power in the Great Lakes. Immediately, the power of Ohio "rebel" Natives and their connection to Pennsylvania traders vanished. By crushing Memeskia's independence movement, the Anishinaabeg reinforced their relationship with New France. In 1749, Céloron had noted disaffection for the French among the Great Lakes Natives. No longer. That the storm that was about to break over the Ohio Valley could be misnamed the French and Indian War—based as it was on the myth that all Native peoples fought for France—was a consequence of the decisive reduction of Pickawillany.

Perhaps the most important shift in 1752 occurred even before the Anishinaabeg warriors had reached home to tell the news of their triumph. A ship carrying a new governor-general for Canada pulled up to the docks in Quebec and off stepped the Marquis de Duquesne with orders to begin France's military occupation of the Ohio. He instructed the Canadian militia to begin drilling exercises and made plans for a series of French forts to be constructed from Lake Erie south. "Ohio" was the Iroquois's word for it, but French traders labeled the river that began at the Forks as La Belle Rivière. Not just *a* beautiful river, but *the* beautiful river. Duquesne wanted such a place to be firmly a part of New France.[59]

Duquesne sent more than two thousand men south in the spring of 1753. The first fort was built on the shore of Lake Erie, with a second a few miles away on a creek that emptied into the Alleghany River. A third, at the Delaware village of Venango, seventy miles north of the Forks, would be ready by autumn. Duquesne next planned to occupy the Forks.[60]

The Ohio Company's men were headed to the same location from the opposite direction. Thomas Cresap enlisted the help of another important trader (and George Croghan's son-in-law), William Trent, to construct the Red Stone Creek storehouse on the Monongahela. The project was completed by the end of 1752, and the Ohio Company was now just thirty-five miles from the Forks.[61]

The summer of 1752 had been a transformative one for George Washington as well. At Mount Vernon, he kept watch as tuberculosis closed in around his beloved half-brother Lawrence. With Lawrence's death in July, the twenty-year-old stood to inherit that estate on the bluffs and his brother's shares in the Ohio Company. Young George was a man on the move in tidewater society. It is perhaps not surprising then that when Dinwiddie decided that Virginia needed to warn the French to cease their invasion of Ohio, he turned to this up-and-coming young gentleman, the newest partner in the Ohio Company.

As Washington, then a major in the Virginia militia, set off for the Forks late in 1753, the waves of change that had been building throughout the region during his twenty-one years suddenly converged. He arrived at the Company storehouse at Wills Creek on November 14, where he recruited Gist and four others as an escort party. They set off north, inspecting the land at the Forks and reaching Logstown by the end of November. There, Washington ran right into Scarouyady, who told him his Iroquois counterpart, Tanaghrisson, was out hunting a few miles away. While they waited, four French deserters strode into Logstown, accompanied by a Philadelphia trader. They had come from a Shawnee town farther down the Ohio and informed Washington about French military activity all throughout the Great Lakes. Washington and Tanaghrisson went to call on the new French installations on the Alleghany.[62]

At Venango, the young Major Washington delivered Dinwiddie's warning letter to the French commander, who replied, "As to the summons you send me to retire, I do not think myself obliged to obey it." Washington might have expected this, but he confided in his diary what he saw around him in the French fort was shocking. He was aghast at how the French were trying to gain Tanaghrisson's loyalty: "I can't say that ever in my Life I suffer'd so much Anxiety as I did in this affair. . . . I saw that every Strategem that the most fruitful Brain could invent was practiced to get the Half King won to their interest." The French were trying to steal the loyalty of the Iroquois, and Washington had accidentally arranged the opportunity! He and Gist packed to leave as soon as possible.[63]

They headed for the safety of Cresap and the Ohio Company, but they were soon ambushed in the woods. As Washington would later write, "We fell in with a party of French Indians, [who] had laid in wait for us. . . . One of them fired at Mr. Gist, or me, not 15 steps [away], but fortunately missed." These lurking Natives were from Anishinaabewaki; their newly reinforced alliance with the French gave them ample reason to stop Virginia's incursion into the Ohio Valley. Washington and Gist started to run, traveling day and night until, at dark on Sunday night, December 23, they reached the Alleghany River, just up from the Forks. They cobbled together a raft and crossed so hastily that Washington ended up tumbling headlong into the freezing water. He managed to swim over to an island in the middle of the river, where, drenched, he and Gist spent a terrifying night.[64]

The plunging temperatures bit their fingers and toes, but it also saved them. Dawn revealed a frozen-over river, and the pair crossed gingerly to the other side. By January 2, they were at Gist's house near Red Stone Creek. Within a week they were at the Ohio Company's storehouse at Wills Creek, and on January 16, Washington arrived in Williamsburg, where he presented the French refusal to Dinwiddie.

Two months later Washington would be headed back to the Ohio, this time at the head of two companies of Virginia militia. Again, he was on his way to Wills Creek, but not before ordering the soldiers to make camp at Thomas Cresap's house. The six-year-old boy Washington had last seen at Cresap's was now twelve. What must adolescent Michael have made of the soldiers camping in his front yard—soldiers who, at daybreak on May 28, 1754, in Jumonville's Glen, would take actions that would affect not only the lives of his family but also those of tens of millions throughout the globe?[65]

The region surrounding the Forks of the Ohio River in the middle of the eighteenth century was a mysterious "blank space on the earth" onto which European imperialists, commercial speculators, and Native peoples all projected power. It fueled the dreams of many who sought to turn that place and all its resources into personal fortunes and patriotic glory. Washington's journal illustrates how quickly Ohio dreams could turn into nightmares. When he scribbled down how he didn't understand what was going on around him, he was just the latest to do so.

Most of the people in this chapter were bewildered. The maps were wrong. The boundaries were vague. People disappeared. Towns disappeared. Witnesses confessed they didn't understand what was going on at Logstown, at Shamokin, at Lancaster, and at Oldtown. Leaders gave away territory over which they had no rights of ownership; others spoke for people they had no right to represent. Loyalties snapped back and forth. These misunderstandings resulted in friction, conflict, and violence. You, too, may have been a bit bewildered reading about all the rivers and settlements, factions, and schemes that marked the eighteenth-century scramble for Ohio.

Some players in this time and place saw opportunity in the bewilderment of the Ohio scramble and made use of it. Sowing bewilderment was often a precursor to resolving bewilderment through an enforced border or a renamed town—a strategy that specifically advantaged one party over another. Violence was often the means the progenitors of bewilderment employed to resolve a misunderstanding in their favor.

Many groups—tribes of Europeans, colonists, and Natives—sought to control the Upper Ohio Valley. Everyone who Washington and Gist saw on their trip had only just arrived. They all had come to Ohio to build a better life; they, too, dreamt of the future. But, once the bloodshed began in 1754, those ambitions would all but evaporate. The scramble for Ohio would devolve into a vicious, retributive war. The Cresap and Shickellamy families would each experience a swirling vortex of violence that engulfed the region for the next decade.

CHAPTER 2

STRAIGHTFORWARD FACTS, 1754‒1759

"For a time I would feel I belonged to a world of straightforward facts; but the feeling would not last long. Something would turn up to scare it away."

—*Heart of Darkness*

We now refer to the conflict that began at the Ohio Forks as the Seven Years' War. But its original name, at least in America, was probably more fitting: the Great War for Empire. It was a war produced by imperial fantasies; a war about which color European mapmakers would use to paint the interior of North America. They assumed that these vast blank spaces would be filled in either with red (for the British) or blue (for the French). The reality on the ground, however, was never that simple. Because of its bewildering nature, people all over the world looked for ways to organize the confusion of this climactic war that would be fought all over the globe and would forever transform North America.

According to the standard telling, the Great War for Empire was a resounding victory for the British in North America. This was not, however, the view held by a host of Native peoples who believed that they had won. Leaders among the Iroquois, Anishinaabeg, Shawnees, and Delawares designed their own maps about who controlled the Ohio country and filled in the region with their own colors and cultural values.

Moreover, even among the British there remained questions about who *actually* won the war. While their soldiers would stand triumphant at the Ohio Forks and across French Canada, British victory was only made possible by significant aid from the American colonies. And those colonies held strong opinions about what victory would mean for them: both Pennsylvania and Virginia vied to establish their right to develop the region once the war was won.

In short, the British "conquest" of Ohio was not a straightforward affair. In fact, it was utterly confounding. Throughout the conflict, as we will see, people across the American backcountry could not tell friends from enemies nor winners from losers. Colonists went out on vengeful raiding parties disguised as Natives, while Natives disguised themselves as colonial militia. Prominent Native leaders thought to be friendly to the colonial governments were found in enemy camps painted for war. With no front line, war swept through the entire mid-Atlantic. Time and again, roads that were cut to carry soldiers and settler families west were choked with refugees fleeing the mountains, terrified that Native bands were close on their heels. In 1756, George Washington captured the mood well: "When I came to this place I found everything in deep confusion; and the poor distressed inhabitants under a general consternation." At the epicenter of all this bewilderment and terror were the families of Thomas Cresap and Shickellamy.[1]

On their journey home from the frozen-over Forks in the first days of 1754, George Washington and Christopher Gist passed a small party on the new road a few miles north of Wills Creek. "We met 17 Horses loaded with Materials & Stores for a Fort at the Forks," Washington noted in his diary on January 6, 1754. The Ohio Company was on their way. This caravan, led by George Croghan's trading partner and kin, William Trent, had traveled thirty-seven miles north from the Ohio Company's outpost at Redstone Creek and set up their camp at the Forks. Soon, they began the difficult work of turning over the hard, frosty soil.[2]

They knew they were in a dangerous spot. With every shovelful, the forty workers must've constantly scanned the winter horizon, anxiously wondering who was watching. Near the end of February, both Trent and

Cresap sent nervous letters to their backers in Williamsburg, reporting fears that the French might show up at any moment. Despite the anxiety, building proceeded apace that spring, with Tanaghrisson acting as supervisor. The Mingos' half-king laid the fort's first log, believing that his involvement in its success would mend fences with the Ohio Indians and help keep this country Native, no matter what any colonists, governors, or army officers might proclaim.

On the morning of April 17, Trent and Cresap's fears materialized. Three hundred canoes and sixty flat-bottom boats—many loaded down with cannons—came into view. Nearly one thousand French soldiers disembarked and assembled in the woods just above the Forks. The forty-one Ohio Company men surrendered without a shot.[3]

A few weeks later, Washington and two companies of Virginia militia slowly made their way there. After having camped at Oldtown, they proceeded northwest, widening the trading path from Wills Creek to Redstone as they went. They had little going for them: Washington's men were undersupplied, greatly outnumbered, and were so loud and slow that they couldn't even count on surprise. By May 23, Washington had his men at the Great Meadows, a large clearing tucked between two mountain ridges about twenty miles from Redstone. Three days later, Tanaghrisson and a group of Mingos informed Washington that French troops were very near. Indeed, the French commander at the Forks had sent out a patrol of thirty-five men to find them.

The skirmish that took place the next morning—halfway between two Ohio Company outposts and sixty miles from Thomas Cresap's house in Oldtown—would signal the beginning of what would become the largest global war yet in human history.

That confrontation on May 28, 1754, took the lives of a dozen French soldiers, and concluded with Tanaghrisson splitting open the skull of a wounded French officer, Ensign Joseph Coulon de Villiers de Jumonville. It was a gruesome act meant to demonstrate that Europeans could not conquer the Natives of Ohio, and it certainly got the attention of the French. The commander at the Forks dispatched a large force to eliminate the Native-colonial group that had killed thirteen of his men. Within

a few weeks, French soldiers demanded Washington's surrender in the
Great Meadows, his miserable attempt at defense—the pitiful stockade
dubbed Fort Necessity—having failed.

A humiliated Washington stumbled back to Wills Creek. The day
after Washington's men surrendered, French troops torched the fort
Thomas Cresap and William Trent had built at Redstone two years
earlier. Virginia and the Ohio Company were vanquished. The French
began to build Fort Duquesne on top of the logs Tanaghrisson, Trent,
and the Ohio Company had laid at the Forks.

———

News of the calamity reached London in early September, and King
George II met with his ministers about how to respond. By month's end,
they had decided to send General Edward Braddock and two regiments
of British soldiers to dislodge the French from Ohio. Braddock was to
have command of not only 1,300 regulars but also of colonial governors
who were to provide him with whatever men and supplies he required to
achieve his mission. Over the last few months of 1754, while the English
made preparations for Braddock's expedition, three companies of colonial
militia set about transforming the Ohio Company's storehouse at Wills
Creek into Fort Cumberland. For the time being, it guarded the fragile
settlements on the Potomac, including Cresap's place at Oldtown fourteen
miles downstream. Once Braddock's redcoats arrived, Cumberland was
to be the launching point for England's offensive into Ohio.[4]

Braddock landed in Virginia in February 1755. That spring, as his
troops began their month-long march to Fort Cumberland, the general
summoned Colonel William Johnson from New York to his headquarters.
Johnson had just turned forty, and over the last decade he had established
himself as one of the most important traders in the Albany area. Like
Conrad Weiser and George Croghan in Pennsylvania, Johnson was an
important broker keeping the peace between New York and the Iroquois.
Braddock had instructions to elevate him to Indian Superintendent,
a powerful new imperial position. For the next twenty years Johnson
would preside over British-Native relations throughout the northern

backcountry. He would be made a baronet for his troubles and become known as Sir William Johnson, but it would prove a tumultuous tenure.[5]

Braddock joined his troops as they tramped through the hill country of western Maryland. On May 8, he and his men made camp next to the Potomac as its shallow, gentle current flowed past Cresap's house at Oldtown. A naval officer attached to Braddock's command wrote about the beautiful vistas that surrounded what used to be Opessa's Town. But the charm of the view did not extend to the people living there. As the officer noted in his diary, "Here lives one Colonel Cressop, a Rattle Snake Colonel, and a damned Rascal." Dislike of Cresap, as well as this derisive nickname, was widespread among Braddock's officers. A month later, another diarist, an English woman who accompanied her brother, one of Braddock's commissary officers, across the Atlantic, *also* referred to stopping "at a Rattlesnake Colonel's nam'd Crisop."[6]

In addition to ridiculing the family in their private journals, Braddock's staff loudly criticized them during those early summer weeks. The English soldiers were near starvation and growing resentful as they made their way west. "We can get nothing but Indian Corn, or mouldy Bisket," one officer wrote home to London. Blame for the lack of provisions increasingly fell on the Cresap family.[7]

The supplies for Braddock's men had been gathered at Daniel Cresap's house in the Conococheague settlement, where wagons were to be loaded down with barrels of meat and flour and sent to Fort Cumberland. When Braddock's hungry troops opened the casks, they found the provisions ruined. Officers were enraged at both father and son: the flour spoilage was "occasioned by the infamous neglect of [Daniel] Cressap" and the "quantity of beef" Thomas was to provide "was no sooner brought to Camp but it was condemned to be buried." Braddock himself complained to the governor of Pennsylvania that "one Cressup . . . had behaved in such a manner in Relation to the Pennsylvania Flower [sic] that if he had been a French Commis[sioner] he could not have acted more for their Interest." The English viewed the Cresaps as emblematic of the bewildering difficulties Braddock's men inexplicably faced in America.[8]

But, no matter what Braddock's circle thought about him, what did

Thomas Cresap think of himself in 1755? The answer can be found in the naval officer's diary mentioned above. The entry in that diary made a significant contribution to American culture. In full, it reads:

> Here lives one Colonel Cressop, a Rattle Snake Colonel, and a damned Rascal; calls himself a Frontier man, as he thinks he is situated nearest the Ohio of any inhabitants of the country, and is one of the Ohio Company. He had a summons some time ago to retire from the Settlement, as they said it belonged to them, but he refused, as he don't want resolution; and for his defence he has built a log fort round his house.

This is, according to one literary scholar, the first time that the term "Frontier man" entered American letters. But Cresap did not merely speak into existence this word that would become so ingrained in American folklore; he embodied the qualities that word would come to signify: the boasting, the defiance of authority, the martial defense of property and household, even the proudly poor diction. He was the rugged individual come to life. To Braddock, his officers, and many in the colonial elite, however, Cresap and his family were merely dirty, rough scoundrels.[9]

One of William Johnson's first duties as the new Indian superintendent was to order George Croghan and his Mingo friends to rendezvous with Braddock at Fort Cumberland. Tanaghrisson had died the previous October, and the Mingos under his leadership had gone to Croghan's estate near Carlisle, Pennsylvania, for protection. Croghan was to bring fifty adult Mingo men with him to act as scouts for Braddock. In a sign of what was to come, the Mingos were displeased when Braddock wouldn't let their families come with them. The gruff British general did not see the point in bringing women and children along on a military expedition. That misunderstanding would contribute to his undoing.[10]

The Mingos accompanying Croghan were joined at Fort Cumberland by a contingent of Delaware Natives from the Ohio country, led by Shingas. The Delawares arrived with an open mind, and Shingas presented Braddock with an impressive gift of goodwill: a diagram of Fort Duquesne that a Virginia militia officer had secretly sketched and the Delaware leader had personally smuggled out. In return, Shingas asked what was going to happen to the land around the Ohio Forks once British troops had used his gift to defeat the French. Braddock's answer was unfortunate. Shingas later stated that the General had "replied that the English Shoul[d] Inhabit and Inherit the Land." When the Delaware leader protested that this might cause his people to join the French, Braddock reiterated that "No Savage Shou[d] Inherit the Land." Moreover, according to Shingas, the general boasted that "he did not need their Help and had No doubt of driving the French and their Indians away." With this, Braddock's Native support evaporated. Shingas and the Delaware departed the next day, some so "very much Enraged" that they immediately did join the French. Only Scarouady and seven Mingos would escort the redcoats to Fort Duquesne.[11]

Braddock and his 2,200 English and provincial soldiers began their torturous 125-mile journey from Fort Cumberland to the Forks a year and a day after Tanaghrisson split open the skull of Ensign Jumonville. Rather than follow the footpath Thomas Cresap had helped blaze from Wills Creek to the Ohio Company's storehouse at Redstone, Braddock chose to cut his own road to the Forks through the mountains and thick woodlands. But that construction effort proved slow, so slow that after a week Braddock decided to divide his forces and rode along with an advance "flying column" that could move unhampered by heavy wagons loaded down with siege cannon and supplies.

On the morning of July 9, a small French force supported by a large Native contingency ambushed that weary, hungry detachment along the banks of the Monongahela. More than six hundred Natives—mainly Anishinaabeg from the Great Lakes—fanned out on both sides of the English and thrashed the lead elements commanded by then-Lieutenant Colonel Thomas Gage. Over the next three hours, Braddock's men stood their ground until a bullet slammed into the general's back. Their courage then collapsed and they fled the field. Braddock, mortally wounded, fell into the care of the man standing next to him, George Washington, who was miraculously unhurt despite several bullet holes through his coat. British expectations of retaking the Forks were dashed. Washington arranged for Braddock's body to be buried in the road and, to hide any evidence of its location, the survivors then tramped over his grave as they returned to Fort Cumberland.

What remained of those English regiments would eventually trudge past Cresap's house in Oldtown as they marched east in defeat. Mere weeks earlier, Cresap saw himself as the gatekeeper of a dawning age of Anglo-American expansion and prosperity. How things had changed in two months. As the shattered army filed by, the "rattlesnake colonel" must have realized his family was in grave danger. His outpost was now an obvious target, as the road that Braddock's soldiers had hacked to the Forks could be reversed. It would almost certainly channel war right to their doorsteps.

The *Maryland Gazette* was already publishing stories about a general flight from the backcountry, with Cresap's neighbors abandoning their homes and fields lush with mid-summer bloom. Looking about his household—which included Hannah, his wife of nearly thirty years, his teenaged daughters Elizabeth and Sarah, his youngest son, Michael, who had just turned thirteen, and a small retinue of servants—he must have feared for their future. Others he cared about would be in danger, too. Daniel (twenty-seven) and his four young sons were not much safer at the vulnerable Conococheague settlement. Thomas Jr. (twenty-two) still lived close by. He could at least bring his young bride and baby daughter to the family compound for protection. As could another nearby woman Thomas Sr. apparently cared deeply for: Elizabeth Lamy. Earlier in 1755, Thomas had taken out a deed "for the better Maintenance and Support of Elizabeth Lamy," giving her the use of a parcel of fifty acres out of the Indian Fields tract, a few hundred yards from his house. In the likely case that Oldtown was attacked, it's equally probable that Elizabeth would've sought shelter at Thomas's compound, as it was the closest stronghold to Indian Fields.[12]

Whatever fear Cresap felt that day would prove well-founded. The area that Braddock's beaten regulars left behind as they retraced their steps and dragged themselves back over the eastern ridges would quickly descend into a zone of death, destruction, and captivity. The sixty miles between Winchester, Virginia, and Fort Cumberland was about to become a central combat zone between two hostile European empires. The scattered settlements along the creeks that emptied into the South Branch of the Potomac, including Patterson's Creek from the Virginia side and Town Creek on Maryland's, quickly became military targets. The most important of these settlements, and the landmark noted on colonial maps, was the Cresap household at Oldtown.

The other epicenter of frontier defense was at Shamokin. As one of his first tasks as superintendent, Sir William Johnson set about trying to keep the Six Nations out of the French interest. They pledged neutrality, while some Iroquois-affiliated groups sided with the colonies. After Braddock's defeat, some of those Native allies went to Shickellamy's former residence to form their own military units to fight the French. Shickellamy's oldest son, Tachnedorus (John Logan Shickellamy), was to serve as captain of one group, with his two younger brothers acting as junior officers. Together, Shickellamy's sons worked with other Native allies and agents George Croghan and Conrad Weiser to keep the peace along the Susquehanna in central Pennsylvania in the months after Braddock's defeat.[13]

Then, in the first days of October, the raids began.

"The Smouk of the Burning Plantations darken the day, and hide the neighboring mountains from our Sight," wrote Washington's second-in-command on October 4. "By the best Judges of Indian Affairs, it's thought there are at least 150 Indians about us. They divided into Small parties, have Cut off the Settlement of Paterson's Creek, Potomac, Above Cresops, and the People on Town C[ree]k about four miles below his house." The "rattlesnake colonel" had been very lucky: even though the parties had come close, they had spared Oldtown this time. Others had not been so fortunate. The attacks at Patterson's Creek alone saw more than forty settlers killed or taken prisoner. Reportage of the damage done by "a Party of these Barbarians," with Cresap himself as a main source, appeared in newspapers up and down the Eastern Seaboard.[14]

The attackers were Delawares from the Ohio country. Led by Shingas and supplied with French arms from Fort Duquesne, they came east early in the fall, splitting into several raiding parties. One group, which was headed toward Shamokin, wiped out a new settlement of farmers at Penn's Creek on the western banks of the Susquehanna. Small bands of Delawares went from cabin to cabin, attacking with their tomahawks, setting fire to the dwellings, and carrying off women and children. At least a dozen died, and twice as many were taken as captives.[15]

Shingas was more than mad at Braddock for rejecting his people's claims at their Fort Cumberland meeting. He was also furious with the Shickellamys, father and sons. A year and a half earlier, Pennsylvania's erstwhile go-between, Conrad Weiser, went up to Shamokin, looking for the three sons of his old friend Shickellamy. Weiser knew there was to be a big meeting that summer in Albany that promised to bring together all the Native leaders in northeastern North America, and he wanted the Shickellamy sons to go and lobby the Iroquois to agree to another massive land deal. The brothers hesitated when they heard what Weiser proposed—the selling of all lands west of Shamokin up to the Alleghany Mountains—but he pressed them: "I told them if they did not now stir, Others would bring it about, and they would then be obliged to sit and kill Lice and Fleas, and repent their Backwardness and Folly." Weiser overcame their doubts, and soon the three sons set off for Iroquoia. With the Shickellamys' help, the Iroquois agreed to the "Albany Purchase" in July 1754. In fact, the Albany deal, in which the Iroquois ceded seven million acres for £400, included many established communities near the Forks—like Shingas's home on the Alleghany River. Shickellamy had started the Delawares' ejection with the Walking Purchase two decades earlier; now his sons compounded their dispossession at Albany.[16]

When Shingas's Delawares struck fourteen months later, they specifically targeted any new colonial cabins within the Albany Purchase, such as those at Penn's Creek. In the days after that attack, John Harris

and Thomas McKee, two Pennsylvania traders living down the Susquehanna, gathered a posse of about fifty men to investigate. When Harris
and McKee stopped in Shamokin on the way to Penn's Creek, the village was in an uproar, with people they didn't recognize milling about.
Shamokin had long been a confusing place, but this was especially bad.
Lots of Natives were painted as for war, and one who was allegedly a
reliable friend informed them that a massive force of 1,500 French and
Indians had left Fort Duquesne sixteen days ago, headed toward the
Susquehanna. He warned them not to cross the river.

The Pennsylvanians didn't know who to trust. They thought they
had allies in Shamokin, but it was also conceivable that this place was
now hostile. Harris and McKee defied the warning, and, sure enough, as
they crossed the Susquehanna and approached Penn's Creek, a volley of
bullets ripped through their party, one smashing into Thomas McKee's
hand. After an exchange of fire and a frenzied swim across the river (in
which several colonists drowned), they returned to Shamokin.[17]

Shingas's raiders next laid waste to the ninety families in the Great
Cove, another new Albany Purchase settlement, taking dozens of women
and children into captivity. These attacks produced a general panic. "Our
Roads are continually full of Travellers," one Pennsylvanian reported.
"Men, women, children, most of them barefoot, have been obliged to cross
those Terrible Mountains with what little they could bring with them."
The *Maryland Gazette* begged for volunteers to build trench defenses
around the town of Annapolis as enemy forces "draw nigher and nigher."
The next week, Marylanders panicked that the enemy was within thirty
miles of Baltimore. The sense of impending doom was reinforced when,
five days later, in the middle of the night, the largest earthquake in
colonial history shook people awake, knocked down fences, and toppled
chimneys all over North America. "A frightful charm this," one Boston
paper opined.[18]

For Shickellamy's sons, these were indeed days when the Earth
trembled. As winter began to set in, they realized the world of negotiation and coexistence their father had crafted at Shamokin was no longer
tenable. As Benjamin Franklin observed in the wake of Shingas's attacks,

"some of those Indians we took for our Friends, I find are suspected by their Neighbors." Franklin could not help the understatement, for he could only acknowledge half of the story. He recognized how colonists now glowered at "friendly" Natives, but he could not conceive of the harrowing ordeals produced by the suspicions that had developed *among* the Native peoples. Shingas's attacks on the Albany Purchase settlements were clearly a judgment on the Shickellamys and their Iroquois sponsors.[19]

Afraid of everyone, Shickellamy's three sons cast about frantically looking for safe places to hide. Tachnedorus (John Logan Shickellamy) left Shamokin to take refuge at a town further up the Susquehanna, which Pennsylvanians suspected was now "the headquarters of French and Indians that have for some time infested our Borders." His disappearance was a mystery. For months, Conrad Weiser anxiously looked for the trio, unable to locate them. Finally, in February, two messengers found Tachnedorus and conducted him to Philadelphia for an interview, careful to avoid the usual route to the capital for they were all "apprehensive that the [Pennsylvanians] would fall upon them" as enemies.[20]

Upon reaching Philadelphia, Tachnedorus had a private breakfast with Conrad Weiser. The aging trader was eager to find out where his friends had been for months. Tachnedorus contended that he was taken away from Shamokin under duress, but since he was "afraid of the back Inhabitants, and much more afraid of the Delawares," he didn't know what to do.[21]

Tachnedorus promised Weiser that he wanted to remain steadfast to the English, despite Delaware intimidation. When Weiser asked whether he or his brothers actually participated on raids against colonial settlements, he admitted that they had. "My two Brothers went with the Delawares to fetch provisions," he said. "The lame one [Soyechtowa], whom you know very well, could not perform the Journey," but the youngest brother, John Petty Shickellamy, went along and exchanged fire with colonists as they tried to get away with stolen hogs. "He told me his Heart did bleed to see Indians and English fight, and he assured me he did not fight against the English but gave way."[22]

The winter of 1756 had been torture for Shickellamy's sons. Nearly everyone they encountered said they wanted to kill them, Pennsylvanians and Delawares. The bewilderment sent them into hiding deep in the highlands. However, with the spring, they hoped those ordeals would be behind them. Tachnedorus left Philadelphia with a clear purpose: he promised that he would "live and die with" his colonial brethren and "fight with and for them."[23]

Alas, the spring of 1757 would not bring clarity. Tachnedorus had sworn he would go to the Susquehanna, reclaim and reconstitute his family, and return to Shamokin where he hoped to be met by Pennsylvania troops who would begin building a fort there. Apparently, he didn't (or couldn't) keep that promise. When Scarouady came upon the Shickellamy brothers in late March, he was shocked to find them in a party of eighty hostile Delawares all painted for war. "We took John Shickellamy [Tachnedorus] aside," Scarouady reported, and "upbraided him with his Ingratitude to this [Pennsylvania] Government which had ever been extremely kind to his father when alive and to them and their Families since his decease." They "charged him not to go along with" the party that was about to "set out against the Inhabitants of Pennsylvania." Tachnedorus's response was the same as it was to Weiser in Philadelphia: he had no choice. While going was against his inclination, "they threatening to kill him if he did not go," Scarouady reported.[24]

In fact, he didn't go, but that only caused another desperate flight. Days later, on the run again, Tachnedorus showed up at McKee's outpost with his family in tow. But he did not feel safe there, either. As another Pennsylvanian visiting McKee's place observed, "John Shickellamy [Tachnedorus] is greatly dissatisfied with being there and has several times been out of Temper," in no small part because he was surrounded by "fearful, ignorant people who have Sometimes told [him] to his face, that they had a good mind to Scalp him." This wasn't just a free-floating, paranoid fear: that very week Pennsylvania had issued a scalp bounty, rewarding $130 to any colonist who presented the scalp of an enemy male Native. With good cause, Tachnedorus worried someone would see his body as a viable asset. Was he an enemy? He didn't know the answer to that question himself, or what that word even meant in those earthshaking, bewildering days. Tachnedorus begged McKee to again shield him from harm, insisting he escort his sick family "down to where his sister and childer is, at Conistogo." When he had first gone into hiding, he had sent his sister to what he thought was a safe place, to live among the Conestoga Indians farther down the Susquehanna, just a short distance from where Thomas Cresap had operated his ferry service twenty years earlier. Tachnedorus thought his extended kin at Conestoga would protect them.[25]

The six months since Shingas's attacks had produced unspeakable terrors along the Susquehanna and Potomac Rivers. Ohio Natives, encouraged and supplied by the French at the Forks, had taken their revenge on all the groups who had sought to evict them from their lands. "It is," one colonist wrote, "impossible to describe the Confusion and distress." Colonel Thomas Gage, having fully recovered from wounds suffered at Monongahela, wrote to Washington about the reports coming from the region through which he had recently marched: "the Accounts we have received of their Barbarities gave me infinite Concern when I reflected on the many poor families that I had seen, when in that part of the World, that had been massacred by these Murderers." Perhaps Gage's empathetic reflections included the young family at Oldtown, at whose house he had rested along the banks of the Potomac River.[26]

By the spring of 1756, the region was awash in ghastly sights. Dead bodies of adult men and young girls lay scattered around the Conoco-cheague settlement. Two members of a Maryland company "were found tied to trees and their bodies horribly mangled," Maryland's governor Horatio Sharpe reported, adding, "it is supposed they were tied while living and put to the most cruel death." The scalped body of another militia officer was found somewhere on the path between the Cresap outpost and Fort Cumberland.[27]

The "cruel robberies, murders, and Devastation among poor back settlers" had become so endemic that parties of volunteers vowed to take their revenge on Natives. But which ones? The *Maryland Gazette* reported the arrival in Baltimore of a party of forty-one people (including thirty children) from Conococheague who had fled "the Fury of the Enemy." One of those refugees reported how "*Thomas* and *Daniel Cresap* (sons of Col. *Cresap*) went out about 3 weeks since, with 60 People, dressed and painted like *Indians*, to kill the Women and Children In the *Indian* Towns, and scalp them, while their Warriors are committing the like Destruction on our Frontiers." Gage's empathy certainly didn't extend to the "poor families" of Natives they were setting out to massacre.[28]

The vigilante party led by Cresap's two oldest sons headed northwest out of Fort Cumberland; by April 23 they had gone about twenty miles west and were lying in wait at the Little Meadows. Someone got too excited and fired too quickly, spoiling the ambush. The Natives they were hunting sprinted into the woods. When one broke off from the rest, Thomas Cresap Jr. and two others ran after him, in hot pursuit for about a mile. "When the Indian finding that Mr. Cresap gained on him and would over take him," the newspaper account related, "he dodged behind a large Tree, and Mr. Cresap stopped behind one smaller." They then fired at one another at "so near together that it could not be distinguished" who shot first. "It seemed like one Gun," another account stated. Cresap had hit his mark, but his opponent had, too. "Mr. Cresap was shot . . . in the Breast and others of his Party coming up, he told them, *Not to mind him, he was a dead man, but to pursue the Enemy*, and then dropped down dead." After finishing off Cresap's assailant and scalping him, they buried the twenty-three-year-old "as privately as they could."[29]

The *Maryland Gazette* summed up Cresap's demise by noting he "has left two little children; and his Death is lamented by all who knew him." Another news account that appeared in Franklin's *Pennsylvania Gazette* was more effusive, using language that would be employed nearly twenty years later for Thomas's little brother: "his Death was reckoned a very great Loss, being a most active Man, an extraordinary Woodsman, able to undergo great Hardships, as good a Marksman as was in the Country, and beloved by all that knew him; and that if he had lived, he would have had as fine a Company of Rangers as was to be met with anywhere." The Maryland assembly introduced a motion to provide for the children of such a hero.[30]

But look again at Thomas Cresap Jr. as he bled to death in the woods that April afternoon. What qualified him as a hero, as someone whose children merited the charity of a grateful colony? The *Maryland Gazette* tells us what he looked like in his last moments: "dressed and painted like an Indian." And it tells us what his purpose was in those woods: he was out to find, kill, and scalp Indian women and children. What separated him from Shingas? Colonial newspapers were already using a phrase that would become more widely used in the years to come: "merciless savages." The Cresap boys were not called that, but they certainly fit the epithet.[31]

What about the man who shot him? We don't have the luxury of knowing who he was, but it's certainly possible a similar encomium could have been made for him: that he was an active man, an extraordinary woodsman, and was beloved by all who knew him. Those same colonial newspapers also employed a phrase that was becoming ever more ubiquitous: "unhappy sufferers." They meant the colonial victims of Indian raids, describing the plight of farmers "flying with their Children to save their lives, many of them having nothing to subsist on . . . and hardly any Clothes to defend them from the cold." But the Native who Thomas Cresap Jr. shot was an "unhappy sufferer," too, and, had the Cresap boys achieved their goal, they aimed to put Indian women and children through precisely that kind of sorrow and pain. The names that colonial institutions assigned to people as they ran through the woods carried with them a distinct set of values: "friends" versus "enemies," "sufferers" versus "savages." Just as the maps were inaccurate, these labels did not correspond to conditions on the ground. Natives suffered from the treatment of these enemy "savages" just the same. Indeed, it was often impossible to know in those woods who was who.[32]

Within a few weeks of his son's death, the rattlesnake colonel and his remaining boys—including fourteen-year-old Michael—led another expedition west. In all, sixty armed men charged out of Oldtown, where they soon met up with Cresap's old Ohio Company partner, Christopher

Gist, and another two dozen men. Cresap himself described what they found as they reached the area where his son died. In a long letter he would send to the *Pennsylvania Gazette*, Thomas described encountering a "very nauseous smell" as they neared the swamp where the body of his son's assailant had been left unburied. "We saw no Bones, but great Signs of Wolves, Turkey Buzzards and Ravens having been at the Plate, and make no Doubt of his dying there." The grief-stricken father learned, too, that hungry animals had "scratched up the Body of Thomas Cresap, and eaten it likewise."[33]

After this gruesome discovery, they were ready to fight but couldn't find any enemies and soon fell to arguing among themselves. They decided to divide into separate parties, with Gist sticking to the road while Cresap's party plunged into the woods. As a news report would later tell it, "soon after their Separation, Lt. Gist fell in with a large party of the Enemy, who not being able to distinguish our Men on Account of their being painted and dressed like Indians," entered into desperate battle. Cresap's men, after getting lost in the thickets, also encountered a small party and fought a running battle along the road. They soon returned to Fort Cumberland, and a messenger carried the scalps they had collected to Philadelphia to be turned in for their cash reward.[34]

A month later, Thomas Cresap set out again from Oldtown. To allay the confusion about who was who out in the woods, he had his men wear red caps. This time they had only reached the "End of the Fence below the Saw Mill," when the cattle they were driving stopped, and the shooting started. Even though this skirmish wasn't much of an event, it was widely reprinted in colonial newspapers. In fact, most of the evidence for these scouting expeditions comes from printers who deemed them important news. Colonists far from this scene of action, in Massachusetts, New York, Connecticut, and South Carolina, read reports of the Cresaps' expeditions in their local newspapers. Cresap himself sent dispatches from the front to Franklin's *Pennsylvania Gazette*.[35]

These print reports attempted to clear up the mess about who was who in the backcountry. They were tools that were supposed to distinguish between heroes and villains, to classify some behavior as just and denounce other behavior as barbaric—even when it was the same action. The spare paragraphs of news from the western frontier that appeared in the pages of a newspaper worked to make sense of the chaos. For a colonial reader who perused the paper in a coffeehouse or at home next to their warm hearth, these stories provided illusions of order in that wild country. But out in the woods, far from the print shops of Annapolis or Philadelphia, bewilderment reigned. Thomas Cresap Jr. and his men dressed themselves like Indians. Friendly Natives were found wearing war paint. Gist's men couldn't figure out who to shoot at. Three weeks after the report of Cresap's men fighting in red caps, a revealing account ran in the *Maryland Gazette*: word arrived "from the Mouth of Conoco-cheague that 4 Indians, dressed in red Caps, and much like Col. Cresap's Men, came down among the Inhabitants there, and killed and scalped 2 people, then made off."[36]

As raids continued to occur all around their compound at Oldtown, the Cresaps decided they could not hold out any longer. The "frontiers-man" and his household packed up and joined the flock of settlers who had been streaming east for months. Thomas temporarily moved them in with his son Daniel's family near the mouth of the Conococheague, about fifty miles away. Whether Elizabeth Lamy rode along in the wagon with Hannah and the family in their flight east isn't known. From there, Thomas would continue to lead scouting parties, arrange for supplies to go to soldiers in Virginia and Pennsylvania, and soon represent Frederick County in the lower house of the Maryland assembly. Michael, who had been sporadically attending a boarding school outside Baltimore, was sent farther east for his own safety.[37]

As it had been for the Shickellamys, the year since Braddock's defeat had been excruciating for the Cresaps. It was even more so for those who were forced to live with them. As Cresap would later report in an advertisement in the *Maryland Gazette*, when the family fled from Oldtown, two indentured servants and a young girl took the opportu-

nity to escape. "The Mulatto's Name is *Isaac Cromwell*," Cresap listed
in his attempt to recover his lost property. About forty-five and "can
talk Dutch as well as English," he was married to an English woman,
Anne Green, "of a middle stature but pretty thick." They ran away with
Isaac's young daughter Susanna on July 25, 1756. Cresap thought they
may have fled to Baltimore, but guessed they probably had gone "either
over the Bay or else to the Northward." That Cresap assumed they were
somewhere in the east is hardly a surprise; Isaac, Anne, and Susanna
had been forced to endure the horrors they had experienced at Oldtown
and now, though fugitives, they chose not to raise their daughter under
such conditions anymore. The Seven Years' War had already exacted a
harsh psychic toll on families living all over the American backcountry.
But it was only beginning.[38]

In the summer of 1757, Pennsylvania troops began building Fort Augusta
at the forks of the Susquehanna next to Shamokin. Scarouady and the
Shickellamy sons had begged Pennsylvania to protect them with such
an installation, but by the time its walls began to rise, conditions were
sufficiently dangerous that they had all fled the area. Scarouady escaped
to Iroquoia and was dead of smallpox a year later. "We have lost ourselves," Tachnedorus (John Logan Shickellamy) lamented. His brother
Soyechtowa (James Logan Shickellamy) had also "suffered himself to
be laid a stray." Tachnedorus promised yet again that he would be "open
and free with you about everything," but reiterated to the Pennsylvanians just how much the trials of the last year had cost him: after being
"cursed by some of the people of Pennsylvania to his face and threatened
to be killed," he had "almost perished in the Woods for want of food."
Shickellamy's oldest son "thought it very hard that there was no Body
that spoke in his favour among them people on Susquahanna, tho they
all knew that he was a Constant friend to the people of Pennsylvania."
Weiser loaded Tachnedorus up with a large assortment of goods, some
for his use, some to "give to the poor, [and] some to Sell" at Shamokin.

He went on his way, and, this time his journey away from Philadelphia would be an extended one. Voluntarily or not, Shickellamy's sons were no longer the center of Native-colonial relations in the region.[39]

For the residents of the Ohio Valley, the Seven Years' War was entering its third year in 1757. If you were a British official in London or a French one in Paris, however, the war had only started a year earlier, in 1756, when their respective monarchs declared it so. And if you were a member of any of the groups of the Great Lakes Natives, then the fighting began not with Washington's surrender at Fort Necessity, but with the ritual torture of Memeskia at Pickawillany in 1752. By that reckoning, this war was already five years old.[40]

The Seven Years' War is thus a rather misleading name for a conflict that lasted longer than that for many of its combatants. "The French and Indian War" is perhaps even worse. Setting aside its internal logic—that Native peoples were junior partners, rating second place—its real deception comes with its totalization: the implication being that all Natives fought, and when they did, they did so for the king of France. Many Native peoples stayed out of the fighting. As much as the British begged, the Iroquois stubbornly remained neutral during these years. Others fought for the British. The Cherokees and Catawbas both offered their services to King George in the late 1750s.

No matter what we call it or how we number it, the war began to enter a new phase after 1757. The devastating, sustained power of Ohio Indian raids had all but brought the proprietary government in Pennsylvania to its knees. As attacks flared up again that summer, they could not afford to lose any more Native support—and that meant listening to (and perhaps even admitting) Native claims that Pennsylvanians had been bad actors, especially by their committing a massive fraud against the Delawares with the Walking Purchase twenty years before. They maybe needed to revoke the Albany Purchase (1754) that Weiser and Shickellamy's sons had orchestrated to secure colonial claim to thousands of square miles west of the Alleghany Mountains, too.

Thus, pressed to the wall, Pennsylvania authorities begrudgingly made some substantial changes to their Native diplomacy, which changed the tide of the war. After those concessions, made in a series of multi-lateral treaty conferences concluding at Easton in 1758, it may be more accurate to call this phase of the conflict the British and Indian War.[41]

There is no evidence that Shickellamy's three sons attended any of the major treaty conferences Pennsylvania conducted in 1757 or 1758. It's certainly understandable why they might not want to show their faces. The Iroquois had a revolt on their hands. To the east of Shamokin, a group of Delawares living in the Wyoming Valley (what is today Scranton/Wilkes-Barre, Pennsylvania) was using the chaos of war to make a bid for independency, a movement that directly defied everything the Shickellamys had worked for since the 1730s. Shickellamy and his sons' political worth with both Pennsylvania and the Six Nations was predicated on keeping revolts like these from materializing. Concerned about this brewing threat, the Grand Council of the Iroquois decided that, instead of using intermediaries, they needed to negotiate themselves. Shickellamy's sons were unwelcome in this atmosphere, so it was probably wise to stay away.[42]

On October 18, 1758, Pennsylvania authorities and Native peoples from Iroquoia and Ohio gathered at Easton, a small village on the Delaware River that lay near the center of Walking Purchase land, to begin the latest in the colony's series of efforts to talk their way to safety. This meeting was the crowning episode of their negotiations: more than five hundred Native peoples from Iroquoia and Ohio attended.

At Easton, the Grand Council neutralized the Delawares' revolt in the Wyoming Valley by trading away some control over the faraway Ohio region, thus shutting down the threatening independence movement much closer to their homeland. The Iroquois agreed to allow Delawares in Ohio to negotiate directly with Pennsylvania (instead of through them) but maintained full control over the eastern Delawares who still lived in the Wyoming Valley. As further evidence that Shickellamy's sons were in trouble, Pennsylvania and the Iroquois also renounced the Albany Purchase. The Penns agreed to restore to the Iroquois all lands west of the Alleghanies and reassured the Ohio Natives that their territory was secure from imperial domination. The vast Ohio country was theirs.[43]

The Ohio Delawares were thrilled. They had won. Their representative at Easton, Pisquetomen, declared the war was over. Within days, he was galloping through central Pennsylvania, reaching Fort Ligonier on November 7. There he found British General John Forbes, seriously ill and in bed. Forbes was in command of another British expedition sent to oust the French from Fort Duquesne. While Forbes tried to preserve his strength, his redcoats were hacking their way to the Forks. Much to the chagrin of the members of the Ohio Company, Forbes's men did not use Braddock's road but were in the process of building a new one, a path through central Pennsylvania protected by a string of forts, including Ligonier, where Pisquetomen found the dying general. Forbes welcomed news of the Easton treaty and hustled Pisquetomen to Ohio to convince the Delawares and all Natives to stand down when the British made their attack on Fort Duquesne. He knew his men stood a far greater chance of success if Natives refused to support the French.

There was no time to lose. The same week Forbes's advance troops had gotten to within a dozen miles from the Forks, Pisquetomen convened his own conferences with Shingas and other Delaware leaders. They were in the process of considering the Easton agreement when the French commander concluded that all was lost and, on November 24, 1758, he gave the order to blow up Fort Duquesne. If anything punctuated the fact that Ohio Natives believed they had won the war, the roar of Fort Duquesne's exploding gunpowder magazines was it.

Thomas Cresap was in Annapolis for the December session of the Maryland Assembly when word arrived of Duquesne's fall. The *Maryland Gazette* urged patience until rumors were confirmed, but confirmation arrived in the capital a week later that Forbes was indeed master of the Ohio Forks. The source of all the evil inflicted on settlers from the Susquehanna to the Potomac—Fort Duquesne—was eliminated, too. It must have been a joyous holiday throughout the entire mid-Atlantic region.[44]

What in retrospect was an obvious turning point—the beginning of the end of New France—didn't seem so throughout most of 1759. Even with all their recent gains, Britain's hold on the Forks remained quite precarious. The French spent the spring planning to recapture Fort Duquesne and negotiated with any Great Lakes or Ohio Natives who would listen. During those same months, colonial governments struggled to transport supplies to the Forks; it took five long months to get a supply shipment over the mountains. Worse, Virginia's commander at Fort Cumberland continued to report attacks all around his compound, including that "Some of the Enemy has been as low as Cressop's."[45]

The surrender of Fort Niagara in July ended French hopes of retaking the Forks, as it crippled their ability to sponsor raids in the area. But it was two events in September 1759 that permanently sealed England's control over Ohio. On September 13, the Canadian citadel of Quebec fell to British General James Wolfe. And three days before Wolfe's legendary victory, the inner walls of Fort Pitt began to rise at the Ohio Forks. Ten times the size of Fort Duquesne, Fort Pitt would be a massive pentagonal fort measuring four hundred feet from tip to tip. It would enclose more than eighteen acres and had barracks enough for a thousand men.

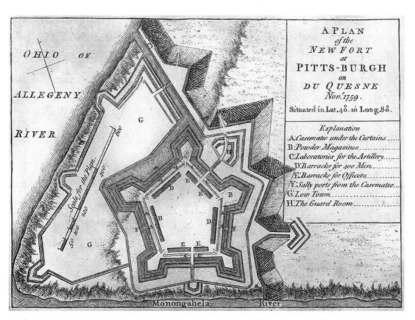

Figure 7. Plan of Fort Pitt, 1759. Published in 1765 by cartographer John Rocque.

Soon there would be more than 150 houses in the surrounding village, Pittsburgh, to shelter the thousands of soldiers and laborers it took to complete this "emblem of empire." Ohio Natives had expected the British to build a trading post at the Forks, a place to gather and get supplies to live better in their own territory. Fort Pitt was no trading post. It was, rather, a sign that the British were planning to dominate the continent.[46]

As the glorious year of 1759 came to a close, Francis Fauquier, who had replaced Robert Dinwiddie as lieutenant governor of Virginia, summed up the current situation to the Board of Trade in London. His letter anticipated many of the problems that would wrack the region—and the empire—for the next two decades. First, there was "the Affair of the Indian Fur Trade"—that is, who would have the right to trade with the Natives in the Ohio country once the war was over. Unless the Board made a ruling, he was sure it would "again prove a bone of Contention between this Colony and Pennsylvania." The best way to prevent this conflict, he argued, was to settle the jurisdictional problem and draw boundaries. Imperial surveyors were needed in the American backcountry, and fast. Second, "the Pensylvanians act" as if Pittsburgh belonged to them, Fauquier complained. "Upon what Authority they proceed I am yet intirely ignorant." This territory, he and his predecessor Robert Dinwiddie had assumed, was Virginia's. Then there was the problem of colonial settlement. "People seem to be very desirous to settle on the fine fertile Lands, lying on the Waters which fall into the Ohio," but "there are some Points which seem to require Consideration." Those lands had been promised to several parties: "By Proclamation from Mr. Dinwiddie all Officers and Private Men who have served in those Parts have a Right to a Certain proportion of those Lands, to which they are daily laying claim. It is also to be considered whether the Crown will renew the two Great Grants." Perhaps it might make more sense, Fauquier suggested, "to make a Separate Government of all the Lands between the Mountains and the Waters."[47]

The concerns Fauquier outlined were no doubt serious, but they all assumed that the British had really won in Ohio. Had they? Fort Pitt suggested one answer, but the Treaty of Easton suggested another. Native peoples rejected any notion that the Ohio Forks were British territory. According to their understanding, this was Indian country, and, with their smashing attacks and diplomatic victories, it was more securely so than it had been for a generation. They had explicitly been promised at Easton that no colonists would settle on these lands.

The fight over the right to map—to control, to possess, to make the rules of—the Ohio country had produced horrific violence in the 1750s. Families were slaughtered. Others were ripped apart. Households and forts were burned. Enemies appeared as friends and friends sometimes dressed themselves as enemies. As much as imperial conceits, like maps, roads, and newspaper columns, tried to sort them into readily identifiable, reliable categories, the experience of war along the Potomac, Susquehanna, and Ohio Rivers made little sense.

This confounding violence had profound effects on the Shickellamy and Cresap families. Shickellamy's sons found themselves cast off from their homes, relations, and friends. Everywhere they went someone threatened to kill them. They didn't know if they should be more afraid of colonists or Natives. The political capital their father had amassed evaporated. No one could classify them—were they friends? were they enemies? There were times during a few of those traumatic seasons when they didn't know the answers themselves.

The family of the first frontiersman had suffered dislocation and loss, too. Wolves had devoured the body of twenty-three-year-old Thomas Cresap Jr. on a ridge of the Alleghany Mountains. His adolescent brother Michael had ridden alongside his father painted as Natives, yearning for revenge.

Despite appearances, neither family was safe quite yet. The Treaty of Easton and the construction of Fort Pitt might have indicated to some in Anglo-America that the long-suffering region had indeed returned to a world of straightforward facts, but that feeling would not indeed last long. Something was already brewing that would scare that notion away. Within a few months of Fort Pitt's completion, the clouds of war were already gathering again, darkening the western sky.

CHAPTER 3

GROVES OF DEATH,
1760–1763

"My purpose was to stroll into the shade for a moment; but no sooner within than it seemed to me I had stepped into the gloomy circle of some Inferno. The rapids were near, and an uninterrupted, uniform, head-long, rushing noise filled the mournful stillness of the grove, where not a breath stirred, not a leaf moved, with a mysterious sound . . ."

—Heart of Darkness

Today, high atop the bluffs that face the confluence of the North and West Branches of the Susquehanna River, is Shickellamy State Park. Gazing down on the wide river from a height of more than three hundred feet, one can see where Fort Augusta used to stand and a replica of the log cabin in which lived the man for whom the park is named. The North Branch, visible for miles as its waters ease their way toward the convergence, remains a captivating sight—despite all the concrete barriers, highways, and four-lane bridges that run alongside and over it.

In Oldtown, Maryland, one can have a similar experience from a much more proximate location. A few yards down from where Thomas Cresap's house used to stand is the oldest privately owned toll bridge in America. As long as your car doesn't weigh too much, for a small fee you can cross the Potomac River on this rather rickety bridge and drive into West Virginia. The river runs just a few feet deep at this crossing and in

Figure 8. The confluence of the North and West Branches of the Susquehanna, taken from the heights of Shickellamy State Park. Directly across on the southern side is a reproduction of Fort Augusta and Shickellamy's log cabin, as this was the site of the original village of Shamokin.

high summer the sun dapples the water between low-hanging branches from trees close to the shore. Eighteenth-century observers frequently noted how bucolic Oldtown—formerly Indian Seat, formerly Opessa's village—was. It still is.

These toll bridges and highway barriers signify more than intrusions on the bucolic, however. They connote order: the enforcement of traffic laws and collection of taxes; the universal recognition of state boundaries and national legal tender. Those roads, bridges, and boundaries are striking in their own way because they represent the resolution of bewilderment in favor of settler colonists and their descendents. But more than just marring pastoral spaces, imposing artificial order, and burying evidence of who came before, the cement and signage obscure what defined those same vistas centuries ago: utterly confounding, brutal violence.

In the middle of the eighteenth century, before the cement, colonists and Natives turned beautiful places such as these into groves of death.

Figure 9. The North Branch of the Potomac River just before it merges with the South, going past Oldtown, Maryland. Thomas Cresap's house was on the hill to the left of the photograph, taken from the toll bridge running across the surface.

The violence that erupted during the Seven Years' War would return with a vengeance in 1763 and devastate many of the same idyllic places that had only begun to recover.

This violence was enabled by and exacerbated a broader collapse of the social order. When war broke out, the categories that settlers had used to set one group apart from another in the mid-eighteenth-century American backcountry broke down almost instantly. For the rest of the war and after, participants struggled to make sense of the muddle. They attempted time and again to reestablish words like "friends" and "enemies," "savages" and "sufferers," and—even more importantly—"winners" and "losers." Natives negotiated these expectations at treaty conferences and, when that failed, they turned to violence. The hard feelings of betrayal that grew during those confusing and gruesome times would climax in 1763, with the vengeance of Pontiac's War and the Paxton Boys' vigilantism. By that time a new set of social categories, based on race, started to emerge from the ashes. As they had in the terrible years of the 1750s, in this new decade the Cresap and Shickellamy families encountered yet more groves of death. Some of them were right in their own front yards.

=====

The discontent that would break into a resumption of conflict in the American backcountry began even before the end of Seven Years' War. In the first days of 1760, Tachnedorus (John Logan Shickellamy) began hearing hostile whispers near his new home on the edge of Seneca country. Although Shickellamy's oldest son had stayed away from politics since moving from Shamokin three years prior, the rumors were sufficiently alarming that he decided it best to tell Conrad Weiser.

In late January 1760, a militia captain wrote to Weiser, telling him that Tachnedorus wanted his father's old friend to come up to Fort Augusta to talk. Weiser replied that he was ill and couldn't travel but invited Tachnedorus and his brothers to visit him at his house. Pennsylvania authorities didn't know what was on his mind, but they were eager to find out. The French had not yet been completely defeated in Canada, as Montreal still held out, and the peace produced by the Treaty of Easton and the capture of the Ohio Forks was tenuous at best.[1]

But rather than travel to Weiser's, Tachnedorus stuck around Augusta for weeks, waiting. Others tried to talk to him, but he would only unburden himself to Weiser. Pennsylvania leaders told Weiser to send his son if he couldn't go, "as it is a very critical time, and if [Tachnedorus] be sincere he may communicate many things which at this time may prove of great Service. It is said the Indians are everywhere plotting to betray the Garrisons, and to do some great stroke." Weiser, who would die a few months later at the age of sixty-four, sent his son with gifts for the Shickellamys. It proved no use. The travails of war had taught Tachnedorus to trust no one but his closest friends, and he refused to share what he had heard whispered in the woods.[2]

This episode captures just how precarious things were in 1760. Pennsylvania authorities treated Tachnedorus's sudden appearance at Fort Augusta as a portent of very terrible days ahead and wrote multiple letters asking how they should handle him. They scrambled to get him the right gifts so not to offend. Inexperienced officers were terrified they might make a misstep. All this to impress someone who by this time was almost entirely out of political power.

The flurry of letters concerning Tachnedorus's extended visit to Fort Augusta in 1760 are revealing in another way. Writers consistently referred to the Shickellamy brothers as living among Mingo Indians. Tachnedorus's father was an Oneida, and his mother a Cayuga, so as per the matrilineal dictates of the Iroquois, the three Shickellamy brothers were Cayugas. At a treaty conference in the early 1760s, the trio would be listed as part of the Cayuga delegation. But it seems that, by 1760, they also identified as Mingos. "Mingo" usually referred to Iroquois-speaking Natives who had allegedly migrated to the Ohio country. But many people who identified themselves as Mingos lived much closer to Iroquoia, on or near the West Branch of the Susquehanna. Whether they had migrated back after the chaos of the 1750s or had never left is unclear. One colonial trader described his efforts going up the West Branch to a town called Paseckachkunk, which was a "Mings Town." If that's so, and if that's where Tachnedorus had come from when he appeared at Fort Augusta, then he did have important news to share: for it was from this region that the earliest seeds of a movement that would become known as Pontiac's War first blossomed.[3]

The Ohio Company partners were also plotting in the early 1760s. In the aftermath of the British capture of Montreal in 1760, the Ohio Company once again looked to cultivate a new government insider, as they had done by taking Robert Dinwiddie into their midst in 1752. Their target was Colonel Henry Bouquet, the new British commander at Fort Pitt. Thomas Cresap, who had dealt with Bouquet before, extended an offer asking if he would like to join his fellow gentlemen in a full and equal membership in the Company and informed him that each member was to have twenty-five thousand acres of their own. Bouquet, leery of the invitation, sat on the rattlesnake colonel's proposal for more than a month.[4]

When he did respond, Bouquet craftily begged for more time, putting him off until they could meet in person. Then, in a rather "by the way" manner, he added:

> you know that by the last Treaty of Easton approved and confirmed by the Ministry at home, we have engaged not to settle the lands beyond the Allegany, and tho' the Government of Virginia and Maryland did not accede to that Treaty, I conceive that they are equally bound to it, and that no Settlement will be permitted upon the Ohio till the Consent of the Indians can be procured.

Bouquet's rejoinder, which we can assume Cresap forwarded to his fellow partners, seemed to have little impact on the Ohio Company's plans. Though Cresap was not in attendance when his associates gathered in Williamsburg a month later, the body resolved nonetheless to have Thomas begin repairs to the old Company storehouse at Wills Creek. Bouquet, the Pennsylvanians, and even Ohio Natives could say what they wanted; the Company acted as if the Seven Years' War never happened. They would rebuild the road from Oldtown to Wills Creek, and from there to Redstone on the Monongahela, and then to the Forks—just as they had in 1754. Indeed, in the May 1761 session of the Maryland legislature, Assemblyman Cresap asked the colony to fund one hundred militiamen for Fort Burd, far more than the tiny stockade built a couple years before at Redstone could hold. The motion failed dismally, but it is evidence that Cresap had Redstone and Ohio Company expansion on his mind.[5]

Cresap continued to try to cultivate Bouquet throughout 1761. Since Bouquet had recently purchased a significant estate near his own along Conococheague Creek, Cresap asked whether his new neighbor wanted to stand with him in the Frederick County election for the Maryland assembly. Winning the election was not in question, Cresap boasted, since he had always had sway enough "to Carry one Gentleman whom I recommended." Bouquet declined.[6]

All this pressure further unsettled the already fretful Bouquet. In February, his boss, General Jeffrey Amherst, the commander of all British forces in America, had forbidden his officers from giving Natives expensive gifts. Within months of this decision, bad news started to land on Bouquet's desk at Fort Pitt. The Mingos caused particular problems, waylaying supply wagons and stealing horses, sometimes right next to the gates of English posts. Then, in June, news reached Bouquet that the Senecas' plotting had developed into a much larger movement. The Senecas had formally invited several Native groups around the Great Lakes to join them in a universal uprising. The whispers that Tachnedorus had probably heard in Seneca country in 1760 had grown into something so serious that Bouquet furiously reinforced the walls of Fort Pitt and ordered his magazines put into proper order.[7]

Natives were very upset about the lack of gifts, but even more about the British allowing further settlement. "Here comes Such crowds of Hunters out of the Inhabit[ants] as fills these woods," a British officer wrote from Redstone in October, "at which the Indians seems very much disturbed." Bouquet decided to take a stand. Without seeking permission, he issued an official proclamation: no colonists would be allowed to settle or even hunt west of the Alleghany Mountains without express approval from either General Amherst, from himself, or from a colonial governor. The diplomatic situation with Native peoples all over the backcountry was as delicate as it had ever been. Thomas Cresap—his lobbying, his political organizing, his sending people to Redstone—might tip the region back into a general war. This would be Bouquet's final answer to the Ohio Company: neither Cresap nor his colleagues were welcome.[8]

Bouquet hoped his proclamation would soothe anxious Native minds in Ohio. It created the opposite condition among political power brokers in colonial capitals. Virginia's Lieutenant Governor Francis Fauquier immediately wrote to Bouquet to let him know how his cordon "gives rise to some uneasiness in this colony." Bouquet replied that it was men like Thomas Cresap who forced his hand: "for two years past these Lands have been overrun by a number of Vagabonds, who under the pretence of hunting were making several settlements in several parts of them, of which the Indians made grievous and repeated Complaints, as being contrary to the Treaty made with them at Easton." He continued, "notwithstanding what I have done they Still . . . continue the same practice," with Natives complaining that they just now "discovered Ten new Hutts in the Woods, and many Fields cleared for Corn." A few weeks after Bouquet sent this reply, a party of Mingos killed two hunters a few miles south of Fort Burd, the Redstone outpost. They were shot, scalped, and their cabins "sett on fier over them," according to George Croghan. Nathaniel Tomlinson Sr., one of Cresap's neighbors from the South Branch of the Potomac, was among the dead. "This affair has frighted the people that was settling" and some fled back east, a British soldier reported from Fort Burd. Redstone was already destabilizing relations in the fragile Ohio country, and the troublesome settlement was likely uppermost in Bouquet's mind when he banned all colonists from the western woods.[9]

If Redstone was high on Bouquet's list of irritants, so was its leading developer. After receiving Fauquier's inquiry, the Fort Pitt commander reached out to Amherst, explaining that another reason lay behind his proclamation, one he was less willing to reveal to the Virginia governor. Writing just days before Tomlinson's slaying near Redstone, Bouquet related that he "had been repeatedly informed that one Col. Cresap, who is concerned in one of the Ohio Companies (the favorite scheme of Virginia) was proposing by way of subscription to several families, to remove from the frontiers of that Colony and Maryland, to form settlements upon the Ohio." Bouquet said he knew this to be true "from an offer made me by that same Gentlemen of a share, or 25,000 acres of those lands," and he did not want to see "those poor people," the unwitting settlers, "ruined by that bubble." He distanced himself from Cresap and his Ohio Company partners, reassuring Amherst that the invitation "did not tempt me," and he could not be "charged with Interested Views."[10]

In Oldtown, Cresap parried Bouquet's proclamation by switching his orientation. Maybe Braddock's road wasn't the best way to Ohio after all. If Bouquet couldn't be bought, maybe the Ohio Company could find their way west by going north. Cresap turned his attention to the other path that lay near his house, the Warrior's Path, one of the most important north-south roads in North America. Since Bouquet had rebuffed his offers and his colleagues in the Ohio Company didn't

show much urgency in pressing their claims, Cresap also began searching for new political partners. His conclusion was a typical one for many
players looking to make work-arounds in colonial America: maybe the
Iroquois could help.

━━

Before the war, when Cresap operated his Oldtown store, he had supplied Native travelers with ample provisions. The upheavals of the 1750s
ended his days as a storekeeper, but that did not stop Iroquois travelers
from coming by in pursuit of goods. In April 1762, when a party of ten
Iroquois stayed three days at his compound, they informed Cresap that
three hundred more warriors "would be along this way at the time that
Corn would be waist high." Cresap wrote to Maryland governor Horatio
Sharpe about how the provincial authorities would prefer he respond to
the request, and whether the province would reimburse him for his losses
in outfitting such a large—and dangerous—party. Actually, he didn't
ask. "As they will have Provision either by fair or foul means," Cresap
said he would "protect my private property either by force or otherwise."
If Maryland authorities dragged their feet, he threatened he would not
be at fault "should the Indians Resentment be drawn on this Province."
Cresap, in no uncertain terms, was extorting the colony to support his
trade—or else. Sharpe forwarded Cresap's letter to Amherst, requesting
how to proceed.[11]

Cresap also decided to advance his own standing by letting his Native
visitors in on his predicament. Maybe they could use their diplomatic skill
to help ensure that he was reimbursed. While we do not know whether
Cresap directly asked, implied, or left it to the Iroquois themselves, at
the next major treaty conference, *they* proposed recognizing the Cresaps
as official traders.

More than five hundred Natives attended the conference, which
was once again held at Lancaster. The Iroquois, along with large groups
of Ohio and Great Lakes Natives, met with Pennsylvania authorities
for two weeks in August 1762. By all accounts, things did not go well.
Pennsylvania authorities started off on the wrong foot, demanding that

Natives return all colonists who had been taken as captives during the war. The Iroquois delegation countered by insisting that the Cresaps be recognized as official suppliers for their expeditions against the Cherokees. "One Daniel Cressap has sent me word by many Warriors this Spring," Oneida leader Thomas King said, "and he tells me that if the Governor would order him to keep a Store there, he would provide everything for the Warriors; for his Father used to maintain all the Indian Warriors that passed and repassed that way." They stipulated Daniel be "the person appointed to receive Messages," and that "the Warriors may pass and repass without Molestation." Pennsylvania governor James Hamilton promised he would forward their request, and did so, as letters crisscrossed between Hamilton, Sharpe, William Johnson, and Thomas Cresap about the propriety of establishing an official, taxpayer-funded trading station at Oldtown. Sharpe was pessimistic about the Maryland Assembly being willing to "subject their constituents to such an expense" but pledged he would present the proposal to them nonetheless.[12]

It worked. By the spring of 1763, Cresap's effort to get himself or his son Daniel established as official traders with the Iroquois had paid off. Bouquet had tried to block his moves at Redstone, but he had further solidified his position in the region in dangerous times. Party after party of Iroquois would stop at Oldtown on their way south; Cresap reported four separate companies visiting his place between December 1762 and May 1763.[13]

But not everything at Oldtown was peaceful and easy during this time. The summer before, Cresap had allegedly challenged a rising Ohio Delaware leader named John Killbuck to a duel. Killbuck had played both sides in the war, sometimes acting as a courier and informer for the British army, while at others he was accused of being a horse thief and "Villain." Killbuck had heard a rumor "there had been a sum of money offered for killing him . . . sent round the frontiers in private letters by subscription," and had reached the conclusion that Cresap was the originator of this contract on his life. In response, at least as popular rumor had it, Killbuck "lay many Days on a Hill Opposite [Cresap's] house waiting to kill the old Colonel." When Cresap found out Killbuck had been stalking him at his home, he issued "a Challenge that he would fight him, each to take a Gun." The challenge seems to have scared Killbuck away. In fact, Killbuck was supposed to attend the recent treaty at Lancaster, but was so "frightened" by Cresap's offer to duel that he did not go. Oldtown was indeed a dangerous place. The next summer it would be a battleground.[14]

———

What came to be known as Pontiac's War wasn't much of a surprise. Natives who were convinced they had been victorious in the last war were justifiably angry at the increasingly shabby treatment they received at British posts.

Because peace was far cheaper than war, British officials knew they had to keep Native peoples happy in the American backcountry. Unfortunately, their primary method of doing so, diplomatic gift-giving, conflicted with their new austerity measures, and once New France fell, British commander Jeffrey Amherst prohibited the practice. For decades, Native peoples had played European empires off of one another, securing food, clothing, arms, and other goods with alternating pledges of friendship. Amherst put an end to this dance, as he believed Britain could dictate the terms of peace to both the French and the Natives. This method of cutting costs on the frontier did not, however, lend itself toward long-term peace and stability.

As a result, since 1760 there had been threats coming from the Seneca in Iroquoia, from Mingos, Shawnees, and Delawares in Ohio, and from the Anishinaabeg and their allies in the Great Lakes country. One rumor followed another, as Tachnedorus was trying to tell the Pennsylvanians. The commissary at Fort Pitt had absorbed so many of these scares that they haunted his dreams. In December 1762, a nightmare had so shaken him that, nearly a week later, he was still thinking about it so much that he jotted it down in his journal. He had dreamed "that a Mingo Young Man told me the Mingoes Go to War with the English next summer." His subconscious proved remarkably accurate. On May

9, 1763, Pontiac and his allies began their siege of Fort Detroit, the first act of what would become a widespread uprising.[15]

Pontiac's War is usually narrated as a war against the forts. Pontiac's men besieged British posts from Michilimackinac to the Alleghany River, almost all of which fell to their attackers, with horrific stories of what happened to the unfortunate soldiers stationed inside. But this conflict did not only occur around the walls of British forts. In a replay of 1755–57, raiding parties fanned out against settlers in the countryside. When the most careful student of the 1763 attacks mapped out the target zone of these raids, he found they mostly occurred within a triangle south of the Forbes Road, east of Braddock's road, and north of the Virginia road from Winchester. The rattlesnake colonel's den sat near the very center of that sector of carnage.[16]

In May, a few days before the war began, another large party of more than seventy Iroquois visited Oldtown. They had a pass from George Croghan instructing Cresap to provide whatever they asked for, but complained when Cresap didn't satisfy all their needs. Even though they left unhappy, Cresap did not consider them hostile. He had worked diligently over the last year to improve his relations with the Iroquois.[17]

A few weeks after they departed, violence engulfed the entire region. By mid-June, raiders launched attacks up the Forbes Road into central Pennsylvania. They moved down Braddock's road, too. The small garrison abandoned Fort Burd, fleeing south to Fort Cumberland, taking most of the Redstone settlers with them. A Delaware named Shamokin Daniel led a band of eighteen warriors east, carrying war into the Susquehanna Valley. As Shingas's people had done before, they made quick, lethal strikes against dispersed settlements to produce maximum psychological shock.[18]

British officers told how the people again faced "the prospect of Starving (being drove from their Plantations & nothing to Subsist on)." Newspapers printed nearly verbatim sentences that had appeared eight years prior: "I assure you it was a most melancholy sight, to see such Numbers of poor People who had abandoned their Settlements in such

Consternation and Harry, that they had hardly anything with them but their Children." A contributor to the *Maryland Gazette* claimed "never was Panic more general or forcible than that of the Back Inhabitants, whose Terrors, at this Time, exceed what followed on the Defeat of General *Braddock*, when the Frontiers lay open to the Incursions of both *French* and *Indians*."[19]

On Wednesday, July 13, the Battle for Oldtown commenced.

It started in the wheat field. Six men were working in the midsummer heat, fighting their own agricultural war against the wheat rust brought on by the heaviest June rains anyone could remember. They were so absorbed that they did not see five Natives sneaking up to unleash a volley at them. One colonist fell dead among the stalks, killed instantly. The shots alarmed the inhabitants of Oldtown, and a number of settlers ran toward the field, returning fire, and keeping the attackers from taking their dead neighbor's scalp. The Natives fled into the woods, but the battle was far from over.[20]

The next day, as sixteen men lounged under a tree at the end of Cresap's lane, one hundred yards from his front door, the same five Indians attacked again. The colonists fired back, wounding at least one Native, and the attackers again took flight into the woods. This time, the more prepared colonists ran after them, following what they claimed was a vast trail of blood. The Natives eluded their pursuers, however, who were only able to recover three bundles of goods.

A few hours later the crack of rifles again shattered the summer afternoon, this time near the livestock pens. As the colonists rushed over, they found three beef cows dead. More shots came from the woods, one slicing into a colonist's body. Settlers plunged into the woods in the direction of the gunsmoke, but to no avail. As night fell on July 14, the residents of Oldtown gathered in their strongest houses, anxiously awaiting what the next day might bring. A few were bloodied, but all had survived the day. The second day of battle had been marked by frenzied chases into the woods.

The worst was yet to come. Overnight, the five Natives who had harassed the town were joined by a party three times their size. The group, now twenty strong, planned a serious assault on the village the following morning.

At ten o'clock, one of Cresap's neighbors, Samuel Stanbury Welder, carefully cracked the door to his house, looked out, and gingerly stepped across the threshold. When nothing happened, Welder figured the danger had passed. He guessed wrong. A few moments later, after Welder, three men, and several women exited the house, the twenty Natives lept from their hiding spots and raced toward them. The Welder household turned on their heels and ran, screaming, in the direction of Cresap's house, three hundred yards away, with their attackers closing the distance quickly. Hearing their cries, the men who had spent the night inside Cresap's stockade grabbed their guns and rushed out, running down the lane to meet them. The three groups collided near the tree that had been the site of the previous day's clash. Welder was unlucky: after a bullet cut him down, one Native stopped to mutilate the body with his tomahawk, "divid[ing] his Ribs from the Back Bone." At very short range, Natives and colonists fired upon one another. Another colonist named Wade was shot dead, and Richard Morris was wounded. Colonial gunmen killed one Native and wounded a few others. More blood fell on the ground at the entrance to Cresap's house. The Natives fled, leaving two rifles, a musket, and a pistol behind on the battlefield as they ran.[21]

After the attackers escaped into the woods, Michael Cresap, now twenty-one, knelt over the dead Native's body. We wonder what went through his mind at that moment, adrenaline still coursing through his body. His young life had already been filled with scenes like this, but not quite like this. Natives had killed his older brother, but that was in the wild woods many miles away. This was at his front door. There were dead, disfigured bodies and pools of blood all around the entrance to the only home he had ever known. Still, they hadn't gotten him or his parents. It was time to take trophies. He took out his knife, and sliced off the man's scalp. He then wriggled the moccasins off his feet. Who was this dead man who lay sprawled in his front yard? Who were his associates? Who had put them through this harrowing ordeal? Michael picked up one of the rifles that had been left behind and immediately recognized the markings on it. He showed it to his father, telling him it belonged to one of the parties of Iroquois that had been at their place only a few weeks before.

We know these details about the Battle of Oldtown from letters Thomas Cresap wrote in a full panic the night after the third fight. As soon as the group had tended to the corpses, the terrified survivors crowded back into Cresap's house and bolted the door. Thomas immediately started scribbling letters to the Fort Cumberland commander and to Governor Sharpe. He told Sharpe that he took "this opportunity in the h[e]ight of Confusion to acquaint you with our unhappy & most wretched situation at this time being in Hourly expectation of being Massicread by our Barberous & Inhuman Enemy the Indians."[22]

Cresap recounted every detail of the past three days. Throughout, he cast the battle as one between Natives and "white men" or "white people." He consistently used race to describe the men who battled the "barbarous and inhuman enemy." Not knowing what Natives he could trust—after all his dealings with them, were the Iroquois really trying to kill *him?*—he lumped them all together as enemies.

Cresap shuddered in fear of what Saturday might bring. He begged for help, having no idea whether his cries would be heard. "I have inclosed a List of the Disolate men, women, & children who have fled to my house," he wrote to the governor, "which is Inclosed by a Small Stockade for Safety by which you['ll] see what a number of Poor Soals destitute of Every Necessary of Life are here penned up & likely to be Butchered without Immediate Relief & Assistance & can Expect none unless from the Province to Which they Belong." That list has not survived, so we don't know if Elizabeth Lamy or her baby's name was on it. Three years earlier, Elizabeth had borne Thomas an illegitimate daughter, who was named Jane Cresap. It's very likely that Elizabeth took shelter in the house with Jane's father and half-brother Michael. It must have been an excruciating few nights for the Cresaps. Although the Native party would not return again, Thomas had no way of knowing that. He believed they might all be killed or captured, so he eventually took the risk of sending Michael east to Frederick, Maryland, to get help.[23]

Is it ludicrous to call the three days of violence at Oldtown a "battle" along the lines of those fought in the 1750s at the Monongahela or outside Quebec? In total, the fighting at Oldtown probably didn't last more than half an hour. It was mostly a series of volleys and chases. Still, for everyone involved—settlers and Natives alike—it was combat just the same.

Moreover, the Battle of Oldtown was *news*. Even while the shooting continued, the *Maryland Gazette* had the story: "We have had repeated Reports, which we hope may prove False, that Col. *Thomas Cresap*, with his Family, and Neighbors, are cut off by the Indians." The following week, they had "the pleasure" of printing a retraction and, having received a copy of Thomas's letter to Sharpe, related the battle's details as Cresap had provided them. A contributor to the *Maryland Gazette* reported from Frederick in the next week's issue that, "on Sunday Afternoon we had the Pleasure of seeing Mr. *Michael Cresap* arrive in Town with Mokosins on his Legs, taken from an *Indian* whom he killed and scalped." "Money has been cheerfully contributed" in Frederick, this correspondent exulted, "towards the Support of 10 Men to be added to Col. *Cresap's* present Force, as we look upon the Preservation of the *Old Town* to be of great Importance to us, and a proper Check to the Progress of the Savages." But this battle was of more than merely local interest. Newspaper printers in New Hampshire, Georgia, Pennsylvania, Connecticut, New York, and Massachusetts all thought the fighting at Oldtown was worth their readers' attention. The desperate combat in Cresap's front yard, printers calculated, encapsulated what many people felt at the height of Pontiac's War. It was shaping up to be another summer of panic.[24]

As it turned out, the Battle of Oldtown happened at the climax of attacks east of the Appalachians. After July, the worst assaults on the colonial countryside subsided, and by August 1, Natives had lifted their siege of Fort Pitt. Bouquet subsequently marched his troops out and brought them to battle around Bushy Run on August 5, an engagement that is normally (and erroneously) considered the end of Pontiac's War. The conflict was far from over, but the tide had turned, aided more by smallpox than victorious British arms. Within a few weeks, the *Maryland Gazette* reported that settlers were returning to their homes.[25]

Emboldened, Oldtown's veterans were anxious to carry the war to the enemy. Michael Cresap and seventeen other volunteers intended to join Bouquet's expedition against Pontiac's allies. By 1763, leading a vigilante party west into the mountains was now a family rite of passage. The band set off from Oldtown in early August and travelled fifty miles to the Youghiogheny River before four of them took sick, and they were forced to turn back to Fort Cumberland. Still wanting revenge, they decided to trek home through the mountains searching for enemy raiders. It was almost their undoing—Michael and the half-starved men stumbled into a remote Pennsylvania fort far from home after having run out of provisions two days before.[26]

Some part of Michael Cresap's furious motivation to seek out and destroy Native peoples had to come from a sense of betrayal. Over the past year, his family home had become an official trading station on the Warrior's Path, assisting the Iroquois in their prolonged war against the Catawbas and Cherokees. If the Iroquois were indeed the perpetrators of the horrific, sustained attack on Oldtown, Cresap deemed that an act that justified merciless retribution.

A similar feeling—that they had been betrayed by Natives they had come to count on as friends—animated another set of vigilantes from Paxton, Pennsylvania. During the same days that the colonists in Oldtown fought for their lives, settlers from Paxton (near Harrisburg, Pennsylvania) formed themselves into several militia companies. They referred to themselves as the Paxtang Rangers. Although intended as a defensive force, they, like Michael Cresap and his Oldtown volunteers, went out searching for the enemy. In August they marched up the West Branch of the Susquehanna to Great Island, very close to the Mingo towns where the Shickellamy brothers were last known to reside. In October they went out again, this time following the North Branch up to Wyoming. In both cases, they returned empty-handed.[27]

Unable to locate Pontiac's allies, they turned their attention to Conestoga Indiantown, forty-five miles down the Susquehanna River from Paxton. Some of the Rangers were especially suspicious of Will Sock, a Conestoga leader who had loudly advocated his people should abandon the small plot of land set aside for them sixty years before. The Conestogas were a gathering of Susquehannock Indians who remained after a generation of fighting with both the Iroquois and Virginians in the last decades of the seventeenth century. They were the survivors of "Fort Demolished," and William Penn (with Opessa's assistance) extended protection to them in 1701 by providing a tract on Conestoga Creek to settle on. Even though their numbers had dwindled to less than two dozen, Sock argued the remaining Conestogas would starve if they stayed penned up on this parcel of land any longer. If the Pennsylvania government wasn't going to provide for them adequately anymore, they had to take steps to protect themselves, even if that meant leaving Conestoga Creek.

The Conestogas had been Pennsylvania's most steadfast friends for six decades. That relationship was what the Shickellamy sons were depending on when they sent their sister and other family members there for refuge during the last war. But despite the fact that the Conestogas had recently pledged not to "harbor any strange Indians," the Paxton Boys viewed them with increasing suspicion. Like Thomas Cresap, they had begun to see the backcountry as divided into two hostile groups, white people and Indians. When they heard rumors that Will Sock and other of his people had perhaps given information or provisions to enemy Indians, they made plans to eliminate the betrayers.[28]

There were only six people in Conestoga Indiantown in the morning of December 14, 1763: three men, two women, and a young boy. At least fifty mounted Paxtang Rangers, having galloped through the night, entered the town at daybreak, and killed them, mostly while they slept. "All of them were scalped, and otherwise horribly mangled. Then their Huts were set on Fire, and most of them burnt down," Benjamin Franklin would later write. "Pleased with their own Conduct and Bravery, but enraged that any of the poor Indians had escaped the Massacre," the Rangers "rode off, and in small Parties, by different Roads, went home."[29]

Lancaster County officials scrambled to locate any surviving Cones-togas. Three married couples and eight children had been out "among the neighboring White People, some to sell the Baskets, Brooms, and Bowls they manufactured," and others on various errands. The Lancaster sheriff, John Hay, "collected and placed them in the Work house of this county," where, he reassured the governor, "they are properly taken care of."[30]

Sheriff Hay didn't even have time to get this letter into the post before having to append a grim postscript. "Since writing the above," he related, "the poor Indians we imagined were placed in Safety are destroyed." Hay informed Governor Hamilton that fifty or sixty armed men, "suddenly, about Two o'Clock, rushed into the Town & immediately repaired to the Work House where the Indians were confined." They shoved Hay and others who tried to stop them aside, "broke open the Work House, and have killed all the Indians there." Then they rode off again.[31]

Shickellamy's daughter was not among the Paxton Boys' victims. Soon after Shingas's raids in 1756, the Shickellamy sons sent their sister—either Cajadis or Koonay, we don't know which—to hide there, but she was no longer a resident of Conestoga Indiantown in 1763. Neverthe-less, when tragedy again struck the Shickellamys in 1774, her brother Soyechtowa (James Logan Shickellamy) included the Paxton murders in his catalog of the horrible things that had befallen his family. "The white people killed my Kin at Conestoga a great while ago," he would say. He was nowhere near Lancaster in 1763, but he claimed to have experienced its trauma profoundly, nonetheless. One of the victims was a Cayuga, and the Conestogas were considered part of the Iroquois' extended family going back at least a half century. The Paxton Boys, in Soyechtowa's eyes, had spilled his family's blood.[32]

Pontiac's War and the brutality of the Paxton Boys' attacks added to evolving notions about racial differences in the backcountry. The category of "whiteness" was a novelty in the eighteenth century, mostly because its inclusiveness went against Europeans' deep-seated prejudices. In his 1751 pamphlet "Observations on the Increase of Mankind," Benjamin

Franklin lamented how "the Number of purely White People in the World is proportionately very small," since there were none in America, Asia, or Africa. Who qualified as white in Franklin's eyes? Not all Europeans, for sure, since "Spaniards, French, Russians, and Swedes, are generally of what we call swarthy Complexion." But even the Germans were a problem, for if "the Palatine Boors be suffered to swamp into our Settlements," Pennsylvania would soon be more German than English.[33]

The brutality of Indian war changed all that. While colonial printers had only sporadically used the term "white people" prior to 1754, they would continually put it in front of their readers during the conflict. George Washington first used the phrase in his correspondence in July 1757. Sometimes this came from Native speech, with Indians using it to protest "white people" invading their lands or attacking them, but as the conflict worsened, colonists began to employ it as a shorthand for *their* suffering. The concept of "white people" became a reed to which colonists could cling during the baffling time of the Seven Years' War. Despite differences in language, background, and religion, the colonists had crowded together on backcountry roads in sheer terror. Willfully ignoring what caused this war in the first place, a shared sense of victimization brought white people together. On their night march, the Paxton Boys galloped past the spot where almost three decades before Thomas Cresap and his Maryland militia had battled Pennsylvanians and spilled their blood. Now, as white men, these factions were on the same side.[34]

Still, the term "white people" didn't clear up much confusion in the backcountry. There were tensions inherent in that emerging concept that would take decades—and a revolution—to work out.

If whiteness was really another way to convey victimhood, that meant it was based on behavior, mostly on things that happened *to* them. "White people" suffered, and, when justly provoked, they inflicted suffering. But this was before ideologies of biological racism, as they would evolve in the nineteenth century, which would dictate that physical attributes marked difference. Not so in 1750. For most at mid-century, behavior still governed how people viewed one another's social status: how you looked, acted, talked, and walked (or, even better, rode) suggested your ranking. To English observers in 1755, Cresap the "rattlesnake colonel" was in no way similar to General Braddock, even though both were "white." The colonists at Oldtown and Redstone purposely disguised themselves like the enemies that they perceived all around them—and not only when they went out hunting for them.

But there were wide differences of opinion on what was legitimate behavior. Emerging racial solidarity did not mean that all behavior on "one's side" was beyond reproach. Benjamin Franklin famously castigated the Paxton Boys' slaughter of the Conestogas as the work of "Christian White Savages." "O ye unhappy Perpetrators of this horrid Wickedness!," he wrote in "A Narrative of the Late Massacres,"

> Reflect a Moment on the Mischief ye have done, the Disgrace ye have brought on your Country, on your Religion, and your Bible, on your Families and Children! . . . All good People every where detest your Actions.—You have imbrued your Hands in innocent Blood; how will you make them clean?—The dying Shrieks and Groans of the Murdered, will often sound in your Ears."

In response, defenders of the attacks denied that the Boys had committed anything like an atrocity. "A mighty Noise and Hubbub has been made about killing a few Indians in Lancaster County," one pamphleteer argued. "The names of RIOTERS, REBELS, MURDERERS, WHITE SAVAGES, &c. have been liberally and indiscriminately bestowed upon them."[35]

The debate over the Paxton Boys' behavior illustrates the instability of the concept of "white people" at the end of the Seven Years' War. Some saw their actions as justified (a group which no doubt included Thomas and Michael Cresap), while others found them reprehensible. These tensions would evolve rapidly in the years after 1763. In the coming decade, even Franklin would change his tune.

The events of 1763, which signaled the start of an "imperial crisis" that would result in the American Revolution, were of world-historical significance. But they also transformed everyday peoples' lives, not least by ending them. Groves of death had abounded during the early, terrible years of the Seven Years' War, at Penn's Creek, Patterson's Creek, and dozens of other scenic locales throughout the American backcountry. These spots were so close to the Cresap and Shickellamy families that both took flight from their homes to seek shelter with loved ones and trusted friends. Michael Cresap had lost an older brother in the woods. The Shickellamy brothers hid in different woods to prevent being murdered by colonists or Natives. But in 1763, the conflict came home, with brutal attacks at Oldtown and Conestoga.

These terrible events, in which former friends attacked one another, were a fitting capstone to protracted conflict. The Seven Years' War, in addition to being gruesome and shocking, had been *confounding*. On the macro level, what started as the French and Indian War became the British and Indian War and then concluded as war between the colonists and their former allies. Native warriors and British soldiers both congratulated themselves for having vanquished the other. On the micro level, friends acted like enemies and those who appeared to be enemies weren't always so. Imperial conceits to legitimize some behavior and denounce others failed miserably.

So, by 1763, colonists began to deploy language in new ways to highlight the differences between "them" and "us." In their search for social and cultural anchors in the midst of horrifying, shocking violence, they found a powerful new tool. Thomas Cresap, the Paxton Boys, and lots of other American colonists began to refer to themselves as aggrieved "white people" who suffered at the hands of all Indians. Deploying the power of words to control peoples' lives was one of the markers of imperialism. They fashioned colonizing words that not only allowed violence but encouraged it. By identifying themselves as victims, rather than aggressors, American colonists had begun to develop a vocabulary of victimhood. In so doing, they had stumbled upon a language that would fuel imperial adventures in the Ohio and beyond.

This new project of race-making was in its embryonic stages in 1763. It would eventually become a force unto itself, seemingly inevitable, irresistible, and universal. It is almost impossible to conceive of America without race prejudice. But it wasn't inevitable. Just like the violent events that gave it its start, it was contingent. It depended on people—men like Thomas and Michael Cresap or the Paxton Boys or the Shickellamy brothers—to give it fuel, to speak it into being. That was another legacy of those groves of death, those beautiful spots desecrated by gruesome human behavior that lay all about the American backcountry in the middle of the eighteenth century. There would be more, soon enough.

PART 2

THE SEEDS OF COMMONWEALTHS

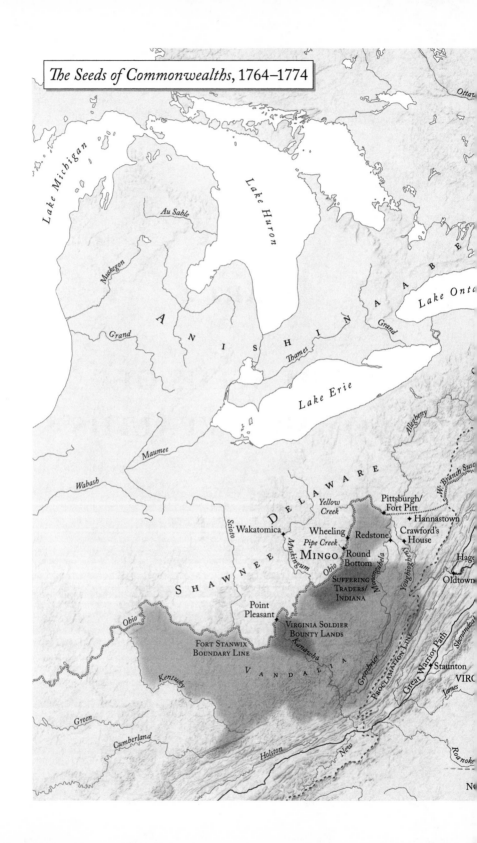

The Seeds of Commonwealths, 1764–1774

Lake Michigan

Lake Huron

Au Sable

Muskegon

A N I S H I N A A B E

Grand

Lake Ontario

Grand

Thames

Lake Erie

Maumee

Allegheny

W. Branch Susq.

Wabash

D E L A W A R E

Scioto

Yellow
Creek

Pittsburgh/
Fort Pitt

Hannastown

Wakatomica

Muskingum

Wheeling

Pipe Creek

Redstone

Crawford's
House

S H A W N E E

MINGO

Round
Bottom

Ohio

SUFFERING
TRADERS/
INDIANA

Monongahela

Youghiogheny

Hag

Oldtown

Point
Pleasant

VIRGINIA SOLDIER
BOUNTY LANDS

Ohio

FORT STANWIX
BOUNDARY LINE

Kanawha

V A N D A L I A

Greenbrier

PROCLAMATION LINE

Great Warrior Path

Shenandoah

Staunton

VIR

Kentucky

James

Green

Cumberland

Holston

New

Roanoke

N

Quebec

Montreal

Gatineau

Rouge

St-François

Chaudière

Kennebec

Penobscot

St. Lawrence

Richelieu

Androscoggin

MASSACHUSETTS

I R O Q U O I S

Black

U. PROCLAMATION Line

Fort
Stanwix

Mohawk

Johnson
Hall

Connecticut

Merrimack

NEW HAMPSHIRE

FORT STANWIX
BOUNDARY LINE

Susquehanna

Hudson

Boston

MASSACHUSETTS

N. Branch

Great Warrior
Path

NEW YORK

Delaware

CONNECTICUT

RHODE
ISLAND

NSYLVANIA

New York

Susquehanna

NEW
JERSEY

'sle

ON-DIXON LINE

Philadelphia

RYLAND

derick

Annapolis

DELAWARE

Mount
Vernon

Chesapeake Bay

ATLANTIC
OCEAN

Williamsburg

N

W   E

S

0   50   100 mi

OLINA

CHAPTER 4

MESSENGERS OF THE MIGHT, 1764–1768

"Hunters for gold or pursuers of fame, they had all gone out on that stream, bearing the sword and often the torch, messengers of the might within the land, bearers of a spark from the sacred fire."

—*Heart of Darkness*

With the French vanquished from eastern North America, Thomas Cresap and his sons believed that the Ohio country had the potential to propel Britain to even greater glories. They saw themselves as messengers of a mighty dominion, bearing the sword and often the torch. As soon as they were able, the Cresaps resumed their efforts to spearhead settlements in the Upper Ohio Valley.

To their surprise, the empire on whose behalf they crusaded did not want them. British officials, who hoped to keep frontier families on the eastern side of the Alleghany Mountains, viewed settlers like the Cresaps as intruders, not torchbearers. The empire told them they were unwelcome in Ohio. This rejection fostered another deep sense of betrayal and contributed to the notion that colonial American interests were perhaps not the king's highest priority. Just as perceived betrayal bred Paxton vigilantism in 1763, it helped spur resistance to imperial reform in the years that followed. Who was this empire for, if not for Cresap's people?

Leading British officials in America, especially Amherst's replacement, General Thomas Gage, and Indian superintendent Sir William

Johnson, quickly found themselves acting as referees between two increasingly hostile groups. Settlers streamed west after Pontiac's War, and Native leaders insisted the British protect them from the likes of Thomas Cresap and his sons. Imperial officials had to listen. They could not support Cresap's machinations on the Ohio because Native peoples still dominated the entire territory. They had to take their interests seriously—or else face another general uprising of Native peoples. Disagreement over who belonged in the Ohio country, therefore, exacerbated Britain's colonial crisis.

For the next several years, indecision and confusion reigned throughout the upper Ohio territory. Many settlers, speculators, and Native peoples tried to turn this bewilderment to their strategic advantage. Just as they had before the climactic "Great War for Empire," people renewed their efforts to make dreams come true along the Ohio. For Natives, this was a defensive campaign, an effort to maintain their space on their terms. For colonists like Thomas Cresap and George Croghan, it was the moment to resume their personal and imperial ambitions. Their previous forays into the region precipitated a world war that led to Britain's triumph in 1763. These colonists now sought to deliver an even greater glory—unto their king, and, especially, unto themselves.

Toward the end of February 1764, the *Maryland Gazette* published a hopeful letter written a month before in Carlisle, Pennsylvania, that perhaps the terrible days that had brought devastation to the area were finally ending. "A Number of Families are again returned to their Dwellings in Shearman's Valley, and some of them begin to talk of putting in Spring Crops in those Parts," the correspondent said, concluding that, "our frontier now rests in Peace."[1]

It was not to be. Less than four months later, Philadelphia newspapers ran another letter from Carlisle: "twice this Week I have had Occasion to write of the sundry Depredations committed in this County . . . You will readily guess at the present Situation of our miserable and unhappy People, and the piercing Applications I must endure from every Quarter, crying for Help." All hopes were dashed; there would be no peace in the summer of 1764.[2]

These attacks were a continuation of Pontiac's War. Even though Ohio Natives had given up their sieges around British forts and been defeated in a battle with British redcoats near Bushy Run, sporadic attacks on settlers living near the Potomac or Susquehanna Rivers did not abate. Only another British military expedition into Ohio would convince Natives to seek a negotiation with Sir William Johnson and British authorities by year's end. Finally, in the spring of 1765, there seemed an actual, if tenuous peace.

Half a century later, one of the people who returned to the area recalled how anxious those first days of peace were. Archibald Loudon had been born on the Atlantic in 1754 while en route from Scotland to North America. His parents, James and Christiana Loudon, believed they had secured a bright future for their baby when they purchased seven hundred acres in Shearman's Valley, one of the settlements in the controversial Albany Purchase. However, no sooner had they begun felling trees on their new tract when Shingas and his Delaware raiding party attacked. The Loudons threw their infant son into a wagon and joined the frontier families choking the roads, running for their lives in 1755. A decade later, James and Christiana finally deemed the situation safe enough to return. Archibald, now eleven, remembered returning to the area. The family couldn't bring themselves to go back to the same spot, so they decided to settle a few miles north of where they had first experienced trauma.

Although it seemed as if peace was indeed at hand, there was very little assurance. Archibald recounted the rumors swirling around their new farm that "the Indians had begun to murder the white people" again. Loudon and his siblings were cautiously playing outside the house when they "espied three Indians coming across the meadow, a few rods from us." They sprinted for the house and "informed our parents, who were considerably alarmed at their approach; the Indians, however set their guns down on the outside of the house and came in, when they were invited to take seats, which they did." The Loudons were terrified. Only one of the Natives spoke English, but when the other two spoke to one another, Archibald interpreted only impending doom. Decades later, a now middle-aged Archibald still remembered, "we conjectured they were saying, [it] would make a nice scalp" after one of them reached out to touch his sister's hair.[3]

Eventually, tensions eased. "After some time, when we saw they had no hostile intentions, I took a bible, and read two or three chapters," Loudon recalled. The one who spoke English "paid great attention to what I read, my father upon observing this took occasion to mention to him, what a great benefit it would be to the Indians to learn to read." To this, Archibald's father received a reply that probably surprised him. "O!," he said, "a great many people (meaning the Indians) on the Mohawk River, can read the Buck [book] that speaks of God." After sitting with the Loudons for a couple of hours, the three Native men said goodbye, crossed over Tuscarora Mountain, and were gone.[4]

While we don't know who accompanied him, the visitor who spoke English and could read the Bible was one of Shickellamy's sons, probably Soyechtowa (James Logan). "He was a remarkable tall man, considerably above six feet high," Loudon later remembered. The afternoon that young Archie spent with him would be one of the few times settlers remembered seeing the Shickellamy brothers in the years after Pontiac's War. After all the suffering they had been through—and with colonial families like the Loudons crossing over more mountains and carving out farms in valleys farther and farther west—the three brothers, along with their aging mother (Neanoma) and sister (Koonay), retreated deep into the Juniata River valley. Shickellamy's sons also shed their previous names. Settlers who came upon them in this time and place referred to Tachnedorus as Captain John Logan and Soyechtowa simply as Logan. They hadn't yet fallen away from the Shickellamy way of negotiation and reconciliation, but they stopped using their renowned surname.

Perhaps this effort to start a new chapter bred discord among the previously tight clan, for the Shickellamy family began to pull apart. Just outside what is now Reedsville, Pennsylvania, Logan (Soyechtowa) made himself a place to live next to a rippling brook still known by the name of Logan's Spring. He lived an isolated life there, separate from the rest of the family, hunting deer and dressing the skins for trade. His older brother, John Logan (Tachnedorus), went forty miles farther into the Pennsylvania forests. He decided to live where Bald Eagle Creek ran into the Little Juniata River (now Tyrone, Pennsylvania). His youngest brother, John Petty, his mother, sister, and son Tod-kah-dos, lived with him for a period in the late 1760s.

Two traders later recalled running into Logan (Soyechtowa) during this period near his home. They had been separated while hunting a bear, and one of them came upon this spring and knelt for a drink. When he looked up he saw the reflected shadow of "a tall Indian." He grabbed for his rifle, but the Native immediately showed his gun was not loaded and "held out his open palm to me in a token of friendship." The trader claimed they remained together for a week and afterward continued to visit him occasionally. "Poor Logan," the account concluded, "soon after [he] went into the Allegheny, and I never saw him again." Unlike many of their contemporaries throughout the American backcountry, Shickel-

Figure 10. Pennsylvania historical marker denoting Logan's Spring, outside Reedsville, Pennsylvania. Note the sign does not indicate which of Shickellamy's sons was Logan.

lamy's sons turned away from exploiting bewilderment as a strategy in the aftermath of this devastating conflict. They retreated.[5]

In a few years, Logan (Soyechtowa) would go even farther west. He didn't stop at the Allegheny but would convince his mother, brother John Petty, and sister Koonay to go with him to Ohio, leaving John Logan (Tachnedorus) and Tod-kah-dos behind in central Pennsylvania. We don't know if the three brothers ever reunited. Soon Logan and his family would be seen living in a small village of Mingos where Beaver Creek runs into the Ohio River.

On October 7, 1763, George III signed what would be known as the Royal Proclamation, a decree that prohibited all colonial settlement west of a line drawn across the crest of the Appalachian Mountains. The proclamation also stipulated that only the Crown and Crown-authorized agents had the ability to negotiate land at official diplomatic treaty conferences. Sales between individual buyers and sellers were illegal, a stunning departure from a century and a half of settler colonial deals. Imperial administrators hoped the king's cordon would be enough to bring an end to expensive war in the backcountry. This effort to try to restrain colonial expansion and keep the peace was deemed so important that British officials held the monthly packet boat bound for New York City four days so they could get a copy of the proclamation onboard. However, any hopes that it would prevent Native-colonial violence would soon be dashed. The same week that colonial newspapers in Boston, Philadelphia, Providence, and Savannah ran the text of the proclamation, the Paxton Boys made preparations for their night ride to Conestoga Indiantown.[6]

Archibald Loudon's parents were among the thousands of colonial settlers who calculated that defying the king and pushing west into the Alleghanies was worth the risk to their young children. Many of them headed to Redstone, the small village Thomas Cresap founded on the Monongahela about fifty miles downriver from Fort Pitt. Redstone had been a thorn in General Bouquet's side before Pontiac's War, and he had tried to evict the settlers living there. Now, with the Royal Proclamation, it was official: King George III proclaimed this settlement illegal.

Pontiac's War taught imperial officials several critical lessons. They now understood that they could not shut off the practice of diplomatic gift-giving wholesale as they had done at the end of the Seven Years' War. They also admitted that, to avoid further conflict, they needed to at least try to enforce the new Proclamation Line that Thomas Cresap and the settlers at Redstone so flagrantly defied. Further orders arrived from London in 1764 that put Johnson and Gage in charge of all Native affairs, a centralizing move that sought to downgrade the colonial governors. But, above all, everyone knew they had to make empire cheaper. Fighting Pontiac's War and then trying to maintain the peace was yet another expenditure on top of the most expensive war so far in British history. The national debt had been growing steadily over the course of the eighteenth century, but the Seven Years' War had all but doubled it, bringing the total to £146,000,000 sterling.

These lessons would also contribute to bringing about what we now call the "imperial crisis," the decade of conflict that erupted as Britain attempted to make significant reforms to how it would govern and distribute authority throughout its empire. In March 1765, the king gave his assent to the Stamp Act, which placed a tax on all paper sold in America, ranging from newspapers and playing cards to legal documents such as wills and deeds. British officials, especially its architect Prime Minister George Grenville, did not anticipate any controversy, especially since the act stipulated that any revenue raised in America would stay in America to help offset the enormous costs of the army that remained to keep the colonies safe from another Native uprising.[7]

Grenville, as we know, was mistaken. The Stamp Act would provoke the first sustained round of protest in the "imperial crisis." Resistance escalated over the summer, with American mobs beginning to take matters into their own hands. Keeping with their effort to cut as many costs as possible, Grenville's plan called for individual merchants in each province to act as stamp agents, distributing the taxed paper from their warehouses and stores. While it was cheaper than hiring dozens of tax collectors, putting this much power in the hands of just a few agents made them easy targets. Across the thirteen colonies, crowds attacked merchants who had volunteered to be the distributors of the hated stamped paper. Those mobs, led by groups of urban artisans and mechanics who called themselves the Sons of Liberty, forced resignations in many colonies.

In Maryland, the stamp distributor was to be Zachariah Hood, an Annapolis merchant who had received his infamous appointment while visiting England. When he returned to Annapolis in late August, crowds led by the Sons of Liberty did their best to prevent him from even coming ashore. On August 26, an assembly of "ASSERTORS of BRITISH AMERICAN-PRIVILEGES," as the *Maryland Gazette* called them, created an effigy of Hood, paraded it through town, hanged it from a gibbet, and burned it over a barrel of tar. A week later, the crowd gathered again to pull "down a House lately Rented by a certain unwelcome Officer." But Hood refused to budge. Only after they gathered again to demolish his warehouse did he flee for New York City, where he thought he would be protected by General Gage. The Sons of Liberty there weren't happy harboring a fugitive stamp distributor and demanded he leave town. Hood slunk back to Annapolis, but his reputation and merchant business were destroyed; he soon left for the West Indies.[8]

The western Maryland town of Frederick—and the Cresap family— would be at the center of multiple protests of Hood and the Stamp Act before the end of that tumultuous year. In the last days of October, Joseph Chapline was hustling to sell lots for Sharpsburg, a new town due west of Frederick he had founded less than two years before. In almost exactly a century this town would be the site of the battle of Antietam, but in 1765 Chapline was hard at work getting sales finalized before the Stamp Act was to take effect on November 1. An express messenger rode up and handed him a "Writing to the People." The express and the petition were from Thomas Cresap. Chapline and Cresap were at least acquainted, since both represented Frederick County in the lower house of the Maryland assembly, and probably more so, since Chapline would soon become a member of the Ohio Company. Chapline read the paper aloud to the assemblage of purchasers. "It expressed a Satisfaction of the Conduct of the Lower House, in Opposing the Stamp Act," one of the listeners later testified, "and intimated a Reliance that they would Endeavour, like the Renowned antient true Roman Senate, to Suppress any future Attempt to deprive them of their Liberty."[9]

But all was not well in Annapolis, either. Cresap's "Writing" went on to suggest that Parliament was not the only threat to the peoples' liberty. There was a financial discrepancy in the Maryland capital that was also disturbing. In Cresap's view of the affair, the clerk of the Maryland council was trying to fleece the public by putting in an exorbitant claim for fees due to him for services rendered. However, since the clerk worked for the Calvert family (the proprietors of Maryland), Cresap and his allies thought that they, rather than the public, ought to cover his bills. Making matters worse, because of this unsettled claim, the two assembly houses (upper and lower) were unable to agree on how to settle *other* claims, most importantly the reimbursement of some of his Frederick County constituents for monies they had spent in defending the frontier during the Seven Years' War and then Pontiac's War. According to Cresap, militia officers who had saved frontier settlers should be repaid before council clerks. Again: or else.

Perhaps, Cresap's circular letter continued, the signers ought to "come down" to the capital "and cause justice to take Place." Chapline "jocularly asked" one of the militia captains who happened to be there purchasing town lots if he would add his name to the petition, to which he "answered, that he did not like Hanging, . . . observing the Writing to be of a Threatening Nature." The Frederick crowd seemingly had a laugh at this, discounting it as "one of the Old Colonel's Schemes."[10]

A few weeks later, however, the situation would escalate. When the Stamp Act went into effect any use of non-stamped paper was illegal. Newspapers were to close their shops unless they had stamps. As were county courts. The Frederick County court, however, defied the Act by opening their session as scheduled on November 15. A week later, on Saturday, November 23, the judges issued a statement, declaring it was the "unanimous resolution and opinion of this Court that all the business thereof shall and ought to be transacted in the usual and accustomed manner." This was the first "repudiation" of the Stamp Act to emerge from a colonial courtroom.[11]

To celebrate the court's defiance, people in Frederick planned a town-wide party they would throw the following week. According to the long account that ran in the *Maryland Gazette*, the "Sons of Liberty" assembled at Samuel Swearingen's house, where they constructed yet another effigy of Zachariah Hood. At 3:00, they marched in a funeral procession through the town up to the courthouse yard, and Hood's effigy was made to give a pathetic gallows speech. After the crowd threw his likeness into a grave, they returned to Swearingen's house, "where an elegant Supper was prepared" and "many loyal and Patriotic Toasts were drank."[12]

The Swearingens, it is worth noting, were Thomas Cresap's extended family, as Samuel Swearingen's older sister Ruth had married Thomas's oldest son, Daniel. While we cannot say with certainty that Thomas was in Frederick that day, he did specifically ask for a leave of absence from the Assembly two days before the parade. It's difficult to imagine him not holding court there as the effigy was constructed, marching in the parade, and presiding over the evening's festivities, probably with his twenty-three-year-old son Michael and his new wife Mary, married in Philadelphia a year before, in attendance.[13]

Whether he was at Swearingen's or not, Cresap's influence was apparent a few days later when another meeting in town, this one at the Charlton's tavern in Frederick, witnessed even more raucous behavior. The matter of the public debts raised by Cresap's incendiary letter was still yet to be resolved, and the petition had circulated in taverns throughout November. One eyewitness later contended that "a number of People" in the tavern, while "in their Cups" resolved to "March to Annapolis in order to intimidate the Assembly" so as to insure they would honor the frontier militia's debts. Their host (and a grandfather of Francis Scott Key) Arthur Charlton confirmed this account, adding that the discontent was not limited to the grumbling and epithets the drunken men hurled around in his tavern. Charlton testified that "he understood that a great

Number of People were assembled on the Roads, in Order to Join the Inhabitants of Frederick Town in their way down to Annapolis."[14]

By the end of November, reports reached the Maryland government that "there were between three and four hundred Men [in Frederick Town]," and "they were about to Choose Officers, and to March down in Companies to Annapolis, in order to settle the Disputes betwixt the Two Houses of Assembly." Informants also named the man who was at the heart of all this trouble: "they heard Colo. Cresap say, that nothing would be done unless the People did come down . . . to see whether the Business was done, and if it was not, they would not return until it was done."[15]

Governor Horatio Sharpe took these threats to storm the capital seriously. For him, these were not patriots, but dangerous, deluded thugs seeking to intimidate elected officials. Over two days, December 10 and 11, he deposed witnesses and investigated rumors. He also received word from county officials in Elk-Ridge, less than twenty miles from Annapolis, who reported that "a great number of people that live in that Neighborhood" were also on the march. Sharpe knew who was to blame. The trouble, he reported, was "Owing to Colo. Cresap's Declaring, as he lately returned home thro' the County, that nothing would be done unless the People did come down." Sharpe sent a message to the assembly houses imploring them not to be fearful and to finish the work of this session.[16]

"The People" never came down to Annapolis from either Elk-Ridge or Frederick. But an atmosphere of threats and vigilantism continued. Sharpe saw this as the natural evolution of the attacks on Zachariah Hood. In a letter to Maryland proprietor Cecil Calvert, Sharpe noted that, after such success in forcing the resignations of stamp distributors, "they begin to think they can by the same way of proceeding accomplish anything that leaders may tell them they ought to do, and I really know not whether the civil power in any of the colonies will be sufficient of itself to establish order." For Sharpe, the Sons of Liberty, with men like Thomas Cresap directing the mob, were threatening to put an end to reasoned governance in America.[17]

From the perspective of Cresap and his allies, they were merely making their voices heard to representative bodies who were not taking them seriously. They demanded justice. Even though Cresap himself was a member of the lower house of the Maryland assembly, he resorted to stirring up insurrection when he could not achieve his aims through official channels. He was willing to be an exuberant crusader for colonialism, but it seemed that both of the polities to which he belonged—the colony of Maryland and the British Empire—were unwilling to back his efforts. He was going to have to start acting like a free agent.

In the quest to dominate trade in the Ohio country, George Croghan was Thomas Cresap's chief rival. It's easy to see why; they did have a lot in common. One historian has described Croghan as "a wily man with often murky motives." That's a pretty fitting description of Thomas Cresap, too. Neither could separate their own self-interests from those of the British Empire as a whole. Both tried to corner the market on land deals and trade networks in Ohio.[18]

Before the Seven Years' War, however, it was not much of a rivalry. Croghan's Pennsylvanians floundered while Cresap and his fellow Ohio Company investors seemed well on their way to success. But a decade later, the situation had reversed. Croghan and his Philadelphia backers raced ahead while the Ohio Company faltered. General Forbes had cut his own road through central Pennsylvania when his redcoats turned Fort Duquesne into Fort Pitt. George Washington knew at the time that pivot away from Braddock's Virginia road was going to be bad for the Ohio Company. Then Croghan was named Sir William Johnson's chief deputy. When George III decided in 1764 to invest Johnson and the new commander-in-chief Gage with primary authority in dealing with Native affairs, George Croghan would find himself with unparalleled opportunities.[19]

At the end of 1764, Johnson assigned Croghan the task of presiding over a peace conference at Fort Pitt with Shawnees and Delawares as part of the ongoing negotiations to bring Pontiac's War to a close. Croghan

Figure 11. Sir William Johnson would conduct many negotiations with the Six Nations at his residence in Johnstown, New York, Johnson Hall.

knew this effort would require considerable gifts and asked Gage for £2000 to buy goods for him to distribute at the meeting. Gage thought that amount would suffice. Croghan saw it as a down payment. He took the king's funds and worked with the Philadelphia merchant firm Baynton, Wharton, and Morgan to finance a shipment about ten times that size. Croghan and his partners had dreams of outfitting Natives not only in the Upper Ohio Valley but throughout the Illinois country farther to the west. If they could corner the fur trade market in the territory recently won from France, they would make an incalculable fortune. All through the winter months, Philadelphia artisans labored to fill their substantial orders. One recent estimate suggests that, by the end of January, the firm had made 5,700 shirts out of 15,000 yards of cloth. Urban laborers loaded a whole ton of sugar and nearly two tons of rum onto a convoy of wagons that headed west in February 1765.[20]

They wouldn't get far. On March 6, as the pack train neared the valleys west of the Susquehanna that had been so burned over with Native raids, a group of vigilantes who referred to themselves as the "Black

Boys" intercepted it. Colonists from Shearman's Valley (men like James Loudon and his neighbors) and the Conococheague (men like Daniel Cresap and his neighbors) did not want these supplies going to people they deemed as erstwhile enemies. In their view, any hatchets Croghan and his Philadelphia merchant friends might give to Ohio Natives would surely end up in their backs. The Black Boys' bold seizure of Croghan's convoy—and then their even more brazen action of *firing on* British soldiers at Fort Loudoun when the fort's commander had the temerity to make some arrests—suggests that the discontent with the British government's treatment of the colonists wasn't just in Boston, and it wasn't just about the Stamp Act.

Croghan was appalled—and financially crushed. The loss had all but broken Baynton, Wharton, and Morgan. By 1767 they would be in receivership and their storehouse in Pittsburgh put up for sale. For Croghan, it was another attempt to strike it rich in the backcountry gone wrong, and he felt once again like a "suffering trader."

The term "suffering trader" arose at the end of the Seven Years' War. It was a sobriquet Croghan and his allies had come up with to garner pity from British officials back in London. The traders, including the Baynton, Wharton, and Morgan firm and one other major Philadelphia merchant house, claimed they had incurred stupendous losses in the raids of 1755–56 and then again in 1763–64. They argued they were innocent victims of French and Native attack, and sought wartime reparations. A gift of free land in the backcountry might help assuage their terrible "suffering": 1,200,000 acres ought to do it.[21]

The traders first lobbied Superintendent Johnson. When he signaled support for their efforts to seek indemnification for their losses, they then met as a group in Philadelphia late in 1763. They decided to name themselves the "Suffering Traders" and elected Croghan to go to England and campaign on their behalf. They extended membership to other Philadelphia luminaries, including Joseph Galloway, Benjamin Franklin, and his son William, to help with political difficulties. In London, Croghan waited patiently in the lobbies of all the government offices he thought could help. Of course, Croghan being Croghan, he also had a separate scheme: to secure the 200,000 acres of land he argued the Iroquois had granted him at a treaty conference back in 1749. He failed to make much progress on either issue and came back to Pennsylvania without having eased anyone's suffering.[22]

Early in 1765, as Croghan began to gather funding and goods for his huge trade expedition to the Illinois country, the Suffering Traders, now a consortium of twenty-three merchants, adopted a new name. Instead of embracing a sense of victimhood from past wrongs, they decided to associate themselves with the possibility of a new colony in the Illinois territory, far to the west around where the Ohio joins the Mississippi River. The Indiana Company, with George Croghan as one of the principal shareholders and Benjamin Franklin as their chief lobbyist in London, became a going concern just as the Black Boys attacked.[23]

Thomas Cresap, though a trader who had suffered greatly during the Seven Years' War, was not invited to join the Suffering Traders. Croghan wanted nothing to do with him. In fact, Cresap posed the greatest threat to the chances that the Crown might award a handsome restitution in land to that faction, and not only because he was one of the principal investors in the competing Ohio Company. Cresap was becoming his very own problem at Redstone; the "monster's" reputation was becoming as infamous in London as it had been in Philadelphia thirty years earlier.

Unlike Cresap, Croghan would never consider himself a free agent. Despite his setbacks, the empire worked to his benefit. He used his contacts in Philadelphia and position as Johnson's deputy superintendent to work within the imperial system to achieve his dreams. Yes, he had cut some side deals that he hoped would redound to his benefit, but for the most part Croghan was the empire's man in Ohio. Thomas Cresap, on the other hand, was becoming a thorn in the sides of many imperial officials who viewed his penchant for striking out on his own as potentially destabilizing an already shaky peace.

Starting in the spring of 1766, General Thomas Gage began to get testy about Cresap and the illegal colonists at Redstone. Just a few weeks before the Frederick Sons of Liberty threw their party at Swearingen's house, the king had issued a new round of orders insisting that colonial authorities "use their best endeavours . . . to put a stop" to any colonists who have "irregularly seated themselves on Lands to the westward of the Allegheny Mountains." That meant Redstone. Johnson warned Gage about the "Lawless and Cruel proceedings of the people on the Frontiers," but he confessed being "utterly at a loss about what to do" in "bringing those lawless Ruffians to punishment." In his reply, Gage predicted that, "These Cursed Villains will Sooner or later bring us into a War." A few days later, Croghan made essentially the same prediction to Gage: "If some effectual measures are not speedily taken to remove those People settled on Red Stone Creek," Croghan wrote, "the Consequences may be dreadful & We involved in all the Calamitys of another general war."[24]

That summer, Native groups continued to visit Croghan at Fort Pitt to "complain loudly" about Redstone, which was growing to the point of becoming out of control. "The settlers at Redstone must be drove away if it is possible," he wrote. "Were they not so numerous it might have been easily done; the garrison of Fort Pitt drove them off once or twice, I believe no later than last year." But given the rising tensions about imperial authority spreading throughout the mainland colonies, Gage perceived the dangers of sending redcoats to Redstone. "If a Skirmish happens, and Blood is Shed, you know what a clamor there will be against the Military Acting without Civil Magistrates," he told Johnson in June. Reading Gage's reports about Redstone, imperial administrators in London ordered a clear response: "The Settlers at Ridstone Creek [sic] seem to have placed themselves not only beyond the Limits prescribed by His Majesty's proclamation, but beyond the Boundaries & consequently out of the protection of every Province." The Secretary of State in charge of colonial affairs instructed Gage and Johnson to have the commander at Fort Pitt, Captain William Murray, go again to warn them away. Ridstone, indeed.[25]

Proclamations ordering those pesky squatters at Redstone to leave kept piling up through the end of 1766. Perhaps literally so: two hundred copies of Pennsylvania governor John Penn's September proclamation ejecting everyone over the King's Line were sent to Fort Pitt for distribution. But no one budged. In fact, more colonists kept arriving. In the first days of 1767, Johnson received a distressing letter that the Redstone situation might be even worse in the new year.[26]

It was Croghan's associates in the Baynton, Wharton, and Morgan firm who took it upon themselves to enlighten Johnson. With bills coming due and their fortunes dwindling, they decided to appeal to Johnson for help neutralizing what they saw as the greatest threat to peace and stability in the region. "By letters from Cumberland County, from Persons, we can rely upon, we are informed," they wrote to the Superintendent, "That Colonel Cressap of Maryland, sometime last summer, held a Treaty with forty [Iroquois] Warriors, in which, they, by deed, ceded to Him a large Extent of Land down the Ohio." This would be right in the territory that the Suffering Traders/Indiana Company had circled as lands they hoped the Crown would give to them. If Cresap was acting under orders from Johnson, they wrote, "we are uneasy, least such Contracts may produce Discontent; for Others will no doubt follow such unwarrantable Practices." They were grateful for all Johnson had done in support of their efforts to end their suffering, the traders continued, "But if Colonel Cressap or any other Persons are permitted thus to bargain with the natives—we are apprehensive your benevolent Intentions may be frustrated."[27]

Johnson immediately picked up a pen and wrote to the Lords of Trade about Cresap's free-agent dealings with the Iroquois. Much as he had four years earlier when he was running into headwinds with colonial and imperial officials, Cresap enlisted the Iroquois to legitimate his claims. If Cresap had indeed gained permission from the Iroquois and turned that permission into the basis for an independent Ohio claim, it could ruin many people's dreams—in London, in Williamsburg, in Philadelphia, and at Johnson Hall. "By letters I have this moment received," Johnson wrote on January 15, "I am informed that a Colonel Cressop of Maryland held some time last year a Treaty himself with several Six Nations [Iroquois] leaders . . . whom he persuaded to grant him a considerable tract of land out of the Government's down the Ohio." His disbelief—

and worry—flowed out onto the page. "If this be true (which I have little reason to doubt) it is a flagrant instance of the little regard paid to authority and will . . . be productive of dangerous consequences." Johnson didn't write that those consequences included danger to his and his associates' bottom line.[28]

There were a few windows in the 1760s in which colonial schemes—whether those of companies or individuals—stood any chance of getting the Crown's approval. Those opportunities corresponded to the brief times when one man, the Earl of Hillsborough, wasn't in power. Hillsborough was the president of the Board of Trade intermittently during this period (September 1763–July 1765; August–December 1766; January 1768–August 1772). When he had the gavel in his hand, colonial speculators need not waste their breaths lobbying for thousands of acres of western lands. Hillsborough's wealth came from rents he collected from his vast holdings in Ireland, and he watched in horror as potential tenants like George Croghan left Ireland for America in the mid-1700s. Peace only multiplied those numbers. Immigration from the British Isles exploded after 1760, with at least 125,000 people crossing the ocean over the next decade and a half, many of them headed straight for the American backcountry.[29]

According to Benjamin Franklin, the Traders' agent in London, Hillsborough was "terribly afraid of dispeopling Ireland." He therefore opposed *all* schemes to organize and settle the trans-Appalachian region. Hillsborough especially did not like free agents. At least the companies respected proper channels. They employed agents who the Board of Trade could interview in London. They asked permission and offered the board the opportunity to reward their favorite schemes. Most importantly, there was usually a chance for peers like him to buy in and line their own pockets. Individuals like Cresap, who tried to circumvent the system, were seen an especially treacherous sort.[30]

The year 1767 happened to be one of those rare windows when Hillsborough was not in power. William Petty, the Earl of Shelburne, had become the secretary of state for the colonies, and he took less of a hard line against American expansion. With Hillsborough out of office, the Pennsylvanians had a real chance to secure claims to vast quantities of land. Thomas Cresap and his fellow "ragtag refugees" at Redstone were the primary obstacle standing in their way.[31]

It was bad enough that Cresap's Redstone colonists defied the king's proclamation. That didn't help the Pennsylvanians' lobbying effort. But, even worse, Cresap's efforts to gain Native sanction for his own personal grant challenged the British claim to the territory over the mountains. It flew in the face of the Treaty of Paris! Even though the Crown had set aside that territory as an "Indian reserve," the government still maintained they were sovereign there. Native leaders didn't have the authority to determine who had right to that land. Only King George did, or so Shelburne and the men who worked for him maintained.

In a panic after having received no reply from Johnson, the Indiana Company (Suffering Traders) men sent another note in March 1767. "We judged it necessary that your Honor should be appraized of such clandestine and impolitick Proceedings, lest others may follow the example," they protested again. The Indian superintendent did respond this time, saying he had indeed written to his superiors about the "affair of purchase . . . about the Ohio."[32]

While the flustered (and all but bankrupt) merchants were busy worrying about the reliability of Johnson's mail, the predictions of Gage and Croghan had come true: there had been murder again at Redstone that February.

John Ryan, another free agent in the making, had brought kegs of rum to Redstone, boasting he was going to sell them to Natives in Ohio. Cresap couldn't brook any more rivals. Witnesses told British officials at Fort Pitt that a "Quarrell arouse thro' the Instigation of Col. Cresap of Maryland who trades on that frontier." Cresap had allegedly threatened Ryan that "if he met with any Traders in the Country or going to it, he should take their Liquor from them & cause the Kegs to be staved."

Cresap asked a Delaware leader named Peter to seize Ryan's rum on his behalf. When Peter challenged him, Ryan shot the Delaware leader dead and then fled to the mountains. He was never seen again.[33]

Why had this happened? Gage partly blamed Peter, since he was "the first aggressor," but, then again, the environment was a poisonous one. This kind of behavior was bound to occur on these "usurped Settlement[s]," Gage scoffed. On the other hand, maybe Cresap had a good reason to have Peter confront Ryan. One recent study suggests Cresap's real motive was to stabilize the unruliness at Redstone. Since Ohio leaders insisted they wanted to curb access to alcohol, perhaps Cresap wanted to stop that item to earn Native backing for his personal speculations. Ryan's kegs might undercut his own diplomacy in the Upper Ohio Valley. Instead of a "ragtag refugee" acting beyond the law, perhaps Cresap was trying to alleviate tensions and win Natives to his side. When Gage thought about Redstone, he was bewildered. Thomas Cresap was trying to use that to his advantage.[34]

Other imperial officials had little good to say about Cresap and Redstone. "The Conduct of that Gentleman is very extraordinary, to say no worse of it," Virginia governor Francis Fauquier sniffed to the commander at Fort Pitt, Captain William Murray. Maryland governor Horatio Sharpe also wrote with disdain about the "parcel of Refugees and outlaws from the several provinces" who had settled there. Sharpe joined a host of British imperial officials who wanted the place eliminated, a move which would thrill Croghan and his allies. Throughout the spring, riders galloped over many colonial roads with orders to eject the Redstone colonists.[35]

In early May, Captain Murray sent word that their warnings had largely worked: "most of the Settlers are removed." But they kept returning. It was barely thirty days before Gage had to write more letters about how colonists "upon the Branches of the Monongahela still remain there." By the fall, there were reports that "there are double the number of Inhabitants" there than "ever was before." "The Emigrants from Pensilvania and Virginia daily increase," Johnson complained in December. Shelburne, on whose London desk all these reports landed, concluded

that "the Abuses committed in the Indian Trade and the Disorders in
the back Settlements have had their Source principally in the fraudulent
Purchases and Grants from the Natives." This is so "detrimental to the
Interests of His Majesty's Provinces," that they needed to be addressed,
and quickly.[36]

A solution would soon emerge to deal with Cresap, Redstone, and
other squatters who defied the king's Proclamation Line: the establishment of a permanent boundary separating Natives from colonists.

Boundaries had not been kind to the Cresaps. The imprecision of American maps was the reason the family was in the backcountry in the first
place. That first controversy over the boundary between Maryland and
Pennsylvania—the one that sparked "Cresap's War" in the 1730s—had
still not yet been fully resolved after nearly three decades. In 1763, the
proprietor families, the Penns and the Calverts, hired the surveyor team
of Charles Mason and Jeremiah Dixon to draw an official boundary line.
Finally, the border dispute that Thomas Cresap had initiated a quarter
century ago was going to be settled.

Mason and Dixon arrived in America in the last few weeks of that
pivotal year; in fact, they had just gotten to Philadelphia when the Paxton
Boys marched up to the city's outskirts and threatened to ransack the
capital. Mason and Dixon were going to have to use all their mathematic
and scientific skills if they were going to bring reason and progress to
this bewildering place.

It took the surveyors several years to finish the project. At the height
of summer 1767, while British officials cursed the Cresaps throughout
their correspondence, Mason, Dixon, and their party of more than three-
dozen assistants stayed the night at the Cresap outpost in Oldtown. They
had heard of Thomas Cresap earlier in their American adventure. Two
years before, in January 1765, Mason and Dixon noted in their journals that they had spent part of their winter break visiting Lancaster,
Pennsylvania. They expressed a "curiosity" to see the place "where was
perpetrated last Winter the Horrid and inhuman murder" of the Con-

estoga Indians at the hands of the Paxton Boys. While they were there, the sheriff of Lancaster took them to see another famous local site, the place where "one Mr. Crisep defended his house as being in Maryland." They learned about the "open war" over the "Boundary line" thirty years before. Now, in July 1767, the survey team pitched their tents on the "monster" from Maryland's storied front lawn. They were impressed with the improvements to Cresap's fortunes, commenting how "he has here a most beautiful Estate."[37]

Over the next few months, the surveying party crossed near to the ridge where Thomas Cresap Jr. had bled to death, mapping and measuring their way west to the Youghiogheny and Cheat Rivers. They soon began to gain the attention of Natives in the area who were not as pleased to welcome them. On September 12, they crossed the Monongahela River about fifty miles upstream from Redstone, where news still poured in to Fort Pitt that summer about how Natives were "greatly Incensed" and "threatened an Open Rupture with Virginia." Two days prior, Cresap welcomed more visitors to his Oldtown estate, hosting a group of Ohio Natives (Delawares, Shawnees, Wyandots) in an independent effort to broker peace between them and Virginia.[38]

Near the end of September, eight Senecas appeared out of the woods to watch the surveyors make their calculations. These Iroquois were the latest in a number of parties of Natives who had been monitoring their progress. On October 9, Mason and Dixon splashed through Dunkard Creek, where they noticed the ruins of some colonists' cabins that had been destroyed in 1755. An ominous sign—and one that had bearing on the present moment. The next day the Native guides accompanying them informed the surveyors that *they* would not go "one step farther Westward," and suggested that perhaps Mason and Dixon should not either.[39]

The English mathematicians got the message: Dunkard Creek was the outer limit. They packed their equipment and retraced their steps. They hadn't gone as far as they had been instructed to go, but that would be the final western point of the Mason-Dixon Line. Cresap's earlier machinations in the 1730s had brought Mason and Dixon across the ocean to start their famous boundary, and his colonialism in the 1760s—

and the Natives' hostility to it—influenced where it ended. Perhaps it
should be called Cresap's Line.

⸻

A year later, at Fort Stanwix (now Rome, New York), Natives and imperial agents discussed another consequential boundary line. There, in the
fall of 1768, Sir William Johnson presided over a treaty conference that
he anticipated would be a turning point in North American history.
After many years of lobbying, he had finally gotten permission from
the Crown to negotiate a permanent boundary line separating Natives
from colonists.

As it stood, the earlier Proclamation Line enacted a vague order that
didn't correspond with geographic or political realities in the eastern
woodlands. George Washington scoffed that the King's line was merely
a "temporary expedient to quiet the minds of the Indians and must fall
of course in a few years." Johnson hoped to gain Native consent and
approval for a real boundary, much like what Mason and Dixon were
gazing at the stars to plot. His plan was to invite Native leaders from all
over central North America and negotiate a landmark treaty.[40]

Events (Pontiac's War and the Stamp Act) had intervened—but so
had indecision and fumbling back in London. Shelburne didn't help.
He was in favor of reversing the 1764 decision to give Johnson and
Gage exclusive power in the west and wanted to return responsibility to
the colonial governments, thus reopening the door to speculators. He
hemmed and hawed. In the last days of 1767, Shelburne wrote Johnson
that "the Completion of a Boundary Line . . . being a Matter so essential
for the Preservation of Peace and Harmony with those People; I was in
hopes to have sent you . . . positive Instructions for effecting this necessary Work without Loss of Time. But as so many different Interests are
concerned in this Affair," it hadn't come together. However, a month
later, in one of his last acts of as secretary of state, Shelburne sent orders
for Johnson to hold his conference "without loss of time."[41]

That autumn, all eyes turned to Fort Stanwix. Delegations from
Virginia, New Jersey, and Pennsylvania gathered in Johnson's house on

September 15 and proceeded to travel as a group to the fort, sixty miles to the west. They were joined there by several members of the "Suffering Traders," who went to press their claims, as well as more than three thousand Native peoples, three quarters of whom were Iroquois. Only a small number came from the Ohio country. There were a few Shawnees and no Mingos present. John Killbuck, the man who Thomas Cresap challenged to a duel when he found him stalking around Oldtown six years earlier, was one of the handful of Delaware deputies in attendance. A rising Seneca leader in the Ohio country named Guyasuta was also there. On October 24, the conference began.[42]

Behind the fort's impressive seventeen-foot-high walls, Johnson and the Natives haggled over where to draw the line. After some hard bargaining, Iroquois leaders agreed to a boundary that protected their homelands but swung out wide to the south and west, following the Ohio River and running all the way to where the Tennessee River joins it (in present-day Paducah, Kentucky), less than fifty miles short of the Mississippi. They ceded huge swaths of southern land, including what is

Figure 12. Built during the Seven Years' War, Fort Stanwix guarded the Carrying Place, a strategic spot between the Mohawk River and the Finger Lakes.

today western Pennsylvania, West Virginia, and Kentucky. But, as they had done for decades, the Iroquois sold lands they had no real power over in order to fortify their political prestige as the only rightful brokers in Indian country. The Six Nations had once again shielded their own lands from colonial incursion by giving away much of the Ohio Valley. They had drawn what they and British officials agreed was a distinct, defined border separating Indian country from colonial settlers. The "line of Property" was set.[43]

On November 5, the parties signed the treaty, Johnson distributed an astonishing amount of gifts and cash—totaling £10,460—and everyone headed for home. The Iroquois relished their victory. But as happy as they might have been, they couldn't have been as jubilant as George Croghan. Much of the work at Stanwix had been done in private, unrecorded meetings, often at night and outside the walls, the kind of dealing that suited Croghan. As a result of these secret arrangements, Johnson's deputy was able to extract assurances that the 200,000 acres the Iroquois had granted him around the Ohio Forks back in 1749 were rightfully his to possess. Even better, Croghan and his Suffering Traders secured what he had been unable to get from his London connections: the exclusive right to a large chunk of the ceded ground. According to the secret deal, the Suffering Traders and no other speculators could possess what would become the top third of West Virginia: 2,500,000 acres, twice as much as the Traders had originally requested from the Crown. The British government had refused to ease Croghan and the traders' suffering, but the Six Nations had delivered. Croghan finally had his triumph.[44]

Johnson was equally pleased. While at Stanwix he had written to New York's governor that "it was my intention to Obtain as Much Land I possibly could." On this front, he had succeeded magnificently. Yet a tricky task lay ahead of him. Not everyone agreed that a massive land grab was the best way to proceed, or that colonial speculators were to be emboldened. He had to write to London with the details, many of them sordid, about what had taken place in and around Fort Stanwix, knowing full well that the man he needed to inform was not going to be happy.[45]

Just two weeks after sending Johnson orders to go ahead with his treaty conference, Lord Shelburne resigned as the American secretary of state. His replacement was the Earl of Hillsborough. In the new ministry that formed in early 1768, Hillsborough was now both the president of the Board of Trade *and* the American secretary of state, key positions he would hold for the next four years. The colonial speculators had not only lost their best advocate in the British government, but the enemy had returned—in force.

As Johnson likely feared, Hillsborough read his letter with fury. The earl had supported the policy of drawing a permanent boundary for several reasons. He hoped it would hem the colonists in and prevent them from spreading all across the continent, thus blunting the promise of abundant land in America for his Irish tenants. The settlement of a line would, moreover, allow him to redeploy the army and evacuate the expensive western posts. The Crown could then quarter those troops more cheaply in or near the eastern cities, which would have the added benefit of being available to quell disturbances when unruly Bostonians or New Yorkers broke out in mobs again.[46]

A line running all the way down the Ohio River threatened all these plans. The negotiated territory opened far more extensive lands than Johnson's instructions had permitted, especially south of the Ohio Valley, thus creating a vast new opportunity for speculators. Even worse, in Hillsborough's view, was the side deal Johnson had brokered for Croghan and the Suffering Traders. Over the next year, the secretary would instruct Johnson to have the Iroquois take back most of their cessions south of the Ohio. Moreover, Hillsborough demanded that Johnson inform George Croghan that unless his company made personal application to the king, their grant wasn't remotely legal.[47]

The Earl of Hillsborough was not the only one upset with the machinations at Stanwix. Johnson had bluntly told any Natives from Ohio that their voices were irrelevant at the conference. Since the Iroquois had sovereignty over the territory, Johnson argued, Ohio was theirs to dole out as they wished, reinforcing the Iroquois' interpretation of how power worked in eastern North America. In the aftermath of the conference, the small groups of Ohio Natives who had witnessed the dealings returned home and reported how they had been ignored and betrayed. The Iroquois had given away their land—and taken their gifts—while they could do nothing but watch.

Perhaps unsurprisingly, the treaty of Fort Stanwix did not settle disputes over land in the region. Instead, speculation schemes that had been closed down by the Royal Proclamation were suddenly revived, just as Hillsborough feared. During the intervening years, however, the context of the Upper Ohio Valley had changed considerably. More and more Natives had moved to the region in the years after Pontiac's War, into the zone, they learned, that the Iroquois had traded out from under their feet at Stanwix. The major groups of Natives living near the Ohio River—Shawnees, Delawares, and Mingos—would not stand idly by while lands they believed they had won through military victory were taken from them. Iroquois who lived in the Alleghany highlands who might have already been disillusioned with the temerity of the Six Nations, joined them in Ohio. As more of these groups gathered in the Ohio country, they, too, found out that—despite what Johnson, Gage, Croghan and other British officials in America had promised them since Pontiac's War—their interests weren't going to be protected. Ohio Natives had again been sold out to reinforce what imperial officials deemed the far greater relationship, the diplomatic alliance with the Iroquois. The message after Stanwix was that Natives living in Ohio were unwanted and unwelcome, too. As the decade drew to a close, many people in the American backcountry—from Cresap's settlers at Redstone to Native groups along the Ohio River—began to ask themselves, who was this empire for, anyway?[48]

CHAPTER 5

FEELING VERY SMALL, VERY LOST,

1769–1770

"Trees, trees, millions of trees, massive, immense, running up
high. . . . It made you feel very small, very lost, and yet it was not
altogether depressing that feeling."

—*Heart of Darkness*

W hen George Washington and his enslaved servant William Lee
set off for the Ohio country on October 5, 1770, they were
relieved to find the skies "clear, warm and remarkably pleasant." Three
days prior, snow and hail blanketed Mount Vernon's roof while a few
former soldiers from the old Virginia Regiment gathered around the
fire in the mansion's well-appointed front parlor to discuss the western
journey Washington was about to undertake on their behalf. Sixteen
years earlier, Governor Dinwiddie had promised the men in that room
and many more like them—those who volunteered to defend the colony
in 1754—that they would receive a share of two hundred thousand acres
at the confluence of the Ohio and the Kanawha Rivers for their service.
Their host was now determined to lead a new campaign to fight for their
(but especially his) fortunes in the Ohio country.[1]

On that bright October morning, just before they spurred their
horses west, Washington posted a letter to the Virginia governor, hoping
to learn whether the surveys he was about to make for his men would
have any value. This, his fifth trip to Ohio, needed not to be a fool's
errand. Virginia's skies might have cleared that October morning, but

there were political clouds troubling Washington's mind as he made his way west.

One of his first stops would be to see Thomas Cresap in Oldtown. It had been nearly twenty years since Washington had grumbled that the way to Cresap's place was the worst road in America. Perhaps that memory was the subject of their opening pleasantries as Washington dismounted and greeted his business partner. Maybe Washington commented on how Oldtown had grown since he had been there last. Three years before, Thomas and his son Michael partnered to develop the settlement, taking out advertisements in the *Maryland Gazette* about how well situated the spot was and how it was "most proper for a County Town." The Cresaps promised that any tradesmen—carpenters, tailors, hatters, smiths, saddlers, and shoemakers—could get lots in their developing town free of charge. While Oldtown had expanded, Cresap's house was now nearly empty, the children all grown. Michael Cresap was twenty-eight and married, with two toddlers and more on the way. A year after the Battle of Oldtown (1763), Michael had finished building his new bride Mary a two-story stone house there, but these days the budding town developer was currently spending most of his time operating a store at Redstone.[2]

Washington wasn't there for a social visit, however, or to sleep in a bed that he had slept in several times before. This was an important stop on his tour. Washington was there for much-needed intelligence—and Thomas Cresap had it.

The summer before, Cresap had gone east: not to Annapolis, as he had done so often as a member of the Maryland Assembly, but to Philadelphia. He had not visited that city in thirty years, since his brief stint in the stone prison on the corner of High and Third Streets. This time, decidedly freer, he was headed down to the wharfs. He secured a berth on the sloop *Endeavour* bound for New York City, where he then boarded a ship for England. Cresap was still rather infamous in the Quaker City, and his political opponents in town noted his presence— and, more importantly, that he was going to London. They were instantly suspicious and worried that the now aging "monster" from Maryland once again threatened Pennsylvania's interests.[3]

Figure 13. Stone house (left) built by Michael Cresap at Oldtown, completed 1764. The addition on the right was undertaken by Michael's former clerk, John Jeremiah Jacob, after the Revolutionary War.

While Cresap didn't leave any evidence about why he chose to cross the ocean in his sixties, it's doubtful he had decided to undertake a trans-atlantic voyage just for pleasure. The Stanwix treaty had recently opened the door for speculators, and Cresap was likely going to see about his affairs. His rivals certainly thought so. It was Thomas Wharton, one of the proprietors of the Baynton, Wharton, and Morgan firm, who first noticed Cresap leaving for London. Worried that Cresap might ruin the firm's carefully laid plans, he mentioned it at the end of a letter to Sir William Johnson.[4]

A few months before Cresap boarded the *Endeavour*, Wharton's brother Samuel and fellow "Suffering Trader" William Trent had sailed for London to secure permission for the lucrative arrangement they had won at Fort Stanwix. Upon arrival, they immediately ran into the wall that was Lord Hillsborough. When the earl dictated his orders to Johnson that the deal the Traders had cut at Stanwix was illegal, Wharton was already in town doing his best to charm the Board of Trade. The Privy

Council, upset with the secretary of state for his overreach in demanding the whole Stanwix deal be scrapped, recommended, over Hillsborough's protests, that the boundary line (absent the Traders' controversial side deal) be sent to the king.[5]

What follows in this chapter will be an account of individuals in 1769 and 1770 advancing several competing interests. Each actor held incomplete information, but they nevertheless tried to bend that confusion to their benefit. It is the exercising of bewilderment as close to real time as the sources allow. Visible throughout are interested parties hedging bets and shading truth, always aware that they were engaged in a game of musical chairs in which there were multiple fiddlers, separated by thousands of miles, and the precise number of available chairs were unknown to every participant. In the aftermath of the Stanwix boundary line treaty, everyone was trying to recapture their Ohio dreams.

Only a few spare months after they thought they had achieved victory at Stanwix, the Suffering Traders' project looked to be smashed beyond repair, wrecked by Hillsborough's obstinance. Not even the prodigious lobbying efforts of Benjamin Franklin could rescue them, though he knew someone who might be able to help. In the middle of June, Franklin introduced the dejected Pennsylvanians to Thomas Walpole. A banker from an impeccable family and a member of Parliament with even more impressive political connections, Walpole was the answer to the Traders' desperate prayers. Over the next six weeks, Wharton and Walpole combined their resources, cajoled their political friends, and scribbled memoranda to put together a new company. The names of several lords and dukes, some of whom sat in the plush seats of the Privy Council, peppered their expanded list of luminaries invited to join. When this now much better-connected company applied to purchase 2,400,000 acres of land out of the Stanwix grant, Hillsborough suddenly found himself dealing with more than just a band of colonial land speculators.[6]

All of these machinations happened as Thomas Cresap made his way east from Oldtown to Philadelphia. These plans were momentous but still quite fragile. Small wonder Thomas Wharton fretted about the damage Cresap might do in London. We know little, however, about how Cresap spent his time in the metropolis. The one thing we know for certain is that he took a meeting with representatives from the Calvert family, proprietors of Maryland. Although Mason and Dixon's line had established the colony's northern boundary, the question of Maryland's western border was still hazy, and the Calverts commissioned Thomas Cresap to undertake a new survey.

Whatever kept him busy in London, Cresap was still in town when the Board of Trade convened its December 1769 meeting. That meeting found Hillsborough in a tough spot. He did not want to encourage vast interior tracts of North American land to be settled with his Irish renters, nor did he want to deal with the headaches of governing colonists so far removed from Atlantic ports. But the list of signatories on the Pennsylvanians' proposal was daunting, full as it was of influential members of government. According to Benjamin Franklin, the wily Hillsborough at some point during the autumn months struck upon a way out: what if he flipped sides, acted as a warm friend of the project and encouraged that illustrious group to go for broke? Perhaps they might just go broke, or get so greedy that they would ask for a ludicrous grant and the king would say no. Either way, he might hold on to his tenants a little longer.[7]

When the Board of Trade reconvened, Hillsborough did just that, suggesting that the partners make their proposal *much grander*. He encouraged them to ask for enough land to create a vast new colony west of the Appalachians, not one that would be an extension of Virginia or Pennsylvania. The group, encouraged by Hillsborough's reversal, met later that week at the Crown and Anchor Tavern and reconstituted themselves under a new name, one which reflected their expanding ambitions: the Grand Ohio Company. The project would more generally become known as Vandalia, which was to be the name of their new interior colony. In their petition, they requested a whopping twenty million acres—encompassing what today is nearly all of West Virginia, the eastern half of Ohio, and even a slice of eastern Kentucky.[8]

Wherever Thomas Cresap was staying in London during that late

December night, if he knew about the meeting at the Crown and Anchor, he was probably up walking the floors until the wee hours. This was disaster. His nemesis George Croghan and the now-saved Traders were going to best him now for sure.

As the audacious Vandalia proposal began to gain traction, Hillsborough must have sorely regretted his ploy. Still, the Vandalia schemers faced significant headwinds, including dealing with the myriad other counterclaimants to that territory. In the spring and summer of 1770, they set about disposing of these challenges. One major competitor was the old Ohio Company, the defense of which was surely one reason Thomas Cresap had sailed to England. The Cresap family had a lot to lose if that now-twenty-year-old enterprise disappeared. The Walpole group offered George Mercer, the old Ohio Company's agent in London, a juicy bribe, consisting not only of Vandalia shares but also hints that he might be appointed the new colony's first governor. Mercer was a critical person to buy, as he was not only the Ohio Company's agent in London, but he also lobbied on behalf of the 1754 grant to Virginia's veterans of the Seven Years' War (known as the Dinwiddie bounty lands) that Washington was just then trying to secure the rights to. Mercer didn't put up much of a fight, and the Ohio Company thus vanished into the ever-expanding Vandalia maw. Mercer never informed the Ohio Company partners, including Thomas and Daniel Cresap, that their investment was now worth far less. The Vandalia investors promised they would honor the soldiers' bounty claims, but that could not have been very reassuring, as there were scores of other competitors. The Walpole group labored to check all these rivals off the list, either by subsuming them within their own proposal or muscling them aside. As they proceeded, they grew increasingly confident the Crown couldn't say no to Vandalia. They thought they would be the sole masters of a vast internal American colony. It was so massive that it might be more apt to call it a kingdom, as colonial newspapers would in the future.[9]

At some point in 1770, Thomas Cresap returned home in utter defeat. Hillsborough might have been unhappy, but Cresap stood to be one of the biggest colonial losers of the rising Vandalia scheme. It looked nearly certain that he would fail to achieve the windfall in land and power that he had long sought. While we don't know exactly when Cresap packed for home, it was most likely before the end of July. He could not have been around when the Vandalia group began to run into obstacles.

In July 1770, a report arrived from Virginia that itemized all the competing claims to Ohio lands. That list was much longer than the Vandalia group had anticipated, and the complications it presented gave Hillsborough a lifeline. Walpole appeared before the Board of Trade to refute and dismiss these competitors, but the secretary seized the advantage and threw a bureaucratic wrench into the works. He announced that this development required investigation—*lengthy* investigation—and called a halt until it could be determined who had claims to what, how valid they were, and what were all the boundaries. That, as Hillsborough knew, could take years.

This brings us back to George Washington and the reason for his stopover in Oldtown on October 8, 1770. More than a year before, Washington had launched his own crusade to ensure Virginia came through on the wartime promises made to him and his men. In early May 1769, Washington attended two dinners at the Governor's Palace in Williamsburg with Norborne Berkeley, Lord Botetourt, the man who replaced Francis Fauquier as Virginia's royal governor after his death in 1768. During those meals, the Virginia regiment's former commander put forward his claim. In the wake of the treaty of Fort Stanwix, there were suddenly many suitors for Ohio country lands. The music had started, and well-connected colonial speculators all over the mid-Atlantic did not want to be standing without a chair whenever it stopped.

Later that year, as Wharton, Franklin, and Walpole spun up their Grand Ohio/Vandalia scheme in London, Washington continued to press his case across the Atlantic. The Virginia House of Burgesses had taken upon itself the task of writing up a summary of all the claims for Ohio lands, the same report that Hillsborough would soon seize upon. Washington personally made himself a twelve-page copy of the council clerk's document and, seeing that there were nearly three dozen claimants, sent Botetourt a long letter on December 8, 1769, outlining the "full and perfect State of the nature" of the soldiers' claim. While Botetourt could not himself grant them title—only the king could do that—he signaled that he supported the soldiers' rights to two hundred thousand acres at the mouth of the Kanawha. Over the next few days Washington scrambled to organize a petition on behalf of his Virginia veterans, and he took out an advertisement announcing a meeting the following summer for claimants to gather and determine their particular shares. In private, he was less optimistic. In a letter to his brother the next month, he observed that there was so much uncertainty "no man can lay off a foot of Land" west of the mountains "and be sure of keeping it." Washington was doing his best to arrange the chairs, but with this much confusion and contingency, one could never know.[10]

It would help, however, to have a man on the inside. As part of the soldiers' petition, they requested that a special surveyor be appointed by the College of William and Mary to go to the Ohio region and record things on their behalf. Washington took no chances about who would be appointed to this important position and lobbied for the job to go to William Crawford, whom he had known for decades. Crawford had served as an officer in the Virginia Regiment during the Seven Years' War and was with Washington when Braddock met his end along the Monongahela. After the war, Crawford, now approaching fifty, lived much closer to Redstone than Mount Vernon, on the Youghiogheny River in what is present-day Somerset County, Pennsylvania.

In 1767, Washington reached out to Crawford to ask if he would act as his chief agent in scouting out western lands, and the two developed a close relationship that would last until Crawford's death in 1782. Washington asked Crawford to find him some good lands close to the place where Crawford then lived. He wanted a bigger spread than Pennsylvania would allow, so Washington hinted to Crawford that he engage in a bit of title chicanery and purchase a number of tracts under false names. Then he asked Crawford to really break the law. Washington instructed him to quietly scout around the Ohio River looking for good bottomlands near the shore, even though doing so would violate the King's Proclamation Line, which Washington saw as a "mere nuisance." He advised Crawford to act like he was out hunting and find the best land in "the King's part," over the line. But please, he begged, "keep this whole matter a profound secret." Crawford was more than happy to oblige. He acknowledged he had recently been thinking the same thing about taking advantage in "the King's part," given how chaotic things were in Ohio, and agreed to keep their partnership a secret.[11]

So, when it came to appointing a reliable surveyor to map out the soldiers' bounty lands, who better than one of their own—who also just happened to be Washington's employee? Luckily, the college authorities agreed; Washington had his man, and the two made arrangements to undertake a lengthy trip into the mountains together.

A few weeks later, however, a letter from Annapolis arrived at Mount Vernon with bad news. Washington's informant had seen a letter from George Croghan that offered the broad outlines of the Vandalia scheme. According to the correspondent, "A new government is certainly determin'd upon in that Western World—& that either Col. Mercer or one Mr. Wharton are to be appointed Governor. . . . He speaks of its Boundaries etc. with Certainty, as a Matter of Fact. Have you heard of it—& the Particulars?"[12]

Washington had not. This was the first time Wharton's name had crossed his desk. If Croghan was right, it meant that someone in London had stopped the music long before he realized—and he might in fact be the unfortunate one without a place in "that Western World." In fact, Hillsborough had already slowed the scheme down to a crawl by the time the news reached Washington, but no one in America knew that yet. For all Washington knew, the deal was sealed.

He wrote to Botetourt about Vandalia. He waited three weeks for a reply, yet received no response. The morning that they set off for Ohio, he tried once again to see if Botetourt could find out for him "how far the grant of Land solicited by Walpole and others will effect the Interest of this Country." Washington worried that, even before he left the yard of Mount Vernon, the Vandalia scheme had "destroy[ed] the well-grounded hopes" of his soldiers. Like Cresap, Washington couldn't rely on deep family fortunes or multiple plantations to maintain his position in Virginia society; he needed western lands to secure his status. With all this confusion over who had right to what in Ohio, there was all the more reason to go and see it personally.[13]

Botetourt had a good excuse for failing to reply: he was dying. The governor was too ill to respond to Washington's September inquiry, and before the travelers reached Fort Pitt, Botetourt would succumb in his bed in Williamsburg on October 15, 1770. For Washington, Botetourt's untimely death only added to his uncertainty about his future prospects.

As the houses of the Oldtown settlement came into sight three days after leaving Mount Vernon, Washington felt reassured that he would finally get some solid information. He went to "Colo. Cresap's in ord[e]r to learn from him (being just arrived from England) the particulars of the Grant said to be lately sold to Walpole and others, for a certain Tract of Country on the Ohio," Washington confided to his diary on October 8, 1770. Alas, there is no more about what the pair discussed. What exactly Washington learned remains a mystery. Indeed, it's not even clear what information Cresap would have been able to provide, as we don't know exactly when he returned to America.[14]

Hillsborough's showdown with Walpole, which led to the scheme's stall, occurred on July 20. For Cresap to have been back in Oldtown by early October, he would've had to have left England no later than the middle of August—figure six weeks of ocean travel, plus more than a week to get from New York to western Maryland. It's possible that he left this late, but more likely that Cresap was well into his voyage before the meeting that applied the brakes to the Vandalia project. Nothing indicates either of them knew of Hillsborough's maneuver. Nor did Cresap offer Washington any reassurance that the Walpole group had promised to incorporate the Dinwiddie bounty claims into their grant (which they had). Without this latest information, it's likely their conversation was heavy and leaden, like the volatile autumn skies that on this night poured rain outside the stone walls of the Cresap compound.[15]

The best evidence of what they discussed came thirteen months later, when Washington reached out to Mercer. "Colo. Cresap, who I have seen since his return from England," Washington wrote, "gave it to me as his opinion, that, some of the Shares of the New (Charter) Government on the Ohio might be bought very Cheap from some of the present Members—are you of this Opinion? Who are they that would sell? And at what price do you think a share could be bought?" Neither Cresap nor Washington wanted to be left out of the potential riches in Ohio.[16]

The next morning Washington and his party bade Cresap goodbye and headed into the mountains. The cold and wet weather certainly didn't boost his mood as the party crossed mountain ridge after mountain ridge, making their way toward William Crawford's place on the Youghiogheny. They spent a few days there, riding out to inspect the 1,600 acres (later known as "Washington's Bottom") that Crawford had misled the Pennsylvania government into collecting as one parcel.

By Wednesday, twelve days into the journey, Washington found himself back at the Ohio Forks. He stored his baggage at Samuel Semple's tavern, the best inn in town, and then went over to Fort Pitt, walking around the grounds and perhaps talking with Crawford about the smoldering ruins of Fort Duquesne that they had witnessed together a dozen years earlier. He had dinner with the British officers, who treated him with "great civility," but he was surely more interested in chatting with another guest at the table: George Croghan. Their conversation spilled over into the next day, when Croghan invited Washington to come up to Croghan Hall. Croghan had also asked a few important Iroquois who lived nearby to join them. Washington recorded in his diary that his reputation preceded him with the Natives, as a few remembered seeing the twenty-one-year-old Virginian on his first trip to the Ohio and most others had "heard of" him. Whether this was for good or ill Washington didn't know, for the Iroquois expressed their concerns about Washington's fellow Virginians: "their Brothers of Virginia did not come among them and Trade as the Inhabitants of the other Provinces did," and therefore "they were afraid that [they] did not look upon them with so friendly an Eye as they could wish."[17]

Here was the problem again, reflected in the mirror from the Natives' perspective: Pennsylvania vs. Virginia. Washington had long suspected this rivalry would prove a problem in Ohio, especially after General Forbes decided to spurn Braddock's road from Virginia and cut his own path to the Forks, which then Croghan and the Pennsylvania traders used to undercut the Ohio Company. Now those same Philadelphia merchants were in London about to whisk the entire region away from Virginia. These Iroquois recognized there were distinct differences, one could almost say tribal differences, between Pennsylvanians and Virginians. "That the Virginians were a People not so much engag[e]d in Trade as the Pennsylvanians," Washington responded, "was the reason of their not being so frequently among them; but it was possible they might for the time come have stricter connections with them." Washington promised he would "acquaint" Lord Botetourt (unfortunately dead four days prior) "with their desires" for the Virginians to be better friends.[18]

Washington did not commit any further details about his dinner at Croghan Hall into his diary, a silence even more fascinating after, in this instance, he had documented Native opinions in detail. It's certain they talked about land because Croghan offered to sell Washington fifteen thousand acres out of the lands he had finagled around Fort Pitt in some of his rather shady private dealings with Ohio Indians twenty years before. Washington was amenable but had some conditions before buying them from Croghan outright.

The next morning, the party, now enlarged to eight plus a Native interpreter whom the colonists called the Pheasant, started to paddle down the Ohio. For the first day, Croghan and his deputy Alexander McKee went along. McKee was the son of Thomas McKee, whom we have met in the confused days of 1755–56, when he got shot near Shamokin and, later, when he tried to protect Shickellamy's sons from the chaos. They stopped to eat at McKee's cabin on the river just down from Pittsburgh, and the next day Washington paid close attention as they paddled past the lands that Croghan had offered to sell. He jotted down something obvious, but quite important to keep in mind: "Note the unsettled state of this country renders any purchase dangerous." Indeed.[19]

Getting a clear title wasn't the only complicating factor. There was also competition. Right as the party floated by Big Beaver Creek, Washington noted that the spot held "a good situation for a House." Others had their eyes on this particular place. In a few months, it would become known as "Logan's Town," with a number of Mingo families making their residence at this promising locale. If he were to go through with his purchase of Croghan's land, he would have to contend with Natives like Logan (Soyechtowa) who saw this as their territory.[20]

Washington and his party awoke to snow that had fallen all night and repacked the canoes in "very raw and cold" conditions. It was easy to feel intimidated as they were about to be on their own, surrounded only by water and trees. Millions of trees. The snow that fell on their canoes, on the trees all around, and on the water's surface dampened both pad-

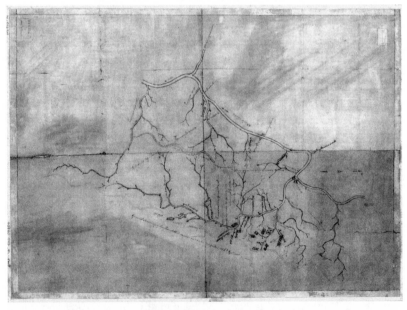

Figure 14. William Crawford's map of Ohio, drawn during his tour with Washington. Note the location of Fort Burd (Redstone), Fort Pitt at the Forks, and Mingo Town on the Ohio.

dlers and noise, heightening the solemnity, the awe. It wasn't altogether a depressing feeling. They knew where they were headed. They hoped they were floating toward a promised land.

After about twenty miles they passed the entrance to Yellow Creek on their right, and Washington noted "opposite to . . . appears to be a long bottom of very good Land." Within four years that place would be called Baker's Bottom, and many people would learn about the terrible things that took place at that spot on the Ohio.[21]

Twenty-three miles below Yellow Creek, they pulled their canoes up at a Native village and took some shelter from the bitter, wet weather. Washington referred to it as "Mingo Town" in his diary, as did Crawford on the map he was drawing of the trip. "This place contains about Twenty Cabbins, and 70 Inhabitants of the Six Nations," Washington noted.[22]

It was becoming a prime destination for Natives looking to escape both colonial and Iroquois authority. Many of these Mingos were Senecas who had drifted away from the politics of the Six Nations and first lived in what is now northwestern Pennsylvania. In the 1760s, they kept moving south, settling on tributaries along the Ohio River. Others, including most of the Shickellamy family, would soon join their migration and come to this place on the river.

As the survey party tried to warm themselves from the elements, they found out the weather was not their only adversary. "Upon our arrival at the Mingo Town," Washington noted, "we received the disagreeable News of two Traders being killed" near to the area where they were heading, "which caused us to hesitate whether we should proceed or not, and wait for further Intelligence." They decided to stick around. The village was bustling just then, as sixty Iroquois men were there headed for Cherokee country "to proceed to war against the Cuttawba's," Washington wrote.[23]

In the middle of the next afternoon, after "several imperfect accounts" came in that only one person was dead and that it wasn't foul play, they decided to continue their journey. Getting on the river before sunrise the following day, the party passed by Wheeling Creek, where Washington noticed good land all around. South of Wheeling lay an overland path that connected the Native villages and the Redstone settlement, and just below that the Ohio makes a broad bend. Washington quite liked the looks of this spot, later called "Round Bottom," and made sure Crawford knew how much he desired it.[24]

After another four days, the party was nearly two hundred miles down the Ohio. They paddled with greater ease once they heard that the trader allegedly murdered had only drowned in the river. Yet there was still good reason to be cautious. When they came upon an encampment of Natives, Washington lamented that they were "under a necessity of paying our compliments." The leader of this hunting party was Guyasuta, a rising leader among the Ohio Iroquois, and someone Washington knew it was unwise to snub. Guyasuta had recently made several trips to Johnson Hall, attended the Stanwix treaty conference, and was considered an essential British ally in the region. He hadn't always been; Guyasuta was a key player in Pontiac's War (1763–65). Since then, however, he had chosen diplomacy over war. Guyasuta's presence along the Ohio during that season was not only to hunt game but also to foster relations between the British, Ohio Iroquois, and Shawnees over what the latter called the "betrayal" at Fort Stanwix.[25]

Washington found Guyasuta very hospitable, but to his frustration heard the same talk about the differences between Pennsylvanians and Virginians that he had heard at Croghan Hall. Guyasuta encouraged Washington to recommend his fellow countrymen to "deal with them upon a fair and equitable footing." "This I promised to do," Washington replied, although he confessed to his diary that he found the whole thing a "tedious ceremony."[26]

Two days later, the party finally reached the mouth of the Kanawha River. They turned and paddled upstream about ten miles "to discover what kind of Lands" lay here. They found the skies thick with fowl and "a great many small grassy Ponds . . . full of Swans, Geese, and Ducks of different kinds." They were pleased with what they surveyed. This was indeed good land—if he and his men could get free and clear rights to it.[27]

On Saturday, November 3, they returned down the Kanawha and made camp at a spot since called Point Pleasant. In less than four years, their campsite would be a bloody battleground between Virginia militia and Shawnees. While Washington couldn't have predicted that exact future as he struggled to stay warm next to the fire on a windy night, many factors that would lead to the battle of Point Pleasant were already making themselves plain: Guyasuta's efforts to placate infuriated Shawnees after Stanwix, Native migrations to Mingo Town and other places lower down on the Ohio, the rivalry between Pennsylvanians and Virginians, and the general Native sense that settlers from Redstone were not to be trusted. New York governor Lord Dunmore hadn't even heard that Botetourt was dead yet, let alone had any notion that he would be the one appointed to replace him in Williamsburg, but the general contours of what would become known as Dunmore's War were already taking shape.

The next morning, Washington's party began the arduous journey home. Getting back to Fort Pitt meant they had to battle the Ohio's current for more than 250 miles. Two days in, they found Guyasuta again, and were again entertained ("detained," as the impatient plantation master put it) "by the kindness and Idle ceremony of the Indians." A few days later it started to pour constant, heavy rain, and the river began to rise. The current ran with "violence" against them. They decided to stop paddling and dispatched a "young Indian express" to Pittsburgh to have someone bring down horses and meet them at Mingo Town. It eventually stopped raining and the Ohio crested, but a frost set in as they again passed Wheeling and arrived at Mingo Town in the middle of the afternoon on Saturday, November 17.[28]

For the next three days they waited for the horses to arrive. With nothing else to do, Washington spent some time with his pen, writing longer entries in his journal. He made notes on the depths of the Ohio and reflected on how Natives used the river. Then, to fill a "long and tedious day," he talked with a trader who had been several times down the Ohio and compiled a master list of the distances on the river, all the way down to the Mississippi, 1,164 miles from Fort Pitt.[29]

Washington also filled time by undertaking a lengthy analysis of the politics of his Native hosts, and what he thought the future of this region might be. It wasn't a positive assessment. "The Indians who live upon the Ohio (the upper parts of it at least) are composed of Shawnas,

Delawares, and some of the Mingos, who getting but little part of the Consideration that was given for the Lands Eastward of the Ohio, view the Settlement of the People upon this River with an uneasy and jealous Eye," Washington observed, "and do not scruple to say that they must be compensated for their Right if the People settle thereon, notwithstanding the Cession of the Six Nations thereto." He did not mention whether any of these uneasy and jealous eyes had been directed toward his scouting party, whose canoes couldn't have been a welcome sign. Washington did not consider himself one, but he understood the mentality of "the people," as he called settlers who were headed to Ohio, and he recognized that things were going to get ugly in Mingo territory soon: "How difficult it may be to contend with these People afterwards is easy to be judg[e]d from every day[']s experience of Lands actually settled." Whether Washington himself grasped his own complicity in the violence that he anticipated was coming, he didn't commit it to writing.[30]

Early Tuesday afternoon, November 20, the horses finally arrived, and the party set off overland for Pittsburgh, reaching Fort Pitt the next day. More dinners welcomed the exhausted travelers. It was Washington's turn to treat, inviting the Fort Pitt officers to dine with him at Semple's tavern. That evening Washington first encountered the tavernkeeper's brother-in-law, the extraordinary Dr. John Connolly.

John Connolly was born just up the Susquehanna River from Thomas Cresap's old house at Pleasant Garden not long after it burned to the ground. His Irish father, a surgeon in the British Army, was his mother's third husband. He died soon after John's birth, and, when his mother passed, he spent his inheritance studying medicine in Philadelphia with Dr. Cadwalader Evans at the Pennsylvania Hospital. While the extent of his medical training is not known, he would thenceforth refer to himself as Dr. John Connolly. He soon followed his father's path by joining the British Army toward the end of the Seven Years' War, and served on Martinique in 1762. He was soon back in Pennsylvania, however, and volunteered to serve in the campaigns to put down Pontiac's War. In the late 1760s, Dr. Connolly claimed to have traveled throughout the Illinois and Ohio country and knew all about the geography there—information that endeared him to George Washington.

"A very sensible Intelligent Man," Washington confided in his diary. It seems he was rather taken with the good doctor, writing extensively about what all they discussed over dinner, especially Connolly's delights about the Illinois country: "he seems to wish for nothing more than to induce 100 families to go there to live that he might be among them." Connolly cut quite a dashing figure in Semple's tavern, even letting on that George Croghan was his uncle, although proof of this family tie has evaded historians. Washington noted that Connolly mentioned how "a New and most desirable Government might be established here" in the Ohio country, which sounded an awful lot like he was well acquainted with Uncle George's letters from London. The dinner certainly burnished Dr. John Connolly's reputation in the developing town of Pittsburgh, and his growing connections would soon include the next royal governor of Virginia. Within two years, Connolly's power at the Forks would surpass even that of his "uncle."[31]

The following morning Washington settled his bills in preparation for heading home. He owed the Pheasant and other Natives for their help carrying canoes, interpreting speech, and pitching camp, and paid them £10 13s. He compensated the Semples for their hospitality, and squared things with the "People that attended me down the River," all except, of course, his enslaved man William Lee, who received nothing for undertaking nearly five hundred miles of dangerous river work.[32]

The party then climbed into the Laurel Highlands and stayed at William Crawford's cabin, where inclement weather forced Washington to yet again stop and take shelter. While more rain and snow came down, he and his surveyor-agent reflected on all they had seen and began to make plans for the future. Washington was having second thoughts about those lands that Croghan offered to sell. Given how fragile the situation was about who owned what in the Ohio country, Washington was not going to commit himself to just any land. It needed to be worth the trouble. He asked Crawford to "examine" Croghan's land "with the greatest care and attention." "The uncertain footing upon which the affairs of this Country seem to rest at present, will prevent me from making this purchase, unless I can get Lands that are really fine," he instructed Crawford. He also wrote Croghan to tell him about these conditions of purchase. If Crawford is impressed, we have a deal. If not, no sale.[33]

At the end of the letter, Washington also gave Croghan a brief recommendation. "If the Charter Government takes place in the manner proposed," Washington added as if a passing thought, "I presume there will be different Districts, in order that the Land may be run out as fast as possible; in that case, I wou'd beg leave to recommend Capt. Crawford to your friendly notice as a person who would be employed, and as one who I dare say wou'd discharge the duty with honesty and care." Even if the hostile Pennsylvanians wouldn't let him join the Vandalia scheme, Washington had struck upon a way in: get Crawford named as an official surveyor, just as he had done with Virginia and the bounty lands. That way he—and Washington—"might come in for a share of this business." He had found a way to ensure he had a chair when the Ohio music stopped. One wonders whether Washington mentioned this strategy to Thomas Cresap three days later when he again stayed over at Oldtown.[34]

On the first of December, Washington was back in his bed at Mount Vernon. The trip was a hard one, but he got exactly what he was sorely lacking at home: information. Washington's inability to ascertain reliable information had left him feeling small and lost—bewildered—when news of the Vandalia scheme arrived. Nine weeks in Ohio had rectified the situation. He learned a great deal, not only about the exact geographic features of the region, but also about the people he was going to have to work with to realize his fortunes.

From the correspondence that had piled up on his desk during his absence, it looked increasingly like the Vandalia scheme would carry the day. He instructed Crawford to keep an eye on Croghan. What he should have added was: and his "nephew," too. Washington had also discovered, from colonists and Natives alike in the west, that there were significant tribal differences between Pennsylvanians and Virginians in the Ohio country. He already knew this from his days during the war, but it had gotten far worse since. It wouldn't take much to spark violence between them. It might only take someone brash, arrogant, and full of their own dreams of western glory. Someone exactly like Dr. John Connolly.[35]

CHAPTER 6

BACKBITING AND INTRIGUING, 1771–1773

"They beguiled the time by backbiting and intriguing against each other in a foolish kind of way. There was an air of plotting at that station, but . . . It was as unreal as everything else—as the philanthropic pretence of the whole concern, as their talk, as their government, as their show of work. The only real feeling was a desire to get appointed to a trading-post where ivory was to be had, so that they could earn percentages."

—Heart of Darkness

In February 1771, Lord Dunmore received word from Lord Hillsborough that the king had named him the new royal governor of Virginia, and he was to leave for Williamsburg immediately. He was crushed. He had been governor of New York for the past year and desperately wanted to stay. Dunmore dashed off several letters to London begging Hillsborough and the king not to send him and his family to miserable Virginia. The climate was terrible, he said, and—worse—there was "little or no society" there. He even tried to get his replacement, William Tryon, to exchange places with him. Finally, eight months after news had arrived, he resigned himself to his fate and boarded a ship for the Chesapeake. On September 25, 1771, he glumly watched fireworks light up the sky over Williamsburg to honor his much-anticipated arrival.[1]

It wasn't long, however, before Dunmore found reason to love his new office in the Old Dominion. With the Ohio Valley up for grabs, his position in Virginia provided an unsurpassed opportunity to secure western land for him and his friends. Soon, Dunmore's letters to London had a different tone. A few months into his tenure, the forty-one-year-old governor confessed he "could not find a better occupation for my leisure hours than applying myself to the settling of some of the vacant lands, which the new boundary line now offers, and which at the same time . . . may be advantageous to my family." Dunmore had more than made his peace with sleepy, stuffy Williamsburg. Within four years, he would bestow upon his newborn daughter the name Virginia.[2]

For someone who wanted to limit colonial expansion over the mountains, Hillsborough could not have found a worse person to put in the Governor's Palace in Williamsburg. He must have read Dunmore's letter about his new hobby of dabbling in "vacant lands" with horror.

After all, Dunmore had been expressly ordered to discourage western expansion. In the instructions for his new posting in Virginia, the Crown had told him to do everything in his power to "induce" Native peoples to "become not only peaceable Neighbors but useful and faithful

Figure 15. John Murray, Fourth Earl of Dunmore. By Sir Joshua Reynolds, 1765.

Allies." The best way to accomplish this was to prosecute fraud in the Indian trade, but also to put an end to devious land sales. "It is therefore our WILL and PLEASURE, that you do not upon any pretence whatsoever, make a Grant or Grants to any Person or Persons of any Lands within Our Colony of Virginia" without a license obtained either from the governor or the army commander-in-chief. Any new licenses were to be only given after faithful surveys with Native observers and were never to be larger than one thousand acres. They bound the new governor to "strictly observe" these "regulations." Despite these rather clear orders, Dunmore was not about to let this unique opportunity slip away.[3]

Dunmore's installation as the new Virginia governor precipitated a new round of crisis in the Ohio country. Since the 1740s, the question of who would control the Forks of the Ohio had seen several contenders come and go. The French had built Fort Duquesne there before they blew it to smithereens four years later. The British celebrated their conquest of the place by turning the ruins into the impressive bastion Fort Pitt, which loomed over the Forks for more than a decade.

By the early 1770s, however, the soaring costs of maintaining a global empire meant that sacrifices had to be made. Near the end of 1772, Gage ordered the evacuation of Fort Pitt as a way to cut costs and streamline the empire. It was their way of resolving imperial bewilderment. But just the opposite actually occurred. That evacuation produced a power vacuum, into which the leaders of Pennsylvania and Virginia heartily plunged. Native peoples watched as yet more factions of backbiting, intriguing men rushed to Pittsburgh in their quest to establish their authority, please their patrons, and secure their substantial fortunes. Who would be able to hold on to power this time?

During 1771, while Dunmore dithered in New York, the Shickellamys, the Cresaps, and others concerned with the Ohio country continued to pursue their plans in the region. William Crawford purchased more lands for George Washington. In the spring, he also completed his inspection of the holdings George Croghan desperately wanted to sell and advised his patron not to trouble with these shaky claims. Another meeting of the former Virginia Regiment officers in March ended with a resolution to send Crawford back to the Kanawha River to conduct a formal survey. In London, the Walpole group quietly gathered resources to rebut the myriad Virginia counterclaimants, and worked to isolate Lord Hillsborough's obstinance, in the hopes of moving their enormous Vandalia project forward. Young men on the make back east wrote letters hoping to get in on the action. The eyes of speculators on both sides of the Atlantic sparkled in anticipation, but, as Benjamin Franklin reminded his son, "Many things happen between the Cup and the Lip."[4]

Meanwhile, more and more people continued to move into the Ohio country. Logan (Soyechtowa), Koonay, Neanoma, and John Petty (Shickellamy) weren't the only ones establishing new residences there. One colonist who visited Croghan and Fort Pitt reported that the area around Redstone was now "full of people," many of whom were headed even farther west. A young clerk in Michael Cresap's Redstone store remembered later that the "tide of emigration" to Ohio had "begun to flow with great rapidity," and people to whom Cresap had extended credit vanished into the west. Cresap's storekeeping venture was a disaster. He had "dealt too liberal[ly]" with his customers and was broke. Worse, he couldn't even stock his shelves. His supplier in Frederick, Maryland, an agent from a London mercantile firm, had not trusted Cresap, fearing that one day he, too, might disappear into the Ohio country. To protect himself, the agent started withholding shipments. When Michael heard about this, he rode east to confront him. "The consequence was a dreadful battle ensued," that same clerk remembered. In the end, Cresap decided to do just what his supplier feared and joined his customers, moving west to Wheeling Creek on the Ohio, where he would specialize as a land scout.[5]

His father also went scouting in the summer of 1771. In the mid-1730s, Lord Fairfax had sent a party up the Potomac, past King Opessa's Town, to look for the river's source, which was the outer limit of his enormous grant. They thought they had found it on the North Branch and laid a stone to mark the headwaters, known as the Fairfax Stone. Yet doubts remained as to whether this truly marked the southwest border between Virginia and Maryland. On his recent visit to London, this was what the Maryland proprietors tasked Thomas Cresap to discover: which branch of the Potomac—the North or the South—penetrated deeper into the American continent and therefore extended Maryland's claim.

Thomas Cresap set off to undertake this new project in the early summer of 1771. As he paddled up the South Branch, he realized the proprietors' hunches were right: this tributary extended much farther, curling and curling for more than one hundred miles deep into the Appalachians, following close to what is today the Virginia-West Virginia border. The map Cresap sketched put the southwest corner of Maryland twelve miles farther west and more than fifty miles to the south of the Fairfax Stone.[6]

In early July, his mission completed, Cresap travelled to Annapolis to submit his map. While there he ran into the man who had tipped off Washington about Vandalia. The two talked about that very topic, with Cresap seeming "quite confident that the new Grant will take place," and "taking his Measures accordingly." Cresap didn't know it yet, but in Lon-

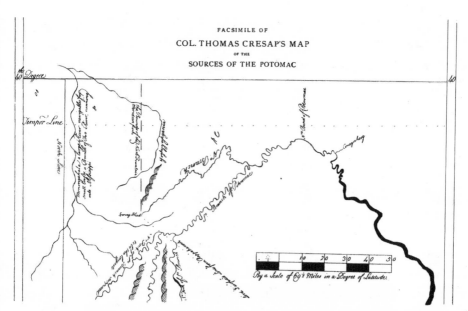

Figure 16. Thomas Cresap's map of the branches of the Potomac, surveyed in 1771 to find the westernmost point of Maryland.

don Samuel Wharton was thinking about him, too. A secret movement to bring down Lord Hillsborough was gaining steam in London—and Wharton wanted Thomas Cresap to help.[7]

Less than three weeks after Cresap's trip to Annapolis, Wharton wrote a trio of letters to Croghan. Putting pen to paper was a risky move, especially with what Wharton had to disclose. It is only "under the mark solemn of inviolable secrecy to tell you," he related to Croghan, but the Walpole/Vandalia group had successfully wheedled every minister in the Cabinet over to their side (except Hillsborough). Still, they needed something further to bring about a revolt against the secretary of state, as there was a "Delicacy" among the ministers not to overrule one of their own. They sought ironclad evidence that colonists desired to settle these new lands, evidence that that they could make public if they were forced to confront Hillsborough directly. Wharton "rejoiced" to hear that setters were "cheerfully disposed to buy" Croghan's lands. "It shows their good sense," he wrote, and encouraged him to keep going. In fact, that was a perfect way to get the evidence they needed of the insatiable American thirst for Native territory.[8]

At a "secret meeting" held on July 20, 1771, the "most leading[,] important, and active of our Partners (who must be nameless)" launched a plot to neutralize Hillsborough. The Grand Ohio partners drew up a petition, made six copies, and gave them to Wharton to send on to Croghan and Thomas Cresap. Without "Loss of Time," Cresap and Croghan were to ride around with these petitions collecting signatures of any frontier settlers who were willing to say they preferred to be under the jurisdiction of Vandalia. Make sure each person's signature looks different, and don't leave any copies laying around, they instructed. "By no Means let any Persons take any Copy of the Petition, nor let any Persons read it, whom you think will not sign it." In particular, they were to "beware all Penn's Surveyors and other Officers," for if the plot leaked, "Every lord would spurn us and instantly dissolve all Degrees of Connection with us and our Partners." Under no circumstances could even the "nearest nor most intimate Friend or Relation you have know that the Petition took its Rise from this Side [of] the water." Wharton was so anxious about this he reiterated the dangers again in *two* postscripts. "The whole Affair of the Petitioning . . . must spring in Appearance from your Side of the Water," he repeated. And then again, just under: If, on their clandestine canvass, the pair sensed any danger that it might "provoke a Counter Petition from the Settlers against a New Government, then by all means drop the plan" immediately. Wharton knew he was swimming in treacherous waters, but he was desperate. For months he had been living in fear of the sheriff's knock at his door. Back in the fall he had confessed to Croghan, "I do not know the moment when I may be arrested for [debts] as that I cannot find Bail for. . . . God only knows."[9]

Keeping with the covert nature of this affair, little evidence exists about Cresap and Croghan's efforts to canvass the Redstone and Pittsburgh settlements for Vandalia in the autumn of 1771. As signers would be putting their names to a document that rejected both Virginia and Pennsylvania authority, the plan bordered on conspiracy, illegality, and secession. Yet one intriguing letter, written by Cresap, has survived. In November, Cresap sent Samuel Wharton's brother Thomas—the very person who two years earlier had wrung his hands about how this particular frontiersman might wreck all their plans in London—an update on their progress. "Colonel Croghan and myself ha[ve] done everything in our Power" to obey the Vandalia effort to "remove Lord Hillsborough's opinion," he wrote. There are, he said, "sundry letters directed to Col. [George] Mercer, they are from different persons Calculated to show the Necessity of a government which are for the use of the Company." They will, Cresap indicated with a wink, "appear as if they came from Indifferent persons unconcerned." He concluded with a sentence that could sum up his entire adult life: "I have had hard Battling with the Friends of Mr. Penn, and the Settlers in his interest, I think I have gained ground on them."[10]

Other than this letter, no trace of the petitions surfaced then or since. Nevertheless, this imaginative maneuver reveals just how far all the players involved, including George Croghan and Thomas Cresap, would go to win the complicated, decades-old fight to control the Ohio country. Long-standing rivalries, like the one between Croghan and Cresap, or the enmity the Wharton brothers felt about the "monster" from Maryland, evaporated with the prospect of such a windfall. The profits from this unlikely partnership stood to be enormous. If they could pull it off.

Native peoples living in the region didn't need to know details about the "secret meeting" in London nor Croghan and Cresap's efforts to spur the Vandalia project to be very concerned. They saw for themselves the colonists scouting up and down rivers, taking notes and extending surveyor's chains around the Ohio. In 1770, Washington thought Native peoples in Mingo Town and its environs appeared anxious. By 1771, they were starting to grow angry.

That spring, Pennsylvania traders began to hear rumors "of an Immediate war" with the Shawnees. The situation was "at Present" very dangerous; emotions were running high, as Shawnees believed the Six Nations had sold their lands out from under them, and yet another Native had been "murdered by the People of Radstone." The "behavior and appearance" of several Native groups along the Ohio were "just the same as it was before the[y] Broke out in 1763."[11]

In an effort to try to defuse the situation, Delaware leaders sent John Killbuck—another of Thomas Cresap's old nemeses—and his son to Philadelphia to meet with Pennsylvania authorities. Killbuck told them he feared that the council fire that had once burned so brightly "between our fore Fathers peoples, is now almost gone out." He begged the Pennsylvanians to help restrain illegal alcohol sales and prosecute murders. They assured him they would. Meanwhile, however, General Gage informed London that Sir William Johnson expected "a rupture with the Indians" at any time. While Killbuck was in Philadelphia, the *Pennsylvania Gazette* printed letters from Pittsburgh that claimed an Indian war was imminent. Johnson maintained throughout the summer that the Senecas who had recently migrated to Ohio were "not our friends."[12]

The council members from Pennsylvania did not let on to Killbuck that they had also recently taken steps that might exacerbate the problem.

In March, the Pennsylvania government sliced off the western part of Cumberland County and formed Bedford County, a new jurisdiction that stretched all the way to the Forks. They appointed fifteen new justices of the peace, including George Croghan's deputy Alexander McKee (whose father Thomas was an old friend of the Shickellamy family), Thomas Gist (whose brother Christopher was an old friend of the Cresap family), a Virginian named Dorsey Pentecost, the ubiquitous William Crawford, and a thirty-seven-year-old Scotsman named Arthur St. Clair.[13]

St. Clair's parents wanted Arthur to be a doctor and enrolled him at the University of Edinburgh, but when war broke out with France in 1756 he left to join the British Army, just like his future enemy, John Connolly. Soon Ensign St. Clair was headed to America, where he saw combat in Canada and served on the staff of General Frederick Haldimand. He was married in Boston the following year, resigned his commission, and took up land near Fort Ligonier in Pennsylvania. When Pennsylvania established Bedford County, St. Clair was not only made a justice of the peace, but he also was recorder of deeds, clerk of the orphan court, and prothonotary of the court of common pleas. The doctor-turned-soldier was now about to become Pennsylvania's leading politician on their western frontier.[14]

Within a few months of their new appointments as Bedford County officers, St. Clair and his colleagues found themselves at odds with settlers pouring into the region. Devastating floods had wrecked Virginia that summer—one estimate put the loss at twenty-five thousand hogsheads of tobacco as the James, Potomac, Shenandoah, and Roanoke Rivers all wreaked havoc on the population. If accurate, this would be an incredible loss of more than one-third of Virginia's annual export. The flood of water surely contributed to the flood of people going into the mountains; for anyone barely hanging on in the struggling Virginia tobacco colony— which was already in the grips of an economic depression throughout the early 1770s—packing up whatever was left and heading west for the Ohio country was perhaps the only option.[15]

By August, the first evidence of resistance to Pennsylvania's authority in what they now called Bedford County began to surface. William

Crawford wrote to the secretary of the Pennsylvania Land Office that "a number of the inhabitants of Monongahela and Readstone" had "entered into a bond or Article of Agreement that Each man will Joyn and keep off all Officers belonging to the Law." Crawford said that this "notion" was "propagated by Col. [George] Croghan," who told the Redstone settlers their territory "would not fall into Pennsylvania" and has "since told those People that they had no right to Obay [sic] any presept [precept] Ishued from" there. Crawford also warned the Pennsylvanians that "it is a great pity" that no one has stopped Croghan from selling off his lands around Fort Pitt, "as it will be attended with very Bad Consequences," not admitting that his patron George Washington had almost been a main purchaser of those lands.[16]

Less than a week later, St. Clair received a letter from a Bedford deputy who had already felt the consequences of the "Articles" Crawford had mentioned. Those papers were "here handing fast about amongst ye people," he said, and signers were to "oppose every one of Penns Laws . . . at the Risque of Life & under the penalty of fiftey pounds." Within a month, more Bedford officials reported fighting with parties of armed men. One warned Sheriff Thomas Woods not to "execute any process or authority" for Pennsylvania on the west side of the Youghiogheny River—"or he might depend on suffering for it." According to St. Clair, Croghan wasn't the only one causing trouble. "A ridiculous story that Mr. Cressap has spread with much industry that this Province did not extend beyond the Alleghany Mountain . . . has taken great hold of the People," St. Clair wrote, and "together with Mr. Croghan's claims and surveys . . . will probably make it very difficult to carry the Laws into Execution." He anticipated it "will be impossible to collect the Taxes" in the western part of Bedford, thanks to Croghan and Cresap.[17]

The "resolves" that St. Clair and his officers kept running into are fascinating, though none have survived. They couldn't have been related to the clandestine Vandalia petitions, for Wharton's sealed letters were still on the Atlantic when St. Clair started writing Philadelphia about how Croghan and Cresap were encouraging settlers not to obey Pennsylvania's laws. When Wharton's instructions found Croghan, he must have thought, we're already doing this. What Croghan, Cresap, and Wharton didn't know is that the new royal governor of Virginia was about to set himself to the exact same task. Dunmore, too, saw a chance to capitalize on the chaos in Ohio. He started making plans to introduce his own order west of the mountains. A new show of force in the Ohio country was not to come from a new colonial establishment, but from the oldest government in North America.

⸗

When Lord Dunmore first sat at the desk in his new upstairs study late that September 1771, the "imperial crisis" was at a low ebb. In Boston, the "massacre" trial was over and British troops had been pulled out of the city. The leaders of Boston's resistance movement found themselves either losing interest, like John Hancock, or losing influence, like Sam Adams. In Virginia, the damage done by spring floods brought an end to the boycotts protesting the Townshend Duties, the set of taxes the Crown had levied on certain colonial goods in 1767. Even in the west, only two issues had generated conflict: the Proclamation Line and the Stamp Act. The Proclamation Line was, frankly, just disobeyed. The Stamp Act protests were loud, sustained, and reached deep into the backcountry, but the complaints from the frontier were just as often directed at local assemblies as they were at Parliament.[18]

At the moment Dunmore became royal governor of Virginia, then, his main concern was not dealing with a sustained imperial resistance movement but rather with contesting Pennsylvania's attempts to claim the Ohio country. Because he had inherited an unstable situation— boundaries that were still unsettled, speculation schemes that had not yet secured royal backing, hundreds of settlers streaming west, and the question of whose authority they would obey in flux—Dunmore saw opportunity all around.[19]

Yet for much of 1772, he laid low. Actually, as he had feared, Williamsburg laid him low, giving him a fever that left him feeling unwell for much of the year. During the summer that Dunmore was in his bed, St. Clair wrote more letters accusing Cresap and Croghan of instigating resistance to Pennsylvania's authority. St. Clair was convinced Thomas Cresap was the "prime mover" in the "associations [that are] forming to oppose the jurisdiction of Pennsylvania," but saw them "chiefly abetted" by Croghan. Croghan, clearly suffering from financial woes, drove off the tax collectors and "threatened to put any or all" Pennsylvania officials "to death if they attempted to touch any of his effects." No matter which of them was in the lead, the pair of Croghan and Cresap were seen as the most important destabilizers on the frontier, perpetrators of what St. Clair labeled a "deep laid scheme."[20]

Other developments occurred during the summer of 1772 that would bear on whether the Ohio country really was going to descend into civil war. In late June, after a year of maneuvering behind the scenes, the Walpole group and their backers in the Ministry made their play to unseat Hillsborough. Appearing before the Board of Trade, the American lobbyists all gave lively testimony about the need for a new administrative structure in the interior. Trent said there were already five thousand families living at Redstone. Wharton said even the British Army couldn't eject them. The old Ohio Company agent George Mercer said there was a fantastic road from Fort Cumberland to Redstone to Pittsburgh. Benjamin Franklin even brought up the dazzling commercial possibilities of growing silkworms in the region. The performance was a smash. A week later the Commissioners of Trade approved the petition and sent it to the Privy Council. The Vandalia colony was finally moving forward. Samuel Wharton sent Croghan detailed instructions—and even a diagrammed sketch—for a new governor's mansion that he "will be so good as immediately set about building for me." Wharton was jubilant that their financial ordeal was finally over. "Keep up your spirits my friend," he told Croghan. "You will soon be, not only a rich, but a publick, respectable man."[21]

A month later, Hillsborough would be out as secretary of state and president of the Board of Trade, and with him went the most important impediment to western land speculation. His replacement, Lord Dartmouth, was far more conciliatory to the American colonies than his predecessor. The news of the change in cabinet must have done much to restore Dunmore's health. The fall of Hillsborough was a victory for more than just the Vandalia group. It removed a barrier for his western aspirations, too.

The final important change that happened in 1772 occurred at the Forks. The Crown had long wanted to reduce the British military presence in the Ohio region, at both the Illinois post of Fort Chartres and at Fort Pitt. Hillsborough wrote Gage at the end of 1771 that the Cabinet had given permission to abandon Fort Pitt. For his part, Gage wanted no part of being drawn into another war: "If the Colonists will afterward force the Savages into Quarrells by using them ill, let them feel the Consequences, we shall be out of the scrape," he wrote with "great pleasure." On October 10, 1772, the garrison loaded its equipment on carriages and prepared to destroy the fort, much to Gage's relief.[22]

This was not, however, welcome news to Pittsburghers. As the Reverend David McClure recorded in his diary, the evacuation was "a matter of surprise and grief to the people around," who had requested that the fortress might remain, "in case of Indian invasion." McClure himself was worried about that possibility: he had just been at Mingo Town, where he was disturbed to see several Natives "frightfully painted" for war and heard rumors of more murders down the Ohio.[23]

McClure had recently run into Logan (Soyechtowa) in the woods near Big Beaver Creek. He found him troubled, too. Only a few days before, McClure had spied him walking around in Pittsburgh, and Logan's appearance in that already anxious place, just before orders arrived for British soldiers to leave the fortress, caused a stir. Someone whispered to McClure that Logan "had been a bloody enemy against the poor defenseless settlers on the Susquehanna" in the Seven Years' War and that he had killed a white man in the mountains, too.[24]

When McClure spoke to Logan in the woods, though, the minister encountered a different man than the one he had observed in town. There, he had appeared "the most martial figure of any Indian that I had ever seen." Now he found him in "distress and agitation." McClure reported that Logan had confessed to him, "My house, the trees, and the air, are full of Devils, they continually haunt me, and they will kill me. All things tell me how wicked I have been." The missionary instructed him to repent and pray for forgiveness from these evil thoughts. "He attended to what I said," McClure wrote in his diary, "and after conversing a little longer, in the same strain, [my interpreter and I] left him, in the same distress as I found him." McClure was perplexed at the behavior of "so renowned a warrior."[25]

The evacuation of Fort Pitt, Croghan told Gage, "made much noise throughout the Country." When word of that "noise" reached Dunmore at the end of 1772, he knew—with Hillsborough gone and a power vacuum at the Forks—that if he wanted to press Virginia's claims to Ohio, the time was fast approaching.[26]

Governor Penn's men in Philadelphia knew it, too. As soon as word of Fort Pitt's evacuation became known, Penn received several petitions from western settlers "expressing their Apprehensions of the dangerous situation." He worried that the removal of troops would not only "depress the Spirits of the Present Settlers, but retard the progress of Settlement." Thinking about the "unspeakable sufferings and distress which attended those unhappy people and their families . . . in the last Indian War," he begged the Assembly to fund a small garrison to rearm Fort Pitt.[27]

The Pennsylvania assembly took it upon themselves to extend their authority west of the mountains. Less than two years after creating Bedford County, they voted to create another county out of Bedford, and thus increase their legal and administrative presence west of the Allegheny Mountains. Westmoreland County was to encompass all of the Forks region, and had its county seat at Hanna's Town, nearly seventy miles farther west than Bedford and thirty miles from Pittsburgh, where they were also to open a new court. They carried over five of the Bedford officers into the new county, including St. Clair, Alexander McKee, Thomas Gist, and William Crawford, and appointed ten new magistrates. One of the new officers was Aeneas Mackay, a veteran who had served in

Bouquet's regiment during the Seven Years' War and had just turned fifty. Mackay would soon find himself at the center of the swirling jurisdictional controversy that was about to engulf Westmoreland County.

These officers were just being notified of their new positions when word began to spread in North America of Wharton's great success in London. South Carolina papers had the story in January; by March it was in the *Virginia Gazette*, which reported that Vandalia would comprise an "immense tract of country, equal to some kingdoms."[28]

That news would just miss George Washington. He had been in Williamsburg a few days before the *Gazette* printers were setting the type for those paragraphs, but he had left town before it became public knowledge. Still, Washington had spent the just-ended House of Burgesses session lobbying the new governor about western lands. Washington dined at the Governor's Palace and listened intently as Dunmore outlined his plans to get away from the sickly Williamsburg climate that coming summer and travel to the Forks. Washington immediately volunteered his expert services to accompany him, and the two began making arrangements to travel together.[29]

Washington had been getting along well with the new governor. The previous fall, right as British soldiers marched out of Fort Pitt, William Crawford had spent a week at Mount Vernon reviewing his surveys of the Dinwiddie bounty lands. Dunmore had signaled already that he was amenable to moving the soldiers' claims forward, and a week after Crawford's visit, the governor and his council readily approved the surveyed tracts amounting to 128,000 acres, 20,000 of which belonged to Washington. Because the bounty land claims were nearly twenty years old, Dunmore viewed them as a way to skirt his instructions not to allow any *new* grants. If that cracked open the door to further approvals of more western grants, so much the better. Washington was of a like mind; it was natural that the pair of them were planning to go to Ohio together. With more news that the Vandalia scheme was a sure thing making its way to Virginia in early June—and that twenty-five thousand migrants from Scotland and Ireland were eager to go straight there—this trip was more urgent than ever.[30]

At the last minute, Washington had to write to Dunmore that he couldn't accompany him after all. His seventeen-year-old stepdaughter Patsy had died suddenly of an epileptic seizure and Washington thought it imprudent to be away from Mount Vernon at such a time. Dunmore sent heartfelt condolences. The governor would have to rely on Washington's man William Crawford as his scout.[31]

After a brief stop to pick up Crawford, Dunmore headed for the Forks. He would (much) later report to Lord Dartmouth how he had found there "upwards of ten thousand people settled, but they had neither Magistrates to preserve rule and order among themselves, nor Militia for their defence in case of any sudden attack of the Indians." Dunmore picked his words very carefully. He deliberately hid the fact that there *were* more than a dozen magistrates appointed there for Westmoreland County, Pennsylvania. He also claimed that he was welcomed as a hero: "Upon my arrival the people flocked about me and beseeched me" to appoint officers "to remove those grievous inconveniences under which they labored."[32]

By August 12, having made his way through apparently thronging crowds, he arrived in Pittsburgh. There he first met Dr. John Connolly. George Croghan's supposed nephew had been busy in the two years since he had dined with George Washington. Connolly had taken another tour in the Illinois country and Lower Ohio Valley, scouted out lands at the falls of the Ohio (present-day Louisville), and sifted through "Elephant Bones" in the midst of large herds of buffalo at the salt licks. Like his "uncle," he was eager to cultivate his relationship with Washington, and sent one of his souvenirs (a woolly mammoth tooth) to Mount Vernon with his compliments. Even more like his "uncle," Connolly had also gotten himself wildly into debt in the early 1770s. Dunmore's arrival in Pittsburgh offered a golden opportunity to revive his financial fortunes.[33]

Connolly gushed about meeting "so considerable a Personage" not long after the governor began his return trip to Williamsburg in the middle of August. In their discussions in Pittsburgh, Connolly found Dunmore a "Gentleman of benevolence & universal Character & not unacquainted with either Man or the World," he wrote to Washington.

The governor and the physician-turned-speculator had indeed formed a fast alliance. Dunmore promised Connolly he would honor his claims of two thousand acres at the falls of the Ohio. In return, Connolly would be the governor's man in Pittsburgh for the next phase of Dunmore's plan to claim the region as rightfully belonging to his newly beloved Virginia.[34]

Dunmore's appearance west of the Appalachians ignited the fires against Pennsylvania that Croghan and Cresap had been stoking for two years. In his wake, resistance gripped the region. On August 17, just after the governor had departed, hundreds of settlers converged on the Redstone settlement for a "grand meeting." There, at least four hundred settlers signed a petition to Dunmore "imploring the interposition of his lordship for a speedy redress" of their complaints. "The general complaint of the people is, that the Pennsylvania officers have done them a great injustice, and they seem determined to give their oppressors a warm opposition." The petitioners claimed they were "extremely willing and desirous" of being under Dunmore's authority until the king had granted them their own civil government.[35]

Perhaps these were the very petitions that Dunmore laid before his council, which he convened in a private session on October 11, 1773. He spread out before them documents signed by hundreds of "Sundry Inhabitants in the Neighborhood of Fort Pitt, Complaining of Encroachments by the Government of Pennsylvania." Dunmore claimed he could not turn a deaf ear to their cries. The council agreed something needed to be done to prevent Pennsylvania from usurping Virginia's right to the Forks, and voted to extend the boundaries of Augusta County, with its county seat more than two hundred miles away in Staunton, to encompass the Forks. Pittsburgh was now under the jurisdiction of both Westmoreland County, Pennsylvania, and West Augusta County, Virginia.

Dunmore appointed seven West Augusta magistrates, nearly all of whom were either George Croghan or someone related to him. John Connolly may or may not have been his nephew. Thomas Smallman was a cousin, and Edward Ward was a half-brother. Another West Augusta justice was Dorsey Pentecost, who had been a Bedford County official but defected from Pennsylvania to join Dunmore's mission.[36]

Dunmore also tapped John Gibson to be a magistrate for West Augusta County. Gibson, an important Indian trader in the region, was part of Croghan's Philadelphia merchant network. He was also recently married—to Koonay, Shickellamy's daughter, who he had met when the family had relocated to the Beaver Creek region on the Ohio. Gibson's cabin was just a few miles upriver from the place becoming known as Logan's Town. When the Reverend David McClure had his strange interaction in the woods with Logan (Soyechtowa) in 1772, Gibson had been the one who introduced them, although the Presbyterian minister expressed disappointment that his "friend" had made the poor decision to "keep a squaw." What McClure didn't (or refused to) see was that—in addition to the real possibility that the relationship was based on true, companionate love—marrying into the Shickellamy family was as savvy a political move as was his association with Croghan and the rising Virginia authority at the Forks. Few in the Upper Ohio region were as well connected as Gibson.[37]

These seven Virginia officials were to administer the Pittsburgh region for Virginia. Dunmore claimed that twenty years earlier, his predecessor Governor Dinwiddie had no doubts that the Forks belonged to Virginia, which was why he sent George Washington there twice, first to scout and then to fight. The players had changed, but Virginia's claim remained just as valid as Dinwiddie had believed it to be in 1754. Now John Connolly was going to be Dunmore's Washington, carrying Virginia's sword to the Forks. Again.

That December, Connolly went to Williamsburg to strategize with Dunmore. The governor bestowed upon him two commissions—one civil, one military—and ordered Connolly to take command of Virginia's claim. He galloped away from the capital in full confidence and giddy with expected success. Just before Christmas, he wrote Washington from Fredericksburg, extending apologies that he wasn't going to be able to swing by Mount Vernon for a visit as he had arranged. He was pressed for time. "I have very luckily succeeded as far as I could well have expected," he wrote, and needed to get to Pittsburgh fast.[38]

Connolly could barely contain himself, for he had another piece of paper in his mind, if not already composed in his bags: a proclamation dated January 1, 1774. This is why he couldn't tarry at Washington's. On New Years' Day, he pasted up copies of his broadside all over Pittsburgh. Now that Dunmore has appointed me "Commandant of the Militia of Pittsburgh and its Dependencies," it said, "and convinced from their repeated Memorials of the grievances at which they complain," he hereby "require and command all Persons in the Dependency of Pittsburgh to assemble themselves there as a Militia" on January 25. Several Pennsylvania officials had already described the situation at the Forks as a state of war. Captain Connolly's advertisement all but declared it.[39]

All through the fall the prospects of peace with Native peoples continued to diminish. The intensifying conflict between Pennsylvania and Virginia, the steady stream of news about Vandalia, and, in Croghan's words, the "great numbers of loose people frequently going down this River [Ohio] to settle and take up lands" together combined to produce a "very alarming jealousy amongst the Western Indians." Croghan worried there is "reason to fear, some mischief will happen." He wrote these words just as he and Alexander McKee met with Shawnee leader Cornstalk at what was left of Fort Pitt in October 1773. Croghan informed the assembled Native leaders that the Vandalia colony was imminent, and a new governor was expected to arrive in Pittsburgh "this summer, to take command of both Whites and Indians upon him." There was a lot of blame thrown around at this tense meeting. Cornstalk and the Shawnees warned that the Mingos were unhappy. They have "stopped up their Ears and will not hearken to us. . . . talking to them is to no purpose." Others said that it was the Shawnees who were stirring trouble and were being unreasonable. When the Seneca leader Guyasuta arrived a few days later, he too pointed fingers. There was trouble lurking at

Mingo Town. A missionary headed down the Ohio had previously noted that "some of" the Mingos who still resided in "this town were wont to plunder canoes," so his party "passed them as quietly as possible, and were so happy as not to be discovered." When he met a few weeks later with Sir William Johnson, Guyasuta led the Indian superintendent to believe that the "wicked Designs and treacherous Conduct of the Shawanese," in addition to the Mingos, was "beyond all doubt."[40]

There was still more resentment. "Your people counteract us by their unfriendly, and hostile behavior towards us," Natives pointed out to Croghan and McKee. "We cannot cross on the side of the Ohio River which you call yours, but our People are ill-treated, and even knocked in the Head and thrown into the River by yours, whereas when your People come on our side they have the liberty to walk peaceably, and quietly whenever they please." In a key turnabout, they rebutted the political maneuvering and divide-and-conquer tactics Croghan and McKee were trying to pull off: "You Pennsylvanians will endeavour to exculpate yourselves, and throw this Charge on the Virginians, but we are convinced you are equally culpable." These Natives invoked liberty and called out the colonists for being bad British subjects: "It is therefore you white People who oppose the good intentions of the King."[41]

One Huron leader offered up a final, prescient summary. "We must also tell you that the Indians will not be altogether to blame for the Trouble shou'd any unfortunately happen, You have likewise foolish People among you as well as us, who pay [no] Regard to the advise and Directions of their wise People." The Huron representative uttered this warning just two days before Virginia organized West Augusta. After John Connolly distributed his proclamation on the first day of 1774, the actions of foolish people disobeying wisdom and direction was all but written in stone.[42]

The bewildering elements of this decades-long story thus far—the intriguing, plotting, and conspiracies; the confusion, mistaken identity, and blundering; the projection of power, bluster, and bluff; the misunderstandings leading to death, destruction, and chaos—pale in comparison to what was about to happen in 1774. John Connolly scampered out of Williamsburg with his commissions just days after thousands of Bostonians gathered around Griffin's Wharf to watch more than six hundred tons of tea get dumped into the harbor. In fact, Paul Revere was on the outskirts of Philadelphia as Connolly wrote Washington, riding hard to deliver the news of Boston's destruction of the tea, just like John Connolly was galloping to Pittsburgh to foment civil war. For many on both sides of the Atlantic, 1774 would be a "long year of revolution," an utterly disorienting experience, as imperial officials intensified their efforts to resolve some of the most bewildering aspects of the British Empire, only to make matters much worse.[43]

For settlers and Natives living in the Upper Ohio Valley, what was about to happen was also an intensification of what had long been their reality. For two decades, the peoples living around the Forks had watched as empires came and went. Dreams of great futures being secured in Ohio had been spun in Williamsburg, Philadelphia, London, Paris, Anishinaabewaki, and Iroquoia, only to have them all fly to pieces, dismantled and destroyed by small-scale raids and continental wars. Authority, such as it ever was, also came and went. The order that Dunmore, Penn, and the Vandalia lobbyists all boasted they could bring to the Forks was just the latest of these fantasies. Meanwhile, thousands of Natives and colonial settlers, Logan and Michael Cresap among them, moved into the area, each struggling to make their claims valid, and above all, trying to survive.

Both Virginians and Pennsylvanians pitched their maneuvers as something more than just naked greed; they insisted that there was a philanthropic pretense to the whole concern. But it was, in truth, simply a way to better earn percentages, just as it had been since the 1740s. The simmering civil war between Pennsylvania and Virginia over who controlled the Forks was about to burst into terrible violence. And this new round of backbiting and intriguing—because it happened in the *unreal* context of that year of revolution, with its tea parties, coercive acts, boycotts, public meetings, and Continental Congress delegations—would be that much more incomprehensible and consequential.

CHAPTER 7

APPROACH CAUTIOUSLY,
1774

"Hurry up. Where? Up the river? 'Approach cautiously.' We had
not done so. . . .Something was wrong above. But what—and
how much?"

—Heart of Darkness

One month after posting his New Years' Day proclamation all over
Pittsburgh, John Connolly found himself in a jail cell. In that proclamation Connolly had ordered all able-bodied men in the Pittsburgh
district to report with their arms to assemble on the parade grounds of
Fort Pitt on Tuesday, January 25, 1774, on behalf of Virginia. Arthur St.
Clair was not about to allow that to happen. Hours before Connolly's
muster was to take place, the Pennsylvania official sent deputies to his
residence to arrest him. Eliminating the ringleader by carrying him off
to the Westmoreland County court in Hanna's Town, they hoped, would
keep Pennsylvania's authority at the Forks.

The maneuver did not have its intended effect. As St. Clair would
later report to Governor Penn, "About eighty persons in arms assembled
themselves, chiefly from Mr. Croghan's neighborhood and the Country
west of and below the Monongahela. . . . After parading through the
Town, and making a kind of feu de joy, [they] proceeded to the Fort,
where a Cask of Rum was produced on the Parade, and the head knocked
out. This was a very effectual way of Recruiting."[1]

To combat this brewing storm, St. Clair drafted his own proclamation and sent the Westmoreland magistrates to deliver it aloud in front of the intoxicated assembly. St. Clair's message gave Pennsylvania's side of things, subtly criticizing the "pains" taken by the likes of George Croghan and Thomas Cresap "to persuade many of you to a belief" that this territory did not belong to the Penn family. Any insistence that Pittsburgh wasn't part of Pennsylvania, St. Clair argued, would inevitably result in "a state of Anarchy and confusion, and a total subversion of Property." It was not well received, and the magistrates fled the parade ground in defeat long before the crowd broke up. Worried that he "should probably have felt their resentment," if he had provoked them any further, St. Clair "thought it most prudent to keep out of their way."[2]

In Philadelphia, Governor Penn couldn't believe the reports of this "very strange affair." When he first learned of Connolly's call to muster, Penn naively responded that this man was clearly "assuming powers which Lord Dunmore had never given him." He sent St. Clair copies of the Riot Act, the mechanism that eighteenth-century British authorities used to announce to crowds that they were in violation of the king's peace. It was a warning that continued assembly would be considered a felony and from this point forward could be met with force. Reading the Riot Act could, however, be seen as a dangerous escalation, so Penn instructed St. Clair to take "great care" with it. The Pennsylvania governor then sat down to write his colleague in Williamsburg.[3]

St. Clair understood that keeping Connolly in a Pennsylvania jail also risked inflaming the situation. From his cell, Connolly had already begun the process of gathering support, writing to his friend George Washington about what had befallen him. St. Clair released Connolly on the promise that he would go home to Pittsburgh, avoid further trouble, and appear before the court in April. Immediately upon receiving parole, Connolly broke his end of the deal. He did not return to Pittsburgh; rather, he headed straight for friendlier environs, Redstone, where his fellow magistrate Dorsey Pentecost was busy enlisting allies and occupying Fort Burd, the abandoned, twenty-year-old fortification there. Connolly stayed with Pentecost and then rode off for Staunton in the Shenandoah Valley to continue marshalling his forces.[4]

If John Penn was having a hard time wrapping his head around this "very strange affair," what must people down the Ohio River have thought when they heard of Connolly's arrest, the drunken muster at the fort, and the escalating confrontation between Pennsylvania and Virginia authorities? The area from Oldtown to Redstone was a "very loose society," near to the action but not able to witness it, and thus dependent on whispers and gossip. The perfect place, in other words, for speculation to go wild.[5]

As winter turned into spring in 1774, there were two topics on everyone's lips west of the mountains. The first concerned the dumping of East India Tea into Boston Harbor. On the day that John Connolly was being hauled off to a Westmoreland jail, a Virginian noted in his diary about celebrations and "general applau[se]" regarding the news of "manly and patriotic resistance" to the tea shipments in eastern cities. The Boston Tea Party was a significant escalation in the "imperial crisis," and not everyone was sure that was the smartest move. Many American colonists—Benjamin Franklin and George Washington among them— had their doubts about the attack Boston radicals had made on private property. There was unease all over America as people waited to hear how the Crown was going to respond to Boston's act.[6]

In the Ohio Valley, however, there was also unease about a topic much closer at hand: the crisis of sovereignty at the Forks. This "loose society" was ripe for misinformation, but it was also primed for individuals to take actions to resolve that uncertainty in their own interest. John Connolly, his allies, and his patron in Williamsburg saw opportunity in bewilderment and sought to exploit the situation, and made moves to secure their authority. Franklin and Washington and their colleagues weren't prepared to resort to violence yet, but that wasn't the case for Dunmore's men in Ohio.

Connolly had no doubts about who was in charge at the Forks. He was. After his release from jail, Connolly made his way more than 250 miles down to Staunton, the seat of Augusta County. There he met militia commanders and got his paperwork in order. When he returned to Redstone later in February, he brought along a dozen blank military commissions, ready to hand out to any volunteers for Virginia. Pennsylvania authorities reported back to St. Clair that there had been three further militia musters in the Redstone district, including one at Pentecost's house. These gatherings were full of "men without character and without fortune," William Crawford scoffed, "and who would be equally averse" to Virginia's "administration of justice" as they proclaimed to be about Pennsylvania's.[7]

For the moment, however, it was St. Clair's deputies who were being confronted with an "open and avowed determination of the People" not to obey Pennsylvania's laws. Westmoreland County official Van Swearingen (a cousin of Samuel Swearingen at whose house the Cresaps had probably delighted in protesting the Stamp Act) had borne the particular brunt of this intimidation, with Dorsey Pentecost threatening him directly that if he continued to administer Pennsylvania's laws, he did so "at his peril." St. Clair still blamed "Mr. Croghan's Emissaries" for all this unrest and noted his astonishment at "how many he has, either duped or seduced to embrace his measures."[8]

If Connolly was certain that he was in charge at the Forks, so was his boss. While Connolly rode about Redstone whipping up support in the last days of February, Penn's innocent letter inquiring about Connolly's actions had arrived in Williamsburg. Dunmore convened his council to show it to them, and then, together, they formulated Virginia's response. The Forks had always belonged to Virginia, Dunmore insisted. He denounced the "violent proceedings" of Westmoreland's officers, especially the "irregular Commitment of Mr. John Connolly, for acting under my Authority." He demanded reparations, apologies, and resignations—including that of St. Clair—for "so great an Insult on the authority" of Virginia. Penn had been reticent to believe that a fellow royal governor would take such a brazen step. He would no longer be so naïve as to doubt Dunmore's guile.[9]

Dunmore, for his part, certainly believed he was winning the game. While he waited for further reports from Connolly, Dunmore got used to the new bustle in the Governor's Palace. After four years apart, Lady

Dunmore and their six children finally arrived in Williamsburg. The town's people lined the streets to greet her carriage, illuminated their windows, and put on another fireworks show. Within a few weeks, his wife would be expecting another child. A few days after his family's reunion—during the same week that Parliament began debate about how to confront Boston's destruction of the tea—Dunmore finally sat down to inform his superiors in London about all he had been doing for the past several months.

He had not filed a single report since the previous summer. He had not told Dartmouth about his trip to Pittsburgh, nor his actions in extending Augusta County to the Forks. It was in this letter, dated March 18, 1774, that he discussed how the backcountry people had "flocked about" him the previous August, begging for better government. Dunmore recounted all that had happened over the winter, enclosed copies of the petition with six hundred signatures sent to him the previous October, and forwarded Penn's letter. He then had the temerity to ask for official approval, and begged that he hoped he would be able to continue "according to the urgent desires" expressed in the settlers' petition.[10]

Over the next several weeks, the governors of Pennsylvania and Virginia would dispatch missives dueling over boundary lines and colonial history. Tempers flared, with Penn referring to Dunmore's demand that St. Clair be sacked as "somewhat dictatorial." Meanwhile, as governors stomped around their houses dictating furious letters, in the Ohio country the onset of spring produced more than blooming hillsides and budding fields. Starting in the last few days of March, the political controversy boiled over into violence. This latest episode of fighting over the Forks would produce scene after scene of threats, intimidation, and chest-thumping bravado. Before April was over, it was war.[11]

On Monday, March 28, Connolly returned to Pittsburgh. Two days later, protected by twenty men from the Chartiers Creek settlement southwest of town—John Gibson's brother George among them—he made his move. The party left Connolly's residence and headed for Fort Pitt. As soon as they heard of this maneuver, the three Pennsylvania magistrates in town, Aeneas Mackay, Devereaux Smith, and Andrew McFarlane, hurried to intercept them. They were armed, too, with the Riot Act, which St. Clair had forwarded them from the governor.

When the trio of Pennsylvanians confronted Connolly, they found him in possession of his own paper weapons. Dunmore had sent Connolly a copy of the angry letter he had sent to Governor Penn, which the captain-commander of West Augusta proceeded to read aloud to the assembled crowd at Fort Pitt. It contained Dunmore's commands for him "to persevere in the prosecution of the plan he beg[a]n upon." After finishing his recitation, Connolly told the Pennsylvanians he would speak to them privately. He informed them, Mackay later reported, that he had no intention of breaking the peace: he was only following Dunmore's orders, and pledged that he would indeed appear for his court date in Hanna's Town the following week. The Pennsylvanians took Connolly at his word and, since they were "averse to violent proceedings," left without having to read the Riot Act.[12]

If the Pennsylvanians went home from the fort thinking they had defused the situation, they were sorely mistaken. The next day, when the Westmoreland sheriff went to serve a writ on one of Connolly's militia officers, peace completely collapsed in the town. Connolly, who the Pennsylvanians suspected was himself holding Virginia arrest warrants for St. Clair and other Westmoreland officials, confronted the sheriff and put *him* in custody. Pittsburgh was devolving into a battleground. "Ever since that time," Mackay reported, "there are parties of armed men in constant pursuit of our Deputy Sheriff and Constables, by which means it is impossible for us to do any business." With Connolly occupying the fort, what had been Fort Duquesne and Fort Pitt was now renamed Fort Dunmore.[13]

George Croghan surveyed the political situation in Pittsburgh and, believing Dunmore's victory to be assured, threw his lot in with Virginia. Croghan's defection to Virginia came about because of another surrender. Vandalia, the scheme that had looked so promising less than a year earlier, had foundered. The Walpole group had run into difficulties over the course of 1773, but the final blow came when one of its leading lobbyists, Benjamin Franklin, fell from grace. At the end of December, Franklin came under fire for arranging the publication of a set of private letters that Massachusetts lieutenant governor Thomas Hutchinson had written in the late 1760s. British officials viewed Franklin's role in publicizing this correspondence as a breach of gentlemanly honor. On January 29, 1774, General Thomas Gage and Franklin's foe Lord Hillsborough watched with glee as the solicitor general raked him over the coals for more than an hour in a room in the Privy Council chambers known as "the Cockpit." It was a public humiliation; the British government was making Franklin into a scapegoat, in no small part because the news of the Boston Tea Party had arrived in town the week before. He was the only leading American they could get their hands on at the moment, so Franklin and all the things he stood for suffered the consequences for America's resistance. By early 1774, even Croghan was aware that Vandalia's fate was sealed. His bending his knee to Virginia was a recognition that Dunmore, Connolly, and West Augusta were now the rising force at the Forks.[14]

The tumult that began in March erupted into violence during the first week of April. One of Connolly's men confronted Aeneas Mackay in his Pittsburgh home. The Westmoreland justice of the peace responded by arresting the Virginian. When the man's friends heard about it, they rushed over and "proceeded to the most violent outrages." They broke through Mackay and Devereaux Smith's back gates, pointed rifles at the family, and threatened to shoot Mackay's wife if she didn't unlock the house door. George Aston, one of Connolly's appointed militia officers— and, in an amazing coincidence, the son of the man who escorted Thomas Cresap to the Philadelphia jail in 1736—chased after her with a drawn sword and stabbed her in the arm. Another Westmoreland official, was also "Abused and Scratched" by Aston.[15]

Two days later, Wednesday, April 6, rumor reached Hanna's Town that Connolly was on his way there for his scheduled court appearance, but at the head of an armed mob, perhaps as many as two hundred. The court ordered the sheriff to "raise as many men as he could collect," but the Pennsylvanians put up a paltry force. Connolly arrived late in the afternoon with a party nearly as large as rumor had it, their "colors flying" and "swords drawn." The justices were out eating dinner, so Connolly posted guards to prevent their returning. Connolly repeated his performance from Fort Pitt the week before, reading Dunmore's letters aloud to the crowd. Supposedly the defendant in this case, Connolly had taken charge of not only the court proceedings but also the entire town. It was, according to one witness, a scene of "clamour and confusion." Connolly dictated to the Pennsylvanians that they had no authority over him or the Forks, and eventually rode away without a major incident.[16]

Late on Friday night, the Westmoreland court having ended a spring session that no one would soon forget, Andrew McFarlane, Devereaux Smith, and Aeneas Mackay trotted the thirty miles from Hanna's Town to their homes in Pittsburgh. At 9:30 the next morning, armed men rushed into their houses with arrest warrants. Connolly's constable grabbed McFarlane by the shoulder and ordered him to go to Fort Dunmore to receive his sentence. When the three magistrates refused Connolly's demand that they pay a bail fee, he had them sent south. "I understand we are to be Guarded by a great Number of Militia to Sta[u]nton Gaol," McFarlane wrote to Governor Penn, "where we are to be Kept in Close Confinement."[17]

The following morning, one of the Westmoreland deputy sheriffs approached a cabin about seven miles east of Pittsburgh. It had been a harrowing few weeks, and the deputy should have been more cautious, but both he and his horse were thirsty and in search of water. As he galloped up, he turned to find half a dozen men emerging from the woods pointing rifles at him and shouting at him to surrender. He immediately snatched his pistols, leapt off his horse, and sprinted into the house. He was shocked to find three men inside being held at gunpoint. It was McFarlane, Smith, and Mackay. He testified later that he immediately recognized the peril he was in, "and rushed out again as quick as possible." He ran back to his horse "with a pistol in each hand, and ordered them to let his horse go, threatening to shoot any of them" who refused. "All but one withdrew a little," and he repeated his threat before firing upon them and wounding one man in the side. He jumped back on his horse and charged into the woods.[18]

As the Westmoreland magistrates headed south under guard, Connolly may have felt like his victory was nearly complete. His winter planning and decisive action that first week of April had given Virginia the upper hand. Until the king determined who "owned" the Forks, Connolly's men rode about the countryside in triumph. Any property owned by people sympathetic to Pennsylvania was fair game. Roving bands of Connolly's partisans "proceeded to shoot down our Cattle, Sheep, and Hogs," the distressed Pennsylvanians later complained, "taking by force of Arms any part of our property he [Connolly] pleases."[19]

A week before he was marched south as a prisoner, Aeneas Mackay had told Governor Penn that Connolly's intrigues were running a significant risk. "The Indians are greatly alarmed at seeing parties of armed men patrolling through our streets daily," he wrote, "not knowing but there is a hostility intended against them, and their country." Mackay's fellow prisoner, Devereaux Smith, recognized this danger as well. Natives on the Ohio, he reported, "expressed surprise to see a number of armed men assembled at this place, with their colors at different times, making a Warlike appearance." "After the Muster of the 25th of January," Smith said, some of Connolly's Virginians "fired on" Natives "at their camps near the mouth of the Sawmill Run," just across the river from Fort Dunmore. A few days after Mackay and Smith were on the road to the Staunton jail, the possibility that this inter-colony dispute might break out into conflict with Native peoples began to seem increasingly likely.[20]

On Thursday, April 14, a canoe loaded with goods belonging to trader William Butler pushed off from Pittsburgh, headed for the Shawnee villages. Three of his employees paddled about forty miles downstream to the mouth of Little Beaver Creek and made camp for the night. On their trip they had met four Cherokee Natives, one woman and three men, to whom they foolishly showed off some of their silver trinkets. The next morning, the Cherokees "waylaid them on the River Bank," killing one of Butler's employees and wounding another. They "plundered the canoe of the most valuable part of the cargo, and made off." A few colonists arrived soon after the attack. One of them, Benjamin Tomlinson, helped bury the dead man, and another tended to the wounded one, a man named Stephens.[21]

Although only twenty-two years old, Benjamin Tomlinson was accustomed to backcountry violence. His family, like the Cresaps and the Swearingens, was scattered throughout the frontier. In fact, his mother Rebecca was a Swearingen, and two of her sisters, Ruth and Drusilla, were married to Daniel and Thomas Cresap Jr., respectively. Natives had killed his uncle Nathaniel at Redstone in 1762. His older brother, Joseph, was living not too far away along the Ohio, and his sister Lucy had married a man named Joshua Baker. They operated a tavern together about a dozen miles farther downstream across from Yellow Creek. In a few years, Benjamin married Rachel Greathouse, whose brothers lived merely a few miles from where he spent Friday morning, April 15, digging a grave.

This incident at Little Beaver Creek transformed the conflict over the Forks. Connolly literally began a new chapter in his journal, which he now titled "commencing from the late Disturbances with the Cherokees upon the Ohio." On Saturday, he sent a detachment of his men in search of the attackers. He then went personally with another group to bring the injured Stephens back to the fort. "This accident occasion'd a great deal of confusion," Connolly wrote. As he would soon learn, however, the colonists at the Forks were even more confused about the situation than he knew.[22]

On that same Saturday, the deputy Indian superintendent at Pittsburgh, Alexander McKee, received what he referred to as "private intelligence" from a Shawnee. "Our great Men" are not telling "all they know to you," he confessed. A meeting was about to take place on the Scioto River down the Ohio involving "Indians from Nations westward and southward" with the aim of "striking the English." The Ohio Senecas—Guyasuta's people—"tho' they may deny it, have their share in this plan, for it is no new one, but has been upon foot many Years." "Whatever Professions of Friendship" Ohio Native leaders make "to the English, it is

from their Lips only, and not from their Hearts." Pittsburghers had spent
the past several months gathering arms and spoiling for a fight to settle
who was going to be in charge at the Forks. It was now clear to McKee
that Natives down the Ohio had been making similar preparations.[23]

The budding crisis on the Ohio consumed everyone's attention during the second half of April. In Philadelphia and Williamsburg, colonial
governors convened their councils to discuss the jurisdictional dispute.
Penn had sent another letter on March 31 protesting Dunmore's protest,
which the Virginians took as "a high Insult." By late April, Penn decided
he needed to dispatch people rather than just paper to Williamsburg
to settle this, and deputized three commissioners to go negotiate with
Dunmore. On April 25, Dunmore wrote a formal proclamation that
ordered his officers in Pittsburgh "to embody a sufficient Number of
Men to repel any Insult whatever" and commanded all subjects to respect
Virginia's authority.[24]

But developments in colonial capitals was nothing compared to the
drama that was brewing on the Ohio River. Connolly had sent a party of
militia down the Ohio in pursuit of the Cherokees who had ambushed
Butler's men, while McKee sent messages to Natives he thought were
friendly that it would be a show of good faith to encourage some Mingos
living nearby to help with the search. Guyasuta, just returning to the
area after another visit with Sir William Johnson, also tried to ease tensions and pull Ohio Natives away from Shawnee influence, but things
were approaching a point of no return. Early in the week, a handful of
colonists living near Yellow Creek "insulted and abused" the Delaware
leader Captain White Eyes. When Connolly heard about this, he took
out his pen and wrote two more proclamations.[25]

The first was to warn traders going down the Ohio that because "certain imprudent . . . Inhabitants down this River have very unbecomingly
illtreated" friendly Natives, everyone was instructed "to avoid a Conduct
of that nature for the future . . . as thereon depends the Tranquility of
this Country." After receiving word from Croghan that the Shawnees
were "ill-disposed and might possibly do mischief," Connolly decided he
would send out a second circular letter to all the settlers of the Pittsburgh

district "recommending them to be on their guard against any Hostile attempts from said people."[26]

Like McKee, Croghan was getting intelligence from Shawnee leaders. A group of Shawnee had wintered over at Croghan Hall, arriving in late December. Since Croghan's place was only a few miles up the Alleghany River from the Forks—and their host was a key player—the Shawnee leaders there witnessed all the machinations in Pittsburgh during those chaotic months. A few days after the attack on Little Beaver Creek, the last of Croghan's guests decided they had better return home. They joined a convoy of canoes of Ohio Natives living between John Gibson's cabin and Big Beaver Creek, what had been called Logan's Town, all headed out of this danger zone for safety several hundred miles downriver. While this party followed the broad turn the Ohio River takes west before turning due south, Connolly's circular letters raced ahead of them, arriving in the Wheeling district early in the last week of April.[27]

Michael Cresap wasn't minding his store in Wheeling during those wild April days; he was out scouting. This is what he did now. On a previous scouting expedition, he laid claim to a valuable spot across from Pipe Creek called "Round Bottom" that Washington also prized—and believed was his. The legal entanglements over who really owned this land would produce headaches for both parties for more than a decade. The following spring of 1774, Michael was out looking for choice lands. While Connolly was busy battling Pennsylvanians at the Forks, Cresap had hired a few men to go out with him down the Ohio, blazing paths, marking trees, and clearing lands.[28]

At that same moment, lots of other colonists also had their eyes on the Lower Ohio Valley region. Daniel Boone's first foray into Kentucky had happened in the fall of 1773, just two days before Virginia established the West Augusta district, and Natives there attacked his party, killing his son and several others. But those murders didn't deter other colonial speculators, like Dunmore, Washington, and Connolly, or scouts, like Cresap, from dreaming about Kentucky.[29]

On April 18, a surveying party working on the soldiers' bounty lands laid out a plot of two thousand acres for Washington way up the Kanawha, nearly fifty miles from its mouth at the Ohio. The next day, they ran into another settler who had news about a skirmish between Natives and a group of thirteen colonists who "intended to settle on the Ohio," in which three Natives died. According to the settler, "this caused the Indians to hold a council and they are determined to kill the Virginians and rob the Pennsylvanians," showing again how Natives discerned between the two tribes of colonists. On April 20, the day Connolly composed his circular letters 250 miles upriver, this party reached the mouth of the Kanawha, Point Pleasant, where they found several other groups of fellow scouts gathering.[30]

One of them was a twenty-three-year-old George Rogers Clark. Born near Charlottesville, Virginia, Clark had come to the Ohio country two years before. The collected body at Point Pleasant, which Clark later remembered as nearly a hundred but others at the time put closer to twenty-five, discussed the news of the recent attack. They decided to retaliate against a Shawnee town near the mouth of the Scioto, another hundred miles down the Ohio. "Who was to command was the question," according to Clark's memory. Someone remembered that Michael Cresap was only about "fifteen miles above us with some hands settling a plantation." They sent for him, and shortly, Cresap arrived to take charge.[31]

What they did not expect was that Cresap would immediately try to talk them out of it. "To our astonishment," Clark remembered, "our intended commander-in-chief was the person that dissuaded us from the enterprise." Cresap thought a war with Natives was certainly in the offing, but he thought striking first would mean "we should be blamed for it, and perhaps justly." He advised going back upriver to Wheeling to discover the latest news. Two hours later, Clark said, the main group pushed their canoes into the river and paddled against the current, headed for Wheeling.[32]

Along the way they encountered a small Native party headed by Delaware leader John Killbuck on the opposite bank of the river. They stopped to talk, but did so without their appointed commander. Killbuck was a sworn enemy of the Cresap family. Michael knew how, when he was a teenager, Killbuck had stalked his father in the hills surrounding Oldtown. Despite being in his early thirties, Michael maintained the family grudge. Clark remembered a quarter century later how Cresap "was afraid to trust himself with the Indians. That Killbuck had frequently attempted to way-lay his father to kill him—that if he [Michael] crossed the river, perhaps his fortitude might fail him and he might put Killbuck to death." Concerned about tilting the region into a general war, Clark said, Michael stayed away for everyone's benefit.[33]

When they arrived at Wheeling, the settlement was in an uproar. "The whole of the inhabitants appeared to be alarmed," Clark said. This was Sunday, April 24. By the end of this week, the lives of the Cresaps, the Shickellamys, and many other people would be changed forever.[34]

As Clark recalled, "By this time we had got to be a formidable party. All of the hunters, men without families, etc., in that quarter had joined our party." When news of the men gathering at Wheeling reached Pittsburgh, Connolly dashed off a message, instructing the growing troop to stay put until they heard further orders from him, but to keep watch on the river. Express riders galloped back and forth over the sixty miles between Wheeling and the Forks on that Monday. Connolly dispatched a second note addressed to Captain Cresap. Lead your scouts out and "cover the country . . . until the inhabitants could fortify themselves," Clark remembered the message saying. "The reception of this letter" to Cresap "was the epoch of open hostilities with the Indians."[35]

Later in the day, Cresap decided that it was time to declare war. He gathered his men for a ceremony "in the most solemn manner." They planted a war post, and each man took turns striking it with his hatchet, pledging his loyalty to the mission and the group. Rumors swirled that Shawnees had killed two colonists nearby, and, later that evening, someone walked up to the group carrying two Native scalps.[36]

The following morning, a lookout saw a canoe coming down the Ohio. In it were three men—a Shawnee, a Delaware, and the unfortunate Stephens (survivor of the Cherokee attack at Little Beaver Creek ten days earlier). His boss, William Butler, had been determined to get his cargo of goods to the Native villages on the Scioto, and had ordered Stephens to resume his journey downriver almost immediately after the earlier attack. Spying their approach, Cresap declared his men should not let this canoe pass and asked for volunteers. Ebenezer Zane, a leading man in Wheeling, opposed this action, but the majority of the group backed Cresap's plan. Two men, one named Brothers and another called Chenoweth, jumped into a canoe with Cresap and went to intercept them. Stephens, rightfully, panicked. He paddled quickly for the opposite shore, but too late. Shots rang out, and the two Natives with him fell dead. Stephens, thinking his assailants were Natives, jumped into the river. But when he surfaced and saw the canoe approaching with three colonists aboard, he hailed them, and they pulled him up.[37]

Had Cresap and his men shot down the Natives in Stephens's canoe? He wasn't sure at first. Stephens thought the bullets had come from the grassy shore, from people who "lay concealed in the Weeds." For their part, Cresap, Brothers, and Chenoweth denied pulling any triggers. When they returned, Zane critically inspected Stephens's canoe, which was splattered with blood and bullet holes. Cresap shrugged and darkly joked that the people inside must've fallen overboard. Stephens later told Alexander McKee that he soon became "well convinced that the . . . murder was done by some of [Michael] Crissop's Associates," for once they returned to Wheeling he swore he heard Michael "using threatening language against the Indians," promising "he would put every Indian he met with on the River to Death, and that if he cou'd raise Men sufficient to cross the River, he wou'd attack a small Village of Indians living on Yellow Creek."[38]

This statement is the basis for the legend of Michael Cresap as a notorious Indian killer that would grow to stupendous proportions over the following century. Thanks to McKee, Cresap's snarling pledge began to appear a few weeks later in newspapers all over the mainland colonies: Virginia, Pennsylvania, Massachusetts, Connecticut, New York, Rhode Island, New Hampshire, and South Carolina. From there it would become canon.[39]

The lookouts who had spotted Stephens's canoe that Tuesday hadn't been as keen the day before. While the colonists at Wheeling fretted and paced, waiting for messages from Fort Dunmore, a convoy of five canoes quietly floated past them. These were some of the Shawnee leaders, including Cornstalk, who had wintered over at Croghan's house, along with others they had picked up along the way. Hearing about the growing posse at Wheeling, they snuck around the back side of the big island across from the settlement and passed Cresap's men without notice.

In the afternoon after the attack on Stephens's canoe, a settler who observed this flotilla sent word to Wheeling. Cresap again called for volunteers and the chase was on, with Clark among the paddlers. Fifteen miles south of Wheeling, right across from the Round Bottom site that Cresap and Washington would squabble over, they identified the canoes at the mouth of Pipe Creek, where the Natives had ditched them to hide in the woods. A pitched battle ensued, with losses on both sides. McKee heard the Natives had one casualty and killed one colonist, while Crawford told Washington he heard that three Natives were dead. Cresap's men scalped the slain and returned to Wheeling after confiscating saddles and bridles, several kegs of rum, and "a considerable quantity of ammunition and other warlike stores" they found in the Natives' canoes.[40]

Returning to Wheeling, Cresap's men regrouped and made plans for their next move. As Clark recalled, "On our return to camp, a resolution was adopted to march the next day and attack Logan's camp on the Ohio about thirty miles above us." The next day, Thursday, April 28, the posse marched north out of Wheeling, headed for Yellow Creek.[41]

Suddenly, however, Michael had a change of heart. Five miles north of the settlement, as the party stopped to rest, Cresap announced to his men that perhaps this was not the best idea. Cresap observed that since "it was generally agreed that those [Mingo] Indians had no hostile intentions, as they were hunting, and their party was composed of men, women, and children, with all their stuff with them," this expedition should be cancelled. They returned to Wheeling that Thursday evening.[42]

Just then, Cresap's men spotted a canoe carrying three traders coming down the river loaded with goods. It was John Gibson and two partners. Gibson later remembered that this party of roughly 150 men hailed him over, told him there was a general Indian war, and boasted of winning several skirmishes with Shawnees. Gibson was skeptical. There had been no talk of war downriver when he was just there, and the Shawnee men were out hunting; this timing didn't add up. He sent off one of his partners to go and check out their story while Gibson stayed with this unsavory lot. Michael Cresap was nearby, they said, and Gibson suggested they send for him. He waited overnight while "they behaved in the most disorderly manner, threatening to kill us, and saying the damned traders were worse than the Indians and ought to be killed."[43]

When Cresap showed up that Friday morning, he greeted Gibson warmly. Michael had heard of Gibson and his business partner Robert Callender, a longtime associate of Croghan and the Baynton-Wharton-Morgan firm. According to Gibson, Cresap seemed wary of this increasingly unruly group that had gathered along the Ohio, of whom he allegedly was in command. Cresap was convinced "the present party would fall on and kill every Indian they met on the river," and advised Gibson not to risk going farther down. "For his part," Cresap told him, he was "not going to continue with them, but go right across the country to Redstone to avoid the consequences."[44]

This is exactly what he did, leaving soon after to head east on the overland path from Wheeling to the Cresap stronghold at Redstone. On Saturday, April 30, witnesses saw him at "Catfish Camp," what is now Washington, Pennsylvania, thirty miles away. Gibson, for his part, didn't follow Cresap's warnings and continued on down the Ohio. By the time he arrived at the Shawnee villages at the Scioto, his wife Koonay would be dead and their child was being taken as a hostage to the same Catfish Camp.

―――

What do we make of Michael Cresap's movements in the last two weeks of April? Many of them were remembered a quarter century or more after the fact, and yet are incredibly detailed and specific. Even though they were recorded much later, they do not contradict one another, but they do suggest that Michael contradicted himself. He seemed to alternatively seek out conflict and then do his best to stop it. He swore he was going to lay waste to Logan's camp on Yellow Creek, but then talked everyone out of it. Which is the real Michael Cresap?

One explanation is that this is legend playing tricks on us again. We know that the Native villages at Scioto and Yellow Creek were not attacked in late April. But as to the reasons why those raids didn't happen, we only have the twenty-five-year-old memories of Clark, Zane, and Gibson to go on, and the controversial legend of what was about to happen certainly shaped their testimony. At century's end, they would be questioned about where they were in 1774 and what they remembered precisely because people had gotten so many facts wrong about Cresap, Logan, and Yellow Creek. They portrayed Cresap as being conflicted, as a man trying to distance himself from his later infamous statement that he wanted to kill every Native he saw. Cresap, in their telling, was trying to hold back the flood during those late April days. He restrained himself from taking revenge on John Killbuck, they said. Were they perhaps overcompensating to clear Cresap's name? As we have been several times in this story, we are yet again in the midst, and mist, of the incomprehensible. We should approach cautiously. Some of the narrative reported above may be wrong. But what—and how much?

It's also possible, however, that he was indeed conflicted. If we accept the evidence we have at face value, Cresap may have uttered that bloodthirsty boast while betraying a more nuanced outlook through his actions. Michael was a complicated figure. He was a leading settler-colonist who had Native blood on his hands from a very young age. He was a prominent member of one of the most prominent settler families on the frontier that fueled Native dispossession and disruption. His family had twice appropriated Indigenous grounds and eliminated any traces of the Natives who lived there before them, turning "Fort Demolished" into "Pleasant Garden" and "King Opessa's Town" into "Oldtown." Michael Cresap, like his father, was a man bent on pushing Natives farther and farther into the interior and claiming their lands as his.

But there is more to his story. Michael was also someone who had suffered deep trauma at a young age. As a teenager, he had found his brother's half-devoured corpse in the woods. He had sweated out a terrifying siege when it seemed very likely that his whole family might be killed inside his childhood home. A man who swore to kill his father stalked them outside that home. This was someone who grew up with violence, war, loss, menace, and blood.

This is certainly not to excuse Michael for his contributions to the long- and short-term forces that brought the Ohio to the precipice of war. We can say he should not have been there. But he was there, and there were enormous consequences to that. There is no doubt that Michael and his family played a significant role in the terrible violence that was about to occur. But many, many people in North America were about to blame him personally, singularly, and unfairly for this carnage. That was exactly what Michael Cresap was trying to avoid when he fled from the Ohio on Friday afternoon, April 29, 1774.

CHAPTER 8

THE HORROR,
1774

"I saw on that ivory face the expression of sombre pride, of ruthless power, of craven terror—of an intense and hopeless despair. . . . He cried out in a whisper at some image, at some vision—he cried out twice, a cry that was no more than a breath—The horror! The horror!"

—*Heart of Darkness*

We have arrived at the horror of Yellow Creek. The perpetrators and victims are familiar to us by now. They were parts of extended, interlocked families who had been engaged in more than a generation of conflict along the Susquehanna, Potomac, and Ohio Rivers. For forty years, alliances of friendship, both real and of convenience, had come and gone. They had negotiated, fought, lied, manipulated, killed, threatened, retreated, and schemed—anything to gain an edge in this bewildering eighteenth-century game. For a few of them, that experience of prolonged, incomprehensible, baffling imperial encounter would end in a cacophony of horrific violence. For more, the terrible sounds of the massacre that happened at Yellow Creek and the reprisals that stemmed from those murders would ring in their ears for the rest of 1774 and haunt them for decades to come.

On Saturday morning, just hours before the ship carrying news of the Coercive Acts entered Boston Harbor, seven Mingos, half of them members of the Shickellamy family, climbed into canoes to try to keep a peace that seemed to be dissolving all around them. They had to be anxious as they paddled the mile down Yellow Creek and then across the broad Ohio, but we know how often they had been in these situations before. They were about to put themselves in mortal danger, and yet they went anyway.

Directly across from the mouth of Yellow Creek was Baker's Bottom, a good spot of flat land that had caught George Washington's eye four years earlier. A house sat up on the riverbank there now, out of which the owners, Joshua Baker (thirty years old) and Lucy Tomlinson Baker (twenty-five), operated a tavern. Lucy's two older brothers, Joseph (twenty-nine) and Nathaniel Tomlinson (twenty-seven), lived nearby, as did her younger brother Benjamin (twenty-two), the latter having finished burying the body of Butler's unfortunate employee at Little Beaver Creek just two weeks ago. Close to Baker's Bottom was a settlement where several members of the Greathouse family lived, including Rachel Greathouse, soon to become Benjamin Tomlinson's wife. Her two brothers, Daniel (twenty-four) and Jacob Greathouse (twenty-two), also lived nearby. There were also a few members of the ubiquitous Swearingen family about, including twenty-year-old Joseph Swearingen. These were the people who had abused White Eyes and convinced Connolly to write his two circular letters on April 20, admonishing them for such imprudent acts in one, and, in the other, advising all settlers in the area to be on guard for any hostile attempts from Natives.

Connolly's second circular letter brought more settlers—and their weapons—to Baker's Bottom. John Sappington (twenty-four), George Cox, and Michael Myers were among them. Much later, when Myers was a very elderly man, he told of how he escorted two men across the Ohio during the last week of April. They forded the river and went a couple of miles up Yellow Creek looking for good land. When a Native tried to steal the horse that they had brought over, Myers shot him. When a second Native came running up, Myers fired at him, too. Whether he hit him, Myers said, he "did not wait to see," since the "Indian camp was only about a hundred yards off." Myers's partners had already fled, sprinting for the canoe as soon as the shooting started. They were halfway

across when Myers reached the riverbank. He scrambled up the shore
to find a low spot where he could swim over, and made it back safely.[1]

Myers suggested later this engagement was the immediate instigation
for the bloodshed that was about to occur. Others, however, provided a
different origin story. Joseph Tomlinson, according to one collector of
frontier tales, sat down with Michael Cresap Jr. in the autumn of 1845,
and told him that Logan's sister Koonay had long been in the habit of
"crossing to Bakers to get milk, and Mrs. Baker was kind in giving her
some for her two children." On Friday, April 29, Koonay told his sister Lucy "that the Indians were angry and would be over next day by
a certain hour, and advised" them to move back to Catfish Camp. The
next day, they did come over, "with their faces painted black," an obvious signal of hostile intentions. John Sappington, one of the assailants,
wove a similar tale twenty-five years after the event, while a third person offered a slightly modified version in 1845, saying that Koonay had
been in Baker's tavern, and told Lucy that Natives "intended to murder
Baker's family." Lucy told her relation Daniel Greathouse, which set in
motion the carnage of Saturday morning. Sappington said that twenty-
one people came over to the Baker's to protect them. Others said even
more were there, and that they had mustered at another's house before
going to Baker's Bottom.[2]

In these renderings, the Yellow Creek massacre had nothing to do
with colonial aggression. They claimed it was a simple case of self-defense.
Given what we know about the people involved—the Shickellamy family
had never to this point struck out in any such belligerence, but rather had
spent the past several decades trying to either defuse or evade tensions—
these aged recollections, coming as they did from accessories to the
murders, if not the killers themselves, are so self-serving that they are
difficult to endorse.

Moreover, it's not what people at the time thought. A more likely
scenario, which one trader in the area believed, was that colonists at
Baker's Bottom "invited a party" of Mingos living on Yellow Creek "to
come over and drink with them," as a way of luring them into a trap.
Thus, they would employ one colonial weapon, alcohol, as an excuse

to use other ones. Moreover, this gesture of goodwill had important resonance with the particular Natives they were seeking to ambush. Crossing the river to engage in a ritual of diplomacy seems more in line with the Shickellamy way than going to execute a dangerous ambush, especially one that Koonay had tipped off and, in doing so, endangered herself, her child, and her entire family. William Crawford and another prominent Virginian named John Neville had indeed heard that Baker and Greathouse had "decoyed" the Mingos to "drink with them" as a premeditation for murder. Another of Baker's neighbors, and an "intimate companion" of one of the assailants, later testified that Greathouse planned the snare after realizing there were too many Mingos on the other side of the river to attack directly. Henry Jolly, a teenager living in the Ohio country at the time, would later assert that no "person of common rationality, [could] believe for a moment, that the Indians came to Yellow Creek with hostile intention."[3]

On Saturday morning, the Mingos fell into the trap. John Petty (Shickellamy), his mother Neanoma, and sister Koonay with her infant child, made up half of the party. Three other Mingo men whose names we don't know were also there. None of their faces were painted black. They went in to Baker's place, said hello to a few colonists inside, and shared a drink. Some accepted Joshua and Lucy Baker's offer of illegal rum; some did not. George Cox, Nathaniel Tomlinson, John Sappington, and Daniel Greathouse were in the front room with the visiting party. "Concealed in the back apartment" were Edward King, Michael Myers, Jacob Greathouse, Joseph Swearingen, Benjamin and Joseph Tomlinson, and others. They listened in silence, their hands gripping loaded rifles. Notably absent from the affair were Michael Cresap, who was thirty miles to the east at Catfish Camp, and Logan (Soyechtowa), who was farther away hunting in the interior of the Ohio country that spring. Neither of the two men most connected to the bloodshed of Yellow Creek were anywhere close to the vicinity.[4]

Someone suggested a shooting contest outside as a diversion. The Mingos who had not partaken in alcohol went first, trying to hit a distant target with their rifles. This had the benefit of emptying the guns of the Natives who were sober. Inside, there was trouble. John Petty (Shickellamy), who, according to colonial witnesses, had imbibed some alcohol, found a military coat hanging on a nail, a British regimental redcoat that Nathaniel Tomlinson probably had purchased from the commissary up at Fort Pitt. John put on Tomlinson's coat and allegedly paraded around the cabin saying, "I am a white man." Sappington remembered John "setting his arms a kimbo [and] began to strut about" saying, "white man, son of a bitch," and "attempted to strike" him. The behavior enraged Tomlinson, whose uncle we know had been murdered by Natives at Redstone twelve years earlier.[5]

Many of them had been drinking, and tensions inside the cabin mounted to the point that George Cox couldn't take it anymore. Michael Cresap Jr. (who wasn't born yet) heard that Cox thought Greathouse's trap "would breed an Indian war and that he would have no hand in it" and abruptly left, tramping off into the woods. He was some distance away when he stopped suddenly. As he had feared, sharp reports of gunfire and screams of terror rent the air behind him.[6]

Tomlinson yelled that he wanted his coat back, threatening John Petty—a man twice his age—that he would kill him if he didn't take it off. There was a scuffle. John made for the door, looking to the colonists like he was going to steal away, and one colonist, Sappington according to some, shot him.[7]

The men hiding in the backroom sprung from their hiding places. Edward King jumped onto John Petty's wounded body and drove a knife into him, allegedly saying, "Many a deer I have served in this way." The Mingos sprinted for the riverbank, with Sappington and the Greathouse brothers in pursuit. Neanoma fell, while Koonay, her infant daughter upon her back, made it to the shore before she was caught. She begged for the life of her child, saying it was John Gibson's baby. A few days later, when Virginia militia leader John Neville asked the man clutching that baby what had happened next, Jacob Greathouse replied that "he was about six feet Distance and just shot her in the Forehead." Neville, shaken by this response, asked whether he was "not near enough to have taken it's Mother Prisoner without putting her to Death in that inhuman manner?" Neville wasn't the only one who instantly judged Greathouse's deed as despicable. The circumstances of Koonay's death would grow into a frontier legend. A rumor spread that Koonay was "very big with child, whom they ripped open, and stuck on a pole." This wasn't correct; Koonay wasn't pregnant. But the story of her body being desecrated lingered on.[8]

Then someone spotted two canoes paddling across the river. Sappington recounted how his men "ranged themselves along the bank of the river" and took aim. The assailants later justified their actions by claiming that the Mingos in the canoes were coming over to help finish off the Bakers. It is far more likely, however, that, as McKee later recorded in his journal, they were simply trying to find out what had detained their kin. When the lead canoe came close, they fired, killing two more. The second boat was able to turn back to safety, with one woman severely wounded and barely able to get out on the other side. From across the river the colonists said they could hear "the Women and Children at the [Mingo] Camp raise a very melancholy Cry." They wailed for the loss of eight murdered Natives.[9]

It was nearly nine. With the ambush concluded, there was an "altercation between those Murderers whether they shou'd put the Child to Death." Jacob Greathouse told Neville he had intended to "have dash'd" the baby's "brains out, but that he was struck with some Remorse on seeing the Child fall with its mother." They decided to "take it along with them," when they left the area, which they did as soon as they had scalped the dead bodies strewn across Baker's Bottom.[10]

By Sunday evening, the perpetrators and their families were at Catfish Camp. It was there that they ran into Neville, who noted Koonay's baby girl with them. The teenaged Henry Jolly was also there, and three-quarters of a century later, he could recall his "mother, feeding and dressing the Babe, Chirping to the little Innocent, and it smiling." Ten days later, the baby was at William Crawford's house, before eventually being returned to her father, John Gibson's, care.[11]

The Baker's Bottom murderers carried with them the haunting memories of the wailing. They were the immediate, vocal reaction to this encounter with men's dark hearts. When the killers reached the shelter of Catfish Camp, they told John Neville about the cries. Did they also share with Michael Cresap what that morning sounded like? About the screaming? Of Koonay's cries for mercy? Of the moans that floated across the Ohio River?

———

The same cries would soon reach Logan's ears. And while he was no stranger to grief, this was different. This weeping compelled him to action. Ohio Natives discussed among one another how to respond, with Delaware leaders advising restraint. But even they knew Logan must obey the cries. He had to be allowed to seek justice for the evil that had visited his family.

There was an uproar on the east side of the river as well. The racket of panic: shouting parents hurrying their children, horses whinnying under pressure from stressed, spurred riders, loaded-down wagons squeaking as they choked the roads yet again. William Crawford's brother told Washington that people were running "as bad as they did in the year 1756 and fifty Sevin." "More than one thousand people Cros[s]ed the Monongahela in one day," he wrote a few days after Yellow Creek. William sent his own letter to Mount Vernon the next day saying "the [w]hole Country Avackquated as far as Monongahalia."[12]

Connolly ordered drums to beat out notice for all militias to muster, in part for defense but also to staunch the panic. Three days after Yellow Creek, Connolly raised the militia and demanded that one-third of the men report directly to Fort Dunmore to make that "Heap of Ruins" ready to withstand a siege. The weather was just as strange as the political situation at the Forks; as the men went to work frantically restoring the walls of the former Fort Pitt, a late spring frost descended on Virginia.[13]

Relations desperately needed their own warming in those frigid early days of May. Brokers like George Croghan and Guyasuta understood how much "emotion work" lay in store for them. Dealing with emotions was an essential part of diplomats' roles on the frontier. They knew the only way to keep peace was by providing outlets for the expression of hard feelings—by holding condolence ceremonies and giving gifts, but most of all, by listening. Croghan, Guyasuta, and several others urged everyone to remain calm until these formalities could be arranged. Connolly desperately dashed off orders to cease all firing of guns. They needed quiet.[14]

In the aftermath of the massacre, people also started pointing fingers. Already, just days after Yellow Creek, the violence that had already occurred and everything that was feared to be coming all seemed to be Michael Cresap's fault. Citing "accounts from Pittsburgh," a New York City newspaper ran an article on May 19, claiming "Col. Crissap, of Potomack, with a party of Virginians, has killed 39 Ohio Indians, in revenge for some murders some time since committed upon the frontiers of the Ohio." The following week, newspapers in Philadelphia supplied more substantial details, including Cresap's alleged oath that he would "put every Indian to death he should meet with on the river." Connolly, too, heard that it was Cresap's skirmishing that brought on this escalating crisis.[15]

In the time between Yellow Creek and his name first appearing in American newspapers attached to the violence, Michael Cresap had left the camp at Catfish Creek, and went briefly to Redstone before heading back to Oldtown. He wasn't home long, for soon he raised a company of volunteers from western Maryland and marched at their head back to Catfish Camp. On May 13, the same day that Samuel Adams called together a large gathering at Faneuil Hall in Boston to discuss their next moves ahead of the British Army's imminent arrival in the city, Michael Cresap convened a "large body of men" to discuss striking out against the Ohio villages and "fall upon the Indians." Although Connolly immediately dispatched a letter telling them to desist, the armed, angry, frightened settlers at Catfish Camp were on the edge of taking things into their own hands. Two days before the Catfish meeting, a small band of disgruntled Virginians had snuck up to Croghan Hall and shot at some Natives who had gone there to negotiate an end to the crisis. Delaware leader Captain White Eyes feared his family was about to be murdered, too.[16]

Then, on May 19, what Connolly described as "an insolent note" was handed to him at Fort Dunmore. Six men who referred to themselves as

those who had "killed the Mingos opposite Yellow Creek," warned Connolly that he had "better order the Indians to remain on their own side
of the [Ohio] River or they would kill more of them." In his response,
Connolly let the signers know that they had "already committed Actions
So Barbarous in their nature, and so Evil a Tendency to this Country in
general that you merit the severest punishment from this Government."
But the six weren't worried about consequences for the murders, nor
were they concerned enough to hide their identities. Daniel Greathouse,
Joseph Swearingen, Nathaniel Tomlinson, Joshua Baker, and two others
proudly signed their names.[17]

Forty-eight hours later, another "very extraordinary epistle" arrived,
this one from the Redstone settlement, signed by Michael Cresap and
his brother-in-law Enoch Innis. Connolly summarized the note in his
journal: Cresap and Innis, the leaders "of a number of people collected
together in a disorderly manner," stated they were "determined to proceed
immediately against the Indians, and consequently involve this Country
in a Calamitous war." Cresap and Innis demanded that unless Connolly
met them personally at Catfish Camp the following Monday morning
at 10:00 a.m. with assurances that the Shawnee danger was really over,
"we shall certainly proceed to distress our common enemies."[18]

Connolly took great offense at his being summoned. "I cannot . . . help
expressing my Astonishment at the manner in which you convey your
Sentiments to us upon what has already happened," he responded, and
then directed his fire directly at Michael Cresap: "I have to acquaint Mr.
Crisop, that in my opinion, he is taking the most immediate steps imaginable to do Himself an irreparable injury, in idly prosecuting what might
otherwise as to himself, been Buried in Oblivion." He railed at Cresap
and his men for the "indignity cast upon the authority of this Government by the manner in which you have illegally assembled yourselves in
arms." Such "imprudence and indiscretion" would only produce a "general
Rupture," he warned, but if Cresap's band "followed the dictates of your
own folly," they should "abide the consequences."[19]

Doubtful that Cresap would follow his orders, Connolly also sent
an express to a nearby militia captain, instructing him to assemble his

company and prepare to march on Catfish Camp and break up Cresap's company if they "will not listen to reason and [be] prevailed upon to desist from their destructive scheme." A confrontation at Catfish Camp between heavily armed militia seemed likely.[20]

The settlers at Catfish Camp and Redstone were afraid. They refused to admit that it was their battles with Pennsylvania, their belligerence on the Ohio River, their abuse of Native leaders, and their murders that had brought them to this precipice. They saw themselves as victims, not perpetrators. So, as an effort to confront their fragility, fear, and bewilderment, white settlers hashed out their own war plans and threatened Virginia's leaders that they better fall into line behind them.

When Connolly refused to follow the Catfish/Redstone vigilantes, Cresap decided to change course. He would face his fears by protecting his household. Two days later, word reached Connolly that Cresap had "discharged his Company and returned Homewards" without a fight. One of Michael's associates remembered that upon receiving Connolly's order, "couched in offensive and insulting language," he swore after disbanding his men that he was determined "never to take any part in the present Indian war, but to leave Mr. Commandant at Pittsburgh to fight it out as he could."[21]

Despite this declaration, Michael would soon be back, changing his mind yet again, to play a significant role in a conflict that people were starting to call another Cresap's War.

≡

During the days that fearful settlers at Catfish Camp and Redstone hashed out war plans, other meetings were taking place all over the Ohio country. At Gekelemuckepuck, the Delaware town on the Tuscarawas River that colonists knew as "Newcomer's Town," Mingos, Shawnees, and other Ohio Natives gathered to discuss what to do after the news of Yellow Creek reached them on May 8. A week later, on May 15, Captain White Eyes and Captain Pipe convened a grand council where they conveyed a message from colonial leaders, reassuring the group that the Yellow Creek killers were not acting on orders from Dunmore. A faction of twenty Mingos and Shawnees were unimpressed. According to a missionary who observed the meeting, the Mingos were "very angry and threaten to kill all white people they met with." The Delawares labored to prevent this escalation and moved to protect all the colonial traders who were nearby. All that week, while Connolly tried to prevent those at Catfish Camp from rushing to violence, Native leaders undertook the same project of pleading for restraint in the hopes of avoiding all-out war.[22]

The border controversy certainly exacerbated a sense of tribal identity. Some thought John Connolly provoked this emergency with Ohio Natives as a way to secure Virginia's authority at the Forks. Arthur St. Clair wondered whether the prospect of Indian war might upend loyalties at the Forks. When he heard about Yellow Creek, and the ensuing panic that he feared might produce "an entire depopulation" of the country, St. Clair and several other Pennsylvania leaders went to Croghan Hall to sign a mutual defense association "in case of danger." Perhaps he could work with the erstwhile turncoat after all. Together, St. Clair and Croghan agreed to "raise, victual, and pay a ranging Company of one hundred men for one month."[23]

When Connolly heard about this new partnership just a few days after he had squelched Cresap's vigilantism at Catfish Camp, he was "astonished." He fired off several furious letters. In his view, this "association was with Men of avowed Principles repugnant to the Welfare & Intentions of this Government," and the "practice is unlawful, unwarrantable, and affrontive." Connolly would not brook an alliance with Arthur St. Clair and feared that if Croghan and other Virginians abandoned him, the growing conflict with the Natives might undermine his power at the Forks.[24]

⸻

While Guyasuta and other Native leaders urged restraint among hostile Mingos and Shawnees, the one thing that all seemed to agree upon was that Logan had the right to exact revenge for the brutal murder of his kin. In the several letters that reached Connolly and Croghan that May from informants in Native villages, many of them mentioned how no

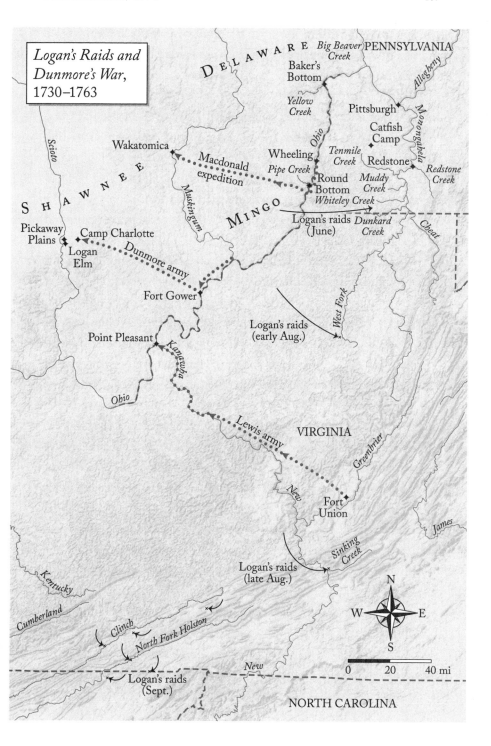

Logan's Raids and
Dunmore's War,
1730–1763

one was able—or willing—to try to restrain Logan (Soyechtowa). While some tried to talk him out of it, nearly everyone expected that he would redeem his family's honor. In the first week of June, he did.[25]

A little more than twenty miles separated Redstone from the spot where Cheat River joins the Monongahela. Between those two places, four small creeks enter the Monongahela from the west: Ten-Mile, Muddy, Whiteley, and Dunkard. This zone had already seen plenty of violence over the previous generation, and commanders at Fort Pitt had sent several warnings to settlers living there that their claims were illegal, and they were squatting on dangerous lands. The warnings would soon prove prescient.

Logan, at the head of a small raiding party, stealthily approached this area during those first June days to scout for potential victims. Despite the near-constant rumors of imminent attack, the Spicer family—William, his wife Lydia, and their seven children—had delayed in taking shelter at a nearby stockade at Muddy Creek. On Saturday morning, June 4, William was in the front yard chopping wood when the Mingos first emerged out of the woods. Spicer couldn't readily tell if they were hostile. He didn't raise the alarm at once, but buried his axe in a nearby log and headed toward the house. The situation changed in a few seconds, however, when Logan's men snatched the axe out of the log and drove it into Spicer's chest, killing him instantly. The Mingos then spread out, yelling and sprinting around the compound. Lydia was inside with Betsy (twelve) and her two youngest siblings. When the door burst open, Lydia and the two small children were knocked down and scalped. Betsy had been ironing clothes with her mother when the Mingos stormed in. She still clutched the iron as she flew out the back door and ran for safety. She flung the iron away and grasped the hand of her brother William Jr. (eleven) as she fled. In the back yard, the other Mingo raiders set upon her siblings. Job (sixteen) and two more of her siblings were killed and scalped. Betsy and William didn't get far. They were soon overtaken and forced to return to the house, which was now a scene of carnage. "The Spicer massacre," as it has become known in frontier lore in this region, was indeed a gruesome event.

Figure 17. Painting of the Spicer Massacre by R. L. Burwell (1895).

Figure 18: Betsy Spicer's iron, which was recovered after the attack and became a frontier relic, is now on display at the Greene County Historical Society Museum, Waynesburg, Pennsylvania.

Something had broken in Logan. Twenty years earlier, when violence swirled all around him, his family was able to talk him out of participating in the worst bloodshed. Now he initiated it. With his older brother Tachnedorus far away and the rest of his kin in the ground, there was no one to get him to reconsider. Logan's grief metastasized. It could not be contained within himself; it would be inflicted on lots of other people. Now it became Betsy and William Spicer Jr.'s grief. It would soon spread to other colonial families.

Word of the attack circulated quickly. "We have a certain Account of some Mischief having been done up Cheat River," Arthur St. Clair wrote two days after the attack, "but whether it is only designed as Revenge, or as really the beginning of a War, we cannot yet Judge." Early reports in colonial newspapers had only the vaguest details, and many of those were wrong, such as referring to the victims as the family of Benjamin Spear. Soon, however, reports from colonists who visited the devastated Spicer house began to arrive. One account informed readers that "some people going to or by the house of William Speir, they discovered him, his wife, and four children, murdered and scalped, with a broad axe sticking in the man's breast, and his wife lying on her back entirely naked." The militia officer who sent these accounts to the *Virginia Gazette* opined that "although he resided" in this region "during the last two wars, he never saw a greater consternation and distress among the people than is at this time."[26]

Reportage of the Spicer massacre fit into the growing genre of the "anti-Indian sublime," a narrative trope that had gripped American culture since the terrible years of the Seven Years' War. Eighteenth-century writers had created certain scripts in how they described attacks like this one, and the details provided about the destruction at the Spicer house followed them precisely: an idyllic settler family set upon by bloodthirsty savages; butchered fathers, violated mothers, scalped babies; household bliss destroyed in an instant. Readers were left with no doubts about who were the victims and who the perpetrators.[27]

Logan and his party continued to menace the settlements around Redstone. The day after the attack on the Spicers, a man near Muddy Creek disappeared after having gotten separated from his party. When his friends heard gunshots and his horse reappeared without its rider, they searched but could only find his coat. The next day, colonists inside Jenkins' fort, a stockade on a creek even closer to Redstone, reported seeing the Mingos skulking about. On Tuesday, June 7, Henry Wall and another man named Keener ventured outside the walls of Jenkins' fort, and Logan's party sprang upon and scalped them.[28]

In response to the attacks, a detachment of a few dozen militia went in pursuit of Logan. The party, led by Captain Francis McClure and his lieutenant, Samuel Kinkade, soon found them. In a short exchange of gunfire, McClure was killed, and Kinkade had a ball pass through his arm. The militia quickly buried McClure's body and retreated. Logan and his party, with Betsy and William Spicer in tow, remained in the area. A few days later, near what is now Waynesburg, Pennsylvania, they killed another settler. Then, having taken twelve lives and two prisoners, they headed back west to the Ohio country, resurfacing at Wakatomica, a Shawnee village on the Muskingum River on June 22. The first screams of Logan's revenge had ceased.[29]

Given the location of Logan's first round of attacks—almost within sight of Redstone—it is clear *he* believed that Cresap and his associates were responsible for murdering his kin. If Logan was hoping to find Cresap, or lure him into an ambush as he did to McClure and Kinkade, he would be disappointed. Cresap was not at Redstone during the first days of June but had returned to the Potomac and the safety of Oldtown.

Logan was not the only one who held the Cresaps personally responsible for what had and was about to happen. In New York, Indian superintendent Sir William Johnson wrote angry letters to General Frederick Haldimand, the man Thomas Gage left in charge of the British Army in America when he went home on leave. Johnson blamed Cresap—or rather, his father. Upset by the "outrageous and Licentious Conduct of Colo. Cressop . . . of which I have had circumstantial Acc[oun]ts of & Information, is likely to prove of verry dangerous Consequence," Johnson warned Haldimand in early June. Haldimand concurred that he, too, was "apprehensive that the unwarrantable behavior of Cressop will draw the Just resentment of the Indians upon us and I foresee nothing to prevent it" except miraculous diplomacy. Correspondents continued to tell Johnson that this was all Cresap's fault. Cresap even had the nerve, one said, of sending "a Blanket and Scalp of a Chief to [Maryland] Governor Eden, as a Trophy of his Valour." Johnson was convinced, he wrote in early July, that "Cressop with others had causelessly surprised & Murdered near 30 Indians, partly Shawnese, but principally of the Six Nations."[30]

Lord Dartmouth, the secretary of state, had received so many letters about the impending violence about to break out in the American backcountry that he too was convinced this was all the fault of "a certain Colonel Cressop, of Virginia, who was instrumental in provoking the last Indian War." Even though there was a great deal of confusion in the letters about whether Colonel Thomas Cresap or his son was to blame, imperial officials were sure they were behind the murders and the "very great trouble" those acts were about to produce.[31]

Colonial newspapers echoed this private correspondence. Back in May, eastern papers had already held Michael personally responsible for the deaths of nearly forty Native people and published news of his boast that he would murder every Native person he saw. In June, reports continued to lay blame at his feet. According to one article in a New York City newspaper, "The destruction lately effected upon the Indians by the son of Col. Cressop . . . we have too much reason to apprehend . . . will terminate in an Indian war."[32]

Philadelphia printers were especially eager to blame Cresap and the Virginians. News of Logan's raids started to appear in Philadelphia papers on June 20, with one report from Fort Pitt relaying that eighteen people had been murdered and that an "Indian war was inevitable." A few days later, the *Pennsylvania Journal* printed several letters from McKee and Connolly in Pittsburgh, noting the "critical situation of the country." The printers then followed this with a letter that unequivocally fixed the blame on Cresap and his compatriots: "All those misfortunes, and the lives and property of the unhappy people who are among them, are owing to the barbarous murder, no other name can I give it, committed by Chrissop and one Backhouse, with their men, on a few Indians who resided or lived near the mouth of Yellow Creek." Then two Philadelphia papers published on July 13 included a long letter from Carlisle that ended with another reference to Michael as the source of all the backcountry's sorrow. "We are informed that young Cressop, who first began the quarrel with the Indians, and murdered a number of them in a cowardly manner," it read, "has received a letter of thanks from Lord Dunmore," and concluded that "land-jobbers" like Cresap were really out to subvert justice at all costs in Ohio.[33]

Philadelphia newspapers also featured letters that attacked Connolly as well as Cresap, one even referring to Connolly's men as a "gang of *worse* savages" than the Ohio Natives. Another article, widely reprinted throughout New England, connected Cresap to the larger controversy with Britain that loomed throughout the summer of 1774. The *Newport Mercury* published a letter from Philadelphia that related the constant "dismal accounts" from the backcountry, the "many white people" who had "already been scalped," and the thousands who were fleeing the area. "People here are not backward in saying," this Philadelphian noted, "that Lord North is at the bottom of all this; for you must know the Indians were first provoked by some murders committed among them by one Col. Cressop, who, it is said, was encouraged in his direful proceedings by a certain great man in power, who is one of Lord North's correspondents, I mean G. D—more of V—g—a." Repeating the error that Colonel Thomas Cresap, rather than his son, was the cause of this conflict, the article connected the family to the villains who were conspiring to rob the colonies of their liberties. The Cresaps' name had been so associated with instability and violence in both imperial correspondence and colonial newspapers—especially those printed in Philadelphia—that they were stock, stand-in villains for all sorts of trouble.[34]

Unsurprisingly, Lord Dunmore did not agree with this assessment. The conflict was neither his, his colony's, nor his empire's fault. Unlike his colleagues, he didn't hold the Cresaps responsible in the slightest. In fact, the governor was about to swear Michael in as a captain in the Virginia militia. But no matter who was at fault for the situation in Ohio, it was quickly becoming Dunmore's top priority. He wrote General Gage in Boston about the "high spirited . . . resolution" that the Virginians had just made protesting the Boston Port Act, but implied that mattered less now because since Natives had "murdered a good number of our

people on the Banks of the Ohio, all our thoughts must now be turned
that way." He issued a letter to all county lieutenants, saying that since
"hopes of pacification can be no longer entertained," they should begin
assembling their militia units to protect the frontier and be ready to
march west. Soon Dunmore would head there himself to orchestrate a
two-pronged invasion of Ohio.[35]

Not long after receiving Dunmore's military commission, Michael Cresap
wrote his first will and testament. That week, as the family celebrated
his thirty-second birthday, he had to know he was becoming a notorious figure on the frontier. The Mingos' initial raids were too close to the
Redstone settlement that he and his family were so intimately associated with for him not to have gotten the message that they might be out
specifically searching for him.

Michael instructed his executors to pay off his not insignificant debts
(a reflection of Cresap's penchants for land speculation, risk taking, and
his youth), and to liquidate most of his real estate to raise cash for Mary
and their three daughters—Maria (eight), Betsy (six), and Sarah (four).
One tract of seventy acres, "Betty's Blessing" in Hampshire County, Virginia, was to be reserved for baby James (two) to inherit when he turned
twenty-one. His father, brother-in-law and fellow instigator Enoch Innis,
and three neighbors witnessed his signature.

But at some point during the day, Michael realized there were more
details than he initially thought. He retrieved the will and added more
instructions. Under the original signatures, he added a postscript that
dealt with the interior life of the Cresap household. "A certain Negroe
Wench named Bett is not intended to be included in the personal estate,
but to be the Immediate property of my Wife . . . without reserve . . . and
as a particular Gift," he added, providing the only evidence we have that
Michael Cresap was an enslaver. We don't know any more about Bett—
where she came from, how she arrived in western Maryland, how long
she had been there, or if she was the only enslaved person in the Cresap
household—but we do know that Michael intended for her to take care

of his wife's every need for the rest of Mary's life. He also gave a second thought to James. Having a small farm to inherit wasn't enough. Michael ordered his executor to sell all the town lots that he had claim to in Oldtown and apply any money raised "to the Education of my son."

Now that he had made these arrangements, Michael was prepared to face what lay in store for him in Ohio. There was some indication that perhaps the danger had passed. Two days after Michael had composed his will, on June 30, a merchant in Carlisle, Pennsylvania, wrote a letter to Governor Penn in which he reported that Logan "is now satisfied for the loss of his relations, and will sit Still until he hears what the Long Knife (the Virginians) will say." St. Clair had similarly heard news by late June that Logan had returned with thirteen scalps and promised

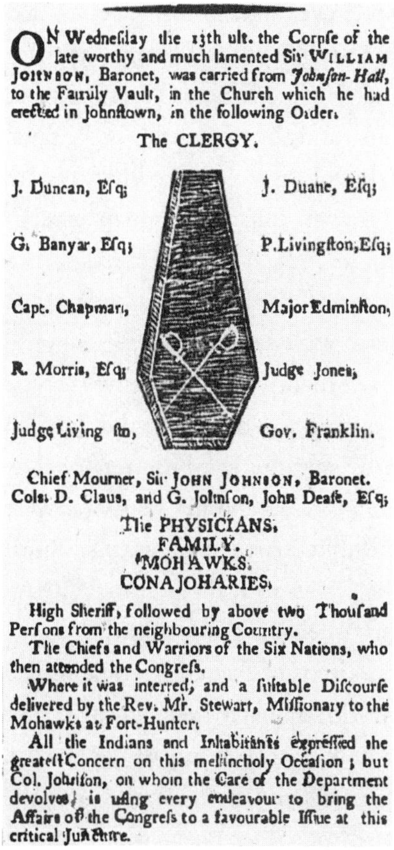

ON Wednesday the 13th ult. the Corpse of the late worthy and much lamented Sir WILLIAM JOHNSON, Baronet, was carried from *Johnson-Hall*, to the Family Vault, in the Church which he had erected in Johnstown, in the following Order.

The CLERGY.

J. Duncan, Esq;   J. Duane, Esq;

G. Banyar, Esq;   P. Livingston, Esq;

Capt. Chapman,   Major Edminston,

R. Morris, Esq;   Judge Jones,

Judge Living fton,   Gov. Franklin.

Chief Mourner, Sir JOHN JOHNSON, Baronet. Cols. D. Claus, and G. Johnson, John Deaft, Esq;

The PHYSICIANS.
FAMILY.
MOHAWKS.
CONAJOHARIES.

High Sheriff, followed by above two Thousand Persons from the neighbouring Country.

The Chiefs and Warriors of the Six Nations, who then attended the Congress.

Where it was interred; and a suitable Discourse delivered by the Rev. Mr. Stewart, Missionary to the Mohawks at Fort-Hunter.

All the Indians and Inhabitants expressed the greatest Concern on this melancholy Occasion; but Col. Johnson, on whom the Care of the Department devolves, is using every endeavour to bring the Affairs of the Congress to a favourable Issue at this critical Juncture.

Figure 19. Sir William Johnson's obituary, *New York Gazette & Weekly Mercury*, 1 August 1774.

he would now "listen to the chiefs." However, both reports turned out to be wishful thinking. Logan would not be finished with his revenge for several months.[36]

Early in July, representatives of several different Native groups, including more than six hundred Iroquois, travelled to Johnson Hall, Sir William Johnson's home, to meet with the British superintendent in a last-ditch effort to keep the peace. After welcoming them with dinner, Johnson opened the proceedings with a speech apologizing for the ill deeds of "some of our ignorant frontier inhabitants." He was almost certainly thinking about the Cresaps when he swore "these men will be sought after and punished."[37]

It was the last speech Johnson would ever make. Feeling very weak, he was carried back to his bedroom to rest. Within two hours, the fifty-nine-year-old superintendent was dead. He had suffered several attacks of acute illness over the past few years, and, like Michael, had drawn up his will earlier that year. In April, he told associates he knew he was dying. The crisis in the Ohio country, however, forced Johnson to undergo the strain of another arduous treaty conference, an unwise exertion for a man in poor health. But this was just part of the job he had undertaken for the last nineteen years. His obituary, published over the next several weeks throughout North America, made mention of how he was "much indisposed," but forced to transact "business with the Six Nations on Account of the Murders committed by some of the Frontier Inhabitants of Virginia." In this interpretation, Cresap and his associates were to blame for this "infinite loss of the Public, particularly at this critical Juncture." The perception that Michael Cresap had sped Sir William Johnson to his death only added to his ignominy that summer.[38]

The day after Johnson died, as hundreds of Iroquois people milled about Johnson Hall wondering what would happen to them now that they had lost their strongest imperial advocate, Logan resumed his attacks. Sixty-five miles south of Redstone, Simpson Creek empties into the West Fork of the Monongahela (West Fork River) near what today is the town of Meadowbrook, West Virginia. On Tuesday, July 12, Logan, with a party of seven Mingos, snuck up on William Robinson, Thomas Hellen, and Coleman Brown working unsuspectingly in a field. Rifle reports broke the low hum of summer insects, followed by the thuds of multiple bullets slamming into Brown's body. Hellen and Robinson started to run. The Mingos overtook and restrained Hellen and Robinson and forced them to go along while they continued to search the area for more victims. Unable to find any more, they decided to carry the two prisoners back to Wakatomica.[39]

A quarter century later, Robinson wrote about his forced march to the Muskingum River. Now the shouts of war were reduced to quiet conversation as they made their way west. "Logan spoke English well," he remembered, "and very soon manifested a friendly disposition" with Robinson. Logan instructed him to "be of good heart, that he would not be killed," but must not try to run away since he would be adopted into one of their families. Robinson recalled talking at length with Logan, but the topic seemed to come back to one thing. "In these conversations," he said, "he always charged Capt. Michael Cresap with the murder of his family."[40]

When Logan's party arrived at Wakatomika, the villagers formed a gauntlet. Yells, taunts, and screams greeted William Robinson and Thomas Hellen as Logan's men shoved them forward in what would be the first of several ceremonial ordeals. Robinson was dragged to the center of the village, where Natives tied him to a stake, and "a great debate arose whether he should not be burnt." Logan, however, insisted he be adopted rather than sacrificed and "carried him to the cabin of an old squaw, where Logan pointed out a person who he said was [now his] cousin." It dawned on Robinson that this was his new family. As was common in Native adoption practices with people taken captive in war, the old woman was now his aunt, and he "now stood in the place of a warrior of the family who had been killed at Yellow Creek."[41]

Three days later, Logan visited Robinson again, this time armed with a pen and paper. Although several witnesses testified over the decades that he could read, it is clear from this episode that Logan was unable to write in

English. He asked Robinson to transcribe a note for him. Making ink out of gunpowder, Robinson transcribed the following from Logan's dictation:

> To Captain Cressap,
> What did you kill my people on Yellow Creek for[?] The white People killed my kin at Conestoga a great while ago, & I thought nothing of that. But you killed my kin again on Yellow Creek, and took my cousin prisoner[,] then I thought I must kill too; and I have been three times to war since but the Indians is not Angry only myself.
>   Captain John Logan

This note has generated profound confusion over whether the man called Logan was Tachnedorus (John Logan) or his younger brother Soyech-towa (James Logan). Since the preponderance of evidence says Logan was Soyechtowa, it is indeed a mystery as to why Robinson signed the note "Captain John Logan." But, aside from the attribution confusion, Logan's dictation reveals several things about his state of mind at that moment, nearly three months after the Yellow Creek massacre.[42]

First, it is clear that Logan was not mistaken about which Cresap he thought had perpetrated the murders. Although several news articles, provincial leaders, and imperial officials had incorrectly referenced Colonel Cresap (as would Logan himself in a few months), in this message, at least, he recognized that it was Michael, thus the address to Captain Cresap.

Second, the premediated brutality of the attack recalled to his mind the Paxton Boys attack on his kin in 1763. But, as Logan pointed out, he didn't take any revenge then. That wasn't the Shickellamy way. But Yellow Creek was a different matter. Surely there had to be a cumulative effect. All the negotiations that his father and brothers had undertaken had failed time and time again. Political disgrace, intimidation, and bloodshed had hounded them out of their homes and split the family into pieces. Yellow Creek was the final act that destroyed the Shickellamy way.

And yet—the last line of the note suggests that some remnants of that search for limiting destruction still remained for Logan. "The Indians is not Angry only myself," he said, insisting that this was a personal vendetta rather than a general war. This seems like a way to contain the conflict, to deescalate and hopefully spare the women and children in Wakatomika and throughout the Ohio country from suffering the wrath of an invading army. Perhaps this note could serve as a signal to colonial leaders that they might not need to launch a bloody, costly expedition into Indian country. It was unnecessary to punish all the Shawnees, Delawares, and Mingos living in Ohio. This was not a fight with Virginia; it was only with Captain Cresap.

Logan folded up the note and left Robinson with his adopted family. Over the next several weeks, Robinson remembered, his aunt "proceeded by signs" to tell him the story of what had occurred at Yellow Creek. She was there, one of the wailers on the riverbank. "Whenever she entered on this subject she was thrown into the most violent agitations," he recalled. Listening to her relate the story, Robinson heard echoes of the groans that hung over the Ohio three months before. Those sounds had dissipated, but they were not gone. Despite his aunt's clear grief, Robinson did not suffer during his time at Wakatomika. Rather, he remembered his adoptive kin were "very kind to him," and "seem[ed] in truth to consider and respect him as the friend they had lost."[43]

Logan's note was still on his person when Dunmore arrived in Winchester over the weekend of July 23–24 to take command of the invasion he had been planning back in Williamsburg. The messages he dictated there would destroy any hopes Logan had of narrowing the conflict. Dunmore sent orders to Colonel Andrew Lewis, the ranking militia officer in the southwestern counties of Virginia, to "raise a respectable Boddy of men" and march them to the mouth of the Kanawha River. Dunmore would go north to Pittsburgh and gather forces to come down the Ohio and join him there, at the place known as Point Pleasant. They would link up and invade Native country.[44]

Even as Dunmore's orders made their way south to Lewis, seven hundred men gathered in Wheeling to prepare for their own strike on Wakatomika. For several weeks that summer, William Crawford had been at the head of a building party of more than two hundred men constructing Fort Fincastle at Wheeling. Then, in the last few weeks of July, more than four hundred men had arrived in town, with Frederick County (Virginia) militia officer Angus MacDonald at their head. Mac-Donald, who fourteen years earlier had been one of a handful of lonely soldiers posted at Fort Burd in Redstone when ominous tomahawks had been found on the road nearby, was in command of what he hoped would be a punishing assault on the Shawnee towns. He organized volunteers into eight divisions. Michael Cresap headed one; other captains included future Revolutionary War heroes George Rogers Clark and Daniel Morgan. Two days after Dunmore issued his orders for a march on Ohio, the MacDonald expedition began their assault on Wakatomika.

The convoy of canoes floated twenty miles down the Ohio to Captina Creek, just past the scene of Michael's initial attack at the end of April. There they stashed the canoes and gave orders for the men to take only what necessities they needed for a seven-day expedition. The Shawnee towns on the Muskingum were ninety miles away. Five days in, on July 31, Natives spotted their column and soon began to engage them. Two settlers died and another five were wounded. When the Virginians reached the shores of the Muskingum, Native leaders and MacDonald conducted a series of complicated negotiations. Pennsylvania traders, John Gibson among them, were in the villages telling Natives "terrible accounts of the Virginians intending to cut them off for the sake of their lands." While Native people struggled to discern between different colonial tribes (Pennsylvanians and Virginians), MacDonald also tried to sort out hostile Shawnees and Mingos from friendly Delawares.[45]

When talks stalled, MacDonald made plans to attack Wakatomika. He sent two companies, one led by Cresap, downriver to cross at daybreak on August 2, where they were to then cover the main body's crossing of the Muskingum. "Old Mike," as one of the eighteen-year-old volunteers in his unit later called him, "was up the whole night among his men, going the rounds and cautioning them to keep their arms in condition for a morning attack which he confidently expected."[46]

Cresap's instincts were correct. His men ran into a party of Natives waiting for them the next morning, attacked them, and drove them off. In the fighting, Cresap "tomahawked and scalped one Indian, and from the quantities of blood on the woods, many must have been wounded." They entered Wakatomika but found it abandoned. Logan and his party had left the week before to go out raiding again, not knowing that the man to whom Logan's note was addressed would soon be strolling through his adopted village. The other inhabitants, including the Spicer children and William Robinson, had fled farther west. "We set fire to the town and destroyed everything of value," summarized one account of Mac-Donald's expedition in Maryland and Virginia newspapers. "From this town we proceeded to the rest, five in number, all of which we burnt, together with about 500 bushels of old corn, and every other thing they had." The human cost of this venture was thankfully meager: MacDonald reported bringing home three scalps and one prisoner, with the loss of two of his own men and six wounded. The torching of towns on the Muskingum, however, added to the intense and hopeless despair many Natives experienced in the summer of 1774.[47]

News of MacDonald's destruction of Wakatomika appeared in the Williamsburg *Virginia Gazette* and then spread all over North America.

Figure 20. An antique dealer near Kingsport, Tennessee obtained this this twenty-two-inch club and sold it as a table leg sometime in the twentieth century. Eventually, a collector of early American arms identified the "IG" markings on the handle's bottom as identifying the club Logan dropped on his way to Sinking Creek.

The short report of his "success" included news that "several parties of Indians are daily seen on this side of the Alleghany Mountains, but they have done but little mischief of late, except scalping one Family on the Head of Cedar Creek." It is possible the *Gazette's* printers got the names of their creeks confused, and what they meant was Sinking Creek.[48]

For it was at the head of Sinking Creek that Logan resumed his revenge raids.

On Sunday, August 7, as MacDonald's hungry men straggled back to their canoes, Logan and three men stalked through the area where Sinking Creek runs into the New River. This was a long way from Redstone, about fifteen miles west-northwest of what is today Blacksburg, Virginia, more than two hundred miles south of the sites of his previous raids. Colonial scouts had seen a few Natives in the area, and one vacated cabin had been burned down. A detachment of twenty militia went in search of them. They found tracks but were unable to locate them. Coming up on another "wasted Plantation," they found a "well made" war club laying in the yard. It had the letters "I G" carved on the handle. Virginia authorities would later realize that they had made a mistake. It wasn't an "I," it was an "L." "LG" on the handle stood for Logan, who had left it on purpose; a calling card to let everyone know he was there.[49]

Two years earlier, Balthazar and Catherine Lybrook had moved to Sinking Creek from Pennsylvania, and built a cabin, grist mill, and blockhouse for protection on top of a steep, twelve-foot embankment overhanging the creek's entrance into the New River. As this was early August, the water around the Lybrook compound was tranquil; the shallow stream offered access to a large rock in the middle of the river where the children could play and sun themselves.

But those first days of August found the blockhouse full of multiple families taking shelter together. The Snidows and McGriffs had crowded into the Lybrooks' makeshift fort over the weekend, as rumors of potential danger rippled through the area. After three days inside, however, the children were tired of being cooped up. Their parents relented and allowed them some recreation outside this Sunday morning.

Logan and his party were watching as Balthazar Lybrook walked around near the shore of the creek and nearly a dozen children bounded out of the blockhouse. Seven boys, ranging in age from very young to teenagers, made their way down the steep banks to enjoy a summer swim. Four girls piled into a canoe, with the two oldest at the helm. Except for Balthazar, who went over to the mill to work, the other adults remained in the stockade.[50]

Soundwaves of violence soon ricocheted through the river valley, shattering this lovely scene of childhood fun. A Mingo appeared above the children up on the embankment, standing between them and safety. The children scrambled in several directions to try to avoid capture. John Lybrook (ten) ran for shore and headed for a break in the cliffbank to try to sprint for the blockhouse. Theophilus (thirteen) and Jacob Snidow (eleven), with Thomas McGriff (thirteen), decided to swim across the New River. Two of Logan's party dove in after them. While his brothers swam for their lives, John Snidow Jr. (ten) was petrified atop the rock in the middle of the water, clutching two Lybrook children who were both less than a year old. The two Mingos stopped at the rock to murder them all before resuming their pursuit across the river. They apprehended the boys on the far riverbank and held them fast.

When the screaming started, Elizabeth (fourteen) and Catherine Lybrook (thirteen) turned their canoe upstream and paddled as hard as they could. When they thought they had gone far enough to be safe, they guided the canoe over to the bank, not knowing that a Mingo was trailing them up the shoreline. When they pulled up, he charged at them out of the woods, swinging his club. Only Catherine made it out of the canoe, darting for the blockhouse. As she ran, a "remarkably fierce" family dog charged out to protect her. Catherine's Mingo pursuer was so close he could almost touch her when the dog leapt on him and knocked him down, saving her life.[51]

The only adult hurt in the attacks was Balthazar, who was consumed with his work while the fourth Mingo snuck up on him at the mill. The Native shot him in the arm but couldn't secure him, and he escaped, taking shelter in a nearby cave. After a short search, his attacker gave up and returned to the house without having taken the father's scalp.

They did have seven trophies, though, all from children, and snatched three prisoners.[52]

Decades later, John Lybrook remembered the heroic dog standing guard over the girls' bodies in the canoe "until the people took them away for burial." Soon they heard another "piteous howl" from the animal, and when they ran to him, they also found another of the Lybrook children, a scalped six-year-old boy, alive but with horrendous skull fractures inflicted by a war club. He lived for only another day.[53]

Was Logan triumphant after such a brutal and ruthless attack? In all likelihood he was, as difficult as this is to face. He was waging his own merciless vendetta. The terrible sounds he caused at Sinking Creek matched those of his people at Yellow Creek. It would not last forever, but while it did, Logan inflicted excruciating pain on colonial settlers— and their young children.

Using "the greatest caution," Logan's party quickly covered their tracks as best as they could and forced their captives up and over the rockiest part of the mountains as they returned west. A few days after they had made their way over the "Stoney Hills, the worst way imaginable," the Snidow brothers and Thomas McGriff noticed their captors had less than ten shots of gunpowder left between them. They decided to make a break for it. A few days later, a patrol of militia discovered two boys in the woods, "entirely naked without either Blankets or match coats." It was McGriff and the younger Snidow boy, Jacob. They had successfully escaped. Theophilus did not; he remained with Logan's men and would go on to live more than a dozen years as an adopted member of a Native family.[54]

Logan's ghastly attack on the Lybrook farm and his marauding throughout the New River settlements was a setback for Dunmore's plans of launching an assault on Ohio. On the day that Jacob Snidow and Thomas McGriff were found wandering in the woods, Lewis convened a council with his subordinate officers to find out how plans were proceeding to gather southern Virginia's forces together for the expedition. Logan's presence in the area had put a significant damper on recruitment. "From the frequent murders committed by the Indians, &

their daily appearance amongst the Inhabitants, the people in general are backward in entering themselves volunteers in the intended Expedition," the officers admitted at their meeting. Men were reticent to leave their households with such danger in their midst. They thought it better to protect their homes from Logan's bewildering raids. Since "it is very uncertain what men the recruiting Officers will be able to raise," they decided to redouble their call to include a greater area of the backcountry. The Virginians were supposed to rendezvous for Ohio soon. It would take more time, now, to get enough men there.[55]

In fact, this seems a likely reason why Logan had come this far south to the New River. It was, after all, a significant departure from his previous raids on the Monongahela. Perhaps he deemed the zone around Redstone too difficult to locate easy targets, calculating that heading south would make for better hunting. But given the proximity to where Virginia militia forces were beginning to assemble, this decision seems especially dangerous. Moreover, Logan was *loud* here. He never left a war club behind before. And the attack at Sinking Creek was deafening.

The nature and location of his attacks thus suggests a particular strategy. Logan was not hiding his presence in the area—just the opposite. He announced he was there. He was playing into his growing reputation as a terrifying figure. For the first time Logan was adopting bewilderment as a state of play. He was sowing confusion and chaos so as to hopefully gain a particular political outcome. The son of Shickellamy had embraced the strategy of Ohio Natives that had terrified everyone living in the mid-Atlantic at the start of the Seven Years' War, including him and his family. Logan had become a son of Shingas.

The nature of the horrific slaughter on Sinking Creek fits with this: he was seeking to shock, to intimidate, and, hopefully, to petrify. Perhaps Logan's tomahawk might stave off or delay another invasion of Ohio and attacks on his people. If enough settlers were too scared to join Lewis, Dunmore's plans would have to be scrapped. This was more than an outpouring of grief, more than uncontrolled, vicious rage. What happened to the Snidow and Lybrook children at Sinking Creek was purposeful bewilderment. Although one militia officer insisted in a report that would be widely published throughout America that the Virginians "declared their Readiness to go out in their Country's Defence, and for the Protection of their Properties and Friends from the Cruelty and Depredations of the Savages," he knew this wasn't strictly the case. Those boasts covered up a deep anxiety. Logan's raids had worked, at least in the short term.[56]

During the middle weeks of August, Dunmore continued to make preparations. He appointed Adam Stephen and John Connolly to lead the forces that were to descend with him down the Ohio. Like Angus MacDonald, Stephen was a long-standing veteran of colonial warfare. He was second-in-command of the Virginia Regiment under Washington during the Seven Years' War and had witnessed the smoke that darkened the sky during the bad days of Shingas's raids in 1755.

Some things had changed since those days. On August 27, he wrote to his friend Richard Henry Lee—the son of Ohio Company founder Thomas Lee—that Dunmore's orders "prevent[ed] my attending the general Congress" then slated to meet in Philadelphia two weeks hence. Stephen badly wanted to go to witness how the colonies were going to defend themselves against the tyranny of the Coercive Acts. Stephen was convinced the "determined system of arbitrary power" recently evinced by Parliament was "intend[ed] to irritate America into a rebellion, then govern us like a conquered people." He advised Lee to "try all means" to avoid conflict, but did conceive that the colonies were going to need to "prepare for the worst as soon as possible."[57]

It is certain Lord Dunmore did not know the contents of this letter or the true feelings of the man he just named a lead commander of his invasion force. It is also very likely that Stephen didn't share these opinions in the many conversations he had with the royal governor as they began their journey from Winchester the following morning, headed for Pittsburgh.

On Tuesday, August 30, they were in Oldtown, and Thomas Cresap yet again hosted a party of dignitaries making their way to Ohio.

The aging frontiersman welcomed his honored guests as a widower, his wife Hannah having died at some point in 1774 by causes unknown. Thomas and Hannah had not enjoyed a perfect marriage. The offspring of his affair with Elizabeth Lamy, an adolescent daughter named Jane, continued to reside in the neighborhood just up the river. Still, they had endured. But, with her youngest son's reputation in tatters, it's likely that Hannah died a troubled woman.

Dunmore, Connolly, and Stephen spent the night of August 30 at Cresap's. Outside the walls of his outpost next to the Potomac river-banks, seven hundred Virginia volunteers pitched tents on the rolling hills nearby, just as Braddock's redcoats had nineteen years before. The governor spent some of his time at Cresap's scribbling more orders for Colonel Andrew Lewis, commander of the southern wing of Virginia's invasion force, unaware of the complications Logan's raids had caused on the New River. Then, in what was becoming an eighteenth-century tradition, the soldiers packed up their gear at Oldtown and marched first to secure provisions at Fort Cumberland before heading for the Forks, as many had done before them over the previous two decades.

It would take ten long days for Dunmore and his troops to reach Pittsburgh. Circumstances there had not improved over the summer. While the Virginia governor was en route, Pennsylvania magistrates busied themselves in taking down sworn statements documenting how Connolly had "grossly abused, threatened, and insulted" one Westmore-land County official a few months earlier. The worsening situation with the Natives, it seems, had not deterred Connolly's partisans from attack-ing Pennsylvanians. Connolly's men invaded and pulled down outbuild-ings in Aeneas Mackay's backyard. A fight naturally broke out, which climaxed with George Aston, Connolly's chief lieutenant, swinging his rifle butt at the head of Mrs. Mackay, less than two months after he had stabbed this poor woman in her arm.[58]

George Croghan's loyalty also came into question. When he offered to partner up with Arthur St. Clair in early June, Connolly and his Virginians were aghast. A few weeks later, when Croghan decided he was going to go personally to Williamsburg to brief Dunmore about

Connolly's actions, inhabitants in Pittsburgh interpreted his leaving as a sign of imminent Native attack. They blocked his passage and forced him to return to Croghan Hall. The near-constant Native visitors he entertained also raised suspicions. Croghan welcomed Delaware and Iroquois representatives to his home to discuss diplomacy right before Dunmore began his march. They had just returned from meeting with Guy Johnson in New York, and briefed Croghan on what they had discussed with the new superintendent.

Thirty-four in 1774, Colonel Guy Johnson had stepped into his Uncle William's role as British Indian superintendent and continued to meet with Native delegations throughout the summer in the hopes of reaching a diplomatic solution to the continuing troubles in Ohio. Like many others, he blamed Michael Cresap for the hectic initiation into his new job. This was all "Cressap's affair," and it had done a great deal to unite the Shawnee into a general—and formidable—confederacy, he said in one of his first letters to General Gage. Native leaders, including Guyasuta, Killbuck, Captain White Eyes, and Captain Pipe, made several journeys from Ohio to call upon Johnson at the new manor home, Guy Park, that he had just completed along the Mohawk River. On the way, they treated Croghan Hall like colonial notables did Cresap's place at Oldtown: an essential political stop along the way. The Virginians, already suspicious of Croghan's motives, eyed this traffic with concern. Some began to concoct plots to eliminate both the patriarch of Croghan Hall and his illustrious visitors.[59]

Croghan's machinations had gotten him into serious trouble that summer in Pittsburgh. His webs of schemes had ensnared his son-in-law, too. Ensign Augustine Prevost had married Susannah Croghan in 1765, not long after Prevost resigned from the British Army. Soon after, Susannah's father had wheedled her new husband into investing in his various land ventures in North America. Being tied to George Croghan's fortunes was a risky business for the young Prevost family, and early in the 1770s, their financial instability forced Augustine to return to the army. He served under his father, Colonel James Prevost, in a battalion stationed in Kingston, Jamaica, while Susannah and their now six children lived in a rented house in Lancaster, Pennsylvania. The threat of bankruptcy loomed so large that James gave his son leave to visit Croghan and press him for relief. Ensign Prevost journeyed to Pittsburgh late in August 1774 to try to straighten things out with his devious father-in-law just as Dunmore was also making his way there. The detailed diary Prevost kept offers a fascinating glimpse into the tumult that gripped Pittsburgh during those dangerous days.[60]

Before heading west, Ensign Prevost had traveled a bit in Maryland and Virginia, where he dined with the Dunmore family on July 4, 1774. He noted how little the imperial crisis had come up in conversation in the Virginia capital, hearing no "undecent reflections upon King or Government" in early July. A week later he was in Lancaster with his own "little family," where he spent six weeks before going to demand some honesty from his father-in-law.[61]

Prevost arrived at Croghan Hall in early September, only to find the man he desperately needed to talk to "laid up with the gout and reumathism." Their discussion would have to wait. Soon after arriving, Prevost was alarmed to find out that Virginians had murdered two Delaware Natives on the road somewhere in the three miles between Croghan Hall and Pittsburgh. Others in their party had managed to make it to Croghan's and thence across the Alleghany River to safety, but Prevost quickly realized this was a very dangerous place to be.[62]

Soon he travelled that short, blood-stained road to Pittsburgh. He went over to Semple's Tavern, where word shortly got out that an important visitor was in town. The tavernkeeper's sister and her husband, Dr. John Connolly, strode in for dinner. A few years earlier, Connolly had been a star at Semple's dinner table, impressing George Washington so much that they maintained a cordial correspondence. Prevost was less taken with Dunmore's man. He had heard many stories about Connolly in his travels that year. He held out hope those myriad "accounts I had heard to his prejudice" were wrong, but he was quickly "convinced of his little worth." Prevost found himself quite persuaded that Connolly could do all the things "he was accused of." But this unpleasant social interaction was not the most alarming matter of the evening. Captain White Eyes had accompanied Prevost from Croghan Hall, and found himself in deep peril. Prevost wrote in his diary that the Native leader "was cautioned to be gone & to take care of himself." "This made me very uneasy," Prevost wrote, and he appealed to Connolly to have someone go and check to see if White Eyes was about to be ambushed on the road.[63]

White Eyes made it—for now. But there was no telling what the "lawless villains" Connolly had gathered at Fort Dunmore would do next. "Both officers and men are people of the most infamous and abandoned characters," Prevost wrote, and he felt no confidence that any Natives or even his father-in-law was "safe from the malignity of the people under Connolly." This wasn't just wild speculation. Less than a week into his visit, Croghan shared with him a deposition he had taken from a man who reported he had been "tampered with to go and assist to kill Croghan and the Indians about him." "Such villainys I never heard of before," the Ensign confessed to his diary.[64]

The next day, Saturday, September 10, Governor Dunmore arrived in Pittsburgh. Prevost chuckled at the comedy of his entrance. Connolly had, "with vast pain and labor introduced a new mode and system of discipline amongst his veterans, and had intended to receive his Lordship with all the pomp etc. imaginable." When the three small canoes carrying Dunmore unexpectedly pulled up on shore late in the evening, all Connolly's plans of a lavish ceremonial display were foiled. Only the sentry was there to greet him, which made the governor "laugh heartily."[65]

Dunmore and Connolly spent the next day and several after meeting with Native diplomats and making preparations to transport his soldiers down the Ohio. While these negotiations were happening in Pittsburgh, Prevost finally had the chance to confront his father-in-law. Croghan responded by letting Prevost read the most recent letters from the Wharton brothers about the latest prospects of the Vandalia venture. They were not optimistic. Vandalia, like all the schemes before it, had fallen to pieces, and debtors' prison loomed large for both Croghan and his daughter's unfortunate husband.[66]

In other places in North America, wheels turned during those very same days that would decide the future for millions of inhabitants across the continent. On Monday, September 5, the First Continental Congress opened at Carpenter's Hall in Philadelphia. Adam Stephen wasn't there, but his former commander George Washington was, along with fifty-five other delegates from twelve colonies (all except Georgia). They gathered to discuss how to craft a collective response to the Coercive Acts, the set of measures Parliament passed in the spring of 1774 to punish colonists for the tea party, including closing the port of Boston and suspending Massachusetts' charter. The Crown had also sent General Thomas Gage back across the Atlantic to enforce what Americans quickly labeled the "Intolerable Acts."

On the following day of business, the Congressional delegates hashed out the rules about how this unprecedented gathering would operate. They discussed procedures for how to talk and cast votes. While they hammered out these details, an express rider from Boston rushed in with shocking news: cannon fire from the Royal Navy had set the city on fire! It turned out not to be true, but at the moment it was unnerving. For the rest of the day, substantive questions crowded out technical ones: Now what? Were we at war?[67]

Four hundred miles away, the advance party of Lewis's invasion force left their rendezvous area on the Greenbrier River that same afternoon. After significant delays brought on by Logan's incursion, the southern wing of the Virginian force was finally on their way to Ohio.

Meanwhile, Dunmore and Connolly continued to meet with Native leaders in Pittsburgh. They received a few Native spokesmen, including Delaware leaders White Eyes and Custaloga, on Wednesday, September 14, at Fort Dunmore. It didn't go well. Dunmore was not very adept at Native negotiation practices. White Eyes and Custaloga made opening ceremonial speeches, the purpose of which were to open Dunmore's ears and prepare him to hear their offers of friendship, their grievances, and their suggestions for keeping peace. Or so they thought. Dunmore was supposed to respond the following day; withholding a response to these remarks would be starting things off poorly. Whether this was the governor's intention, whether he was fatigued from his journey, or whether he was otherwise indisposed, negotiations did not reconvene the following day. Those who knew Dunmore recognized this behavior. He liked to keep people waiting on him. The Natives were the latest ones to feel the frustration of being put out by the governor, getting increasingly offended as the hours ticked away.[68]

Finally, the following morning, it was only after the wise Native broker Alexander McKee warned Dunmore that he should act with more urgency that he graced them with a response. The governor's answer, Prevost noted, was "evasive," and this made the Natives "prodigiously uneasy." Moreover, he did not offer them any "provisions, powder, and other necessities." It was plain to all involved: Dunmore wasn't here to conduct diplomacy.[69]

Nevertheless, he went through the motions, convening more talks at Fort Dunmore and at Croghan Hall. In each meeting, he delivered stinging rebukes to the Shawnees, listing all the colonists *they* had killed over the past decade. Meanwhile, Lewis's men continued to tramp west. By September 21, they had marched eighty-five miles to reach the mouth of the Elk River (today Charleston, West Virginia).

Logan, too, was on the move. He had returned home to view the damage colonial militia had inflicted on Wakatomika. It joined Yellow Creek as another ruined place for Logan. He offered Theophilus Snidow for adoption into his people, rested for a few days, and then headed back south on another raid. On September 23, Dunmore had another meeting with Captain Pipe. The Delaware leader insisted he had news from Shawnee leader Cornstalk that he had told his people to cease and desist. It didn't help. "The country is now in the greatest anarchy imaginable," Prevost confessed to his diary.[70]

Logan and his small band of raiders went even farther south than before, probably to skirt Lewis's invasion force, now within fifty miles of the Ohio River. To protect the settlers, that summer Virginia militia leaders had ordered the construction of a chain of four forts along the Clinch River, a hundred miles to the southwest of Sinking Creek. At one of them, Lieutenant Daniel Boone commanded a dozen militia men. Rumors reached them that a Native war party was in the area, followed by reports of cattle and horses gone missing. Then, at the next fort a few miles farther down the Clinch, Natives kidnapped two enslaved men working out in a nearby field and proceeded to use them as bait. Just beyond the fort's walls, Logan's party made these captives run through a gauntlet, beating them up and knocking them about, in the hopes of luring the men inside into an ambush.[71]

When this ploy didn't work (perhaps because the frontier Virginians were less concerned about African Americans being abused), Logan's party then trekked farther south, through Big Moccasin Gap to some colonial settlements near the Holston River. The area was so far removed from any previous Native attack that John Roberts and his young family did not feel compelled to take shelter at any of the nearby forts. This would prove a costly mistake, as the day after taunting Virginians along the Clinch, Logan's band struck the Roberts farm.

The unsuspecting family was going about business as usual when Logan attacked. The Mingos killed and scalped John, his wife, and their three daughters. They took another ten-year-old boy, John Roberts Jr., captive. A tomahawk strike to the back of the head of John's younger brother left him badly wounded and therefore diminished his value to them as a prisoner. They scalped the still-living young boy but left him behind. Despite his terrible injuries, which included a fractured skull, the youngest Roberts boy was able to run away, calling for his uncle to save him. There was hope that he might survive, and they sent for a doctor. Unfortunately, this "active, wise boy" only lived another two weeks. He was, Virginia militia officer Arthur Campbell wrote, "an extraordinary example of patience and resolution to his last, frequently lamenting 'he was not able to fight enough for to save his mammy.'"[72]

When they first heard about the attack on Roberts's farm, Virginia militia leaders in the area worried that the perpetrators might be

Cherokees—a potentially distressing development if this was evidence of a Cherokee-Shawnee alliance. However, we know it was Logan, for it was here at the Roberts farm that he finally dropped Robinson's note.[73]

After having carried it for hundreds of miles, Logan tied his note to Michael Cresap around another of his war clubs and dropped it on the ground near the bodies of the Roberts family. When the maimed Roberts boy led his uncle back to the scene of carnage, they found the club and the note. As neighbors tried to save the boy's life, the note began to make its way up the official chain of command. Roberts's brother gave it to the commander of a patrol that had come by. That militiaman sent it to Major Campbell, who enclosed a copy of it to his superior in his October 12 report. A quarter century later, Harry Innes remembered an express galloping up to Smithfield, Colonel William Preston's plantation home, where he happened to be visiting, with the club tucked in his satchel. Innes, who had just graduated from William and Mary, was so impressed with this war relic that he copied the note's contents down in his memorandum book as a memento.[74]

As the club and note began to circulate, Logan's men slipped back through Big Moccasin Gap and returned to stalk the Clinch River forts again. They had three captives with them—the two enslaved men they had previously taken and John Roberts Jr.—and were looking for more. At dusk on September 29, they fired on three men who were a few hundred yards away from Fort Byrd, killing one. Post commander Daniel Boone sent off a party in search of them but had no luck.[75]

These early October incidents along the Clinch River were the last of Logan's raids. They happened just as the climactic battle of what some at the time called Cresap's War, but would become better known as Dunmore's War, happened along the Ohio River. If Logan had intended his note to change things, he'd released it too late.

⸻

While Logan menaced the Clinch and Holston Rivers, the lead units of Colonel Lewis's Virginians reached the mouth of the Kanawha. Dunmore and Connolly had also been on the move, floating their men down the Ohio to join up with William Crawford's men at Wheeling, and then

Figure 21. Monument to Charles Lewis and the other Virginians who died at the Battle of Point Pleasant, erected in 1909.

on to the mouth of the Hocking River, where they began to construct Fort Gower (named for the Earl of Gower, Dunmore's brother-in-law, chief patron, and the president of the Privy Council) on October 2–5. Over the weekend, messengers paddled the several dozen miles that separated the two bodies of soldiers carrying orders about how they would coordinate their attack on the Shawnees.

Cornstalk, the Shawnee leader, watched Lewis's men make camp at Point Pleasant. The main body of Lewis's force had arrived late in the day on October 6. The next morning he held a council of war. Cornstalk knew about the two Virginia invasion forces and the likelihood that, in just a few days, they would join and become insurmountable. It made better sense to engage each wing of the invaders individually. The drums of war beat through many Native villages in Ohio. Hundreds of Shawnees and Mingos, along with some Delawares and Wyandots, snuck across the river on rafts and assembled a few hundred yards north of Point Pleasant. As White Eyes put it when he informed Dunmore of their decision, they were going "to speak with" Lewis and his 1,100 Virginians.[76]

Figure 22. Map of the
Native towns along
the Scioto River. The
Logan Elm is due south
of Cornstalk's Town on
Congo Creek. See also
Camp Charlotte.

Map of Locality of Logan Elm.

The number of combatants on the field made the Battle of Point Pleasant resemble a "conventional" clash between European armies. Estimates vary, but most accounts agree that Cornstalk led seven hundred to eight hundred men in battle at dawn on October 10. They fought all day, with the firing only slackening late in the afternoon. When it was over, Andrew Lewis's brother Charles and seventy-five other Virginians were dead, while an additional 140 were wounded, including Colonel William Fleming, whose lung protruded out of a hideous hole in his chest. As one Virginia officer put it, "We had a very hard day." The Virginians were unable to ascertain how many of Cornstalk's men they had killed. The Natives were defeated but not annihilated. The size and scope of the fight surprised the colonists. "Such a battle with Indians, it is imagined, was never heard of before," one wrote in a letter that ended up being published all over North America.[77]

The noise of Point Pleasant reverberated over the river's surface. More than forty miles away, Dunmore could hear the gunfire. On the battlefield the sounds of human suffering—endemic throughout Ohio that year—soon replaced the clatter of war. "The Hidious Cries of the

Enemy and the groans of our wound[ed] men lying around was Enough to shudder the stoutest heart," wrote one haunted Virginian. Another was equally unnerved by the racket: "The cries of our wounded prevented our resting any that night."[78]

The political consequences of what had happened that day also resonated throughout Ohio. Dunmore immediately ordered his men to march west from Fort Gower to the main Shawnee villages on the Scioto River, eighty miles away. When they arrived on Pickaway Plains, near to Cornstalk's Town and other principal Shawnee settlements (today between Circleville and Chillicothe, Ohio), they began to build an armed camp, which they named Charlotte in honor of the queen.

While the Virginians marched through his homeland, Cornstalk held another council. The Shawnees' capacity to resist wasn't destroyed, but Lewis was also making plans to move his bloodied, infuriated soldiers across the Ohio River and would soon reinforce the governor. Cornstalk

Figure 23. The elm tree that would become known as the Logan Elm, photographed by the Ohio Writers' Project in the 1930s.

knew it was unwise to continue. In order to prevent further destruction, he sent a messenger to Dunmore that the Shawnees would sue for peace.

Cornstalk's initial request was that Dunmore send a friendly envoy, someone he could converse with who "understood their language." The governor happened to have someone in his entourage that fit the bill perfectly: Koonay's husband, John Gibson. He dispatched Gibson to the Shawnee villages to meet with Cornstalk. About three miles to the southwest of Dunmore's encampment, the Shawnee leadership had gathered near a small tributary that meandered through the Pickaway Plains called Congo Creek. Even today, this is a broad, open, beautiful space. As Gibson, Cornstalk, and other Native principals sat together and discussed arrangements for the peace conference, Logan arrived.

It's not clear whether Gibson had seen his now infamous brother-in-law in the six months since Yellow Creek. Gibson had often visited the Ohio villages and was in Wakatomika shortly before its destruction in August, not long after Logan had arrived there with his first captives from the Monongahela. Logan was, however, clearly upset when he found Gibson. He interrupted their deliberations and asked Gibson to go for a walk with him. He had more "emotion work" to do.

What happened next would become one of the most enduring controversies in American folklore. In 1800, Gibson testified that he and Logan "went into a copse of wood, where they sat down" together underneath the branches of an enormous elm tree that purportedly was over a hundred feet tall and spread out more than 150 feet across. "After shedding [an] abundance of tears," Logan delivered to him the speech that would become celebrated as Logan's Lament.[79]

Logan began his testimony with Scripture. Recall how one of Shickellamy's sons, probably Logan himself, retorted when a settler assumed that Natives were not familiar with the Bible. "O!, a great many people (meaning the Indians) on the Mohawk River, can read the Buck [book] that speaks of God," he said to Archibald Loudon's father nine years before. Logan's remarks started with a paraphrase of Matthew

25:35–36—Jesus's instruction that Christians must take care for one another if they wanted to ascend into heaven: "For I was an hungred, and ye gave me meat: I was thirsty, and ye gave me drink: I was a stranger and ye took me in: Naked and ye clothed me."[80]

Logan cleared his throat and began, "I appeal to any white man, if he entered Logan's cabin hungry, and he gave him not meat; if ever he came cold and naked, and he clothed him not." Then Logan shifted from Christian charity to history, specifically his refusal to take part in the traumas of the 1750s–60s which had engulfed him and his brothers. "During the course of that long and bloody war, Logan remained idle in his cabin, an advocate for peace," he insisted. He was right: the Shick-ellamy brothers had tried to stay out of the fighting during the Seven Years' War and Pontiac's War. "Such was my love for the whites, that my countrymen pointed as they passed, and said, 'Logan is the friend of white men,'" he continued, perhaps recalling to mind the hunters in the remote woods along the Juniata River who befriended him a few years before he migrated to Ohio.[81]

But then he reached his limit.

I had even thought to have lived with you, but for the injuries of one man, Col. Cresap, the last spring, in cold blood, and unpro-voked, murdered all the relations of Logan, not sparing even my women and children. There runs not a drop of my blood in the veins of any living creature. This called on me for revenge. I have sought it: I have killed many: I have fully glutted my vengeance. For my country, I rejoice at the beams of peace. But do not harbour a thought that mine is the joy of fear. Logan never felt fear. He will not turn on his heel to save his life. Who is there to mourn for Logan?—Not one.

Logan had said all he needed to say. Gibson put down his pen. This speech, unlike Robinson's note, was not intended for a specific audience, although it is assumed Logan meant it for Dunmore. Logan would not attend the Treaty of Camp Charlotte. If the governor wanted to know why he would not participate, here was his explanation. Logan promised his revenge was complete. He again hoped for peace.[82]

Many at the time and since depicted Logan's revenge as an outburst, an emotional release of pent-up grief, rage, and frustration. His rendering of his actions as "fully glutting his vengeance" in the lament contributed to this, adding to the notion that this was how a savage would react to trauma. But it was also something more than just an eruption of emotion. Logan's raids, especially in August and September, were not simply a paroxysm of murder. The screams of the Roberts, Snidow, Lybrook, and Spicer children certainly stayed with Logan, but he also knew that those could very easily be replaced by even more screams from the children of his own people, as they had been at Conestoga and Yellow creeks. There was strategy and purpose behind the vengeful deeds that he claimed in the lament.

Gibson folded up his transcription, the two kinsmen bid one another good-bye, and the trader returned to his meeting with Cornstalk and the other Shawnee leaders. The words he had spoken and the translations Gibson made were eloquent, but both speaker and transcriber knew that what Logan was saying was not truthful. Both knew that Logan's family was not extinguished at Yellow Creek. His brother Tachnedorus, nephew Tod-kah-dos, and Koonay's infant daughter all still lived. Moreover, it's probable that Gibson also knew Logan's fixation on Michael Cresap was equally incorrect. Someone had brought his now motherless daughter from William Crawford to Gibson in the weeks after Yellow Creek, perhaps even Crawford himself. It is unlikely they didn't discuss how she had come into his care and who was to blame for it. Even if they didn't, it is just as unlikely that Gibson hadn't personally inquired into the details of his wife's murder. He had to know that this was not the doing of just one man, but the actions of Greathouse, Baker, and many accomplices.

But Logan clung to his conviction that it was all Michael Cresap's fault. Ohio Natives remained convinced that he had orchestrated the massacre. All Logan had said and done since Yellow Creek suggested that he believed Cresap was solely responsible. He had gone first to the Redstone region to begin his raids, and in his first rehearsal of this speech, Robinson's note, he had addressed all of his words directly to Cresap. Witnesses who engaged with Logan in 1774 reported he was clearly obsessed with this one man.

Logan's fixation of blame for Yellow Creek onto Michael Cresap in this speech would generate controversy for decades. As we have seen, Logan was not the only one to pin on Cresap all the bloodshed that the massacre at Baker's Bottom spawned. Colonial leaders and the most influential imperial officials alike did so, too. Anyone who read a colonial newspaper in the last half of 1774 likely read his name in connection with the ongoing troubles in Ohio. And, as Logan or Gibson did in transcribing the speech, newspaper printers also confused Captain Michael with his father Colonel Thomas Cresap. In the decades to come, many parties—either because of their connection to the Cresap family, because of politics, or because they were fascinated with the epic drama that had played out on the Ohio in 1774—would criticize Logan and his promoters for slandering the name of Michael Cresap. At the time, however, it is important to point out that many Americans, not just Logan, believed he—and he alone—was responsible for the horrors of Yellow Creek.

Logan's Lament was a speech only a Shickellamy could give. The second-born son of the Shamokin ambassador delivered it, but it was decades in the making. For generations this family had tried to encourage coexistence, even to the detriment of their own people. They had bent—contorted, really—themselves to find peace and common ground. While many others around them had sowed bewilderment and chaos to try to better their positions, they had chosen not to do so. They had suffered for this and watched all their family's influence dissolve.

Either Logan said it or Gibson translated it this way, but race was the central trope of Logan's Lament. It captured how more and more Americans had begun to conceive of the differences between colonists and Natives in the years since Shickellamy's death in 1748. The horrific violence of the past quarter century had contributed to the emergence of a new barrier. Now, more than land divided them. Ideologies of race had started to surface and drive them apart, too. White people and his people could not do it; they could not get along. What Logan also lamented was the death of what his family had tried for decades to achieve. Not only would the Shickellamys be extinguished, Logan realized, but the Shickellamy way had died, too. Settler colonists like the Cresaps had finally provoked him to terrible things, including acts that mimicked those of Shingas the avenger. The destruction of his kin at Yellow Creek was a harbinger of the future. Soon he feared there would be no more Native people left alive.

Gibson walked the three miles back to Camp Charlotte, arriving at dusk with the good news that Cornstalk and the Shawnee agreed to discuss terms and that a prisoner release was in the offing. He informed the governor that Logan and several of his Mingo followers would not participate. One officer remembered hearing both Gibson and Dunmore read Logan's speech aloud multiple times in the camp. George Rogers Clark would later say that when it was recited to the soldiers it produced a laugh. "The army knew it to be wrong" that Logan blamed everything on Cresap, he said. Logan's Lament "displeased" Michael, Clark recalled. He remembered telling the accused Michael "must be a very great man, that the Indians palmed everything that happened on his shoulders." Twenty-five years later, Clark hadn't forgotten Michael's startling response to his joke: "He smiled and said that he had an inclination to tomahawk Greathouse for the murder."[83]

With feelings running this high, it was probably for the best that Logan declined to participate in the proceedings at Camp Charlotte. Not only was Michael there—and sulking—but there were three other Cresap boys in his unit. Three of his older brother Daniel's sons—Lieutenant Michael Cresap (twenty-four), Lieutenant Daniel Cresap Jr. (twenty-one) and Sergeant Joseph Cresap (nineteen)—were with their uncle's company. Nor was that all. Two Cresap cousins on their mother's side who *had* killed Logan's kin were there. Another of the actual Yellow Creek murderers, Benjamin Tomlinson, was officer of the day at Camp Charlotte. Had Logan accompanied Gibson back to camp, it would've been Tomlinson he would have met first, as he was the outward sentry.

He would have faced many of the people who he thought had killed his family, and some of those who actually had done so.[84]

As a sign of good faith, Logan promised to release any of the captives he had taken. Betsy Spicer, John Roberts Jr., and William Robinson chose to return to colonial society. The two enslaved men taken at the Clinch River went back also, although whether they did so of their own volition is unclear. Theophilus Snidow and Betty's brother William Spicer decided to remain with their adopted Native families.[85]

With the news that Lewis's men would arrive at any moment, Cornstalk and the Shawnees were motivated to work quickly. The Treaty of Camp Charlotte concluded two days after Lewis had gotten the main body of his army across the Ohio. In order to end things now, Cornstalk agreed to each of Dunmore's demands: to cede to Virginia all the lands south of the Ohio River, to deliver up all prisoners, to open trade with Virginia (not just Pennsylvania), and to allow free passage on the Ohio River.

Because of the hurried nature of things, the Camp Charlotte agreement was more of an interim accord than a settled treaty. Both sides agreed that they would revisit issues again the following spring in a subsequent meeting at Pittsburgh. To ensure the Natives would hold to this agreement, Dunmore demanded Shawnee hostages. He stipulated that a few leaders or their sons were to be sent to Williamsburg and another dozen were to be detained in Pittsburgh to ensure peace. Cornstalk assented. It was done. On October 20, the same day the delegates to the First Continental Congress approved their most consequential measure—the wide-ranging, stinging, non-consumption, non-importation boycott known as the Continental Association—the Treaty of Camp Charlotte concluded. Dunmore's War was over.

The governor rode personally to Lewis's approaching force to inform them they wouldn't be plundering and pillaging Shawnee towns on the Scioto after all. They did not take this news well. Long after, Lewis's son remembered his father telling him how upset his men were at this; he recalled having to triple the guard around his tent to protect him from the wrath of angry Virginians who felt betrayed that they weren't going to lay waste to the Shawnee. Dunmore ordered them home.[86]

It is an understatement to suggest that Lord Dunmore was an arrogant man. What he achieved at Camp Charlotte, however, was worthy of pride. Dunmore could've unleashed the very willing Virginians on the Scioto villages and inflicted much more violence on Ohio. It is to his credit that he didn't. When word got out of the lenient deal he struck with Cornstalk, Dunmore's imperial colleagues were pleased. His enemies were surprised. It must've left a bitter taste in Arthur St. Clair's mouth when he admitted the conflict had "come to a much better end than there was any reason to have expected."[87]

Dunmore packed quickly to return east. In his baggage, filed away among his papers, was a copy of Logan's speech. The governor didn't wait for his troops to strike camp; he would travel back alone. He had pressing business back in Williamsburg—and a triumph to celebrate.

In the last week of October, the members of First Continental Congress wrapped up their business in Philadelphia and returned home. At that same moment, the Virginians were also returning to their camps on the Ohio River and then to their homes. On November 5, some of Dunmore's officers gathered back at Fort Gower. Without the governor among them, they felt free to discuss the other issue on their minds: what was going on in Boston and Philadelphia. The officers even decided to write up resolutions in support of colonial resistance: "We can live weeks without bread or salt . . . [and] sleep in the open air without any covering but that of the canopy of Heaven," they crowed. "Our men can march and shoot with any in the known world. Blessed with these talents, let us solemnly engage to one another and to our country in particular, that we will use them to no purpose but for the honor and advantage of America in general, and of Virginia in particular." In what became known as the Fort Gower Resolves, the officers, which included Adam Stephen, William Crawford, Angus MacDonald, Daniel Morgan, George Rogers Clark, and four members of the Cresap clan, pledged their "most faithful allegiance" to the king, but:

as the love of Liberty, and attachment to the real interests and just rights of America outweigh every other consideration, we resolve that we will exert every power with us for the defence of American liberty, and for the support of her just rights and privileges; not in any precipitate, riotous, or tumultuous manner, but when regularly called forth by the unanimous voice of our countrymen.

What Michael Cresap and his colleagues wrote up at Fort Gower was the first public statement issued in America that suggested colonists employ arms against the British. As much as it pledged fealty to George III and promised to operate within the bounds of civility, the Fort Gower Resolves were a military threat. The officers who just defeated Cornstalk's Shawnees thought they could easily take on British redcoats. Whether other Americans agreed—or actually wanted men like Michael Cresap to come to their rescue—remained to be seen.[88]

Lord Dunmore arrived back at the Governor's Palace late on Sunday afternoon, December 4, where he was introduced to his new daughter, born the morning before. The newspapers reported that the "young Virginian is in perfect health." Her father arrived home to a hero's welcome. The town officers of Williamsburg published their appreciation, taking "the earliest Opportunitty of Congratulating your Lordship on the Conclusion of a dangerous and fatiguing Service." He was flush with a newfound love for the province he tried so hard not to govern. Given these warm feelings for kith, kin, and colony, it made perfect sense that Lord and Lady Dunmore would bestow upon the infant the name Virginia.[89]

While Lady Dunmore's enslaved servants took care of baby Virginia, the governor gathered himself to write the long, involved, detailed report to Lord Dartmouth about all he had been doing over the last several months. Keeping with Dunmore's custom, he kept his superiors waiting for weeks after his return. This delay was perhaps partly explained by the significant rebellion that was beginning to take hold. As he was on his way home, the Continental Association went into effect, ratcheting up resistance to him and other imperial officials. Throughout December, Virginia counties gathered together to create local committees to monitor Congress's boycott. Notices of their elections filled the columns of the Williamsburg newspapers that month. Even more distressing, on December 22, Dunmore must have been aggravated to read in the *Virginia Gazette* threatening resolutions drafted by the officers of the army that had gathered under his authority, at a place named for his patron, just after he left them.[90]

On Christmas Eve, he finally wrote his report to Dartmouth. This was an important letter, especially as the last dispatch Dunmore had received from London, dated September 8, was a sharp rebuke: Dartmouth reminded the Virginia governor that it was the Crown's express order not to grant any lands. What he was doing was met with the king's "just displeasure." This was a warning, a way of putting Dunmore "more upon on his guard for the future."[91]

Dunmore, of course, had not complied with the directive and went ahead with prosecuting an unlicensed war. He had, therefore, quite a bit of explaining to do. Like Logan, Dunmore went back decades to recite the full history of why relations had devolved in Ohio this year. He confessed that Americans were impossible to restrain from going west. "They acquire no attachment to place" and "wandering about seems engrafted in their nature." They ignore all prohibitions, and conflicts naturally arise.[92]

He then recounted what happened at Yellow Creek. Dunmore knew that British army officers had told Dartmouth that the April 30 massacre was all Cresap's doing and assured him that this intelligence, fueled by Pennsylvanians, was incorrect. Dunmore said that Michael Cresap had committed violence on the river before Yellow Creek, but insisted he had nothing to do with the "extraordinary degree of cruelty and inhumanity" Greathouse and Baker displayed that morning.[93]

Dunmore didn't need any more ammunition to increase his anger at Pennsylvanians, but he had recently gotten just that. At some point shortly after his return to Williamsburg, Dunmore received a letter from Thomas

Cresap. Cresap informed the governor that the Pennsylvania traders were already trying to undo his glorious achievement in Ohio. They were sending "large quantities of Powder and Lead" and doing their best "to spirit up the Indians to go to war against your government" again. "They tell the Indians that your Lordship intends to fall on them in the spring," Cresap wrote. If only Dunmore would've "hanged some of them who Deserved it!" Thomas vented his long-standing hatred of the Pennsylvanians who he knew had "represented me and my son in very dark Colours to the Board of Trade" and anyone in London who would listen. "It is no more than what they have done before. Did they not in the year 36 burn my house and all that?" If only he could go directly to the Board of Trade, he "could make" the Penns "as Black as the greatest villain that was ever hanged at Tyburn."[94]

We can't be sure that Cresap's vitriolic letter reached the governor before he dispatched his report, but it does seem so: Dunmore's fury toward the Pennsylvanians—and his efforts to shield the Cresaps from blame—were on full display in his missive to Dartmouth. "The trade carried on with the Ohio Indians has been almost engrossed by the province of Pennsylvania," Dunmore told the secretary of state, all but paraphrasing Cresap. "The traders in general are composed of some of the most worthless subjects such as fail in all other occupations and have become in a manner outcasts of society. These men, we have full proof, have made it their constant business to discredit the Virginians . . . and make the Indians consider them in the most odious light." The Pennsylvanians, he continued, had attacked him, John Connolly, and the poor Cresap family, and they have been duping everyone with bad information. To counter these lies, Dunmore foisted his own falsehoods. "I make no doubt," he exclaimed, that certain British officers "will be ashamed" when they learn that "there is no Colonel Cressop except an old man of ninety years of age and who is and always was an inhabitant of Maryland." Dunmore knew quite well that his friend Thomas Cresap, the man at whose house he stayed a few months back and was his chief source of information in the backcountry, was far more active and involved than this portrayal of him as a doddering old man.[95]

But this was essential. Dunmore used the Cresaps to blur the real issue. He skirted the real problem of his granting lands where he was not authorized, and instead focused on reputations and calumny. By attacking the Pennsylvanians as character assassins and manipulators of news, he shifted attention away from the war he had prosecuted without permission. Dunmore hadn't initiated the conflict, but, by reacting the way he did, emboldening the men he did, and carrying the sword to Point Pleasant and the Pickaway Plains, he did turn it into Dunmore's War, a stunning victory for Virginia, for Britain, for speculators—and for settler colonists.

＝＝＝

January 18, 1775, was a banner day for the Dunmore family. In the morning, they went to Bruton Parish Church for the baptism of the baby Virginia, and that evening they hosted a gala. Ostensibly, the ball was a celebration of Queen Charlotte's birthday—and parties such as these were happening throughout the empire that day—but the guests who crowded into the Governor's Palace that night were really there to celebrate Dunmore's triumph and peace in the west.

It is likely that at least some of the conversation at the ball that evening was about Logan. More than twenty years later, Thomas Jefferson remembered the stir Logan's Lament made in Williamsburg. "When

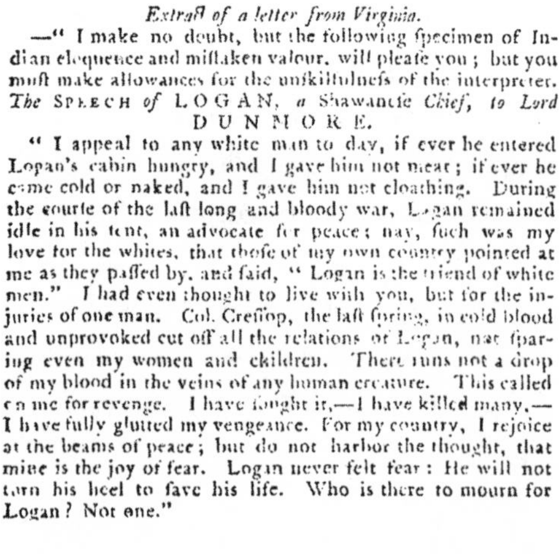

Extract of a letter from Virginia.
—" I make no doubt, but the following specimen of Indian eloquence and mistaken valour, will please you ; but you must make allowances for the unskilfulness of the interpreter. *The* SPEECH *of* LOGAN, *a* Shawanese Chief, *to Lord* DUNMORE.

" I appeal to any white man to say, if ever he entered Logan's cabin hungry, and I gave him not meat ; if ever he came cold or naked, and I gave him not cloathing. During the course of the last long and bloody war, Logan remained idle in his tent, an advocate for peace : nay, such was my love for the whites, that those of my own country pointed at me as they passed by, and said, " Logan is the friend of white men." I had even thought to live with you, but for the injuries of one man. Col. Cresnop, the last spring, in cold blood and unprovoked cut off all the relations of Logan, nor sparing even my women and children. There runs not a drop of my blood in the veins of any human creature. This called on me for revenge. I have sought it,—I have killed many,— I have fully glutted my vengeance. For my country, I rejoice at the beams of peace ; but do not harbor the thought, that mine is the joy of fear. Logan never felt fear : He will not turn his heel to save his life. Who is there to mourn for Logan ? Not one."

Figure 24. Original publication of Logan's Lament, with Madison's introduction, *Pennsylvania Journal*, 1 February 1775.

Lord Dunmore returned from the expedition against the Indians," he would write in 1797, "he and his officers brought the speech of Logan and related the circumstances of it. These were so affecting, and the speech itself so fine a morsel of eloquence that it became the theme of every conversation, in Williamsburg particularly, and generally indeed wheresoever any of the officers resided or resorted." With everyone talking about it so, Jefferson jotted down the text of this remarkable speech early in 1775.[96]

He wasn't the only young Virginian impressed with Logan's Lament. Two days after the governor's gala, James Madison, then about to turn twenty-four and just elected to Orange County's committee to uphold the Association, sent a copy of Logan's speech to his friend from Princeton, William Bradford. Where Madison had obtained a copy of the speech is not known, but he thought his college friend, whose brother and father were co-printers of the *Pennsylvania Journal*, would want it. "I have not seen the following in print," Madison wrote, "and it seems to be so just a specimen of Indian Eloquence and mistaken Valour that I think you will be pleased with it." Bradford was, indeed. He "admired the nervous and untutor'd eloquence of it." The last line, Bradford replied to Madison, "is particularly pathetic and expressive; it raises a crowd of Ideas & at once sets in strong light the Barbarity of Cressop, the sufferings of Logan, and his contempt of death." He immediately sent it to his brother.[97]

On February 1, 1775, Logan's Lament made its first printed appearance in Bradfords' *Pennsylvania Journal*. It was introduced with Madison's line about eloquence and mistaken valor, albeit without naming the contributor. Three days later, a slightly different edition appeared in the *Virginia Gazette*. From there, it went across North America, published in Connecticut, New York, Massachusetts, and Rhode Island, usually prefaced with Madison's words. It even, as Jefferson later recalled, "flew thro' . . . the magazines and other periodical publications of Great Britain." In the following decades, it would become one of the most famous speeches in American history.[98]

1774 had been a year full of disturbing sound. We know this in reference to the imperial crisis. In the growing rift with Britain, colonists listened to strange noises: speeches and resolutions condemning Parliament, the clamor of British military operations in Massachusetts, the odd notion of making "common cause" with Boston being shouted throughout the land, and the gaveling to order of a Continental Congress in Philadelphia. Those sounds were dissonant at the time, but because they would soon become associated with liberation and national independence, they would be remembered as sweet harmonies.

In Ohio, there had been many different sounds that year. The people living west of the Appalachians screamed and shouted, groaned and wailed. They endured the noises of massacre and flight, the unnerving sounds of wounded men crying out after battle, villages going up in flames, families being slaughtered, and tramping soldiers on the march. The echoes of clubs crunching bones and rifle reports bounced off hillsides and skipped across the water. They spoke to one another in private about their grief, made public accusations and justifications, delivered messages at treaty conferences, and barked bitter recriminations.

By the winter of 1775, the cacophonous assault of noise that was Dunmore's War had tapered down to whispers. It had been a year filled with expressions of sombre pride, ruthless power, craven terror, and intense and hopeless despair. But now, all that remained was nearly inaudible. One legacy was a new way to achieve silence. Natives turned Michael Cresap's "detestable" name into a way of "quieting or stilling their children," one missionary living in Ohio remembered long after Dunmore's War. "I have heard them say, Hush! Cresap will fetch you, whereas otherwise, they name the Owl."[99]

The other remnant sounds of the horror of 1774 were of printers' journeymen quietly reciting Logan's Lament to themselves as they set the types into place, and the squeak of the printing press as it impressed those characters into the pages of newspapers throughout America.

That act, however, turned the evanescence of utterance into the permanence of print. The publication of Logan's Lament captured the sounds of 1774, fossilizing them in amber for generations to come. Logan's mournful confession—that he had finally reached the breaking point with settlers, that his heart was broken not just because his family was dead but also because his father's dream of getting along with colonists was just as gone, and that, because of the shocking violence of one man, he would die alone, unmourned and unloved—would survive. It did not dissipate under the branches of that elm tree. His intense and hopeless despair would resonate for generations, long after anyone could remember the other sounds of 1774.

This preservation of Logan's speech would have consequences. He had spoken these words in a very particular, very personal context. They were the result of the horror that he beheld in 1774. Logan saw, heard, and felt the darkness that lurked in men's hearts, and in his own, during that terrible time. It confronted him. It compelled him to do despicable things. To children.

The horror, the horror. That was the context of Logan's Lament. Logan recited his speech to Gibson with all this history on his mind: his father's, his kin's, his people's, his own. Gibson later reported how tears streamed down his face as he spoke. What went through his mind? All the violence he had experienced and inflicted? If he closed his eyes could he see the blood and hear the screams of his own people and those upon whom he took his revenge? That trauma found expression in every line of his moving oration.

But now those words were about to enter a new, strange realm. They would be wrenched away from the shady place under the elm tree. They would be removed from the many groves of death that had materialized in 1774, near Yellow, Muddy, Sinking, and Reedy Creeks. Logan's words now entered the notebooks and newspapers of settler colonists; spheres he had no input in or control over. There, they existed in very different, context-free worlds that could and would be replicated over and over, with colonial printers, writers, and readers creating meanings that were far from what Logan intended that October afternoon. His history would be eliminated. His lament would now be used to serve other purposes, to impress all sorts of different audiences, to make comprehensible the incomprehensible. Even he, Soyechtowa, James Logan Shickellamy, would be turned into something else: the mythological Logan, the Mingo Chief. Logan's words now entered the realm of the eternal. His speech, especially the agonizing final line, would soon take on a new history all its own.

PART 3

THE GERMS OF EMPIRE

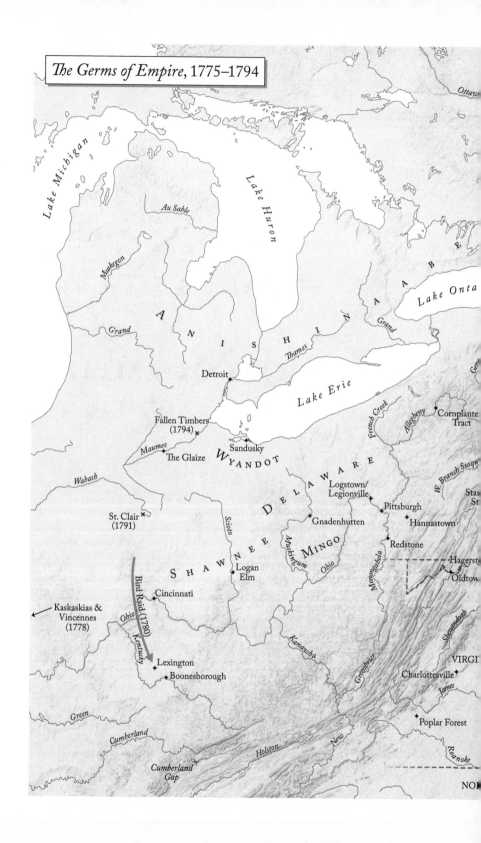

The Germs of Empire, 1775–1794

CHAPTER 9

ON THE THRESHOLD OF GREAT THINGS, 1775–1776

"'I had immense plans,' he muttered irresolutely. . . . 'I was on the threshold of great things,' he pleaded, in a voice of longing, with a wistfulness of tone that made my blood run cold."

—*Heart of Darkness*

A year to the day that Logan made his speech under the elm tree, Michael Cresap breathed his last in a New York City boarding house. He was three hundred miles from Oldtown, and six hundred from that tree, when he slipped into unconsciousness. In his mind, he was on the threshold of great things. He was thirty-three, with a two-week-old son that he hadn't met. The impending loss of all he had killed for must have burdened his mind in that strange sickbed in that strange city in that strange autumn. For the New Yorkers who hefted this unfamiliar yet famous man's coffin into a wagon and paraded it through the city streets, it must've been just as bizarre. By nightfall on October 19, 1775, that casket would lie under freshly turned Manhattan soil, in a privileged spot right up next to Trinity, the oldest Anglican church in the city, at the corner of Broadway and Wall Streets.

Newspapers in New York heaped praises upon the dead man. The summer before, New York printer James Rivington had accused him of killing nearly forty Natives in Ohio. Another printer, Hugh Gaine, had too, declaring that the "destruction lately effected upon the Indians by the son of Col. Cressop . . . will terminate in an Indian war." Printers had called him a cowardly murderer. The obituary that ran in both Gaine's and Rivington's papers struck quite a different tone: "MICHAEL CRES-SOP, Esq., eldest son of Col. Thomas Cressop, of Potomack, in Virginia" had "eminently distinguished himself by his Prudence, Firmness, and Intrepidity as a brave officer" in the recent conflict with the Shawnees. Now, printers opined "by his Death his Country is deprived of a worthy and esteemed citizen." Rivington's *New York Gazetteer* referred to him as "a gentleman of great reputation as a soldier," while the *New York Constitutional Gazette* observed that "his loss is greatly lamented by every well-wisher to the liberties of this once happy country." In the course of a year, Michael Cresap's reputation had been thoroughly—radically—transformed. Or, to be more accurate, it had been revolutionized.[1]

Thirty-eight weeks separated the first appearance of Logan's Lament from the funeral procession in New York City. At any other moment in eighteenth-century America, employing so small a scale of time to measure the transformation of Michael Cresap's reputation would be inconceivable. But during revolutionary times, days and weeks stand in for months and years. When the delegates to the First Continental Congress adjourned in late October of 1774, they made arrangements to reconvene on May 1, 1775, to check on the progress of the resistance measures they had adopted. At nearly the same moment, Shawnee leaders and Lord Dunmore made a similar plan: they would restart negotiations in Pittsburgh the following spring to settle any outstanding disagreements. None of them knew that by then they would be entering the warp speed of revolution time. With the onset of war, all prior plans had to be scrapped.

Revolution time was, for people all over North America, "a time of creation, marked by . . . contingency, fears, and openness," as one historian has written. It was no less a time of uncertainty and confusion. While our efforts to impose order on this moment typically focuses on a select group of people—George Washington, Thomas Jefferson, and the like—the truth is that everyone on the continent had to consider what war with Britain would mean for them. Every actor in this story—Cornstalk, Guyasuta, White Eyes, Captain Pipe, John Killbuck, Lord Dunmore, Guy Johnson, John Connolly, George Croghan, George Rogers Clark, Thomas Cresap, and Logan—had new calculations to make. Each spun up new plans and started negotiations anew in 1775. Michael Cresap had done so, too, which is why he met his end in a place he had never been before. The start of the Revolutionary War initiated an unprecedented period of bewilderment all over the British Empire.[2]

Moreover, the redemption of Michael Cresap, at the end of his life and after death, reveals more than just the bewilderment of 1775 as a state of mind. The celebration of Cresap's march to Boston and his Manhattan funeral also illustrates how Revolutionary leaders embraced it as a state of play.

Patriots broadcast that they grieved Michael Cresap in terms of the loss to his country because he was such a "worthy and esteemed citizen." No one really knew what those words meant in 1775: "country" or "citizen." The process of defining those terms was an essential part of the creativity of the American Revolution. As patriot leaders worked to resolve Revolutionary bewilderment by writing constitutions based on republican citizenship and building a confederated union of states, they also developed cultural efforts of resolving it through the promotion of a new national American patriotism. They had to simultaneously define *both* "country" and "citizen." The turning of Michael Cresap from a "worse savage" to an "esteemed citizen" accomplished just that. He embodied what this new thing, a republican American citizen, looked and acted like.

Cresap's transformation into a hero, however, was an early sign that this confusing civil war might not be good for Native peoples living in the Ohio Valley and elsewhere. Although it was at no time inevitable, leaders of the Revolution boasted that with the creation of a new republic, America stood on the threshold of great things. The union of republican states would resolve imperial bewilderment, but only to the advantage of white settlers. The benefits of the Revolution would apply to all of them, whether Pennsylvanians or Virginians, in the backcountry and everywhere in the United States, but largely for no one else. The Revolution would change many thousands of peoples' lives in Native North America. If Logan wept under his elm tree in 1774 about how his people had suffered from the wrath of colonial subjects of the Crown, he had little clue what would lay in store once they became American citizens.

It took six days for the news of the fighting at Lexington and Concord to reach the Shenandoah Valley. At 5 p.m. on April 25, a printer in Lancaster, Pennsylvania, published a broadside announcing the event. It would not take much longer for the wagon roads leading south out of Lancaster to carry the word to Cresap family members on the Potomac and then over the mountains to Redstone.[3]

The news collided with people already in a hurry. With peace restored in Ohio, in the spring of 1775 colonists began to scurry over the mountains, laying claim to valuable Kentucky lands. The cessation of war with the Shawnees didn't translate into an end to hostilities between Virginia and Pennsylvania at the Forks, though. Dunmore's victory emboldened Virginians to double-down on their claims to the Upper Ohio Valley. In February, the court for the West Augusta district of Virginia met for the first time at Fort Dunmore to dole out rewards. George Croghan, having transferred his loyalties once more back to Virginia, gaveled the court to order, with John Gibson and John Connolly also serving as magistrates. Michael Cresap was another recipient of these fruits of victory, as the new court issued him a license to operate the first ferry service across the Monongahela River at Redstone. Family history repeated itself almost exactly: as his father had done four decades earlier, Michael became a ferryboat operator in a context of vicious intercolonial conflict.[4]

Using both legal and extralegal methods, Dunmore's men tightened their grip on Pittsburgh. Arthur St. Clair reported that a party of armed Virginians had broken into the Westmoreland County jail in late December to free some of their friends, and then returned to do it again in early February. Pennsylvania magistrates begged Governor Penn for his assistance, crying, "Our difficulties on account of the Connolly Party is now grown to an Extreme." Things were so tense in February that Connolly, who had started on a trip to Williamsburg to meet with Dunmore about Native matters, only made it as far as Winchester before being compelled to return immediately. He sent a servant in his place armed with a packet of papers, including a letter for Washington that he would personally deliver to Mount Vernon. It is very likely that the servant Connolly trusted with this political errand was an Englishman named William Cowley; if so, as we will see, this would not be the only time his path would cross George Washington's.[5]

Michael Cresap also felt a deep sense of urgency that spring. Even though he had a pregnant wife in Oldtown and a brand-new business venture in Redstone, he made hasty preparations to head west. He needed to hustle if he wanted to secure valuable lands in the territory that he and his fellow settler-soldiers had wrested from the Shawnees. "What a buzzel is amongst the people about Kentuck," one Virginian commented in the spring of 1775. "To hear people speak of it one would think it was a new found Paradise." Another estimated that five hundred people were on their way to this "paradise." Michael couldn't afford to hesitate. He hired a party of laborers and headed down the Ohio to Kentucky.[6]

One of the people Cresap was racing to stay ahead of was a young Englishman named Nicholas Cresswell. Soon after his ship landed in America, Cresswell began to note distressing developments in his diary: "all was confusion," the king was "openly cursed" and "everything was ripe for rebellion" in Alexandria, Virginia, at the end of October 1774. Cresswell struggled to keep his disapproval of this behavior to himself. "It is as much as a person's life is worth to speak disrespectfully of Congress," he recorded. As the committees proliferated, they began to target spies, and soon Cresswell found it best to leave the tidewater and make his way west. "The people are arming and training in every place. They are all liberty mad," he wrote in February 1775.[7]

Cresswell signed on to become a trading agent in the Illinois country. In April, he had crossed the Alleghanies, bound for Pittsburgh. Two days before the battle on Lexington Green, he met John Connolly for the first time, finding him a "haughty and imperious man." A few days later, as the news of the fighting in Massachusetts began to spread, he climbed into a canoe to go down the Ohio, where he witnessed the aftermath of Dunmore's War. He paddled by Yellow Creek on almost the exact anniversary of the massacre, and found it deserted. "Not a house to be seen in forty miles," he noted. All around, he said, the area was "very thinly inhabited. The few there is are in general great rascals."[8]

Cresswell arrived in Wheeling on May 4, 1775. By then, Williamsburg knew of the bloodshed at Concord Bridge. The news was thundering through the Shenandoah Valley during those very same hours, reaching Augusta County the next morning. At Wheeling, Cresswell's party ran into George Rogers Clark. Soon, Clark would become a Revolutionary hero, earning the nickname Conqueror of the Illinois, but at that moment he only considered himself to be, like his friend and associate Michael Cresap, a scout, ranger, and land speculator. Cresswell liked Clark, calling him an "intelligent man," and they decided to join forces and go together to Kentucky. A few days later, Clark and Cresswell cooked supper at Fort Gower, also deserted, and met with a few scared colonists who "gave us very bad encouragement" for what was happening downriver. So many colonists were sprinting west that the Natives had "broken out again," they said. Cresswell confessed his men were frightened, but they continued. At Point Pleasant, Cresswell and Clark found a hundred men. There the rumors were even darker, and Cresswell's "companions were exceedingly fearful" of Native violence. They had a meeting to decide whether to continue. "After much altercation," they resolved to proceed down to the Kentucky River.[9]

Cresswell thought his party a "set of Dammd Cowards," but this mystifying journey was starting to test his mettle, too. As they drifted into unfamiliar territory, he soon "did not know where they were." He was completely unused to this country. Ticks and rattlesnakes plagued their party. One night, stampeding buffalo plunged into the river right where their canoes were tied up, leaping over one sleeping man and smashing a canoe full of provisions. Cresswell claimed that he "slept sound and undisturbed, tho' some of the company were kept in perpetual alarm by the barking of the dogs and their own fears." When it was his turn to walk on the shoreline to scout out territory, he found it "disagreeable[,] clambering over gullies and wading amongst the weeds as high as my head in some places and raining all the forenoon." On May 21, they found the mouth of the Kentucky River, and turned into it, heading deeper into the continent. Confronted with a swift current and several sets of rapids, they slowly made their way upriver.[10]

Three days later, a figure approached the nervous party. Whether he emerged out of the weeds or paddled across the water, Cresswell didn't say. In the diary, he just materializes in the middle of this strange place, as if appearing out of thin air: "About noon, Captain Michael Cresap met us." Clark greeted his friend warmly. Cresap told Clark he was heading back upriver to Redstone, leaving his men behind. Clark offered to go along, a decision that on its face is a bit perplexing, since it casts him as rather unfocused and peripatetic. Granted, joining Cresap did present Clark with the opportunity to ditch this fussy, suspicious Englishman, but perhaps there was more to the offer than a chance to be with a comrade. Did Clark sense his friend was going to need help getting home?[11]

Neither Cresswell nor Clark let on that Cresap appeared ill, but in a few weeks, he would report feeling "indisposed." It seems likely he had contracted malaria. He certainly had spent lots of time on the water over the last year; in both peace and war, he had been busy clearing shore lands, paddling canoes, marching through marshes, and splashing through creeks. No one, however, reported that Cresap was in anything except peak physical form in 1774. It stands to reason, then, that it was a Kentucky mosquito, of springtime origin, that had infected him.

But mosquitos were not the only danger threatening these explorers. After a few more weeks scouting, Cresswell glumly noted he had to return to Pittsburgh, too. The rumors of Native hostility "had struck such a panic," he wrote in his diary, "I cannot get anyone to go down the Ohio with me on any account. . . . Much provoked at my disappointment." Soon after Cresswell's small group joined the stream of settlers fleeing back to Pittsburgh. They fell in with and joined forces with "nine of Capt. Cresop's people," which increased the size of their party to fourteen. Together, this crew of "two Englishmen, two Irishmen, one Welshman, two Dutchmen, two Virginians, two Marylanders, one Swede, one African Negro, and a Mullato" decided they were better off protecting one another on what might prove a perilous return to the Forks.[12]

By the time Cresswell's party arrived back at Point Pleasant, the camp had been "evacuated." The few remaining colonists did greet them with fresh (though wildly inaccurate) news: "the New Englanders have had a battle with the English troops at Boston and killed seven thousand." After ten more days of arduous paddling, Cresswell was back at Wheeling. He dropped his oar and went overland to Catfish Camp and then on to Redstone, arriving there on July 14. What he found there was the beginning of a world transformed.[13]

While Cresswell was in Kentucky, the first military moves of what would become the Revolutionary War had commenced. The Second Continental Congress had opened at Philadelphia and decided to create ten companies of riflemen—six from Pennsylvania and two each from Virginia and Maryland—to march for Boston. Since they were the first units created outside New England, these rifle companies, drawn from backcountry settlements, were the first foray into creating an American army that was actually "continental." More than that, these were to be the patriots' secret weapon against British redcoats. "These are all said to be all exquisite marksmen," John Adams wrote, and he was gleeful they could "send sure destruction to great distances." On June 15, Maryland's delegates to the Congress wrote to the Frederick County Committee of Correspondence with details about the two units they were responsible to raise. When the committee convened to determine who would command Maryland's rifle companies, they agreed that Michael Cresap was an obvious choice.[14]

One member of the Frederick Committee of Correspondence undoubtedly helped secure Cresap his captain's commission. Thomas Cresap, now nearing eighty years of age, represented Oldtown for the county committee. He also ensured his grandson, also named Michael Cresap (Daniel's oldest son), would serve as lieutenant. Two more grandsons, Daniel Jr. and Joseph, would serve as sergeants in their uncle's company. The four Cresaps who had marched into Shawnee country would now go together to Massachusetts.

As soon as enlistment orders went out, the elderly Cresap immediately started riding around getting his family's military unit organized. He paid a visit to Horatio Gates, a former British officer who had served with Braddock in 1755 and had recently purchased a plantation a few miles south of what is today Shepherdstown, West Virginia. One of the most experienced soldiers in the colonies, Gates was making his own plans to head first to Philadelphia and then on to Boston to join the army. On Monday, June 19, Cresap told Gates they were almost ready to go. Finding volunteers wasn't a problem.[15]

All they were waiting for was Michael. As soon as Thomas had secured a commission for his son, he immediately sent a messenger, John Jeremiah Jacob, Michael's longtime business associate, to find him. Jacob later remembered, "I was dispatched in all haste to give Captain Cresap notice of his appointment, and met him in the Allegheny Mountains on his way."[16]

Jacob was surprised by Michael's reaction. "When I communicated my business and announced his appointment," he remembered fifty years later, "instead of becoming elated he became pensive and solemn, as if his spirits were really depressed." Aided by hindsight, Jacob knew what this trip would ultimately mean for Michael, so this may have shaped his recollection that Cresap "had a presentiment" in their mountain encounter "that this was his death warrant." Then again, maybe Michael did think this trip would kill him, as he was by now showing signs of illness. Jacob recalled that his reluctance at this news stemmed from his feeling that he was "in bad health, and his affairs were in a deranged state." When Jacob told him that Thomas had "pledged himself" that *he* would march at the head of the company if his son couldn't go, "let the consequences be what they might," Michael knew he was stuck. His father wasn't bluffing, not about this. Thomas had informed Gates, too, that if Michael didn't return from Kentucky in time, he would lead the company to Boston personally. When Gates arrived in Philadelphia, he told Connecticut congressman Silas Deane about the elder Cresap's fantastic boast. In a letter home to his wife, Deane related the story, saying "the brave old Colonel," who Deane took to be "ninety-two years of age," was "determine[d] to join the Army, at their head, if his Son should not arrive in Season."[17]

Michael Cresap instructed Jacob to head for Redstone to gather all the men he could find there, while he continued to Oldtown. Jacob went among Cresap's "old companions in arms" in Redstone early in July, right before Nicholas Cresswell strode into town. When Cresswell rested his paddle-weary shoulders at Brown's Tavern in Redstone, he learned that Jacob was "[en]Listing the best riflemen that can be got to go to Boston under Capt. Cressop for the humane purpose of killing the English Officers." To Cresswell's chagrin, Jacob drummed up twenty-two volunteers and accompanied them back to Oldtown to join the others the Cresaps were raising. "Confusion to the Scoundrels," Cresswell sneered to his diary.[18]

Soon after the initial reports from Boston, news began to cross the mountains that another crisis had shaken Williamsburg in late April. During the third week of April, just as British commander General Thomas Gage prepared his redcoats to march for Lexington, enslaved Virginians across five counties along the James River threatened insurrections, and local authorities began to make arrests and mete out executions. In part to prevent its capture by either rebellious slaves or patriot rebels, Dunmore ordered all the gunpowder stored in the capital's magazine to be removed to a nearby British warship. Williamsburg city officials howled in protest, and a confrontation developed. Dunmore, furious at his being questioned, threatened that unless Virginians acquiesced in the removal of the powder, he would "declare freedom to the slaves and reduce the city of Williamsburg to ashes." City officials backed off, but enraged Virginians, including a militia force led by Patrick Henry, threatened to march on the capital.[19]

Throughout May and June, relations between Virginians and their governor would continue to deteriorate. As recently as March 25, Virginia leaders had lavished upon their governor "cordial thanks . . . for his truly noble, wise, and spirited conduct" in the west. Seventy-five days later, on June 8, Dunmore and his family took refuge upon the *HMS Magdalen*, a Royal Navy vessel in the Chesapeake Bay. They would never return to baby Virginia's birthplace.[20]

The onset of war also created new political imperatives for the Forks. The factions in Pittsburgh had forced settlers to choose in 1774 whether they stood with St. Clair/Penn or with Connolly/Dunmore. War in Massachusetts required them to make a further choice: Whose side were they on now in the imperial crisis? "We have nothing but masters and committees all over the country," St. Clair concluded a few weeks after the news of war arrived, "and every thing seems to be running into the wildest confusion." St. Clair had often complained about "confusion," but this was an entirely new level of bewilderment. The problem of identifying who was a patriot and who was a tory intersected with who was for Virginia and who for Pennsylvania. Over the past three decades, collections of powerful interests—trading firms, land companies, Native confederacies, colonial legislatures, European monarchs and their armies—had all tried to dictate terms at the Forks. But what Nicholas Cresswell watched in horror at Redstone was something utterly new: colonists assembling to kill British redcoats.[21]

What would this escalating conflict mean for John Connolly—a man who owed his entire status, position, and authority to the soon-to-be exiled governor? Connolly began plotting as soon as the news of war in Massachusetts reached Pittsburgh. The confrontation in Williamsburg had prevented Dunmore from following through on his pledge to return to Pittsburgh and finalize arrangements with Ohio Natives, so Connolly assumed the role of lead diplomat. He sent out invitations for Ohio leaders to come collect the Mingo hostages at Fort Dunmore and sit down with him to talk. In a memoir that Connolly would write years later, he boasted that this meeting was his first foray into subverting the "machinations of the Republicans." He claimed he worked diligently "cultivat[ing] the friendship and insinuat[ing] myself into the favor" of the Mingo hostages, "and convinced them of the advantages . . . [of] adhering to the British government." Connolly was sure he could secure the military support of Ohio Natives. If there was to be a split between Dunmore and the Virginians, it stood to reason that Natives might fare better siding with the imperial government rather than men like Cresap and Clark.[22]

But what about the colonists at the Forks? Connolly worried that the "spirit of sedition" was everywhere, but he needed to be certain. He put on "an entertainment" in Pittsburgh and gave "such of my friends as I could best depend on" an opportunity to speak their minds. To his relief, they were "universally enraged against the arbitrary proceedings of the Republican party," and they expressed "a high veneration for his Majesty and the constitution." Reassured that the "demagogues of faction" had not seduced everyone in Pittsburgh, Connolly proceeded to spin up his plans.[23]

Connolly wasn't as sly as he thought he was being. As May turned to June, settlers around the Forks became increasingly concerned about what was being discussed in and around Fort Dunmore, especially as news of the confrontation between Virginians and their royal governor grew more dire. When it became known that Connolly was packing his bags to call on Dunmore, partisans from Westmoreland decided they needed to put an end to the threat Connolly posed to Pennsylvania, as well as to America.

Two days before he was to set off for Williamsburg, a knock on the door roused Connolly's servant out of bed. Under the ruse that he was an express rider from Dunmore, a member of the Westmoreland raiding party was admitted into Connolly's bedroom. As Connolly would later recall, "I drew my curtain, received [the letter] and was breaking open the seal, when the villain seized me by the throat, presented a pistol at my breast, [and] told me I was his prisoner." Connolly submitted, and rode off with a posse of Pennsylvanians into the night, reaching his familiar lodgings in the Westmoreland County jail at ten o'clock the following morning.[24]

News that Pennsylvanians had seized Connolly spread quickly in

Pittsburgh. Connolly's Virginia allies were not going to accept this escalation without a response. A few days after Connolly's arrest, another party of vigilantes gathered to take their revenge. Led by John Gibson's brother George, the settlers who lived on Chartier's Creek had been fierce Virginia partisans throughout the boundary crisis and subsequent war with the Shawnee. "On Major Connolly's being taken," William Crawford's brother wrote to George Washington, "the people of Chartier's came in a company and seized three of the Pennsylvania magistrates," and carried them "in a leaky boat" down to Fort Fincastle at Wheeling "under guard." The political situation at Pittsburgh rested on yet another knife's edge.[25]

George Gibson and the Virginia partisans dispatched a letter to St. Clair demanding Connolly's release, threatening vengeance. St. Clair realized how precarious this situation was and relented, exchanging Connolly for the three Westmoreland officials being held at Wheeling. Connolly immediately sent for George Gibson to thank him personally for securing his freedom. Dunmore's man viewed the Gibson brothers as fellows, and assumed they would be willing partners in the scheme he was planning.[26]

In the last week of June, Michael Cresap spent a few days resting at home in Oldtown. That Thursday, he turned thirty-three. Mary was showing with their next child, who would have to be fitted somewhere into the stone house he had built a dozen years earlier, which was already bursting with young children: Maria (eleven), Elizabeth (seven), Sarah (five), and James (two). She depended on the labor of her enslaved woman, Bett, to make it through. On his previous birthday, he wrote his will. If they held a celebration for Michael this year there would have been far more to cheer, despite the still-recent loss of his mother. The family did have a great deal of business to discuss, as Michael's three nephews and his father conferred about organizing this new rifle company.

There was a palpable sense of urgency. Other companies were mustering nearby, and the Cresaps didn't want to seem laggard. One volunteer remembered that "great exertions were made by each Captain to complete his company," to better gain the glory of being the first to arrive in Massachusetts.[27]

This did appear to be a moment of rhapsodic martial spirit all over the colonies. A young itinerant preacher named Philip Vickers Fithian witnessed it not far from Oldtown, near Winchester, Virginia. "Mars, the great God of Battle, is now honored in every Part of this spacious Colony," he wrote that June, "but here every Presence is warlike, every Sound is Martial! Drums beating, Fifes and Bag-Pipes playing." They looked formidable, Fithian noted. "Every man has a hunting-Shirt, which is the Uniform of each Company—Almost all have a Cockade, & Bucks-Tale in their Hats, to represent that they are hardy, resolute, & invincible Natives of the Woods of America." Fithian, for one, wasn't confused about what would happen next. There was no chance, he wrote, that a few thousand "hireling Regulars" stood a chance against "Millions of America's hardy sons."[28]

There was another face to this martial display and bustle, however. Not two weeks after hearing all the bagpipes and drumming, Fithian captured a more disturbing reality in his journal. On June 17, the day of the tremendous battle at Bunker Hill, Fithian was in Winchester, where he met up with his mentor from New Jersey. He learned from him that the potential civil war that loomed over America had produced a slave insurrection there. The minister told Fithian "the Negroes have, in Pittsgrove [NJ], murdered one Mr. Sherry, and Many are in this Conspiracy." Fithian didn't doubt it. All around him in the Shenandoah Valley, he recognized, "Slaves are running off daily—Servants skulking about, and pilfering—Horses & many other things stolen weekly. Riots on many occasions in most Parts of the Continent—And in every Place much Anxiety and Debt & almost no Attention to Business." Fithian wrung his hands in worry. If "these are only some of the most beautiful Out-Lines of 'Civil Discord'—Great Lord! What then is her real Self!"[29]

There is a considerable amount of American mythology compressed into the spring and early summer of 1775. George Bancroft, the renowned nineteenth-century historian, helped in its construction. "With one impulse the colonies sprung to action," he marveled, as the "voice" of

Lexington and Concord redounded throughout America. This sound "breathed its inspiring word to the first settlers of Kentucky; so that hunters who made their halt in that matchless valley of the Elkhorn, commemorated the nineteenth day of April by naming their encampment LEXINGTON." The journey that the riflemen were about to undertake would also add to this legend, as it would become renowned as the "Bee Line March" to Boston.[30]

But what Fithian and his mentor also understood—and we should also strive to rediscover beneath the obscuring haze of this mythology—was that everyone in North America was trying to figure out what the news of war with Britain would mean for them. Enslaved people in New Jersey, Virginia, and throughout the mainland colonies were considering how this news might affect them, and trying to take advantage of this confused and anxious moment.

So, too, were the Native peoples who lived not only in the "matchless valleys" of Kentucky, but also throughout North America. A few days after his release from the Westmoreland jail, John Connolly convened another treaty conference in Pittsburgh with more than a dozen Ohio Native leaders. White Eyes was there, as was Guyasuta, Captain Pipe, Killbuck, Newcomer, and Custaloga. No Pennsylvanians were invited, but Croghan was present, as was Alexander McKee and Pennsylvania defector William Crawford. They met for more than a week, with Connolly presiding. They begged the Natives to remain "united in friendship" with them and "not to be shaken," but with so many witnesses, Connolly wasn't about to openly make a plea for them to consider taking up arms for the Crown. They talked about Dunmore's War, but not the Revolutionary War. Still, many in the region worried about what role Ohio Natives might play in this new conflict.[31]

They weren't the only ones. The anxiety produced by the so-called "voice" of Lexington centered on Natives almost reflexively. In those same hectic days, while settlers readied their rifles in backcountry settlements and George Washington rode north to take command of a "Continental Army," colonists began to clash with imperial officials over accusations that the British were trying to involve Native peoples in the conflict.

In New York, patriot committees in Schenectady and Albany turned their attention to Indian superintendent Guy Johnson. Johnson's transition to his uncle's job had gone well, and his position with the Six Nations was so solid that he warned patriots not to dare try to take him prisoner. A standoff emerged late in May, with the Mohawks sending a message not to do anything hasty. "He is our property, and we shall not part with him," they informed the Albany Committee of Safety. Concerned patriots in the Upper Hudson region wrote to the Continental Congress, begging for guidance.[32]

At the same time, patriot leaders in South Carolina found themselves in an identical position with Johnson's colleague, the Indian superintendent in the south, John Stuart. Visiting Charleston in June, some Catawba Natives talked openly about offers Stuart had made to them and the Cherokees in exchange for taking up arms against the patriots. The Charleston committee of safety immediately dispatched someone to demand Stuart surrender his letters. Unfortunately for Stuart, those papers contained instructions to his deputy to "use his influence to dispose those people to act in defense of his Majesty and Government, if found necessary." This caused a storm in the capital, and Stuart fled immediately for Florida before patriots could pull down his house and take him prisoner.[33]

Allegations of Stuart and Johnson "tampering" with Native peoples soon became common in American newspapers. Stories about Johnson's having "retired" into Indian country and Canadian Natives "taking up the hatchet" began to circulate late in June. On July 3, Philip Schuyler, the commander of American forces in New York, informed the Continental Congress that, according to prevailing reports, Natives in Canada "have accepted the hatchet offered them" by the governor of Canada, Guy Carleton. This was, Schuyler added, "an evil of the most alarming nature."[34]

Three days later, Congress issued its first address to explain its side of the conflict. Written by Thomas Jefferson and John Dickinson, the "Declaration of the Causes and Necessity of Taking Up Arms" listed the grievances Americans had endured over the past decade, and especially over the past few weeks, even including Schuyler's breaking news from Canada in the last paragraph. Its final justification for why colonists were forced to use arms was in defense against malicious British agents. "We have received certain intelligence that General Carleton, the Governor of Canada, is instigating the People of that Province and the Indians to fall upon us," the address stated. In their private correspondence, delegates asserted these rumors as fact. An appalled Benjamin Franklin wrote to a friend in England the next day that Carleton "has been very industrious in engaging the Indians to begin their horrid Work. This is making War like Nations who never had been friends, and never wish to be such while the World stands." Another delegate wrote, "It is certain" that the British government "has endeavored to let loose the Indians on our Frontiers."[35]

Patriot leaders in Virginia took steps to find out how receptive Ohio Natives might be to these offers. In early July, Virginians appointed six commissioners to go to Pittsburgh to conduct negotiations with Ohio Natives. Even though Connolly was about to open a conference, patriot leaders in Virginia wanted to steer negotiations their way. They wanted to talk to Ohio Natives about the Revolutionary War, not Dunmore's War, with the hopes of getting Shawnees, Delawares, and Mingos to forget those very recent, painful memories. They may have also suspected that John Connolly was another of those Crown officials "tampering" with Native loyalties.[36]

One of the six commissioners, Captain James Wood, was tasked with going into Native villages in the Ohio region to invite leaders to come yet again to Pittsburgh. Wood was at the Forks during the last days of Connolly's conference, and he didn't report any chicanery from Dunmore's man. A week after this conference, Wood then went into the Ohio country to visit the villages, inviting anyone who would listen to return to Pittsburgh for another meeting set to begin on September 10.[37]

Ohio Natives must have found this bewildering. Wood told Cornstalk and other Shawnee leaders he intended to ratify the Camp Charlotte treaty at this upcoming meeting. They were confused—they had just come from a meeting! Who were these patriot commissioners? Were they "Virginia" now? If so, who was Dunmore? Suddenly, there was *yet another* layer of political authority at the Forks. As the colonists split into more and more factions, it was a confounding situation, but not perhaps a terrible one: from the Natives' perspective, this bewilderment might bring new political possibilities.

Along with an interpreter, Wood set off for the Delaware towns in mid-July, talking friendship and peace with anyone who would listen. The strange war with Britain was a frequent topic of conversation. Natives told Wood about how they were "Much Surprized to hear that we were at War with ourselves" and that "they would be glad to know the Cause of the dispute or whether we Expected or desired their Assistance."[38]

It wasn't long before he ran into Logan. Wood was not far from the ruined village of Wakatomika, and it was obvious he and his people were not about to forget what had happened there the previous year. Wood found Logan in company with some of the Mingos who had recently been released after being held as hostages in Pittsburgh since last November. "They all appeared to be Pretty Much in Liquour," Wood wrote in his journal, "and very inquisitive to know my business." They told Wood "the Indians were very Angry," and he saw that "many of them Painted themselves black" when he arrived. While Wood slept that night, a Native kicked him in the head, which woke him, and he saw "several Indians with Knives and Tomahawks" whispering nearby. A sympathetic Native woman "informed us privately that they intended to kill us" and "advised us to hide ourselves in the Woods, which we did till Morning."[39]

Having survived the night, Wood then talked to Logan. Despite all that had transpired over the fourteen months since Yellow Creek, Logan's mind was still singularly fixed on that traumatic April morning. He offered Wood another recitation of his lament: "Logan repeated in Plain English the Manner in which the People of Virginia had killed his Mother, Sister, and all his Relations, during which he wept and Sung Alternately, and concluded with telling me the Revenge he had taken." Much to the disappointment of Wood, Logan had not moved on from the horror of the previous year, and neither, it seemed, had his people.[40]

But this was exactly what the patriots wanted Logan and the Mingos to do. The Virginians were now in revolution; they had entered an entirely new stage, and they wanted Ohio Natives to do the same. Revolutions often require undertaking significant mental gymnastics, including a level of forgetting so thorough that it can resemble cognitive impairment. Insensible experiences—reputations transformed, ancient prejudices overturned, political compromises wholly recalculated—were happening all over America in 1775, as Michael Cresap was about to find out. What Wood and the Virginia patriot leadership asked was for Ohio Natives to inflict collective memory loss upon themselves. Nearly in sight of the wrecked village, the patriots wanted the Mingos, Shawnees, and Delawares not only to forget who had torched Wakatomika, but also to side with them in this new conflict. It was quite a request—and a dangerous one. Logan, who boasted he never felt fear, asked Wood if he was afraid for his life.[41]

Though hostile, the Mingos with Logan allowed Wood to continue his fact-finding/public relations tour of Ohio Native villages. He continued to discuss the Revolution, finding that many had already heard "alarming accounts" that the "White People were all preparing for war." He looped around the settlements along the Scioto and Kentucky Rivers before heading back to Pittsburgh in early August, making his last stop at John Gibson's house. Reporting back to patriot authorities in Richmond, he offered a disturbing prospect for future relations with Ohio Natives. "From every discovery I was able to make," he wrote, "the Indians are forming a General Confederacy against the Colony [Virginia], having been led to believe that we are a people Quite different and distinct from the other Colonies."[42]

The border controversy that had gripped the Forks for the last three years had convinced many Natives in Ohio that colonists were not all alike; they were equally as tribal as they were. This competed with the idea that all whites and all Natives were fundamentally, racially distinct. Logan had reached the latter conclusion after his excruciating trials, and some other Americans in the middle of the eighteenth century had, too. However, it was still plain to most colonists and Natives living in Ohio in the summer of 1775 that Pennsylvanians were not the same as Virginians. The Revolution was about to make an essential intervention into the history of race-making in America, but, at this moment, the inhabitants of the Forks still watched the same story unfold as it had throughout the 1770s: Connolly's partisans faced off against St. Clair's; Penn's men battled Dunmore's.

Making matters worse, Wood pointed out that Pittsburgh was in a "most defenseless situation" since Dunmore and Connolly had disbanded the garrison at the Forks. With all this confusion, Ohio Natives found themselves in a curious position. Perhaps now might be an apt time to strike—either a deal or a blow. In the "Declaration of the Causes and Necessity of Taking Up Arms," Virginia's Thomas Jefferson and Pennsylvania's John Dickinson had boasted that "our union is perfect." Natives knew this was a lie. They were well aware that Virginia and Pennsylvania had been at one another's throats for the past several years, and this animosity had not abated.[43]

The other delegates to Congress actually knew it, too. Though they would never admit so publicly, they recognized this border controversy could spiral into internecine warfare. In July, while Wood was out promoting the patriot cause, nine delegates from the two rival colonies signed a letter imploring the "inhabitants west of the Laurel Hill" to "remove . . . every obstacle that may prevent" them "from co-operating as vigorously as they would wish to do" to defend "the liberties of America." Two of the signatories were Dickinson and Jefferson. They, along with Franklin, Richard Henry Lee, and the other delegates from the rival colonies, begged the colonists to get along. Disband "all bodies of armed men," let everyone out of jail, and establish "public tranquility," they charged, before it's too late.[44]

In short, the Revolution was much more vulnerable at this moment than American mythology admits. Beating drums, marching men, and martial ardor feature in the stories we like to tell ourselves about the response to Lexington and Concord. Those legends belie the confusion of that summer. No one knew what might happen next. People experiencing revolution time had an urgent need to impose sense on disparate and uncertain facts, and most intended to do so in ways that advanced their interests or, at least, mitigated anxieties. Philip Vickers Fithian was deep in the Alleghany Mountains in the middle of July when he heard an "alarming report" of Natives carrying eight horse loads of gunpowder into the woods. "It is shrewdly guessed they have in view some infernal Strategem!" Where was that gunpowder going? Who sent it? Where might it be used? The slightest incident could be an omen of imminent war with British-allied Natives. When colonists found a dead body in a field in Butternuts, New York, they immediately wondered if this was the "commencement of hostilities." Newspaper printers spread that story far and wide. Franklin, Jefferson, Dickinson, and their colleagues in Congress knew the union wasn't as perfect as they boasted. They also knew that Guy Johnson, John Stuart, and Guy Carleton were doing their best to end the rebellion.[45]

Patriot leaders understood they had difficult work to do defusing any and all threats to the imperfect union. Telling the right stories would help the public make sense of the strange circumstances. They had villains. They also needed heroes.

Captain Michael Cresap started his trek to Massachusetts a few days before Wood began his into Ohio. On July 19, Cresap, accompanied by a personal servant, went to Hagerstown to purchase thirty-three rifles. With this final errand, the company was finally ready. Since it was clear their unit wasn't going to have the honor of winning the race to Boston (several companies were far ahead of them), the officers decided the nearly 150 men needed to train and drill, so they made camp in Frederick, Maryland, for a week. Listed among their ranks was Sergeant Daniel Greathouse. One wonders what the four Cresaps made of that particular officer. Michael may or may not have been kidding, but a few months earlier he fumed to George Rogers Clark that he wanted to murder Greathouse for what he had done to the family name. Now Greathouse was a sergeant in Cresap's own rifle company.[46]

The gathering of the riflemen was, for many colonists, a sight to behold. An early summary of what would grow into a phenomenon that year appeared in a Philadelphia paper in mid-July. The rifle companies had "had so many applications," that the recruiting officers could take their pick of the best marksmen. "With a piece of chalk," the observer stated, the officer "drew on a board the figure of a nose of the common size, which he placed at the distance of 150 yards, declaring that those who should come nearest the mark should be enlisted." Sixty men allegedly hit the nose directly, prompting the correspondent to quip, "General Gage, take care of *your* nose!" The fascinating bands of riflemen from Pennsylvania, Maryland, and Virginia marching through their villages captivated colonists who had never seen the like of them before. Many of the rifle companies received a great deal of public attention, but none were more noticed, celebrated, and heralded than Cresap's unit.[47]

A year earlier, Pennsylvania traders and politicians invested in the boundary dispute had fed partisan reports about Michael Cresap to the printers of the *Pennsylvania Gazette*, David Hall Jr. and William Sellers. The *Gazette*, along with other newspapers in Philadelphia and New York, had featured his name as the instigator of mayhem in Ohio all through the summer of 1774. In the columns of the *Gazette*, Cresap was a scoundrel and a coward. He was a ringleader in John Connolly's "gang of *worse* savages."[48]

Now, Hall and Sellers abruptly reversed course. They published a long letter from Frederick with lavish details about Cresap again, but this time as a potential savior of America. This remarkable letter, which also appeared in another Philadelphia paper, a New Haven paper, two in New York City, three in Virginia, and one in both North and South Carolina, reads like a stock description of what would become the quintessential American frontiersman, the word Thomas Cresap had coined to describe himself:

> Painted like Indians, armed with Tomahawks and Rifles, dressed in hunting Shirts and Mockasons, and tho' some of them had travelled near 800 Miles from the Banks of the Ohio, they seemed to walk light and easy, and not with less Spirit than in the first Hour of their

March. Health and Vigour, after what they had undergone, declared
them to be intimate with hardship and familiar with Danger—Joy
and Satisfaction were visible in the Crowd that met them.

Savages no longer, these were natural men, sturdy pioneers. But more
than that, at this particular moment, they were precisely the fighters
that the Revolution needed. "Had Lord North been present," the writer
continued, "and assured that the brave Leader could raise Thousands of
such like to defend his Country, what think you, would not the Hatchet
and the Block have intruded upon his Mind?" The prime minister, in
other words, would've been found guilty and executed in the face of such
a formidable enemy.[49]

The letter also heaped praise upon the company's commander. "I had
an opportunity of attending the Captain during his Stay in town, and
watched the Behavior of his Men and the Manner in which he treated
them." The "brave Leader" received "the most willing obedience," and they
saw him as a "Friend or a Father." Cresap, the writer gushed, took care
of their every want "without any apparent Sense of Fatigue or Trouble;
when Complaints were before him, he determined with Kindness and
Spirit, and on every Occasioned condescended to please without losing
his Dignity."[50]

The letter also exalted the skill of the company. One evening they
held a performance "to show the Gentlemen of the Town their Dexterity
in Shooting." A circle "the Size of a Dollar" was pasted onto a board, and
the men scampered about shooting at it. "Some lay on their backs, some
on their breasts and side, others ran 20 or 30 steps and firing." All struck
true, the writer claimed. One especially brave soldier then grasped the
board and held it over his head while his brother "very coolly" shot at the
mark. "But will you believe me when I tell you that one of the Men took
the board and placing it between his Legs, stood with his Back to the
Tree," while another took aim and shot right in the center of the board.[51]

The writer was overcome with all that he had seen. He provided
the only conclusion that could be drawn from such a display of heroism,
valor, expertise, and power:

What would a regular Army, of considerable Strength in the Forest of America do with 1000 of these men, who want nothing to
preserve their Health and Courage, but Water from the Spring,
with a little parched Corn, and what they can easily procure in
Hunting; and who, wrapped in their Blankets in the Damp of
Night, would choose the Shade for a Tree for their Covering and
the Earth for their Bed?

With men like these, America couldn't possibly lose.[52]

On August 1, Cresap's riflemen broke camp in Frederick, Maryland,
and began their 560-mile journey to join the growing Continental Army
camp besieging Boston. Three days later, they pitched their tents in Lancaster, Pennsylvania, a place long connected to the Cresaps. The family
still owned land there, along the Susquehanna. In fact, this is where
Thomas Cresap Jr.'s grieving widow went to raise their young daughter
Charity after her father's death in the mountains in 1757. Moreover, the
men and women of Lancaster had extensive experience with the vigilantism people like the Cresaps advocated. The Paxton Boys had invaded
their town in 1763 and committed murder in broad daylight.

But that was a very different moment. Now, as Cresap's riflemen
pitched their tents near the center of town, these weren't marauders
threatening to upend justice and defy authority. They were liberty's
defenders. No, they were demigods. "On Friday evening last arrived
here, on their way to the American camp, Capt. Cressop's Company of
Riflemen, consisting of 130 active, brave, young fellows," began a letter
published in the *Pennsylvania Packet*. "They bear in their bodies visible
marks of their prowess, and shew scars and wounds, which would do
honor to Homer's *Iliad*." Comparing these men to the most famous warriors in Western literature was an easy reference, given how often patriots
claimed their fight against British tyranny was similar to ancient heroes
in Greece and Rome battling for liberty. But this writer would venture
even further: "One of these warriors, in particular, shews the cicatrices
of four bullet holes through his body. These men have been bred in the
woods to hardships and danger from their infancy. They appear as if they

were entirely unacquainted with, and had never felt, the passion of fear. With their rifles in their hands, they assume a kind of omnipotence over their enemies." Clearly, the upswell of adoration regarding the riflemen phenomenon had swept some observers off their feet.[53]

Over the weekend, Cresap's men repeated the shooting performance to stupefied crowds. The brothers broke out the board again, and pasted on another circle "about the size of a dollar. . . . While one of them supported this board perpendicularly between his knees, the other, at the distance of upwards of 60 yards, and without any kind of rest, shot eight bullets successively through the board and *spared a brother's thighs!*" They offered to overcome any final doubts by putting apples on their heads, in the style of William Tell, but onlookers "declined to be a witness of this."[54]

Cresap's riflemen continued the festivities into the night. They put their rifles away and, more than a century before Buffalo Bill Cody, played Indian for the people of Lancaster on that hot August night:

> A great fire was kindled round a pole planted in the courthouse square, where the company with the Captain at their head, all naked to the waist and painted like savages (except the Captain, who was in an Indian shirt) indulged a vast concourse of the inhabitants with a perfect exhibition of a war dance, and all the maneuvers of Indians holding council, going to war, circumventing their enemies, by defiles, ambuscades, attacking, scalping, etc. It is said by those who are judges, that no representation could possibly come nearer the original.

The very people who had watched helplessly a dozen years earlier as a mob of settlers rode into town to murder every peaceful Conestoga Native—Logan's people—they could find, now watched very similar men pantomime the acts of ferocious Indian warriors. Colonial history, Lancaster's history, was turned upside-down. And no one played the part better than Michael Cresap. "The Captain's agility and expertness, in particular, in these exhibitions, astonished every beholder."[55]

This report in a Philadelphia newspaper concluded by noting that in the morning, Cresap and his men were to "set out on their march to Cambridge." Before we document the remainder of their long journey, however, we must pause and consider the importance of what had taken place, and the language used to describe it, in Frederick and Lancaster on those summer evenings.

There were significant gender and class dynamics at work here. Every description of how Cresap and his riflemen looked and acted exuded masculine bravado. Their hunting shirts also served as a particular kind of democratic uniform; each wore a linen tunic that reached down to the knees and was cinched at the waist with a leather belt. Even though hunting shirts proved especially excellent incubators for lice (and therefore typhus), they became a powerful Revolutionary symbol: since they did not carry any stripes connoting rank, they were seen as the opposite of British redcoats. Americans deemed the men who donned one as slavish hirelings, the other, free, independent, equal men.[56]

The attention writers paid to the politics of the riflemen's shirts was purposeful, as was their obsession with describing their bodies: clothing and physique were markers of masculinity in the eighteenth century. Effeminate men dressed as fashionable fops, were cowardly, didn't marry, and were scrawny and weak. The accounts of Cresap and his scarred, grizzled men reassured the public that America was full of warriors who were none of those things. These men clamored to protect colonial households from the "slavery" of British tyranny. All the descriptions of their health, power, and strength dripped with machismo. They needed no shelter, little food or sleep, and could (and did) march for hundreds of miles. Bullets couldn't kill them. Observers repeatedly exaggerated the distances which they had walked, commenting all the while that they could seemingly keep going forever. And then there's the daring one another to shoot at targets held precariously between their legs.[57]

At the same time, there is a great deal of cultural appropriation evident with every step they took that intersects with and complicates the long construction project of American race-making. Flashpoints like Pontiac's War and the Paxton Boys sharpened notions of racial animosity and added more material to long-standing scripts of difference. Notions of "whiteness" and "Indianness" were defined in relation to these events, and "race" as a cultural construct gained momentum as the eighteenth century went on, especially as the American colonies became ever more involved in the enslavement of African peoples. Logan himself focused on inherent differences between white people and his people in the lament. In the next century, biological or "scientific" ideologies that insisted that race determined human behavior would become dominant—but they did not emerge out of thin air.

The American Revolution played an essential role in that project. This was especially true with regard to Native peoples. In all the moments of interaction between colonists and Native peoples thus far documented in this book, at no point was there a concept of "America" as a political or cultural identity that existed separate from or in opposition to "Britain." Prejudicial attitudes about "whiteness" sat inside a colonial identity; there was no reason or imperative to define it *against* "Britishness." For colonists, the British were us.

But now—in this moment of revolutionary transformation—the need to redefine these boundaries suddenly arose. Colonists in mainland North America had to figure out a new identity. Who were "the American people"? What did such a notion mean for people who had displayed fierce local or provincial loyalties to Pennsylvania or Virginia? In Ohio, the fighting between settlers from these colonies undermined any notion that the union was at all "perfect." What did it now mean to be "an American"?

This question led to others. How, for example, did Native peoples fit into that conception? Could Natives be Americans? Could Americans be Natives?

The Revolution forced colonists to upend their notions of "us" and "them." Since the 1500s European iconographers and illustrators had used Native peoples as shorthand for representing the New World. When British artists used the figure of an Indian to connote America, they intended to suggest it was a foreign and inferior place. In the 1770s, colonists inverted this sense that America was degenerate or exotic because it was full of Native people. They insisted, rather, that those differences were what made it great. As the confrontation with Britain over imperial reform reached a crisis, "England became a them for colonists, Indians became an us."[58]

Rebellious Bostonians had disguised themselves as Mohawks before dumping tea into the harbor. They merged colonist and Native, whiteness and Indianness, into one symbol of American freedom and steadfast resistance. For Bostonians it had been a performance, a projection of a one-dimensional caricature of Native-ness they could appropriate for their own purposes. This was one thing in peacetime, but with the news of Lexington and Concord there was a reflexive, almost automatic embrace of the symbol that America was powerful because it could marshal and deploy Native power.[59]

As we have seen, the Cresaps and their neighbors had dressed and painted themselves to look like Natives in the 1750s, to disastrous results. This wasn't a political act then, but part of the exigencies of a bewildering colonial conflict. It was a key element of what one scholar called America's "first way of war," whereby colonists increasingly adopted Native military practices in their myriad struggles with Indigenous peoples in the seventeenth and eighteenth centuries. In 1775, that way of war had a wholly new political valence, however. This wasn't a colonial war; it was the start of a revolutionary war. Everything about how people saw one another was in the middle of transformation, a splitting and recasting of old forms into new ones.[60]

By the eighteenth century, Europeans in both the Old and New Worlds had developed two such forms about Natives: the "noble savage" and the "merciless savage." Both existed simultaneously in pre-Revolutionary America; some Natives could be noble, others not. Their behavior—changeable, fluid, and personal, not permanent, universal, or determinative—largely shaped how settler colonists interpreted them.

The cultural demands of the Revolutionary War interrupted this. Suddenly in 1775, colonists began to ascribe to *themselves* the qualities of noble savagery. They appropriated the qualities they admired and respected about Indigenous peoples and made them their own. Logan leaned into the notion of noble savagery when he claimed he "never felt fear" in the lament. Now these were the heroic attributes of Cresap's riflemen. Men like Michael Cresap, Daniel Boone, and George Rogers Clark merged settler colonialism and noble savagery into a potent new creation: the American pioneer. That character had been in development for decades—Thomas Cresap, the "rattlesnake colonel," could certainly be cast for the role as far back as the 1740s—but now, with the Revolution, it had the official stamp of a new cultural force, American patriotism. Pioneer-citizens like Cresap were now the ones who never felt fear. The Revolutionaries were attempting to capture this part of Indianness, the fruit of nobility, and leave the husk behind.

That husk was all the qualities they hated, feared, and despised about "merciless savages." Because of the particular moment and circumstances of the Revolutionary War, they were able to fuse those hateful, fearsome tropes onto their British enemies, thus solving the most nettlesome problem of all: How do you get British colonists to make war on Britain? How do you motivate, animate, and mobilize emotions so that enough colonists will take up arms against their cultural cousins? Assigning onto the British all the prejudices, attitudes, fears, and loathing of "merciless savages"—whom the British were constantly accused of recruiting to their side—did a tremendous amount of political work for the patriots. For the first time, looking like an Indian but fighting them—and their British allies—made you an especially beloved American. Michael Cresap thought he was marching to defend American liberty. What he didn't know, and couldn't know, was that as he was walking he was helping to create a new American identity. That identity featured Americans acting like Natives. It left no room for Natives to be Americans.

During these sweltering summer days in 1775, we can see this cultural transformation happen right in front of our eyes. Michael Cresap's men did their best to look like Natives. They painted themselves and adopted their clothing. They did their best to act like Natives, too, pantomiming their rituals for all to see. "No representation could possibly come nearer the original," observers said. The lavish, detailed, widespread coverage of these particular men at this particular place and time speaks to the importance of this cultural project. Not only did the people of

Frederick or Lancaster need to view Michael Cresap as the Revolution's noble savage, but people all over North America did, too. Nearly half (48 percent) of newspapers in the mainland colonies included reports about Cresap and his riflemen, either exchanging the letters about the performances in Frederick and Lancaster, or mentioning their arrival at the army camp in Watertown, Massachusetts. Patriot political and publicity leaders ensured that families all over America could rest easy: men like Michael Cresap would protect them from merciless savages. The patriotic sacrifice, valor, and power they embodied meant Cresap and his men—and therefore the Revolution—were impossible to beat.

Alongside the letters lionizing Cresap, those newspapers also ran stories that continued to draw connections between British agents and potential merciless savages. A week after Cresap arrived at camp, there was another shocking report that the Crown had given £40,000 to insidious agents to "disperse among the Canadian Indians, to induce them to fall upon the colonies." Worse, they accused Samuel Wharton's former partner and Ohio Company man William Trent of accepting another bag filled with "the like sum of £40,000 to set the Indians to cut our throats." This erroneous story went from Virginia to New York and all throughout New England. At the same time, a summary of Captain James Wood's tour through Ohio also began to circulate, beginning in Baltimore and then all over the northern colonies. The account was taken straight from Wood's journal, including the rumors he had heard that British officers at Detroit had warned Natives not to trust Virginians, and noted how "many other diabolic artifices had been used by those tools of Government to instigate these Savages to attack our frontiers."[61]

People were worried about what would come of all these wicked plots. Two weeks after Cresap left Lancaster, Philip Vickers Fithian was a hundred miles to the west, in the Pennsylvania settlement known as Standing Stone (today Huntingdon), and he was terrified. "Many in this Town and Neighborhood are under present alarming Apprehensions of Danger from the Indians!," he wrote. "It is certain that the Indians have strong Temptations, the Governor of Canada, with all his Agents are employed & bribed to set them on us!"[62]

In this context, the juxtaposition of Cresap's Native qualities to the potential of real Indigenous people acting against the Revolution threw into stark relief the distinction between "good" (noble) and "bad" (merciless) Natives and their wicked British friends. By appropriating the noble savage's natural virtues, Cresap became a particular Revolutionary hero. He incorporated and encapsulated noble savagery into an American identity while at the same time highlighting how merciless savages were allies with—and were the same as—their British enemies. That Cresap and his riflemen were not actually Indians was the best part of all. Here was a superman: a white American settler who possessed the best qualities of Native peoples *and* a masculine fortitude to defend his country's rights. Americans needed men exactly like these, at exactly this moment, and patriot political leaders and publicity agents did their best to make as many people in the colonies aware of them as they could. The pioneer hero was born, and in a miraculous, instantaneous about-face, Michael Cresap was thus redeemed; his checkered history as the perpetrator at Yellow Creek vanished.

During the same days that Cresap and his men marched through New York, New Jersey, and Connecticut, John Connolly was with Dunmore onboard the governor's flagship afloat in the Chesapeake Bay after he had to flee Williamsburg in June. Connolly had sought out his patron to seek approval for his big idea: he would return to Ohio, rally the Natives who he claimed were not only the king's friends but also his own, and lead them in an assault over the mountains. They would venture even farther than they had in 1755, raiding up the Potomac Valley all the way to Alexandria, Virginia. Dunmore, reinforced with troops from Canada and Florida and bolstered by loyalist and possibly enslaved allies, would sail up Chesapeake Bay and join forces with him. They would rendezvous at Mount Vernon. Where better to cleave this illegal rebellion in half than at the home of its alleged commander?

Dunmore packed Connolly off on a ship bound for Boston. This scheme needed clearance from General Gage. Before departing, Connolly and Dunmore wrote a letter to White Eyes telling him (and Cornstalk and also the Mingo leaders) to ignore all the terrible things the Virginians were saying about their governor. Don't let their falsehoods make any "Impression on your Heart until you hear from me fully," which would be soon, he promised. Dunmore enclosed this letter in with a friendly note that Connolly penned to John Gibson, who they calculated would be the safest person to carry this potentially explosive message to Native leaders. Dunmore's words to White Eyes were hardly damning, but given what was being said about Carleton, Stuart, and Johnson all over North America at that moment, this was a risk, and they knew it.

Connolly thought Gibson was on his side, and was chummy with him in his letter. This familiarity would be his downfall. Despite his advice that Gibson "avoid an Over Zealous exertion" when the topic of politics arose, Connolly failed to heed his own advice in the cover letter to Gibson, discussing his run-ins with the "enemies to their Country [and] to good order and government," meaning the patriots. Connolly thought he was communicating this to a fellow loyalist. He would soon learn he was wrong.[63]

On Sunday, August 20, the tender *Arundell*, with John Connolly aboard, sailed from Norfolk. He landed in Boston a few days after Cresap's company arrived in Roxbury, Massachusetts, the latter of which was noted by *Boston Gazette* printers John Gill and Benjamin Edes: "Some of this Company, we hear, have travelled from the Mississippi," thus greatly multiplying the distance these mythical warriors had actually walked.[64]

As soon as he got to camp, witnesses reported Cresap immediately went looking to shoot British soldiers. The next night, Cresap, another captain, and a party of thirty riflemen snuck down a ditch and crawled through the grass until they were less than two hundred feet from one of the British sentries opposite a patriot outpost at the base of Plough'd Hill, not far behind the battlefield of Bunker Hill, the site of a colossal fight two months before. Spotting something moving, the guard fired, missed, and ran away. In an hour, a British patrol came out to investigate what was out in the grass. Just then, a thunderstorm blew up; lightning flashed, and wind and rain pelted the soldiers. Cresap and other riflemen fired on them, but they were soon forced to retreat. One Maryland rifleman said they thought "there was about 200 of the Regulars by the appearance of the different ways of shooting at us." The riflemen ran so fast that "one of our men Lost his Gun by falling into a Hole in the marsh." The next day, American lookouts "saw them Carry two persons from that place," and British deserters said that one redcoat had been killed and two wounded.[65]

This lone stormy night was all the action Michael Cresap would see in the Revolutionary War. Perhaps he rushed to the front because he knew he was dangerously ill. In spite of all the Revolutionary hymns sung to Michael, he must've been sick on the march. No one breathed a word that he might not have been anything but in the greatest of health, a perfect human specimen.

That image was hollow, as were other claims about the riflemen, such as their steadfast politics. The American public could never know about it, but they would've been shocked to learn how quickly after their arrival British authorities began to receive deserters from the rifle companies. A British officer reported one Virginia rifleman deserted on July 25, almost immediately. Another surrendered on August 16, and a third a few days later. Then, a few days after Cresap's thunderstorm engagement at Plough'd Hill, Gage's brother-in-law, Major Stephen Kemble, noted in his journal: "At 10 o'clock a Rifle Man came in from them, by Name _____, Servant to Capt. Cresap, Captain of the Company, they come from about Fort Pitt and are near 130 strong." Kemble judged him to be "a Stupid Lad, an Englishman born in Oxfordshire." This must've been a blow to Michael, personally and professionally. Servants had fled from the Cresaps at times of crisis before, but losing his aide at this particular time, with all this attention on him—with his name and reputation being bandied about in colonial newspapers all over America at that very moment—had to have been embarrassing.[66]

Still, stupid or not, Cresap's servant wasn't the only rifleman fighting against the Revolution. Major Kemble heard rumors that desertion among the riflemen had gotten so bad that they hanged one, "which checked the spirit of their People coming over to us." The army officers on the American side hadn't actually taken such draconian precautions yet, but they did make an example out of one rifleman by tying him to the whipping post. A confrontation ensued, which soon turned to mutiny. Nearly three dozen riflemen took up arms, broke their comrade out of prison, and fled into the woods. Washington gave orders to pursue them with loaded weapons and fixed bayonets. "You cannot conceive what disgrace we are all in," one Pennsylvania rifleman wrote in a letter home, "and how much the General is chagrined" that the only troops under his command not from New England should "set so infamous an example." After this, Washington was forced to move the rifle companies to the rear. As much as the public worshipped them, Washington's staff despised the unruly, problematic frontiersmen. "They do not boast so much of the Riflemen as heretofore," one general wrote to John Adams. "Washington has said he wished they had never come."[67]

Michael Cresap was not a party to this uprising, for he was in a make-shift army hospital at the Peacock Tavern. Not long after the mutiny, a group of riflemen decided to spend their Sunday afternoon visiting the celebrated captain, and to inquire "how he does who lies here sick." We can't know for sure what had brought Cresap to the Peacock, although malaria seems the most likely culprit. Disease was all around. Smallpox was so rampant across the lines in Boston that British officials would, a few days after Cresap's men visited their sick commander, shut down ferry services out of the city. Cresap didn't have smallpox (yet), but all sorts of other camp disorders might have contributed to his illness; if he had brought malaria with him to Massachusetts, there was likely a combination of maladies raging through his body.[68]

While Cresap battled fever at the Peacock and the riflemen caused trouble in the American camp, over the lines in Boston, Connolly had his meeting with General Gage. The commander listened as Connolly detailed his plans of leading a Native-loyalist army over the mountains. Having very little to lose, Gage had no reason to reject it. He had, after all, just written to Governor Carleton begging him to "strain every nerve to rouse both Canadians and Indians." This was perfect. Connolly and Dunmore would assume all the risk and danger; all he had to do was write a few letters. On September 10, Gage wrote to Dunmore affirming that Connolly did indeed have his permission. Then he set about letting Johnson, Stuart, Carleton, and the fort commanders at Detroit and Chartres in Illinois know they should be on the lookout for John Connolly and to give him all the support he needed.[69]

Connolly thought he was on the cusp of his own greatness. Examining his maps, he plotted the best way to get into the backcountry without getting caught. Little did he know that on September 24, the man he first recruited in the scheme, John Gibson, had turned over his and Dunmore's letters to patriot authorities in Pittsburgh. His plan was already starting to unravel even before it got started. To make matters worse, his servant betrayed him too. Cresap's man had gone over to the British in Boston just a few weeks before Connolly's servant ditched him at Newport, Rhode Island, and made a dash for General Washington's headquarters in Cambridge.

Connolly had let William Cowley, his servant of two years, in on his scheme in Boston. He asked if Cowley was "willing to go with him into the Indian Country" to help "raise the Indians and French" with the intention of attacking Fort Pitt, "after which he supposed all that part of the world would join him, especially since he had orders to give 300 acres of land to every man that would enlist under him." The servant was appalled at this information. Perhaps sensing Cowley's hesitation, he also told him about the other scheme he was mulling, one that he thought might entice him: he would "proclaim freedom to all convicts and indentured servants." Cowley was not tempted.[70]

On the last day of September, Cowley had started writing a secret letter to Washington to relate this news, but he had no way to get word to the general. When Connolly's ship stopped in Newport on October 5, Cowley "left all [his] clothes and all that [he] had" and made his escape. In fact, it's possible that Cowley and Cresap passed one another on the roads outside Boston, for he, too, was in motion during the first week of October. Cresap, too ill to remain at the Peacock, traveled with a few of his riflemen to a place he had never been before, New York City. Far away, in Oldtown, the Cresaps celebrated as Mary safely delivered their second son, a baby they would name Michael Cresap Jr.[71]

A patriot leader in New York City wrote to John Adams that Cresap had collapsed into a sickbed at a Manhattan boarding house around October 10, just as Cowley convinced Washington's guards that he needed to see the commander. It's unclear whether Washington remembered, but he had probably met Cowley a few times before. Cowley had worked for Dunmore at the Governor's Palace, where their paths may have crossed, and, more recently, he had delivered Connolly's letters to Mount Vernon. He listened as Cowley unburdened himself, taking in what by that time was just more incredible news.[72]

Washington's headquarters was already afire that week with reports that his surgeon general and one of the inner circle of Massachusetts patriots, Benjamin Church, had been spying for Gage. Now John Connolly, Washington's business associate and correspondent for five years, was planning to make Mount Vernon the focal point of a Native incursion into Virginia! "A person who has lately been a Servant to Major Connolly, a Tool of Lord Dunmore's," a beleaguered Washington wrote to Congress the next day, "has given an Account of a Scheme to distress the Southern Provinces, which appeared to me of sufficient Consequence to be immediately transmitted." He also forwarded Cowley's deposition to Lund Washington, the cousin he had authorized to manage Mount Vernon in his absence. Washington's Fairfax neighbors needed to know what they might be in store for. Lund immediately sent the news to George Mason, who also alerted patriot authorities across the Potomac in Maryland.[73]

<hr />

On Wednesday, October 18, 1775, Michael Cresap died. He was on the threshold of great things. This Revolution was going to be the best thing that could possibly have happened to the Cresap family. There was a new baby waiting for him at home. Surely, the praises heaped upon him would redound upon future generations of Cresaps. The riches that child stood to reap! If these were his thoughts, they would be his final ones. Michael had predicted this trip to Massachusetts was going to kill him, but he could never have guessed that by the time he died, his reputation would be so utterly transformed. Had he died only a year before, he would have been remembered primarily as the vicious and cowardly murderer of Logan's family. But now he was an American hero. If he ever came to grips with the fact that he was never going to get out of that bed in New York City, given all he was losing, his last shallow breaths must have been torture.

Patriot leaders in New York quickly realized that Michael's loss could be their gain. His body still contained extraordinary symbolic power, and the patriots in the city needed political encouragement at that moment. New York had long been seen as a "nursery of loyalty to the mother country." The city had seen Sons of Liberty and crowds protesting both the Stamp and Tea Acts, but, when there was an upswell of vocal support *for* the Crown in the winter of 1774–75—what one historian has called the coalescence of a British "common cause"—New Yorkers led the way. Throughout the imperial crisis, supporters of British policy were safer in Manhattan than in Boston or Philadelphia. The most rabidly loyalist newspaper printer, James Rivington, enjoyed a wide readership in the city and its environs, at least until the news of Lexington arrived.[74]

Reports of war created turmoil in Manhattan. They caused a riot at City Hall, which then enabled patriot leaders to seize municipal control. By August "the mob and the militia were becoming indistinguishable" in New York. Patriots threatened Rivington and menaced his print shop. British authorities were aghast as patriot crowds took more and more provocative actions over the summer, but they did so not from a position of strength, but rather of desperation. Unlike in Boston and Philadelphia, the robust loyalist faction in New York City had not dissipated. Patriots took every opportunity they could find to demonstrate the righteousness of *their* "cause."[75]

When one of the biggest celebrities of the Revolution died in their midst, then, New York patriots were not going to allow such a golden opportunity to stage a political performance go to waste. Performances had been the secret to Cresap's revolutionary redemption in 1775; it fit that one more would seal the deal. And while New Yorkers might not have known the man, they made sure to let everyone know that the deceased warranted their utmost reverence. As one New York printer put it in an issue that came out on the day of the funeral, Michael was "a gentleman of great reputation as a soldier, and highly esteemed as a citizen." Such a figure demanded they pull out all the stops to show their respect.[76]

On Thursday, October 19, the day after Michael had succumbed to his fever, they slid his casket into the wagon and proceeded to march. A sergeant major and members New York's first militia battalion were out front holding their muskets upside-down. Next, drummers, fifers, and other members of a military band beat a rhythm, followed by several members of the city's clergymen. Behind them rolled the carriage, surrounded by eight captains serving as pallbearers. Trailing the funerary caisson were mourners, "probably Army friends of the deceased," and

Figure 25. An early rendering of the oldest Anglican church in New York City, Trinity, not long after its construction in 1698. Cresap was buried in the yard very close to the door on the left of the drawing.

then the rest of the military units that patriot leaders in New York City could muster that day: five more groups of soldiers, noncommissioned officers, ward officers, and battalion commanders. At the rear marched the "Citizens of New York," described as a "vast concourse" of people in one paper and "a large assemblage of civilians" in another, and "the most respectable inhabitants" in a third. The crowd headed down Broadway on its way to its intersection with Wall Street, and the graveyard at Trinity Church.[77]

We know all this because New York City printers outdid themselves in providing details about the day's spectacle. Underneath a lengthy obituary, which boasted of Cresap's "prudence, firmness, and intrepidity" in both fighting Ohio Natives and in "the Present Contest," Hugh Gaine produced a lavish graphic depiction of the funeral procession that appeared in his *New York Gazette & Weekly Mercury.*

Stretching nearly a whole column of print, the illustration is striking. Eighteenth-century colonial printers rarely put together such involved graphics. Taking on a project like this was labor-intensive, as Hugh Gaine's staff would have to precisely carve wood blocks that would then be locked into the press. It impressed James Rivington. When he saw it, he walked around the corner to Gaine's shop to borrow the design, which he inserted into the paper he was putting together that week. This may seem odd, given how Cresap had become a patriot symbol, but the aggressive, outspoken loyalist printer felt very vulnerable in New York by the autumn of 1775, as well he should have, given that partisans were at that moment planning another attack on him and his shop. Rivington's attention to Cresap was very likely an effort to save his own neck.

Close readers of Gaine's or Rivington's papers might have recognized the symbol used to depict Cresap's coffin: the crossed swords. The wooden block Gaine used to depict Cresap's coffin was the same one he had used a year earlier to illustrate the casket of Sir William Johnson. Some had insinuated that Michael Cresap's heinous actions in Ohio had so strained the beloved British superintendent that it killed him. Now the

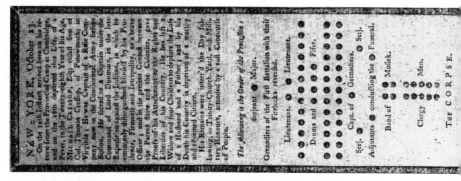

Figure 26. Funeral procession for Michael Cresap, *New York Gazette & Weekly Mercury*, 23 October 1775.

same symbol that adorned Johnson's casket in Gaine's and Rivington's newspapers was used to celebrate the man who had indirectly caused his demise. Both on the streets and in print, Cresap ranked alongside the most important officials in North America.[78]

Had George Washington died in New York on that October day, it is unlikely that he could've been given a bigger funeral. In fact, four days after Michael died, the president of the Continental Congress, Peyton Randolph of Virginia, collapsed of an "apoplectic fit" at dinner and died a few hours later. Philadelphians marched this Revolutionary hero through their streets less than a week after New Yorkers did Cresap. Apart from the presence of Congressional delegates and other Pennsylvania political officials shuffling behind the casket, it was virtually the same occasion. Revolutionary soldiers, clergymen, and thousands of the city's inhabitants would flank each carriage. Cresap's revolutionized reputation was now on a level equal to the head of the Continental Congress; their losses to the American "cause" were the same.[79]

The paeans showered on Michael Cresap were not limited to New York, either. News about the death of this "worthy and esteemed citizen" went up and down the Eastern Seaboard. Either choosing Rivington's October 19 notice of Cresap's death, the *New York Constitutional Gazette*'s October 21 summary of the funeral, or Gaine's obituary, a remarkable number of colonial newspapers called attention to this event. Decades

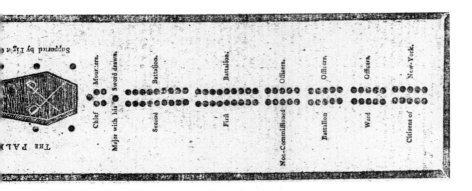

later, Thomas Jefferson remembered how Logan's Lament flew through all the public papers. The news of Cresap's funeral was an even larger phenomenon. Ten (or 31 percent) of a possible thirty-two newspapers then operating in the thirteen mainland colonies printed Logan's speech in early 1775, whereas more than double that number (22 or 69 percent) mentioned Cresap's death. The coverage was impressive: three of four Connecticut papers, three of six in Rhode Island and Massachusetts, both Maryland papers, five of six Philadelphia prints, and all the *Virginia Gazettes* informed their readers. Even the Lower South took notice, with papers in Charleston and Savannah publishing the description of Cresap as a "gentleman of great reputation."[80]

Gaine brilliantly fused together Cresap's twin claims to fame: that he fought Natives *and* British redcoats. These two things together made him essential, and a crippling loss to his country. All colonial readers had to do was turn the page or move their eyes to see reports of British agents plotting with Natives. The week before Cresap died, in fact, yet another conniving British official added his name to the list, when a report from Charleston appeared that South Carolina governor William Campbell had also fled to Royal Navy ship when it was discovered that he had "employed one [Alexander] *Cameron* . . . to engage the Indians in the ministerial service, who had actually enlisted 600 of them, and furnished them with every necessary in order to butcher the back inhabitants." This story circulated through northern papers, including New York, just as Cresap succumbed. Another article would soon appear connecting "those two arch plotters against the rights of America, *Guy Carleton* and *Guy Johnson*" with the most notorious man in English history, Guy Fawkes, the man who almost blew up King James I and all of Parliament in 1605. That reference needed no explanation, as Fawkes remained an iconic villain for Anglo-Americans. In fact, this article insisted, their "villany exceed[s]" even his.[81]

Therefore, according to common opinion, men like Michael Cresap were indispensable to defeating America's multiplying, treacherous enemies. This, as we have seen, flew in the face of what the riflemen were really like: troublesome, mutinous, and some even deserters. Here again, just as during the allegedly patriotic upswell of support in the "glorious" weeks after Lexington and Concord, reality did not match up with myth. In truth, during these bewildering days as many people as possibly could took this unprecedented opportunity to reassess their status. Philip Fithian learned from his mentor that the news encouraged enslaved people to rebel in New Jersey. Just such a chasm between fact and fiction emerged about the riflemen. Despite the stupendous things written about them, riflemen were not impervious supermen, nor were they all patriots. The reality that the union was in fact far from perfect underscored just how imperative the need was to proclaim it to be so. The bewildering reality of 1775 was also *why* such ludicrous statements were written about Cresap and his riflemen: patriot leaders worked hard composing and publicizing letters, obituaries, and funeral processions to establish the idea—to make it a matter of common opinion—that these particular men, dressed like Natives and acting like Natives, were coming to rescue American liberty. They undertook this work, not because of a confident logic or teleology, but to address the particular necessities of union in 1775.

In such a context, even the previously despised Paxton Boys had a chance at redemption. Two weeks before he printed the notice of Cresap's death, *New York Journal* printer John Holt published a story from Hartford, Connecticut, that "a number of Paxton Boys, dressed and painted in the Indian fashion" had come through town on their way to Cambridge. Back in 1763, Benjamin Franklin thought they were despicable and mobilized Philadelphians to oppose their vigilantism. But now, Franklin and his patriot colleagues no longer cast them as unsavory, bloodthirsty killers. "Several of these we hear are young gentlemen of fortune," the *Journal* and several others reported. Cresap, his riflemen, and even the Paxton Boys were an essential projection for patriot leaders who knew support for the Revolution was far from universal. The contingency of this utterly new imperative—the notion that there needed to be a "perfect" union—decidedly changed the calculations of power all over North America, but perhaps no more than in the backcountry.[82]

The political need for Revolutionary unity constitutes a twist in the story I have been telling to this point. Thus far, over the course of two generations of the Cresap and Shickellamy families, we have watched empires come and go, vast land schemes inflate and collapse, and violence explode and subside. Conflicts over hazy and unclear boundaries have escalated into bloodshed, and arguments about the essentialism of race or ethnicity have waxed and waned. We have witnessed colonial invasion and Native counterattack. There was no indication, however, that any of this would cease in the near future, nor that there would be a fundamental shift in how people interacted with each other in the backcountry.

What was happening in these news stories about Michael Cresap was one of the earliest indicators that a new imperative was indeed in the making. The celebrations of Cresap and his riflemen as quintessential models of American citizenship were among the first manifestations of a new national force that would become known as American patriotism. In 1774, many in the east would have agreed that there was little difference between settlers on the frontier and Native people. Printers in Philadelphia and New York called them "worse savages." From their perspective men like John Connolly, George Rogers Clark, and Michael Cresap were even more removed from the boundaries of civilized society than Natives.

The Revolutionary War challenged this conception. Within months, the demands of war with Britain forced patriots to make decisions about those "wild" backcountry settlers. Like them or not, patriot leaders needed their support, and therefore they had to see them in a whole new light.

One of the patriots' primary tasks was to create and give meaning to the notion of utterly new, ill-defined concepts, especially what it meant to be an American citizen and to belong to "the American people." The particular demands of the Revolutionary War forced those who were uncomfortable with the behavior of frontier wild men to nevertheless embrace them as part of the infant nation. By celebrating Cresap's walk from the Ohio River to Boston and mourning his death as a devastating loss to the country, patriots put men like him at the center of their definition of who were the rightful "American people."

This conceptual project was threatened by places like the Forks of the Ohio, where the potential for internecine conflict was extraordinarily high. Patriot political leaders worried that Pittsburgh could play host to a domestic civil war inside an imperial one. We would like to think that the Revolutionary War ended these intercolonial disputes; that patriots in Pennsylvania and Virginia closed ranks and put aside their differences immediately, especially with dangerous loyalists in town. They didn't. Months into the Revolutionary War, witnesses reported that "colonial disputes are very high between Virginia and Pennsylvania, and if not timely suppressed will end in tragical consequences." Three days later, one wrote, "great commotion amongst the people about the boundaries . . . Expect some lives will be lost on the occasion." Three days after that: "Nothing but quarrelling and fighting in every part of the town."[83]

Michael Cresap's patriotic sacrifice offered American leaders an opportunity to hide, to paper over, to whitewash such real political divides. In city streets and in print, they worked hard to promote examples such as these as a way to broadcast unified purpose, of an actual "common cause." Cresap's funeral was another way of proclaiming "our union is perfect," even though it wasn't. It was a clear example of the Revolutionaries trying to resolve bewilderment to their advantage.

As such, there was therefore a deep and lasting consequence to these public and symbolic displays. They featured frontier settlers at the center of American nationalism and patriotism. The alleged murderer of Logan's family, they argued, was now one of "us." This particular resolution of bewilderment, a product of revolution time, would last far beyond 1775.

=====

On Saturday, October 21, the day before Peyton Randolph died, Congress opened Washington's letter and read William Cowley's deposition. Earlier that month Congress had recommended that each of the colonies "arrest and secure every person . . . whose going at large may, in their opinion, endanger the safety of the colony, or the liberties of America." This news put John Connolly at the head of the Revolution's most wanted list. On Monday, still reeling from the shock of their colleague's abrupt death, the Virginia delegates sent the news of Connolly's plot to the committee of safety in Richmond, and instructed them to forward the news to their peers in North Carolina. They didn't know where Connolly was, but they stipulated he should be arrested as soon as anyone could find him.[84]

As it turned out, perhaps Connolly didn't fully trust his servant after all. Cowley told Washington that his master intended to go by sea to Florida and then make a wide arc around the Appalachians, visiting the Cherokees and then Ohio Natives on his way to Detroit. Patriot search parties should look for him in the Deep South, Cowley advised. But those weren't Connolly's actual intentions at all. As word fanned out about the scheme, he was much closer than patriot leaders realized.

Rather than travel to Florida, Connolly had gone back to Dunmore, with whom he stayed for a few weeks. Connolly had also come down with some illness while in Boston and spent time in the Chesapeake recovering. During those days, as Connolly and the governor finalized plans (which included Connolly's being promoted to lieutenant colonel-commandant), Dunmore decided he was going to enlarge his forces to feature freed and armed slaves. Although he wouldn't issue it until after Connolly left, Dunmore had written and prepared his emancipation proclamation. Like Lincoln ninety years later, Dunmore had been looking for an opportune time to publicize his decision to declare freedom to enslaved people who could reach his lines. After his forces smashed

Virginia militia at the battle of Kemp's Landing on November 15, he had his moment. Patriots who accused British agents of scheming with Natives to put down the rebellion now had the opportunity to howl about Dunmore's Proclamation. British agents would apparently stop at nothing to destroy America, they said loudly and frequently.[85]

Before he set off, Connolly and Dunmore settled on a date by which they would join forces at Alexandria: April 20, the day after the anniversary of Lexington and Concord. Connolly would bring Ohio Natives; Dunmore would meet them there with regiments of emancipated slaves.

Connolly left the governor on November 13, two days before what Dunmore thought would be the beginning of his stunning turnaround, with two companions, Lt. Allen Cameron and Dr. John Smyth. They went up the Bay to Port Tobacco, and then through central Maryland, but Connolly knew he soon needed to move deep into the wilderness before he could be recognized. He planned to head for Standing Stone, the place that Philip Vickers Fithian found wracked with terror at the prospect of imminent Native attack only a few months earlier. From there, he would trek over the mountains, going through the Juniata River valley, where Tachnedorus (John Logan) and his son Tod-kah-dos still lived, and eventually reaching Lake Erie.[86]

The route might have carried them safely to Detroit, but inclement weather intervened. "A furious north-west wind" drove them off course, and they had to stay on the road "like ordinary travellers." They made it through central Maryland "unmolested, till the evening of the 19th, when we were on the very border of the frontier, and almost out of danger," he recalled. They took a room at an inn a little past Hagerstown, Maryland, near Conococheague. Connolly carefully inquired whether anyone in Hagerstown knew what business he was on. The landlord told him that it was around town that he had been with Dunmore, but it seemed that no one was aware of his visit to Boston.[87]

Right before they reached their inn, they encountered a young man who had been a soldier under Connolly's command in Pittsburgh a year earlier. As they passed by, he saluted Connolly and called him major. This prompted Cameron and Smyth to exchange a panicked look, and they debated whether or not to waylay this unsuspecting Virginia partisan. They should have. When darkness fell, the thirsty traveler from Pittsburgh went into a tavern and started boasting about the celebrity he had met on the road. Although Cowley's intelligence hadn't yet arrived in Hagerstown, two days earlier, copies of Connolly and Dunmore's letters to John Gibson and White Eyes had reached the hands of local militia officers. Once they heard that that scoundrel was in their neighborhood, the patriots resolved to snatch him.[88]

In an incredible coincidence, Michael Cresap might have played a role in fostering the resolve of the men in this tavern. Two weeks earlier, as Connolly and Dunmore finished their plans, patriots in Hagerstown put on one final performance "to commemorate the death of the late worthy Michael Cresap, Esq.," their homegrown hero. On Saturday, November 4, the militia captains, each "having a scarf on their left arm, the drums muffled and covered in black, and the colors in mourning," called the soldiers to order. They formed three columns and then "marched in Indian file [single file], through the town to the muster ground, where, after performing the whole Manual Exercise, evolutions, etc., they proceeded into town in the same manner." The drums continued to rap out "a solemn sound, and fifes playing accordingly" as they marched. Without a casket to bury, the officers honored their patriot with a silent march: "after they were dismissed, orders were given to beat no drum . . . but to behave in a manner suitable to the occasion." The mourners carried a quiet melancholy with them back to their hearths in the fading November daylight, pondering with heavy hearts all the promise—to his young family, to the Revolution, to America—now lost.[89]

It is not impossible that the inhabitants of Hagerstown were still talking about this latest public performance, only a few days past, in the minutes before they convened their committee meeting to read Connolly and Dunmore's suspicious notes to Gibson and Native leaders. Two days later, when one of those villains was spotted in their town, now they had an unbelievable chance to act like the man they had just honored and to take bold action to save American liberty.

At two o'clock in the morning, a posse of patriots rousted Connolly,

Cameron, and Smyth from their beds, and held them fast. They rode them back to Hagerstown, put them in three separate houses, and discussed what to do with them. Connolly remembered they "suffered the kind of disturbance and abuse which might be expected from undisciplined soldiers, and a clamorous rabble, at such a crisis." Smyth said they "abused us perpetually." Connolly tried to insist that the letters to Gibson and White Eyes were harmless; but he knew that if they found the one piece of paper that he had secreted away in the sticks of his saddle, they would be doomed. His bargaining went nowhere, though, and the Hagerstown militia sent the prisoners to Frederick for further examination.[90]

Connolly found that his meeting with Gage in Boston was well known in Frederick. Continued searches for his papers still turned up nothing, however. The trio had managed to destroy all the damning evidence except that single carefully hidden document. As Connolly later recalled, "There was a manuscript that had been wrapt round a stick of black ball by my servant, so soiled and besmeared, as to have escaped the search committees" at both Hagerstown and Frederick. The Frederick committee was determined, and continued to tear his saddle apart. Eventually, the scrap of paper was identified: it was a "rough draft of propositions." The first sentence began: "As I have, by directions from his Excellency Lord Dunmore, prepared the Ohio Indians to act in concert with me against His Majesty's enemies in that quarter . . ." They didn't have to read any further. "We were now decidedly prisoners," Connolly knew.[91]

They stayed locked up in separate houses at Frederick for a month, at which point patriot leaders ordered Connolly, Cameron, and Smyth to be better secured in the Philadelphia jail. After traveling in the bitter cold, they entered the city on New Years' Day, 1776. By the time they arrived in the capital, the trio were infamous all throughout America. Initially reported in the *Virginia Gazette*, news of their plot and arrest had been published by two-thirds of colonial newspapers in December. Rather than the mournful drums playing in salute of Michael Cresap, Philadelphians beat "the rogue's march" for Connolly on his way to what would be a very long incarceration.[92]

"Thus you see, a part of the diabolical scheme is defeated," concluded the most widely reprinted account of Connolly's arrest. Stories of Connolly's plot being foiled appeared at the same time—and often in the same newspaper columns—as shocking news from the Chesapeake about Dunmore's emancipation proclamation. The story also shared space with accounts from Canada documenting Guy Carleton's pleas for Natives to "feast on a Bostonian and drink his blood." The damning of British officers negotiating with Natives and enslaved people reached a fever pitch as the new year began. Congress certainly helped this along: they gave orders that colonial printers should print both the "feast" letter and Connolly's papers.[93]

"How sunk is Britain!," wrote an essayist calling himself "An American" in the *Virginia Gazette* in the first week of 1776.

> Why make use of every base and inhuman stratagem, and wage a savage war unknown amongst civilized nations? Surely whoever has heard of Carleton's, Connolly's, and Dunmore's plots against us cannot but allow they must have been authorized by a higher power, and whoever believes this cannot but wish to be instantly and forever removed from such a power. . . . Most freely would I *cut the Gordian knot.*

"An American" begged for a declaration of independence, weeks before Thomas Paine would also demand it in *Common Sense*. This essay, published in several of the more radical patriot newspapers, did not mention republicanism or representation as why America must leave the British Empire. "An American's" justifications for cutting ties with Britain were based strictly on the behavior of wicked British agents and their foul methods of allying themselves with Natives and African Americans.[94]

This reasoning foreshadowed the argument that lay at the heart of the actual Declaration of Independence seven months later. The twenty-seventh and final grievance of the Declaration captured this notion of enslaved and Native peoples potentially being "activated" to quell the rebellion. At the climax of the Declaration, Congress said, King George had "excited domestic insurrections among us and has endeavoured to bring on the inhabitants of our frontiers the merciless Indian savages, whose known rule of warfare is an undistinguished destruction of all ages, sexes, and conditions." Over the past year, Congress had participated in the fixing of this argument in public opinion. They had put it in the "Declaration for the Causes and Necessity of Taking Up Arms" and other formal addresses. They had ordered colonial printers to insert it into their newspapers stories of British agents working with Natives. Now they cemented it in the American Revolution's primary statement of purpose.

The featuring of this accusation in the Declaration was an essential development, a formalization of the transformation that the Revolution wrought. While revolution time is marked by contingency and openness, there are moments when that time freezes and becomes fixed in mythological amber. There are instances when what was bewildering and confounding to many is given meaning and explanatory power by a few. The Declaration captured the revolutionary changes of 1775–76—the shifting conceptions of friends and enemies, us and them, noble savages and merciless ones—and featured them in the cornerstone of the new republic based on the hazy principle of citizenship.

The inclusion of these particular words in the Declaration, moreover, further accentuated the heroism of people like Michael Cresap. The Declaration castigated one side of the trope of Indianness—the merciless savage—as being the polar opposite of what it meant to be an American patriot. The "we" of "we hold these truths to be self-evident" was juxtaposed in the Declaration against "he," the tyrant king. It was a powerful statement of who "the American people" were, another way of using the pronouns "us" versus "them." As a pioneer, Michael Cresap was now featured at the center of "we," the American people. His version of Indianness was not banished or rejected; rather, it was worshipped. The Revolution's "noble savage" was the opposite of the king's "merciless savages." The Revolutionaries severed these two tropes, made one the center of American patriotism and cast the other off as treasonous. American liberty depended on the "Prudence, Firmness, and Intrepidity" of men like Michael Cresap, and it could not afford to lose such a "worthy and esteemed citizen." On the other hand, according to the Declaration of Independence, anyone who worked with merciless savages was an enemy of the American people.[95]

Cresap had no idea just how great, how immense the threshold was that colonists stood on in 1775–76. He couldn't know how he was a critical participant in the creation of a new republican regime, and that, even in death, the settler colonial impulse—complete with the cultural appropriation of Native culture—that he represented would become a core value to the independent United States.

———

What, then, about Logan's people? Where did they fit within these new narratives? Despite what the Declaration said, to this point in the Revolutionary War, Natives throughout America—and especially in Ohio—had been nothing but merciful. At the treaty conference held in Pittsburgh in the fall of 1775, Captain James Wood and his commissioners begged Shawnees, Delawares, and Mingos to ignore British entreaties and stay neutral. They promised they would, and had stuck to their word throughout 1775–76. As the Revolution continued, Natives would continue to hold their own discussions about these pressing political and military issues just as Wood had heard them doing in the fall of 1775. The question of what role they would play in this strange war would become increasingly divisive for Natives in Ohio, and eventually violence would return to their villages. The strain over how to deal with all of the Revolution's bewildering transformations consumed Logan. And, like his nemesis, he would die before seeing where these immense changes led.

CHAPTER 10

WHATEVER HE WAS,
HE WAS NOT COMMON,
1776–1794

". . . as it turned out I was to have the care of his memory. . . . He won't be forgotten. Whatever he was, he was not common."

—*Heart of Darkness*

The surveyor had on moccasins, and so walked undetected up to the lone Native camped next to the edge of French Creek, not far from the Allegheny River and seventy-five miles north of the Forks, in the fall of 1794. To his surprise, tears were streaming down the man's face. "After viewing him a few moments for fear he might observe me, and think I was improperly intruding on his privacy," the visitor stepped on a stick to announce his presence. Suddenly aware he was not alone, the crying man whirled and stood. The surveyor introduced himself as John Adlum. The Native said he was called Logan. The surveyor was in his mid-thirties, but the Native was older, in his early fifties and embarrassed that Adlum had caught him crying. He apologized for his tears. He said, Adlum remembered, that he was suffering from "a disease of the mind." The two then launched into a lengthy conversation on a number of topics, including past and present events in Ohio. They talked themselves hungry, and stopped to prepare a meal.[1]

While they broke bread, the surveyor inquired about another who shared the name of Logan. As a younger man, Adlum had spent some time working in Frederick, Maryland, where he had heard stories of Logan and Cresap. He asked the man whether he had ever met a "great man, a namesake of his called Logan." Of course, the Native said. He was my uncle.[2]

Adlum was speaking to Tod-kah-dos, the oldest son of Tachnedorus (John Logan). But could this be true? This man was small, not at all someone of the alleged towering stature and fame as the "great Mingo chief" Logan.

Is your famous uncle still alive, Adlum asked excitedly?

No, he is dead.[3]

Then the interview took a turn Adlum did not expect. "How came he by his death," the surveyor asked.

"I killed him."

Thunderstruck, Adlum pressed on. "You killed him for what?," he responded. "It was the order of the nation," Tod-kah-dos said. "He was too

Figure 27. A portrait of John Adlum painted in the same year as his meeting with Tod-kah-dos, attributed to Charles Willson Peale.

great a man to live. . . . He talked so strong, that if he differed in opinion on any subject or business, [Logan] made them believe they were wrong and that he alone was right." Logan (Soyechtowa) thwarted too many plans: "nothing could be carried contrary to his opinions, his eloquence always took all the young men with him," Tod-kah-dos said. So they wanted to have him silenced. Whether there was an actual *order* or merely an intimation or mutual agreement, Tod-kah-dos certainly believed that the Six Nations wanted him to eliminate his troublesome uncle.[4]

Adlum was still not over the shock. "But why did the nation order you to kill him . . . could they not have got some other one to do it?" "If any other man had killed him," Tod-kah-dos insisted, "I would have put him to death." It had to be his "nearest relation living." Were you "very sorry to be ordered to put your Uncle to death," Adlum implored. "Not much sorry," said the formerly weeping Native man.[5]

Adlum couldn't believe this blithe response. He had, after all, witnessed the man's streaming tears. His answer made no sense. "How so you say not much sorry, what do you mean by saying not much Sorry?" Tod-kah-dos, for his part, wasn't surprised Adlum couldn't understand. Tod-kah-dos explained that Logan was "a very, very great man, and as I killed him, I am to fill his place and inherit all his greatness," just as at some point he had adopted his family's name. Adlum wrote that Tod-kah-dos put his hand over his heart and emphatically stated "when I am so great a man as he was, I am ready to die, and whomsoever puts me to death will inherit all my greatness, as I do his."[6]

Conducted near the upper Allegheny River in 1794, this remarkable interview is the most reliable account we have of what happened to Logan (Soyechtowa) during the Revolutionary War. Other stories, taken third-hand and recorded a half century after this one, portray Logan as a drunken mess, abusing women, cursing and yelling, and getting shot in disgrace. But Adlum's notes from the time he spent talking with Tod-kah-dos are the only ones that feature a Native source. The time and place are correct, further lending it authenticity. Somewhere near the shores of Lake Erie, when Logan and his beloved brother's son were alone in the woods, Tod-kah-dos delivered the fatal blow.[7]

Why did a nephew have to murder his uncle? Logan's brutal end was indicative of the violence that engulfed Ohio in the years after American independence. Just as it had for decades, the precarious politics of the Ohio Valley in the late 1770s had swept Logan, Tod-kah-dos, and the larger groups they belonged to—the Iroquois, Shawnees, Delawares, and Mingos—into another vortex of bewilderment, violence, and horror. The same war that created the United States and reified the status of men like Michael Cresap resulted in drastic, unprecedented, and permanent changes for the region.

Around the time that Michael Cresap perished in New York City, a woman staying with Pennsylvania trader Richard Butler accosted John Connolly's sister Susanna Semple on the streets of Pittsburgh. Despite the pleas of the Continental Congress imploring colonists to stop fighting one another at Pittsburgh, they had not. Shouting turned to blows, and the tussle between the two women quickly escalated into a riot. When Connolly's lieutenant George Aston arrived on the scene, he encountered his old bête noir Devereaux Smith, one of the Westmoreland County (Pennsylvania) magistrates. The two foes fought once again, but this round ended with Smith's dagger buried in Aston's chest, and a bullet in Smith's leg, which would have to be amputated. The political controversy over war with Britain did little to curtail intercolonial rivalries that had turned personal and now, for Aston, lethal. The union was still not perfect at the Forks at the end of 1775.[8]

Natives experienced similar crosscutting pressures as the war between Britain and the colonies continued. American political leaders did their best to maintain neutrality among Shawnees, Delawares, and Mingos in the Ohio Valley, but they had a new rival with which to contend: Henry Hamilton, the lieutenant governor of Canada stationed at Detroit. Two factors kept peace in the valley early in 1776: the American naval blockade of Canada via the St. Lawrence River, and the political decision of the Six Nations to stay out of the war.

Colonial strategists knew that blocking access to the St. Lawrence would complicate supply lines deep into North America as it had in all previous eighteenth-century wars with France. As long as American troops laid siege to Montreal and Quebec, Hamilton's supply of gifts with which he could bribe Ohio Natives to join the British cause was limited. After smallpox and poor leadership put an end to the American invasion of Canada in the spring of 1776, however, the collapse of that front meant fresh opportunities for Hamilton. Still, this didn't mean all Natives automatically went over to the British. For Ohio Natives who considered themselves under the jurisdiction of the Six Nations— Guyasuta's people—the increased capacity for British intrigues at Detroit meant little as long as the Iroquois held to their strict neutrality.[9]

For their part, Mingos were anxious to eradicate the settlements that had multiplied over the past two years south of the Ohio River in Kentucky. Scores of canoes carrying settlers, including those of Michael Cresap and George Rogers Clark, added to the stream of overland colonists who followed Daniel Boone through the Cumberland Gap to establish settlements at Boonsborough, Harrodsburg, and Lexington, Kentucky. In the summer of 1776, Mingos began leading raids against these colonists.

Meanwhile, the Continental Congress dispatched more commissioners to Pittsburgh to find out about the loyalties of Ohio Natives. No sooner did they arrive in town when they began to hear disturbing rumors about Hamilton's growing influence in Detroit. By summer's end, patriot leaders reported Hamilton "has been straining every Nerve to excite the Indians to take up the Hatchet against the Americans." Hamilton's name was soon added next to Stuart, Connolly, Johnson, Carleton, and Dunmore as evil British plotters seeking to wreak havoc in the American backcountry, and he earned himself a hideous nickname. Patriots alleged the lieutenant governor had a particular desire for the scalps of murdered American settlers, so they began to refer to him as Henry "the Hair Buyer" Hamilton.[10]

In the spring of 1777, civil war in the British Empire finally came home to Iroquoia, as a British invasion of New York from Canada forced Iroquois leaders to choose whether to remain neutral or not. That decision caused a split in the Six Nations, with the Mohawk, Cayuga, and Senecas choosing King George, while the Oneida, Tuscaroras, and part of the Onondagas sided with the Americans. Soon, Iroquois warriors would fight one another.

Civil war in the Six Nations would have important ramifications in the Ohio Valley, especially among the Mingos (who were primarily composed of Seneca and Cayuga transplants from New York and Pennsylvania). Virginia leaders wanted to avenge Mingo attacks on Kentucky that started in 1776, but the Continental Congress demurred, afraid of widening the war. Instead, they kept summoning Ohio leaders to Fort Pitt (no longer Fort Dunmore) for conference after conference. Patriot leaders at Pittsburgh grew more desperate, especially after settlers shot and killed some Senecas who were in town to attend a meeting. Frontier militia had also murdered Cornstalk inside Fort Randolph (at Point Pleasant) in the fall of 1777. This act drove Shawnees toward the British, who began attacking settlements along the Kanawha and Greenbrier Rivers in March 1778. The patriots had lost Guyasuta, too, as the Seneca leader took up arms for the Crown. Early on in 1778 nearly all of the most significant Native brokers in the Ohio Valley, including Alexander McKee and his leading interpreter, Simon Girty, had gone to Detroit to curry favor with Hamilton. The patriots were running out of friends in Ohio.[11]

As a result, the Americans made several panicked, confused moves in the summer and fall of 1778. They arranged a strike force to attack Detroit, and then canceled it. They held another conference and extended a number of promises to Delaware leaders White Eyes, Captain Pipe, and Cresap's old adversary John Killbuck, in the hopes they would not follow their colleagues into the "Hair Buyer's" outstretched arms. This agreement even included a startling provision that the Delawares could "join the present confederation" and become a full-fledged member of the United States, if Congress agreed. They didn't; in fact that surprising invitation of American statehood never came up for discussion in Philadelphia. Such an offer was inconceivable in the eastern part of Pennsylvania, but not in Pittsburgh. At the Forks, patriot leaders were willing to agree to anything, much like the desperate situation at Easton two decades earlier.[12]

Their feelings of panic were only made worse when frontier militia killed White Eyes merely a few weeks after the Delaware signed their alliance with the United States. Patriot leaders did their best to cover up this disaster by saying White Eyes had not been murdered but rather had contracted smallpox. No matter what, their best friend among the Delaware was dead.

Luckily, George Rogers Clark came to the rescue. Michael Cresap's friend and partner had long been lobbying Virginia governor Patrick Henry for permission to strike the poorly defended British installations in the Illinois country, especially Kaskaskia on the Mississippi. He promised he could do it very cheaply; all he needed were a few intrepid volunteers. Henry approved the mission early in 1778, and Clark's force of 200 militia headed west. Their trek didn't go well, as they were nearly starved when they reached Kaskaskia. Nevertheless, they managed to capture the outpost on the second anniversary of American independence without firing a shot. Flush with this success, Clark immediately pivoted to march on Vincennes, another former French settlement 180 miles away on the Wabash River. That town quickly surrendered, too, and Clark had earned for himself the nickname Conqueror of the Illinois.

Clark's adventures drew Henry Hamilton out from the safety of Detroit. As soon as he heard of the incursion, Hamilton began to put together his own force to regain British control of Illinois. By October, they were ready to march, and Hamilton led 175 British and loyalist soldiers south, gaining the support of more than 300 Native allies as they went. In December, the Union Jack again flew over Vincennes, as Clark had returned to Kaskaskia. Hamilton thought that the weather had secured his victory, as Clark would never attempt a winter attack.

He was wrong. Six weeks after Hamilton retook Vincennes, Clark set off on a hazardous winter march. Late in February, an ugly siege began, with Clark promising no quarter until Hamilton surrendered. He backed up this threat by butchering five captured British-allied Natives right in front of the main gate. Hamilton sent up a flag of truce and negotiated surrender with Clark, whom he said was still covered in Native blood. Two weeks later, the "Hair Buyer" and 26 of his party would be on their way east, headed to Williamsburg to be put on trial for war crimes.[13]

Hamilton's capture secured Clark's conquest of the Lower Ohio Valley. The news of his victories, combined with the larger British move to shift the theater of war to Georgia and the Carolinas, encouraged Washington to do what he had long wanted: invade Iroquoia. Early in 1779, he put General John Sullivan in command of an extensive, three-pronged assault on the hostile settlements of the Six Nations. Sullivan's forces outnumbered the Iroquois five to one, and as the invasion force entered their homelands, the Natives wisely did not give battle, but fled. Deprived of fighting, Sullivan's men set fire to the countryside. This was precisely what Sullivan's commander intended. "The immediate objects are the total destruction and devastation of their settlements," Washington had ordered Sullivan. "It will be essential to ruin their crops now in the ground and prevent their planting more," he directed. In town after town, they burned anything valuable they could find, along with 160,000 acres of pumpkins, corn, beans, and squash basking in the late summer sun. Sullivan's men finished their destruction in the middle of September, and by November more than three thousand Iroquois were already taking shelter at Fort Niagara, the only food coming from British army rations. The Iroquois began referring to George Washington as "Town Destroyer."[14]

What this thumbnail sketch of Ohio's Revolutionary War over the first few years of independence reveals is an extraordinary degree of contingency. Uncertain as to what would happen next—or even what was to be wished for—British and American interests inflated and collapsed on almost a week-to-week basis. Patriot and British leaders would write letters sometimes within the same month that went from high hopes to utter despair. Native leaders moved from one side to the other and back again. Loyalties to any larger political group—to the Iroquois, to Pennsylvania, to Virginia, to the Continental Congress, to the king, to other Ohio Natives—were constantly in flux. The Americans were so worried they floated all sorts of ideas to maintain control, even incorporating Natives as the fourteenth member of the United States.[15]

In such perilous times, a man with political skill and powers of persuasion could either be a great asset or a significant risk. It is little wonder that, in 1780, after their homelands had been devastated, after they were fractured and fighting with one another, and after they had seen their ally Henry Hamilton hauled off for trial, Iroquois leaders decided to send word to Tachnedorus's son that his uncle must be silenced.

⸻

The evidence of Logan's participation in Ohio's Revolutionary War reveals a man conflicted. For instance, according to one account, late in the war, Logan explained to a loyalist officer that "he had two souls, one good and the other bad; when the good soul had the ascendant, he was kind and humane; and when the bad soul ruled, he was perfectly savage, and delighted in nothing but blood and carnage." Perhaps Logan did say this; years earlier, he had related something similar about feeling beset by devils all around him—and that was before the horror of 1774. The Moravian missionary John Heckewelder, when asked to look back on his memories of Logan, reported that the Mingo would often say that life "had become a torment to him." Logan thought "it might be better if he had never existed . . . [and] declared he would kill himself," Heckewelder said at century's end. He "went to Detroit, drank very freely, and did not seem to care what he did, and what became of himself."[16]

At the time, however, Heckewelder didn't mention Logan being suicidal. In 1779 he told John Gibson, now a general in the Continental Army and the commander of a fort in the Ohio country, that Logan was rebuilding his family. Ohio Natives had captured a daughter of one of the soldiers in Gibson's garrison, and Heckewelder sent word that she was alive and "adopted in the family of Logan, as his Sister, where she is much thought of." Doing the work of finding a replacement for Koonay and incorporating her into his kin contradicts the image of Logan wandering about Ohio cursing his existence.[17]

Other memories from these years also suggest Logan wasn't disconnected or disengaged from politics. In the fall of 1778, Ohio Natives captured Simon Kenton, a scout for Clark in Illinois, and dispatched him to Detroit, where they would decide whether to execute him. On the journey Kenton entered Logan's village on the Scioto River, where he spent the night pleading his case. According to reminiscences taken down in the nineteenth century, Logan dispatched two runners to the Upper Sandusky region where British officers conducted much of their trade with Ohio Natives, to put in a good word for the prisoner. When they got to Sandusky, the British agent spoke on Kenton's behalf, and asked for him to be remanded over as a prisoner at Detroit rather than killed. Kenton—and many in Ohio—attributed his life being saved to Logan's intercession.[18]

Another recollection of Logan during the Revolution underscores this affection for doomed captives. Logan would become renowned in the 1800s as a "friend of the whites," a reputation which must have shaped many of these memories, for nearly all of them revolve around the Mingo leader saving white prisoners from being murdered. William Robinson commented on how Logan's kindness saved him in 1774, as did James Wood in 1775. Others remembered how Logan frequently visited William McMillen, a settler who he had captured along the Greenbrier River not far from Sinking Creek, and sent to Detroit to work on the farm of Alexander McComb, one of the city's most prominent traders.[19]

But as the war stretched on, all was not well between Logan and the British. After Clark and Sullivan's victories, it seems Logan had begun to waver in his support for the Crown. He never appears in the records as being an avid fighter for the British; like many Natives in Ohio, he triangulated between the two sides. In 1780, when he did participate in a British-led strike on Kentucky, imperial agents insulted him, and this disrespect pushed him away from the king.

In an effort to regain the initiative, Crown officers encouraged Natives to fight back after the disasters of 1779. They helped the Iroquois raid American settlements in New York, and worked with the Natives to press

the war in Ohio. In 1780, British commanders at Detroit ordered Captain
Henry Bird and a detachment of 150 British and loyalist soldiers to invade
Kentucky, aided by all the Natives Alexander McKee could muster. A
total of 700, including most Shawnees, Mingos, and other Natives from
the Great Lakes joined Bird's force. Logan was among them.[20]

They attacked Kentucky outposts up the Licking River, about twenty-
five miles northwest of Lexington, and took nearly three hundred prisoners, some of whom were enslaved African Americans. By the time they
returned to Detroit, the number of captives in their party had swelled to
470. In addition to being a military victory, the strike was also an economic boon for the traders in Detroit who had financed it. One of them,
Alexander McComb, the captor of Logan's friend William McMillen,
helped put up the money to pay the soldiers and was repaid with captives. Another, the prominent French trader and Native agent Jacques
Duperon Bâby, had accompanied Bird, in part to help shore up Native
allies but also to monitor his investment.[21]

It's clear Logan also saw his participation in these attacks as trans-
active. Bird noted in one of his reports that Logan was dissatisfied with
the goods Bâby had arranged to secure his participation. "Mr. Baby
delivered me on setting out, three or four strands [textiles], some wor-
sted, and some other little things for Logan," Bird wrote to his superior
officer, but they were "all broke and spoil'd." These paltry things, in such
a condition, he judged, "would never have answered as a present," and
Bird "told Logan" he would receive proper treatment when they returned
to Detroit. By being stingy, Bâby and Bird signaled to Logan that he
wasn't a valuable ally.[22]

When Bird's men returned to Detroit later that summer, Logan
vented his fury about how he had been mistreated. According to one later
account, Logan "got into a drunken frolic and became so troublesome
that Captain Bawbee [Bâby], the commissary of the Indian department, kicked him out of the store-house" and called him a dog. These
were extraordinary fighting words. As historian Brett Rushforth has
explained, when Natives in the Great Lakes called someone a dog, they
were calling you their slave. As Bâby was not only a French trader but

an enslaver of both Native and African people, he knew exactly what he was saying.[23]

Instead of striking out at Bâby on the spot, Logan decided to change his political loyalty. According to one later account, he once again visited his friend William McMillen, to whom he declared, "I won't fight for the British any more; they have treated me very bad. Now, Bill, take this tomahawk and tell me how many prisoners and how many scalps I have taken from the Big Knives [Virginians] for the British.'" There were, according to McMillen, more than seventy notches on his tomahawk. "'Now Bill,' continued Logan, 'I would go back to the Big Knives, if I thought they would not kill me, and would kill and take as many of the British as I have done of the Big Knives; but I dare not go." He would sit the rest of the war out. "I will go home and hunt deer, raccoon, and beaver."[24]

This was the last McMillen ever saw of Logan. Charles Cracraft, a prisoner who worked alongside McMillen, and to whom we owe these recollections, believed that on his way home from Detroit Logan had gotten mixed up in a domestic dispute with a Native woman and got himself shot by her husband, a story that others often repeated in the centuries that followed. But it seems more likely that soon after his falling out with the British at Detroit he met up with a familiar face who was to be his executioner.

How long had it been since Logan had seen Tod-kah-dos? We know it had been a decade since the family had parted ways in the Pennsylvania mountains, with Tachnedorus and his son staying in the Juniata River valley while the rest of the Shickellamy clan tragically went to Ohio. Logan had travelled all over the region, but we have no evidence that he had ever returned to central Pennsylvania. When they reunited, did Logan know the reason for his nephew's sudden appearance? Did he suspect that Tod-kah-dos was there on a political errand, sent by "the nation"?

We don't know exactly where or when Tod-kah-dos fulfilled his mission. When he was made a prisoner at the end of the war and was on his own journey to Detroit, missionary John Heckewelder said his Native captors paused to show him "the spot between Detroit and the Miami

River where" the Mingo had been killed, which happened at some point in the latter half of 1780. It was Logan's own grove of death.[25]

Nor do we know the method of execution. Tod-kah-dos would later recount to the surveyor John Adlum the reasons why the Six Nations wanted Logan executed, but he didn't relate how he actually ended his uncle's life. Local historians in the twentieth century used their imagination, speculating that the two had a quarrel and, "while he was sitting by his camp fire with his elbows on his knees and his face between his hands in deep meditation, Tod-kah-dos stole up behind him and tomahawked him." This rendering, a stereotype of how savages killed one another, fits with and reinforces the mythological Logan, deep in thought and pondering the death of his people and his own mortality. But the truth is we just don't know.[26]

Adlum's incredulous question remains. Why did Logan have to die? Put simply, he was too dangerous to keep around. The politics of the Revolutionary War in Ohio were so uncertain that "the nation" began to see him as a liability. Perhaps he was a "violent sot" surrounded by demons that made him do terrible things. Several people who remembered running into Logan during these years mentioned him being under the influence of alcohol, but this was another easy settler stereotype used to discredit Natives who didn't conform and were deemed troublemakers.

Logan didn't have to be a drunk for political leaders to want rid of him, however. He was "a great man," a persuasive man, Tod-kah-dos said. He had a power that could not be reliably harnessed or controlled—and that constituted a critical threat in the Ohio backcountry in 1780.

Thirty years earlier, when Logan's father Shickellamy had experienced a similar fall from political grace, no one had insisted that he be assassinated. But those were drastically different times. The creation of the new American republic introduced a whole new dynamic to the Ohio Valley, creating new structures, new frameworks for understanding the past, present, and future that would profoundly remake life there. Chief among these was the political theory of republican citizenship. Patriot political leaders reflexively embraced the concept that, instead of subjects, Americans would be citizens. But no one really knew what that status entailed at the moment; there was no consensus on what rights citizens should have, who qualified, and what place those who were not citizens had in the United States. The Revolution also gave birth to American patriotism, a cultural force all its own. The stories told during the Revolution featured heroic riflemen like Michael Cresap and denigrated anyone who fought against the Revolution. That especially meant the peoples who helped the king, including "merciless Indian savages," as the Declaration would refer to them.

Such stories made Ohio a very dangerous place for White Eyes, Cornstalk, Killbuck, or other Ohio Natives who tried to help the patriots or supported the Revolution. There was no asterisk in the Declaration next to "merciless Indian savages" that said, except for those who are our friends. Native people were all lumped together as enemies of the republic. As such, settlers often murdered them, like Cornstalk and White Eyes. Logan knew if he went to fight for the Big Knives they would kill him. At the same time, their own people also saw pro-American Natives as threats to be eliminated. Persuasive men like Logan who endangered the political moves British-allied Natives might make were just as unwelcome. Ohio had been a lethal place for decades, but the Revolutionary War was of a whole different magnitude. This new concept of American republican patriotism that prized white pioneer-citizens and lumped all Natives together as merciless enemies was, as one historian has put it, "turning the world upside down."[27]

The greatest change in Ohio came from the young republic's embrace of frontier settlers. Rather than directing people where they could go and where they could live, as previous imperial and colonial regimes had tried to do in Ohio, the United States proclaimed they would promote an "empire of liberty" west of the Appalachians. Individuals were now emboldened to maximize their potential, to pursue their happiness. American frontiersmen, disdained before 1776 as destabilizers and violent savages, were now pioneer-citizens. Government would follow behind them and largely support their efforts rather than seek to restrain them. Men like Daniel Boone, George Rogers Clark, and, had he lived, Michael Cresap were the future of America and the republican experiment. They were "worthy and esteemed" citizens. Seeds no longer, these were the fruits of commonwealths. The republic had incubated its very own germ of empire.

Ben Franklin, despiser of the Paxton Boys in 1763, now dressed like they did when he went to Paris in 1777, donning a fur cap to the delight of French crowds. The pioneers were the embodiment of an emergent American patriotism, the offspring born of the nation-making—and race-making—project of the American Revolution. The changes that engulfed the Ohio Valley throughout Logan's lifetime would continue to swirl, but the American Revolution marked a turning point from which history would proceed very differently than it had since he was a boy.

The end of the Revolutionary War in Ohio reveals the consequences of these changes already at work. Logan hadn't been dead for two years when the force of American patriotism—with its veneration of hardy pioneer-citizens and its opposite, the notion that all Natives were the republic's enemies—turned Ohio into the bloodiest ground of the Revolution.

A few months after Tod-kah-dos ended his uncle's life, British-allied Wyandots ordered Christianized Delaware Natives living in three settlements along the Muskingum River in eastern Ohio to leave or be destroyed. The Wyandots were convinced these Natives, influenced by the Moravian missionaries John Heckewelder and David Zeisberger, were aiding the Americans. The Christianized Delawares obliged, left their villages and went west, while the Wyandot used their lands on the Muskingum to launch raids on American settlements. During the winter of 1781–82, some of the Delawares returned to their villages to salvage food and supplies, as their sudden ejection had meant they hadn't been able to prepare for the season ahead. Rumors spread east of the Ohio River that the Delawares were back, and some settlers interpreted this as a sign that they had betrayed the Revolution and were now themselves in the British interest.

Two hundred settlers living near Catfish Camp (about to be incorporated as Washington, Pennsylvania) volunteered to march on the Muskingum. Led by Colonel David Williamson, they reached the first of the Delaware towns, Gnadenhutten—"huts of grace"—on March 7, 1782, and decided how to deal with these "enemies." Williamson called for a council of war, and the majority voted to execute the offending Natives on the spot rather than take them to Fort Pitt as prisoners. In the morning, the militia forced the men into one of those huts, and the women and children into another. They then led ninety of them, one by one, to slaughterhouses, where they killed them all, many by bludgeoning them to death with coopers' mallets.

Like at Yellow Creek, the noises must have been unreal. Since this was no ambush, witnesses reported that the Delawares, once their fate was known to them, spent their last night singing hymns and chanting prayers. The next morning, different sounds redounded among the "huts of grace": the pop and crunch of skulls cracking open, the spray of blood up and onto the walls, audible gasps and moans from the condemned, the screams of children. When the carnage was over, Williamson's men scalped the corpses, set the buildings on fire, and returned to their homes. It was yet another horror in Ohio, this one ten times the size of Yellow Creek.[28]

The effects of how the Revolution's war stories had changed things are evident in the newspaper response to Gnadenhutten. Before the Revolution, when settlers like Daniel Greathouse, Joshua Baker, and their associates did things like this, the public called them cowards and savages and excoriated their heinous acts. Eight years later there was little criticism of Williamson and his militia. In 1774 colonial newspapers clamored over Yellow Creek, uniformly denouncing its perpetrators. In 1782, by contrast, the public response to Gnadenhutten was not only tepid, but it bordered on support.

Accounts that did describe the mass murders usually appeared in papers that had recently featured news of the Wyandots' initial attacks the summer before on the Delaware towns. Or they offered a justification for what Williamson's men had done, setting their acts in the context of Wyandot attacks that had "so alarmed the people . . . they therefore came to a determination to extirpate the aggressors." The Natives were to blame; their hostility had produced this collateral damage. As one Philadelphia paper put it, the Natives' "innate barbarity instigated [the militia] to the cruel massacre of the harmless unarmed Indians." No newspapers in 1774 blamed Koonay and John Petty Shickellamy for incurring colonists' wrath. In the eight years since, patriot leaders had spent a great deal of time, money, and ink blaming the British and the "merciless Indian savages" for trying to destroy the Revolution and it shaped the response. Now, the American public was told, the Natives had brought this on themselves. Cruel, yes, but justified.[29]

Consider, for example, the fake newspaper issue that Benjamin Franklin produced seven weeks after Gnadenhutten (but before he heard the news), on a printing press he had in his residence on the outskirts of Paris. The single-sheet newspaper issue featured a letter from an American officer, who discovered near Albany eight packages of scalps "taken in the three last years by the Senneka Indians from the Inhabitants of New York, New Jersey, Pennsylvania, and Virginia" and sent to the Governor of Canada who was supposed to forward them on to the king. A British officer supplied a careful invoice of the packages, which were divided into scalps belonging to boys, girls, women, infants, farmers, and "Congress soldiers" totaling 743 dead Americans. A letter from the Seneca accompanied the invoice in which they hoped the king "may regard them and be refreshed, and that he may see our faithfulness in destroying his Enemies, and be convinced that his Presents have not been made to ungrateful people." A second letter on the news sheet came from American naval hero John Paul Jones, who recited the grievances of the Declaration in his claim that his fight was a just one. "If" King George "engages savages to murder their defenseless farmers, women, and children," Jones argued, "does not so atrocious a conduct towards his subjects dissolve their allegiance?" Faced with eight bags dripping with the scalps of murdered women and children, how could any reader disagree?[30]

The "Supplement to the Boston Independent Chronicle" was a hoax. Franklin invented every word. When he passed the fabrication among his American and French colleagues, he said, slyly, that he "doubted" its contents, but insisted "the substance is truth." Franklin did this at exactly the same time, half a world away, that American readers learned a few bits about what happened at Gnadenhutten. Soon, his concoction would appear in British and American prints, many of them unaware that it was a fake or who its author was. Franklin, then serving as the American minister to France, had created this piece of propaganda because he worried that Americans were too ready to forget all the atrocities they had endured during the Revolution. As a treaty conference with Britain was in the offing, he didn't want his countrymen in a forgiving mood. Thus Franklin did what he and his colleagues had so often done to rile up Americans: they broadcast the connection between the king and "merciless savages." In so doing, they reinforced the notion that all Natives were against the Revolution.[31]

Franklin didn't approve of what Williamson had done, but neither did he blame him. When the news of Gnadenhutten reached Paris, Franklin instantly accused King George. "It is he who has furnished the Savages with hatchets and Scalping Knives and engages them to fall upon our defenceless Farmers, and murder them with their wives and children," Franklin wrote to an English merchant, "paying for their Scalps, of which the Account kept already amounts I have heard to near *two thousand*." This was an exact recitation of the scalp hoax he was currently sending to his friends in London. "Perhaps the people of the Frontier exasperated by the Cruelties of the Indians have . . . been induced to kill all Indians that fall into their hands without distinction, so that even these horrid Murders of our poor Moravians may be laid to his charge." Men like Williamson were only protecting America from *both* the tyrant king and his savage allies. This idea was synonymous with the lavish funeral procession New Yorkers put on for Michael Cresap. Patriot militias were now "killing women and scalping children" because, as one historian has written of Revolutionary Ohio, "behavior no longer betokened . . . human worth. Color did." Franklin's disgust with Paxton vigilantism was the colonial past. Now it was what intrepid, white, republican citizens were supposed to do.[32]

Ohio Natives were, understandably, furious about Gnadenhutten. Anticipating their response, the American commander at Fort Pitt ordered Colonel William Crawford, now sixty years of age, to organize a strike on Upper Sandusky, the place where Tod-kah-dos killed his uncle and the center of British-Wyandot opposition to the patriots. Crawford, with Williamson his second-in-command, put together a force of five hundred militia drawn from western Pennsylvania and Virginia counties, and rendezvoused just south of Yellow Creek at Mingo Junction. In a few days they marched the two hundred miles to Sandusky, where they met disaster on June 4, 1782. The main body fell back in a rout, having been beaten soundly by Wyandots and Shawnees. Crawford and a few wounded men were captured.

Washington's longtime inside man would pay the price for the horror of Gnadenhutten. Carried to Sandusky, Crawford learned from Indian agent Simon Girty that he was to be ritually tortured and killed. He begged Girty for mercy, but there would be none. Captain Pipe, the Delaware leader who had been among the most pro-American Natives in Ohio, now demanded that the Delawares slaughtered on the Muskingum be avenged with Crawford's life. Even if Logan were still alive, it is doubtful he could have saved this condemned white man.

They stripped the old veteran of his clothes and beat him. They fastened him to a pole in the center of the village and bound his hands. Then the torments started. According to observers, they sliced off his ears, and made him run around the pole by shooting gunpowder at him, poking him with burning sticks, and throwing hot coals on the ground under his feet. Crawford begged Girty to shoot him and end his pain, but he would not, responding "examples must take place, the Moravian towns were destroyed, and the inhabitants murdered by our militia." The ordeal lasted for two hours. Spent, Crawford laid on the ground and was scalped alive, and then Native women poured hot coals over his back and exposed skull. Finally, they threw him into the fire, where he roasted to death.[33]

The grisly details of Crawford's torture would become "the stuff of frontier legend." When two witnesses to the execution stumbled back to Pittsburgh a few weeks later, they ran into the writer Hugh Henry Brackenridge, who took down their statements and turned them into a pamphlet that was to instruct American readers of the "sufferings of some of her citizens by the hands of the Indian allies of Britain." Brackenridge added that he hoped readers "will see that the nature of an Indian is fierce and cruel, and that an extirpation of them would be useful to the world, and honorable to those who can effect it." This was what Williamson's men were trying to do at the "huts of grace."[34]

After Crawford's torture, Ohio Natives continued their offensive. Guyasuta led forces deep into Pennsylvania, sacking the county seat of Westmoreland County, Hannastown, a full thirty miles east of Pittsburgh, in the late summer of 1782. Ohio Natives struck south, too, driving to within five miles of Lexington, where Daniel Boone, his son Israel, and 180 other Kentuckians fought them at the Battle of the Blue Licks. Half of Boone's forces, including Israel, died. George Rogers Clark tried to avenge this incursion in November 1782, but was only able to make it as far as Chillicothe, near to Logan's elm tree, before retreating back to Kentucky, regarding his actions as "fruitless." Even though Cornwallis had surrendered at Yorktown the October before, 1782 witnessed some of the bloodiest fighting of the Revolution.[35]

When it came to ending the carnage, British diplomats in the Paris peace talks betrayed Native peoples by ignoring them completely. As much as patriot leaders had proclaimed that the two were firm partners, the British did not take their Native allies into any consideration in the negotiations or in the final Treaty of Paris agreed to late in 1782. They were abandoned—but not defeated.

In subsequent years, Americans followed Brackenridge's "honorable" advice and kept trying to "extirpate" Ohio Natives. It did not go well. Either as representatives of their states or the United States, military forces repeatedly marched on Ohio for more than a decade after Crawford's death. Natives kept beating back all American attempts to conquer Ohio.

When several invasion attempts in the 1780s proved just as fruit-less, the job fell to Arthur St. Clair. After spending years engaged in skirmishes with John Connolly and his Virginia partisans, St. Clair had gone on to become a general in the Continental Army, where he had a checkered career. He was with Washington at Trenton, but faced shame and a court-martial when he surrendered Fort Ticonderoga without fir-ing a shot in 1777. Washington kept him in the army, and he was on the field to watch Cornwallis's surrender at Yorktown. St. Clair later served as president of the Confederation Congress in the 1780s, and became governor over the Northwest Territory in 1788. This was power in title only, however, since the United States had precious little command over the region they claimed as theirs.

In 1790, President Washington and Governor St. Clair sent Colonel Josiah Harmar on an expedition against Ohio Natives who had prepared for such hostility by beginning to put together their own confederacy. Led by Little Turtle (Miami) and Blue Jacket (Shawnee), this incipient alliance would grow in strength, especially after they overawed Harmar's troops and forced them to retreat with significant losses. The next fall St. Clair tried again. This time he personally took charge of an invasion force of 1,500 men. Few came back. Natives destroyed one-third of the entire American military in what became known as "St. Clair's defeat" near the Wabash River. More than 600 American soldiers died, ten times the number of Ohio Natives killed. It was one of the biggest disasters in the history of the US Army, but a huge victory for what would become known as the United Indian Nations. In a strange twist, John Gib-son's brother George, the man who helped spring John Connolly from St. Clair's Westmoreland County jail in 1775, was among those who never returned thanks to his former enemy's negligence. These failures infuriated George Washington. When the news of St. Clair's disaster (or, more properly, Little Turtle's triumph) reached him, the President's personal secretary said he nearly lost control, and was shaking, shout-ing, and cursing.[36]

The Revolutionary War had only increased Washington's obsession with the trans-Appalachian west, believing it to be the secret to American glory. Throughout the 1780s, Washington spun up plans to develop the Potomac, including improvements to reduce rough currents at Harpers Ferry and sketching out what would eventually become the Chesapeake and Ohio Canal. He believed the Potomac was vital to America's future in part because Spain would not allow American farmers free access to the Mississippi River, and prohibited trade at New Orleans. The Potomac, Washington believed, could be the main economic artery into the continent's interior.[37]

When Washington dreamed about the west, he could not differentiate between national pride and personal interest. Washington still held the claims he had Crawford arrange from his previous trip to Ohio in 1770, which included several tracts along the Ohio River and others up the Kanawha. One of the more valuable of these was "Round Bottom," the bend on the Ohio River that saw much action in 1774 but today is the location of the Moundsville (West Virginia) Country Club. Washington had heard rumors in 1773 that Michael Cresap thought the valuable four hundred acres of Round Bottom were his, so he had sent off a cease-and-desist letter. "I can conceive no reason why you or any other person should attempt to disturb me in my claim to this land," Washington chastised Michael. His warning did not have its intended effect. Long after Michael was dead, his heirs continued to fight for this claim, and they thought they had won when they petitioned for, and received, a certificate for Round Bottom in 1781. Washington never wavered that his was the only valid claim, and all these entanglements aggravated him.[38]

So, in 1784, less than a year after he had retired from army service, Washington decided to take another trip to Ohio. His journey brought him back to a place he had camped as a teenager with Lord Fairfax, then as a young militia officer with General Braddock, and then as a hungry land speculator. Now fifty-two, Washington again watched the rippling waters of the North Branch of the Potomac as they drifted past Thomas Cresap's compound at Oldtown.

He hadn't seen Thomas Cresap in a long time. While Washington was becoming one of the most famous men in the world, a lot of changes had occurred among the Cresap clan at Oldtown. The family had donned their best clothes for several funerals—and weddings—after Michael never returned from his march to New England. Despite being in his eighties, Thomas had remarried not long after Hannah's death. Little is known about his second wife, Margaret Milburn, but in 1779, when Cresap disposed of some land, she was listed as a party to the sale. The historical record has even less to say about what became of Elizabeth Lamy, though their now adult daughter still lived close by.[39]

The Cresap women seemed to have had their fill of fighting men by the end of the Revolution. After Michael's death, his widow Mary had married another military man, Colonel David Rogers. In the 1760s, when the Cresaps tried their hand at being town developers, one of the people who responded to their advertisements and came to settle in Oldtown was Rogers, a recent emigrant from Ireland. Rogers and Mary Whitehead Cresap were married in 1777. A year later, Rogers would die in an ambush along the Ohio River trying to bring a supply of gunpowder from New Orleans up to Fort Pitt. In 1781, Mary went in a decidedly different direction, taking Michael's former clerk John Jeremiah Jacob (the man to whom Michael confessed he was going to die in 1775) as her third husband. After the war Jacob became a Methodist minister, and much later a staunch defender of the Cresap family name. Michael's sister Sarah followed a similar path a year later when *her* soldier-husband, Colonel Enoch Innes, also died unexpectedly. She, too, would take a minister as a second husband shortly thereafter. And, on Christmas Day, 1783, Michael's oldest child, Maria, married the most renowned attorney in Maryland and the state's attorney general.[40]

Originally born in New Jersey, Luther Martin had graduated from Princeton College near the top of his class three years after his bride was born. He then went on to study law and, in 1771, became qualified to practice in Virginia. That summer he, like many aspiring, calculating gentlemen of his generation, decided he wanted to see the west and went on a journey into the Appalachians. He arranged for a scout, George Brent, to help him navigate the mountains. Brent had recently married Thomas Cresap Jr.'s daughter Charity and he brought Martin by to introduce him to his famous in-laws. The Cresap family made a distinct impression on the budding lawyer.[41]

In the decade that followed his visit to Oldtown, Martin gained prominence in the revolutionary politics of Maryland. He briefly served as a soldier but soon became the state's first attorney general in 1778, a position he would hold for nearly thirty years. At war's end, Martin was living in Baltimore when he heard that Michael Cresap's eldest daughter, Maria, had completed her studies at Ann Brodeau's celebrated boarding school in Philadelphia and was visiting town before returning home. He had met Maria on his memorable western tour when she was five and he was twenty-three. Now that little girl from Oldtown was a seventeen year old debutante. Martin was immediately smitten. He later insisted he called on her "*solely* from the motive of" repaying the "kind attentions" and "friendly civilities" that he had "received from that truly hospitable family," but by Christmas they were married. At age thirty-five, Martin was thrilled to become "the happy husband of the amiable daughter of the one, and granddaughter of the other" famous Cresap pioneers.[42]

Figure 28. Luther Martin (1748–1826). Etched by Albert Rosenthal in 1905 after a miniature owned by a Mrs. Garrett of Baltimore.

Thomas was apparently just as pleased with his granddaughter's romantic coup, for merely three weeks after the ceremony he made this new member of the family an executor to his estate when he drafted his will in January 1784. Thomas then accompanied the newlyweds back to Baltimore, where he would live with his granddaughter and her new husband for several months. Maria's marriage was an auspicious union for the Cresap family, one that only would become stronger when Luther's brother Lenox married Maria's younger sister Elizabeth. The Martin-Cresap connection would be an essential development for the future of the family's reputation, and, in the decades that followed, the quest to understand what really happened at Yellow Creek.[43]

When Washington returned to Oldtown in September 1784, Thomas Cresap, the patriarch who had presided over all these family changes, was showing his age. Another visitor to Oldtown a few months later thought "the Celebrated Colonel" looked "more than one hundred years old." This man—who was on his way to *finally* draw the official boundary between Virginia and Pennsylvania—recorded that Cresap had suddenly lost his vision "about 18 months ago" (thus the reason he drafted his will in January 1784 and signed it with an "X"), but the old man's "other faculties are yet unimpaired, his sense Strong and Manly and his Ideas flow with ease." Luther Martin would later write that Cresap was deaf as well as blind by this time, but was still "a most entertaining and agreeable companion, still possessing a strong and vigorous mind, and as free from the fretfulness and peevishness of old age, as I ever knew a man of twenty-five." If Martin can be trusted, these praises of Cresap's continued prowess into his advanced years were not just words. Martin stated that Thomas had spent most of 1783 travelling to Nova Scotia to inspect land "near the mouth of the river Saint Croix" in Passamaquoddy Bay that he was interested in buying, returning disappointed to Baltimore in December. How the old man might have pulled this off, given that he was "a very great degree blind and deaf," defies belief.[44]

Washington didn't leave any details in his diary about what his reunion with his aged friend was like. There were greetings all around, and Washington certainly expressed his condolences to Thomas for the loss of his wife, and especially his son, who had died under his command. Washington met Margaret and the other new Cresap spouses who lined up to meet the celebrated general. Though Washington had been coming to Oldtown since he was a teenager, this visit in 1784 from America's savior was an event that surely brought out everyone in the area. It's possible that he even met Thomas's illegitimate daughter, Jane, now in her mid-twenties, her new husband Charles, and their two-year-old son, Charles Cresap Weeks.[45]

But yet again Washington had more than a social call on his mind. The ongoing conflict over Round Bottom troubled him. This, too, had to have been one of the reasons why Washington decided to pass through Oldtown in September 1784 on his western tour. The subject of land matters involving family was a common conversation for the old Ohio Company partners, so it's likely Washington discussed the issue of Michael's case for Round Bottom at some point during the evening he spent at Oldtown.[46]

Whether they confronted the issue or not, the next morning Washington bade farewell to Thomas and continued his trip west, passing through unsettling vistas that surely recalled even more unsettling memories. Two days after leaving Oldtown, Washington noted in particular one disturbing place that since Braddock's time had been called the Shades of Death. He certainly had experienced—and helped to perpetuate—lots of death in the backcountry throughout his life. When Washington did say his goodbyes to the elderly, impaired rattlesnake colonel and rode deep into the eerie woods that he had spent so much time in, he surely knew he would never see Cresap again. When he returned from this, his last trip to Ohio, Washington did what he always did when he got back to Mount Vernon: fought for the lands he desired. He filed papers to get Michael's claim to Round Bottom dismissed. Though it took some time, a grant securing Washington's claim was finally in hand on February 3, 1791. It helped that he was by then president of the United States.[47]

Native resistance, however, threatened Washington's dreams both personal and national. If he could not control Ohio, the Potomac would be as useless as the Mississippi. His friend Crawford had died horribly trying to break Native power there, and every subsequent effort had failed miserably. In 1792, flush with their stunning military success over St. Clair, Delawares, Miamis, Shawnees, Mingos, and a number of Native groups from the Great Lakes gathered at a place called The Glaize (today Defiance, Ohio) and formalized the United Indian Nations. If Washington wanted to conquer Ohio, it was becoming an even more difficult prospect.[48]

St. Clair's disaster did not deter the fuming president. While Ohio Native leaders prepared for their meeting at The Glaize, Washington was gathering his own forces. He interviewed all the Continental Army officers he had served with, picked "Mad" Anthony Wayne out of what he judged a rather lousy bunch, and put him in charge of an overhauled US Army— now named the Legion of the United States. As he had when he commanded John Sullivan to destroy Iroquoia in 1779, Washington ordered Wayne to pacify Ohio. Wayne was everything St. Clair was not, especially when it came to military command. His courage during the many battles he led troops in during the Revolutionary War bordered on recklessness, thus earning him his nickname. "Brave but nothing more," Jefferson wrote about Wayne during the officers' meetings with the Cabinet.[49]

Wayne's "Legion" made camp at what used to be called Logstown, the Mingo village where Tanghrisson had lived and George Washington had visited in 1753, a few miles up the Ohio River from the Forks. When he was a trader—before becoming an army officer and politician—John Gibson also used to live nearby, as did Logan. Now it was "Legionville," the first official training base for the US Army. Over the winter of 1792– 93, Wayne drilled his men here. Guyasuta and Cornplanter came to negotiate peace, but talks went nowhere. In the spring of 1793, Wayne's men started the slow process of moving downriver to Cincinnati and then, the following summer, they began yet another invasion of Ohio.

Wayne's expedition reached its climax, a decisive victory over the United Indian Nations at the Battle of Fallen Timbers, near what today is Maumee, Ohio, on August 20, 1794, just as John Adlum approached Cornplanter's Town on the Alleghany River, two hundred miles to the east.

When Adlum arrived, he found the Natives on the Upper Alleghany preparing for war. He watched Cornplanter bury his tomahawk in the war post. This was not good: if the Americans had lost Cornplanter, Native resistance was far more widespread than they thought. Cornplanter, a Seneca leader, had been a strong advocate for neutrality in the early years of the Revolution, but went with the British in 1778, fighting at most of the significant engagements in the northern backcountry. At the war's end, Cornplanter made an enemy of many of his people by signing the harsh Treaty of Fort Stanwix (1784), which accepted defeat and ceded a huge amount of Iroquois land. In 1790, Cornplanter visited Philadelphia to meet with Washington. It was he who told the president that his name among the Iroquois was Town Destroyer, and that "even to this day," when they spoke Washington's name "our women look behind them and turn pale, and our children cling close to the neck of their

Figure 29. Born of a Dutch father and a Seneca mother, Cornplanter became a war-captain for the Six Nations during the Revolutionary War. His agreeing to cede significant portions of Iroquois lands at the Treaty of Fort Stanwix (1784) led to his ostracization, and his resettling in northwest Pennsylvania on land known as Cornplanter's Tract. Painted by Frederick Bartoli in 1796.

mothers." Nevertheless, Cornplanter also recognized the diminished political power of the Iroquois and negotiated three tracts of 1,500 acres for his people on the Allegheny River. In 1791, Pennsylvania would designate "Cornplanter's Tract" as the first reservation in US history. It would become the residence of Tod-kah-dos, who married Cornplanter's daughter, Annie, as well as his aging father, Tachnedorus.[50]

But, as it had with other leaders who could have potentially become loyal friends of the United States—Guyasuta, Cornstalk, White Eyes, Captain Pipe—the United States looked as if it was squandering its relationship with Cornplanter, or so it seemed to John Adlum in August 1794. Cornplanter warned Adlum that "we are at peace now but in a few days it will be otherwise." He gave the surveyor a pair of moccasins so that he might be prepared to run when war started. However, a few days later, expresses carrying word of Wayne's smashing victory at Fallen Timbers arrived at the Allegheny River. The political calculus all over Native America changed instantly with that news.[51]

With that sudden transformation, Adlum didn't immediately don Cornplanter's moccasins to flee. Instead, he felt safe enough to stick around and investigate the Alleghany region further. Three days later, Adlum found himself sneaking up on a man weeping next to French Creek.

Early in their lengthy conversation, Adlum and Tod-kah-dos discussed the current war between the United States and the United Indian Nations. Tod-kah-dos did not approve and would not take part, even if his father-in-law did. Having seen him weeping, Adlum asked him why he "looked sorrowful," and Tod-kah-dos then gave his reply that it was a "disease of the mind."

They discussed what Tod-kah-dos meant by that. The explanation that Tod-kah-dos gave was part family history, part American history. Tod-kah-dos had so many reasons to be sorrowful, and Adlum was caught off-guard by the response. He was not expecting to hear a recitation of settler-Native relations going back decades.

"I will without reserve relate to you the whole of my griefs," Tod-kah-dos answered. "It has now but a few years since you laid us and the British on our backs," he began. "I know that your power is at least double to what it was then, and ours has diminished in nearly the same proportion—The British had large Armies in your Country, and strong garrisons on their frontiers, now they have neither." But, he warned, even though his people were reduced, they would still "fight desperately." Then Tod-kah-dos launched into what amounted to a refutation of the Declaration of Independence. "We are not so savage," he told Adlum, "we only killed so long as we found resistance . . . and as to women and children we never injured them." It was you, Tod-kah-dos insisted, who "destroyed our towns and sometimes by surprise, and you never spared any."[52]

Adlum was appalled. He had joined the Continental Army at the age of fifteen and had been one of the thousands of American soldiers captured when the British took New York City in 1776. He wouldn't stand for such lies against the republic he helped make independent. Adlum demanded Tod-kah-dos "to point out one instance" where Americans had done such a thing. "He gave me a look of surprise and indignation," Adlum recalled, "and said if you do not know I will tell you of one, and he began—There was a town on the Muskingum river, settled by some of your good white people amongst the Indians." Tod-kah-dos proceeded to lecture Adlum about the Gnadenhutten massacre, relaying "with great energy, the horrible massacre of those innocent people." Adlum remembered feeling properly chastised. Tod-kah-dos had gotten through to the proud republican citizen. "As I consider it a disgrace to our Country," he confessed decades later when he collected these notes into a memoir, "I will here let it drop and not relate it as he gave it to me."[53]

Then, principally to change the subject, Adlum asked Tod-kah-dos to have dinner. While they ate, Adlum inquired about his name, and the surveyor's shock instantly returned. You killed your uncle?!

CHAPTER 11

THE PERSISTENT WHISPER

"I was on the point of crying at her, 'Don't you hear them?' The dusk was repeating them in a persistent whisper all around us, in a whisper of a rising wind. 'The horror! The horror!'

... But I couldn't. I could not tell her. It would have been too dark—too dark altogether."

—*Heart of Darkness*

In the decades following the Revolution, white Americans developed many feelings about Natives. They hated them, they loved them, they ridiculed them, they cherished them, they mourned them, they despised them, they dressed up like and "played" them. In the middle decades of the 1800s they bought James Fenimore Cooper's *Last of the Mohicans* (1826) and wept for the "vanishing Americans," like Uncas and Chingachgook, but loathed the bloodthirsty Magua. They crowded theaters to see famed English actors perform *Metamora: The Last of the Wampanoags*. It was a contradictory, convoluted relationship.[1]

At the same time, white Americans after the 1780s were still sorting through what they thought about pioneers and the frontier. Some claimed they were the secret to an exceptional new American identity. No European novelist could get away with putting Natty Bumppo in the forests of the Old World. The Revolution, moreover, had turned real men like Daniel Boone and George Rogers Clark into republican heroes, and bestowed a new cultural, political, legal, and economic power upon those who acted like them. Some skepticism remained, however, especially as the United States continued to fight seemingly endless wars against Native peoples, conflicts that vigilante frontiersmen usually instigated.[2]

It is impossible, therefore, to divine precisely what Americans thought about Logan and Cresap when they came across their story in the many, many texts where they might have encountered it between the Revolution and the Civil War. There was no singular "American mind" about them, as scholars used to argue. Having a wide range of feelings about Native peoples and pioneers in general, they had, it is safe to say, just as varied a reaction to Logan the Mingo Chief and Captain Michael Cresap, in particular. They certainly did talk about them, though.

After 1787, Logan's Lament became one of the most widely reprinted, recited, memorized, and debated pieces of writing in early American culture. It was in newspaper articles, magazine pieces, novels, histories, ethnographies, poems, songs, anthologies, travel guides, and plays. Schoolteachers and parents across North America forced millions of boys to stand up and deliver Logan's words as an essential part of training young men to become virtuous citizens. It was brought forth to settle transatlantic philosophical debates and featured in decades of political discourse. By the middle of the 1800s, the final line of Logan's speech— "Who is there to mourn for Logan? Not one"—had grown so omnipresent and universal that it had become a punchline, a flippant aphorism spouted off to ridicule and tease.

With each passing year after independence, the confusion and uncertainty over who did what and why in the Ohio Valley became less pressing for white Americans than resolving a different confusion: Who were they and what did this new republic stand for? Even for the issue of republican citizenship, Logan remained useful as a way of resolving this new bewilderment. But it wasn't about him, his family, or his people. White Americans made Logan's words about *them*. They created many different Logans to justify a host of agendas that were important to them: a natural American Demosthenes, the noblest of savages, a worthless drunk, the quintessential "Vanishing American," a violent resister of "civilization." White Americans occupying the lands where Mingos used to live founded the Logan Historical Society, a group whose actual purpose was to preserve and cherish pioneer history.

Ripping Logan's Lament away from the deeply personal context from which it arose was an exercise in redirection. It allowed white Americans to avoid facing the persistent whisper of what really happened in Ohio in 1774 and why. They wouldn't confront the horrible reality of Yellow Creek, Sinking Creek, Gnadenhutten, and all the groves of death that preceded them. That history surrounded them, but it was too dark altogether. To satisfy the needs and desires of settler colonists, Logan and his speech became a lie, something wholly divorced from its true context.

But it was more than that. This effort was the second phase of the "double dispossession." In order to occupy the Ohio Valley and permanently take it away from Native peoples, white Americans had to sever what they did, felt, and experienced there. They had to eliminate Logan's history and replace it with their own.

What follows may seem like small details, especially in comparison with the "scramble for Ohio," the Seven Years' War, Dunmore's War, or the Revolution. Admittedly, the particulars of this chapter are far more mundane: correspondence going back and forth, people writing down remembrances, the publication of numerous books, and the founding of historical societies. We need to recognize, however, how those efforts, conducted almost exclusively by white Americans, constituted a different kind of violence. This was how the celebration of pioneer-citizens as American patriots evolved after 1783. While real violence between settlers and Natives was still ongoing in early nineteenth-century Ohio, there was a perpetual history war being waged about eighteenth-century Ohio that was also vastly destructive. In the decades following the Revolution, white Americans separated Logan's Lament from its context to make it their own. In doing so, they strove to complete the project begun more than a half century earlier—of making Ohio their own.

And it all began with Thomas Jefferson.

In his body and in his soul, Thomas Jefferson was in pain in June 1781. As his tumultuous term as Virginia's governor was coming to a close, a British invasion had not only taken Richmond but also advanced on Charlottesville to raid his home. Several of the people he enslaved left with the redcoats. But even before British cavalry stomped through Monticello, Jefferson had been awash in grief. His infant daughter had died a few weeks before. Heartbroken and in political disgrace, he fled to Poplar Forest, the plantation in Bedford County, Virginia, he had inherited from his father-in-law, about seventy-five miles southwest of Charlottesville. There, a fall from a horse compounded his suffering, breaking his wrist and banging up his body so much that he laid in bed for several weeks.[3]

To pass the time while he healed, Jefferson decided to spend the summer completing the only book he would write, *Notes on the State of Virginia*. A year earlier, not long before Tod-kah-dos ended Logan's life, the secretary to the French delegation in Philadelphia, Francois Marbois, had drafted a list of twenty-two queries to provide the French government with some details about America. The French had been so desperate to punish their English rivals that they had leapt to America's defense in 1778 without knowing even the basics about their new allies. The answers to Marbois's questions would provide the French government with information concerning the borders, peoples, geographic features, animals, minerals, laws, and government of the former English colonies.

Marbois sent his questions to all the states. Virginia's eventually landed on Governor Jefferson's desk. Beyond merely providing basic factual data about Virginia, Jefferson used the opportunity to compose his thoughts about natural history, race, commerce, slavery, agriculture, government, freedom, and human nature—all subjects that currently preoccupied philosophers throughout the Atlantic World. Jefferson turned what was "essentially a statistical study" into what one scholar wrote was "the most important scientific book written by an American before 1785." *Notes on the State of Virginia* became Jefferson's intervention into what we call the Enlightenment.[4]

The first question Marbois posed seemed simple enough, but, as we know, it was anything but: provide "an exact description of the limits and boundaries of the state of Virginia." Jefferson gave a short, numeric answer of latitude and longitude, but he didn't go into all the details, especially the bloody ones, about how these numbers had been reached. In fact, the exact boundary between Pennsylvania and Virginia still had not been finalized in the 1770s. Jefferson's last piece of business as governor in 1781 would be to write to Pennsylvania authorities, advising them to postpone for yet another year the final survey that would extend Mason and Dixon's line and fix the southwest corner of Pennsylvania. In this first chapter of *Notes*, Jefferson provided a list of treaties, grants, and negotiations conducted throughout the seventeenth and eighteenth centuries, but did not include the shattered families, dead children, and traumatized people that the process of trying to fix Virginia's boundaries had produced. Later in the manuscript, he would refer to the Ohio as "the most beautiful river on Earth," but he was thinking of its gentle current, not all that Natives and settlers had done to one another along its banks over the past decades.[5]

Marbois's sixth query asked for "a notice of its mines and other subterraneous riches; its trees, plants, fruits, etc." Jefferson called this chapter "Productions Mineral, Vegetable, and Animal" and began with an exhaustive list of all the resources that might interest French investors. He also used his response to launch an attack on the pernicious ideas of French naturalist Georges LeClerc, the Comte de Buffon, which had gained traction in Enlightenment circles throughout Europe. Buffon had written several volumes of natural history that posited all the animals and plants found in the New World were of a lesser stature than those found in Europe. America's colder and wetter climate had stunted their growth, according to Buffon. His "degeneracy theory" enjoyed significant influence, and it was getting worse: Buffon's protégé, the Abbé Raynal, had extended the "degeneracy" idea to include the peoples native to America and the colonists who had moved there.[6]

In turn, to refute Buffon's theory, Jefferson gathered as much material as he could find about American animals—fossils, animal skins, teeth, horns, and even an entire moose carcass. He sent out his own queries, asking several people he knew had explored the American interior, including George Rogers Clark, to verify his findings. Jefferson was anxious to get this section correct, and continued to add material to it throughout the early 1780s. In the end, Query VI would comprise one-quarter of *Notes on the State of Virginia.*

He also set out to defend America's people, as well as its nature, from Buffon's disparaging theory. In Query VI, and elsewhere in the manuscript, Jefferson gushed with admiration for Native peoples. He respected their natural affection for one another and their children, their capacity for strong friendships, and their moral sense of justice. Because they were "uncorrupted by civilization," he thought, they had no need for coercion or compulsion to keep their communities together. They were, in this telling, cast as "natural republicans." And when he turned to their "eminence in oratory," the proof he needed was right at hand: his memorandum book. Jefferson flipped back to 1775 and found the speech he had taken down when it had been all the conversation in Williamsburg. Yet, just as he had severed the context of Virginia's boundary controversy from its messy, bewildering reality, so too did Thomas Jefferson manipulate for his own purposes the deep and painful family, colonial, and imperial history that produced Logan's Lament.[7]

"I may challenge the whole orations of Demosthenes and Cicero, and of any more eminent orator, if Europe has furnished more eminent, to produce a single passage superior to the speech of Logan, a Mingo chief, to Lord Dunmore when governor of this state," Jefferson announced. He then introduced the speaker by giving some background. As it is the source for Logan's celebrity in the years that followed, Jefferson's introduction as originally published is worth quoting in full.

In the spring of the year 1774, a robbery and murder were committed on an inhabitant of the frontiers of Virginia, by two Indians of the Shawnee tribe. The neighboring whites, according to their custom, undertook to punish this outrage in a summary way. Col. Cresap, a man infamous for the many murders he had committed on those much-injured people, collected a party and proceeded down the Kanhaway in quest of vengeance. Unfortunately a canoe of women and children, with one man only, was seen coming from the opposite shore, unarmed, and unsuspecting an hostile attack from the whites. Cresap and his party concealed themselves on the bank of the river, and the moment the canoe reached the shore, singled out their objects, and, at one fire, killed every person in it. This happened to be the family of Logan, who had long been distinguished as a friend of the whites. This unworthy return provoked his vengeance. He accordingly signalized himself in the war which ensued. In the autumn of the same year, a decisive battle was fought at the mouth of the Great Kanhaway, between the collected forces of the Shawanees, Mingoes, and Delawares, and a detachment of the army of the Virginia militia. The Indians were defeated and sued for peace. Logan however disdained to be seen among the suppliants. But, lest the sincerity of a treaty should be distrusted, from which so distinguished a chief absented himself he sent by a messenger the following speech to be delivered to Lord Dunmore.

Jefferson then inserted the entire text of Logan's Lament into his manuscript, seeing it as the perfect response to Raynal's accusations of Native degeneracy. "Before we condemn the Indians of this continent of wanting genius," Jefferson wrote just after the lament, "we must consider that letters have not yet been introduced among them." Jefferson assumed Logan could not read and had no education, which made his words all the more impressive. Logan was a *natural* Cicero. Buffon, Raynal, and anyone else who might suggest that American flora, fauna, or humanity was inferior, were clearly mistaken.[8]

Jefferson's introduction to Logan's Lament was, of course, riddled with errors. Some of this was purposeful. Jefferson wanted Enlightenment readers to empathize with the weeping, tragic Mingo unburdening himself with such stirring words under the elm tree. He thus eliminated the decades of pain, failure, violence, and trauma that the Shickellamy family had endured long before Yellow Creek, presenting Logan's revenge as the reflexive act of a justly provoked Indian brave.

The word "chief," which Jefferson invoked twice, helped establish this image for Europeans, even though Logan's actual political status was nothing approaching a sachem. Jefferson also refused to elaborate about what it looked like for Logan to have "fully glutted his vengeance." He did not want his readers, mainly people who saw themselves as part of an enlightened, transatlantic republic of letters, to see "Chief Logan" as a terrifying presence that lurked near Muddy or Sinking Creek about to slaughter children. Jefferson needed Logan to be a noble savage, not a merciless one.

Other mistakes were likely unintended. Jefferson reported that he jotted down the speech "as taken from the mouth of some person whose name, however, is not noted, nor recollected." That source, however, shouldn't have been so casually relied upon. What seemed like a definitive account of the lament and the details surrounding its speaker was actually based on whispers, guesses, suppositions, and rumors about what had happened the previous spring. Jefferson didn't know it, but what he had transcribed turned out to be a very shoddy and confused account of what had taken place along the Ohio in April 1774. He turned the premeditated attack at Baker's Bottom into a single musket volley that mowed down Logan's family in an instant. Moreover, as newspaper printers had done in the summer of 1774, Jefferson intertwined several details of the attack Cresap did make on Native canoes at Pipe Creek with the Yellow Creek massacre that happened a few days later. Jefferson compounded Logan's mistake by also referring to Michael as Colonel Cresap, his father's militia rank. But, most of all, he hastily and sloppily assumed that the accusations that swirled throughout Williamsburg and in other American towns in 1774–75 were true: Michael Cresap was indeed to blame for Logan's rage.[9]

At first glance, an astute reader might interpret Jefferson's rather blithe transference of what he wrote in 1774 into a manuscript prepared at the end of the Revolution as refuting a central argument of this book. If the Revolution had so thoroughly transformed how Americans conceived of men like Michael Cresap, how could Jefferson simply copy this

colonial indictment of a settler acting like a savage? If Jefferson judged
Cresap an infamous murderer of much-injured people in the 1780s, had
the Revolution *really* changed anything?

This is where Jefferson's primary motivation for *Notes* must be kept in
mind: the reason for this project was to repudiate any notion that America
was inferior. He had a case to make and he needed it to be airtight. Jefferson didn't know in the 1780s that Michael Cresap had not actually
been the cause of Logan's grief, but even if he had, saying so would've
weakened his claim that Logan was America's Demosthenes. A talented
natural orator would never get such crucial facts wrong. Questioning or
qualifying Logan would have undermined the sentimental pathos Jefferson worked to build around Logan's Lament and thereby threatened
the scholarly points he was trying to score. It was vital for him to take
Logan's side, even if it meant making an exception to the otherwise
revolutionary nature of *Notes on the State of Virginia* to do it.

For that was the other thrust of Jefferson's project. In every other
part of the manuscript, *Notes* served as a justification and defense of the
American Revolution. Jefferson thought American independence had
made it possible for Virginians to realize their dreams of living in a truly
happy society. In order to reach perfection, he wrote in *Notes*, all they
had to do was undertake a few more modifications: amend their constitution, abolish slavery, and establish a broad-based education system to
train virtuous citizens. Then, he wrote, they could usher in a republican
millennium for all white people to enjoy.[10]

And he meant all: in some of the most radical parts of *Notes*, Jefferson "leveled up" common white farmers and argued they, "the people,"
should enjoy the same status as kings or aristocrats. Jefferson rejected
the class prejudices of his fellow planters, proclaiming that the common white folk who "labor in the earth" were "God's chosen people."
Jefferson's adoration of independent, white yeoman farmers fit with the
Revolutionary plaudits lavished upon Michael Cresap and his fellow
pioneer-citizens. As a group, they were not unworthy cowards but the
future of republican liberty and the redeemers of mankind.[11]

The glorification of individual, yeoman farmers, first explicated in

Notes, would become one of the central tenets of the political philosophy known as Jeffersonianism. By the early years of the 1800s, Jeffersonianism would give even more power to the image of pioneer-citizens taming the American wilderness and bringing proper civilization and cultivation to North America. This "leveling up" of white farmers into the epitome of America was the transformation the Revolution produced. Although many of Michael's descendants and heirs did not consider themselves Jeffersonians—indeed, they would come to hate Jefferson for the things he wrote about the family in *Notes*—they nevertheless benefited immensely from a political philosophy that lionized white settlers. Logan's people would find that these notions would have far greater consequences for them and their happiness than any accolades about Native eloquence.

Jefferson continued to revise and expand his manuscript after sending his initial responses to Marbois in late 1782. Few had seen it when, in 1784, he was appointed minister to France and took *Notes* with him to Paris. The next spring he arranged for a Parisian printer to make two hundred copies, which he began sharing with friends, students, and scholars in Europe and America, always with a handwritten request that they not be published. Very quickly, he lost control, as a French bookseller who had gained access to one of the copies commissioned a translation, much to the author's frustration.[12]

Realizing there was little he could do to stop publication, Jefferson began negotiating with a London printer to bring out an authorized version of *Notes on the State of Virginia* in the summer of 1787. From there, it was soon excerpted in periodicals and books on both sides of the Atlantic. Of all the passages from *Notes*, publishers focused their attention on Logan, his story, and his speech. It was, for instance, the only piece of Jefferson's text extracted in the 1787 edition of the *Annual Register*, the landmark English reference work first established by Edmund Burke in 1758. Other English journals and encyclopedias picked it up from there. In America, Noah Webster put the speech in his *American Magazine* in 1788. John Lendrum also included Logan's Lament among the documents he compiled for his *Concise and Impartial History of the American Revolution* (1795).[13]

After the Revolution, a market flourished for educating Americans about the geography and language of the new American republic. Booksellers in several American cities featured a wave of new atlases, geographic textbooks, spellers, and oratory primers. Many of the best-selling editions of these books included Jefferson's introduction and Logan's speech. In the decade after the publication of *Notes*, readers could find the lament in Jedidiah Morse's *American Geography* (1789), William Guthrie and John Knox's *A New System of Modern Geography* (1795), and William Winterbotham's *An Historical, Geographic, Commercial, and Philosophical View of the United States of America* (1795). These books went through many printings, with Logan's Lament often carrying forward in edition after edition.[14]

But the most important of these new works was Caleb Bingham's *American Preceptor*. Bingham's textbook was a wildly successful instruction manual for aspiring American orators. It went through more than seventy printings, sold at least 640,000 copies in the thirty years after its first appearance in 1794, and remained in use into the 1870s. Logan's speech first appeared in Bingham's book in 1795. It remained—complete with Jefferson's introduction—through the next sixty-six editions, published into the 1820s.[15]

In all these early excerpts, both Jefferson and Logan told these students that Michael Cresap was an infamous killer. Within a few years of the publication of *Notes*, as Jefferson's political star rose higher and higher in the 1790s, Logan and Cresap had become fixtures in early American culture.

═══

Logan's increasing popularity pained the Cresap family. Luckily for him, Thomas didn't live to see it. When he died on January 31, 1787, he was at least eighty-five, but he may have been into his nineties. The family buried him near the house and stockade complex he had built nearly five decades earlier, and his body would remain atop the long, majestic hill that slowly sloped up from the Potomac. The gentle rise of that hill from the river to the Cresap compound had seen a great deal of activity in the eighteenth century: Shawnee women tended vegetables there, and, when they left, colonial livestock grazed there. Hundreds of British redcoats pitched tents there on their way to battle the French, and so did Virginia soldiers before heading west to fight the children of Opessa's Shawnees. Native dignitaries, colonial diplomats, imperial agents, a royal governor, and a future president of the United States had walked over the spot on the crest of the hill that would become Thomas's final resting place. His family marked the grave with a squat fieldstone marker that simply read "TC, dcd January 31, 1787."[16]

In the months and years that followed, Cresap's heirs followed the extensive provisions of Thomas's will. His executors disposed of lands he wanted sold and cleared the 120 acres of lands at the mouth of the South Branch of the Potomac and arranged for his grandson, Michael Cresap Jr., now twelve, to inherit not only his father's lots in Oldtown and other plots in Virginia, but also for him to co-own (with Luther Martin)

Figure 30. Gravestone of Thomas Cresap.

the 500 acres Thomas still held on the Susquehanna. This land, Cresap dictated in his will, is "'said' to be in Pennsylvania."[17] Even at the end of his remarkably long life, the "monster" from Maryland was unwilling to let go of his half-century-long grudge against the Pennsylvanians.

As the Cresaps moved on without their famous patriarch, the increasing popularity of Logan's Lament festered. Thomas died without knowing what more and more Americans were saying about his family, but his children and grandchildren were not so fortunate. They were going to need a public defender. Before the 1790s were out, they would have one.

———

Since marrying into the Cresap family, Luther Martin had become a leading political figure in the early American republic. He represented Maryland in the Constitutional Convention, but was so thoroughly dissatisfied with the proceedings that he left early. Martin became a prominent anti-Federalist and fought a losing battle in Maryland's ratifying convention to reject the Constitution. Despite his earlier misgivings—in 1788, he publicly declared the Federalists a group of conspirators who sought "to abolish and annihilate all State governments, and to bring forward one general government, over this extensive continent, of a monarchical nature"—he later became a member of that political party. Such was the depth of his hatred for the author of *Notes on the State of Virginia*.[18]

Daniel Cresap Jr., Michael's nephew and member of his uncle's expeditions in both 1774 and 1775, had long meant to vindicate the family name. But when pneumonia took him in 1794, he bequeathed to Martin what the latter would later refer to as "a sacred trust": the task of defending the Cresaps from Jefferson's aspersions. "He intended to have performed [it] himself, to rescue his family from this unmerited opprobrium," Martin wrote, but now it was up to the outspoken Maryland attorney general to set the record straight.[19]

Martin didn't fulfill his obligation right away, though. Two years went by and his own family increasingly absorbed his attention. After giving birth to three daughters in rapid order, his wife, now thirty, became gravely ill. Maria Cresap Martin, Michael's oldest child, died of cancer in the winter of 1796, and Martin found himself a widower and the sole caretaker of three young girls.[20]

Martin was still grieving a few weeks later when he saw an advertisement in a Philadelphia newspaper for a stage performance that featured a recitation of "The Story of Logan, the Mingo Chief." He suddenly remembered his "sacred trust" and used it as a way to vent his anguish. He took up his pen and set himself to become the public avenger of his dead wife, her father, and grandfather. The actor who had taken out the advertisement had no idea what he had stepped into by including Logan's speech in his repertoire.

James Fennell was a noted stage actor in London, but his gambling habits kept him constantly on the edge of ruin. In 1797 he came to America to escape debts and raise cash. He played theaters in New York and Boston to some success and planned a series of lectures in Philadelphia. He took out advertisements in Philadelphia newspapers over the course of the winter informing the public of all the different poetry and prose he planned to perform at College Hall. One attendee reported Fennell had brought in a "numerous audience" who were "greatly delighted" with his recitations. At the end of March, he informed Philadelphians that Logan's speech would feature in his next performance.[21]

With his shows going well, Fennell must have gone pale when he saw the threat lodged inside the April 3 issue of William Cobbett's Philadelphia newspaper, *Porcupine's Gazette*. It wasn't a bad review; it was far worse. Cobbett had published an open letter from the Maryland attorney general addressed directly to him.

Martin's letter to Fennell began with passive aggression. Surely the English thespian didn't intend "to wound the feelings of a respectable family in the United States," by including Logan's speech. No, Fennell wasn't a villain. He was a dupe: "You found that story and speech in Jefferson's Notes on Virginia; —you found it related with such an air of authenticity, that it cannot be surprising that you should not suspect it to be a *fiction*." This wasn't Fennell's fault; it was Jefferson's. Having dispatched with the unsuspecting actor, Martin then turned on his real prey, the man who just two weeks before had been inaugurated vice president of the United States.[22]

Martin started with snide insinuations that Jefferson was a poor scholar. "For the want of better materials he was obliged to make use of such as came into his hands," Martin informed Fennell, "and we may reasonably conclude whatever *story* or *speech* he could pick up calculated to destroy the hypothesis of Buffon, or establish his own, . . . instead of being scrutinized minutely, would be welcomed with avidity." Martin then launched into a history of Thomas Cresap's early life through the 1770s, documenting his consistent battles with Native peoples, but always defending them as justified. "As to Logan," Martin concluded, "the *real* Logan of *nature* had but little, if any more likeness to the *fictitious* Logan of *Jefferson's notes*, than the brutified Caffree of Africa to the enlightened philosopher of Montecello." Ostensibly a warning to Fennell, Martin's fiery letter left no doubt that he believed Jefferson's reputation as a philosopher was unearned.[23]

Having found himself mixed up in a fight between the attorney general of Maryland and the vice president of the United States, Fennell did his best to get out of it as fast as he could, dashing off a note begging Martin's pardon that same day. He was wise to steer clear, as Martin's war on Jefferson was just beginning.[24]

When Martin sent his first letter to Cobbett, *Porcupine's Gazette* was only a month old, but it had quickly become one of the most radically conservative and vitriolic Federalist papers in the country. It's doubtful, therefore, that Jefferson came across Martin's letter there. But he did see it. Jefferson's friends tried to reassure him that Martin "must have been in a state of drunkenness from which he is scarcely ever free." Jefferson tried to dismiss it as a political smear. The venue it appeared in, and the timing—he hadn't been vice president for a month yet—struck Jefferson as no coincidence. Still, it clearly bothered him.[25]

Six weeks after Martin's initial salvo, Jefferson reached out to John Gibson. If anyone knew the truth about what had happened on the Ohio in 1774, it was the man who had been with Logan under the elm tree. He told Gibson, "I do not mean to enter the newspapers with Mr. Martin," still he wanted to know if "any mistake has been committed to the prejudice of Colo. Cresap." With this query, Jefferson launched his own campaign to get to the bottom of Logan's Lament. His letter to Gibson would be the first of many he would send all over North America from 1797 to 1799; it was the beginning of an intensive investigation of the Yellow Creek massacre and its consequences. Even if they were just another Federalist attack on his character, Martin's charges cut Jefferson to the quick. If he had made an error, he was determined to fix it.[26]

In late June, Martin again took up his pen. This time he dropped the façade of talking to an actor and directed his fire straight at the vice president. An open letter to Jefferson appeared in the June 24, 1797, issue of *Porcupine's Gazette* demanding answers to three questions: 1. Where did you get the speech? 2. Who did you mean by "Col. Cresap"? and 3. Where did you get your information that "*any person of that name*" was infamous as a murderer of Native people? Martin fumed that Jefferson owed it "to the world at large" to resolve these questions.[27]

Five months passed and Martin got no satisfaction. "I have waited sufficiently long for your Answer," Martin insisted in another open letter that appeared in Cobbett's paper on December 14, "but that you have not thought proper to give me. You have preserved obstinate, stubborn Silence." Since Jefferson would not come forward to acknowledge his error, Martin announced there would be future letters. He swore he would continue "through the medium of the publick papers" until he had successfully "effac[ed] from the name of Cresap the Stain you have attempted to fix thereon." Jefferson was never going to give Martin the gratification of sparring with him in the press. That type of combat was not his way. He did, however, ramp up his own investigation two weeks after Martin's latest letter.[28]

On December 31, 1797, Jefferson reached out to the newly elected governor of Maryland, John Henry, who, though a Federalist, had signaled he might mediate this squabble between his attorney general and the vice president. Jefferson informed Henry that had Martin come to him privately, he would've "cooperated in every means of investigating the fact," but "he chose to step at once into the newspapers" and "adopted a style which forbade the respect of an answer." He then gave a lengthy statement to Henry, saying that he "was not the author of the injury," but had only included what he had written down, which had been "the theme of every conversation in Williamsburg" after Dunmore's return from the west. Jefferson explained he "knew nothing of the Cresaps, and could not possibly have a motive to do them an injury with design." He informed Henry that Gibson had already verified that Logan did take him "to a neighboring wood, sat down with him, and rehears[ed] with tears the catastrophe of his family." Thus, Jefferson said, "the speech of Logan is genuine." But, he told Henry, he would "continue to inquire into the evidence." He planned on collecting testimony and then would publish it in future editions of *Notes on the State of Virginia*.[29]

On New Year's Day, 1798, both Martin and Jefferson were at their writing tables scratching out letters about the other. "You have probably seen or heard of some very abusive letters addressed to me," Jefferson wrote to his old college friend John Page from Philadelphia. "I do not mean to notice Mr. Martin," he said, but still "I must pray you to rub up your recollection and communicate to me as fully as you can what you can recall" about Logan and his speech. Meanwhile, in Baltimore, Martin spent the holiday scrawling the first of what would be six open letters to Jefferson that would appear in Cobbett's paper throughout the winter.[30]

"It has been repeatedly suggested to me by my friends" to leave this subject alone, Martin began. He could not. Jefferson had to account for his libel. He could not hide behind Logan: "it is *you*, sir, who in the *Story* pledge your character as a man and historian, for the *Truth* of the savage's assertion." Martin then announced his series of letters would prove "the *falsehood* of those allegations, which you as a *gentleman* and a *man of honor* ought to have *authenticated* or *retracted*."[31]

They started to appear weekly over the mid-winter. The first three focused on establishing Thomas Cresap's reputation, reciting his early history up through the Seven Years' War. Martin also added personal recollections about his grandfather-in-law, describing Thomas's trip to Nova Scotia in his eighties, and his loss of sight and hearing. He provided documents from the 1740s testifying to Thomas's character and said he had "examined the archives of Maryland and can find no complaint or insinuation made by the Indians of his having committed any acts of violence whatever against them." Martin's information was correct; he must've had access to Cresap papers and the support of family and friends.[32]

Martin then pivoted to Michael's defense. He described Michael's upbringing, alleging the infant boy had been only "accustomed to see [Natives] treated with kindness and humanity," and described his education, marriage, and early forays in business. In the spring of 1774, Martin argued, Cresap did carry war to Shawnees and Mingos, but only after he had heard they "were about to take up the hatchet, and to commit immediate hostilities." He included two contemporary letters from settlers begging Michael to help defend them from imminent attack.[33]

Martin dove deeply into sentimental prose when he discussed Michael's actions in 1774–75, veering into hyperbole. Michael volunteered to join Angus MacDonald in the raid on Wakatomika in the summer of 1774, Martin argued, because he could not ignore "the dying groans" from "that infant country['s] . . . butchered inhabitants[;] the flames ascending from their dwellings through the dark horrors of the night could not afford music to his ears or pleasure to his eyes," but rather filled him with "the most poignant anguish" and made him take up arms to fight the Shawnees. He made an even greater sacrifice the following year:

> he tore himself from the tender embraces of a beloved wife, and the endearing caresses of four lovely children, the oldest of whom, the late Mrs. M[artin], was then but eight years of age. It was their last adieu! Their longing eyes were no more to be blest with the sight of an affectionate husband, a tender and indulgent father! He marched with his company to the siege of Boston—he lived not to return.

New Yorkers received "all of him that was mortal." Martin continued to rhapsodize about his father-in-law: "His generous spirit, that portion of ethereal flame which during their union warmed and animated it here, ascended to the bosom of its Creator, where the shafts of malevolence cannot assail it; nor the envenomed calumnies of philosophers disturb its repose." Martin's exuberance is a bit much, but when he said that Michael in 1775 was "*more* than beloved and esteemed; he was by many of them even idolized," he captured the feelings of that moment quite well. "Is *this* the man, whom of all others you selected to declare him an infamous murderer!," Martin thundered at the vice president.[34]

On March 3, 1798, Cobbett published Martin's eighth and final letter to Jefferson. At nearly five thousand words, it examined the reasons for the Yellow Creek massacre and tried to prove that Logan and his people were far from innocent victims. It included allegations from Benjamin Tomlinson, saying the slaughter was "more *immediately occasioned* by the insolence of Logan's younger brother (John Petty Shickellamy), who was about to carry off the coat of one of the Inhabitants." Martin didn't admit that the coat in question belonged to Tomlinson's brother, or that this witness was married into the Greathouse family, two facts that may have influenced his testimony. Tomlinson also charged that Gibson wrote the whole of Logan's speech. Martin also provided a statement from Michael's nephew and fellow soldier Joseph Cresap. Michael's nephew insinuated that Logan's family had it coming: "The Indians in particular at Yellow Creek were so uncommonly impudent" that the neighboring settler families, including the Bakers, had sent their women and children away from fear. Martin layered on more testimony to condemn the Mingos and excuse the murders. He also seized upon Tomlinson's statement that John Gibson had composed the speech, which, Martin called "entirely fictitious." The "celebrated Mingo chief," Martin concluded, "was an ignorant, insignificant, worthless savage, without merit and without consequence."[35]

With these vicious words, the Maryland attorney general believed he had achieved his mission and brought his case to a close.

> Thus having done, I call on you, *Thomas Jefferson, Esquire, Vice-President of the United States;*

You have been *solemnly arraigned* at the bar of that *august* tribunal, *the public*, on a charge of *foul calumny*.—You have *refused* to plead, and *stood mute*; of this no *advantage* has been taken; you have been *put upon a fair*, a *candid*, and an *impartial* trial; the *evidence has been heard*; you *stand convicted*.

Waiting for Jefferson's response to this verdict, Martin finished by saying "Here for the present I *pause*."[36]

In all, Martin submitted more than 17,500 words to *Porcupine's Gazette*. It had some effect. Francis Corbin, a Virginia politician who had been defeated in several elections by some of Jefferson's friends and was trying to make a comeback in 1798, wrote to Cobbett in March that Martin had "absolutely vindicated" the Cresaps, and said Jefferson should "forfeit his title" to be "a republican and a philosopher" if he refused to respond. Martin's Federalist friends salivated, hoping they could draw Jefferson out.[37]

He didn't take the bait. Jefferson knew fighting in the public papers would be a losing cause. When one of his friends sent a rebuttal to John Fenno's *Federal Gazette*, an even more rabidly Federalist paper than Cobbett's, saying that no one in the Ohio country "ever called into question . . . Mr. Cresop's being the perpetrator" of Yellow Creek, it never appeared. This was not a fair fight, and it would've been disastrous for him to respond point-by-point in the press. "While I should be collecting evidence to refute one lie," Jefferson wrote John Page, "the Porcupines would publish twenty new ones."[38]

So, while Martin screeched in "the Porcupines," Jefferson quietly gathered materials. His friends sent him their recollections of Yellow Creek and Logan's speech. They wrote to others on Jefferson's behalf and forwarded any responses. His file of statements and alternate versions of the speech swelled. He reached out to strangers, including the Moravian missionary John Heckewelder. Interestingly, he never wrote to James Madison, his closest friend and political ally, about it. Madison was the original source for the first printed edition of the lament, and his version was slightly different than the one Jefferson copied down in his memorandum book, so there remains an unanswered question as to where Madison got it. Jefferson and Madison were unacquainted in 1774, but it's curious that while Jefferson scoured the Virginia countryside looking for verification of the speech in the late 1790s, there is no evidence he ever mentioned it to Madison in writing.[39]

In the first few months of 1800, Jefferson was able to give his historical research project a bit more attention after pressing political business forced him to set it aside for much of 1798 and 1799. He made a few more inquiries, received some last-minute testimonials, and organized his papers to send off to Samuel Harrison Smith, a reliable Republican printer. Since the new appendix was so long—more than eleven thousand words running to fifty printed pages—Smith initially published *An Appendix to the Notes on the State of Virginia Relative to the Murder of Logan's Family* as a stand-alone pamphlet in April 1800. Initially, it consisted of Jefferson's letter to Governor Henry, followed by fourteen documents and then a final statement summarizing his three-year investigation. Jefferson received a shipment of what he called the "Loganian Appendix" from Smith and started distributing copies to specific people. A list of more than one hundred Americans (but no European philosophers) to whom he sent them remains among his papers. Madison's name is on it; Luther Martin's is not.[40]

Readers of the "Loganian Appendix" found a great deal of details about what had happened along the Ohio in the spring of 1774. From Jefferson's collected evidence, we know much more about Cresap's attacking Natives downriver and especially significant new information on the trap Greathouse and his men set at Baker's Bottom. Since the captive William Robinson was one of Jefferson's informants, we also know about the note Logan dictated to him and tied to the war club later that summer. Not everything Jefferson collected was accurate, and some of it unfortunate, including Robinson's corroborating as truth the mistaken rumor that Koonay's pregnant body was ripped apart.[41]

Heckewelder's narrative was especially important. Not only did it provide significant information about Logan's early life and his untimely

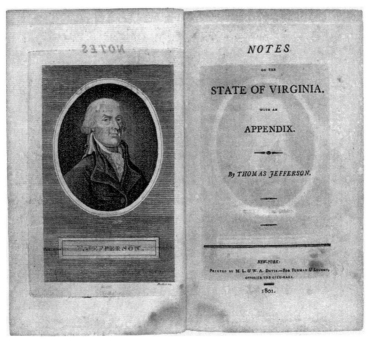

Figure 31. Starting in late 1800, as its author stood for election to the presidency, all future editions of *Notes* included the appendix, and the title page of his book would read *Notes on the State of Virginia with an Appendix.*

death, but it also illuminated what Mingos believed had happened at Yellow Creek. Unlike Jefferson's other sources, Heckewelder and his fellow Moravian missionary David Zeisberger had lived in Native villages and listened to their accounts. It was as close as Jefferson would get to having an actual Indigenous source. Ohio Natives, the missionaries said, were convinced Cresap was "at the head" of the murders and that Greathouse was just his accomplice. This helps explain Logan's unwavering belief that everything was Cresap's fault. Nor did the Mingos move away from this interpretation after 1774. Heckewelder testified that he remained a demon in Mingo culture. "So detestable became [Cresap's] name among the Indians, that I have frequently heard them apply it to the worst of things," even using it to frighten their children into obedience.[42]

In the summary Jefferson composed about his investigation, he declared that Michael had killed Natives on the Ohio River, but was not at Yellow Creek, and that Gibson had confirmed Logan's speech as genuine and accurately represented in the original text of *Notes*. Moreover, people who knew Logan testified he possessed "superior talents." Zeisberger "doubted not the least" that Logan had sent the speech, and said he was "a man of quick comprehension, good judgement, and talents."[43]

In the end, Jefferson largely exonerated himself. His original account was "imperfect and erroneous in its details," he admitted, but he had not been substantially negligent. Since Logan "imputed the whole" murders of his family to Cresap, Natives in Ohio "generally imputed it" to him, Lord Dunmore and his officers "imputed it" to him, and even "the country, with one accord, imputed to him," Jefferson believed he couldn't be blamed for getting it wrong. Nevertheless, to placate Martin, Jefferson promised to delete the phrase "a man infamous for many murders" in Query VI, and added Daniel Greathouse's name. Going forward, the introduction to Logan's speech would say "Captain Michael Cresap and a certain Daniel Great-house . . . surprised, at different times, travelling and hunting parties of the Indians, having their women and children with them, and murdered many."[44]

Although Luther Martin did not mount another campaign after the publication of Jefferson's *Appendix*, it's highly unlikely that it satisfied him or his in-laws. American children would continue to read about how Cresap was a "man infamous for many murders" in new editions of their textbooks, as neither Jedidiah Morse nor Noah Webster followed Jefferson's revisions. Moreover, it wasn't much of an admission of error. Jefferson's excuses probably rankled the Cresap family. Still, Martin might've taken pleasure out of the fact that he had forced the vice president to undertake such a laborious probe. Jefferson did not engage in public combat, but he had done exhaustive work to investigate Yellow Creek, and only did so because Martin had called him out. Others had criticized Jefferson's *Notes*, most importantly the African American mathematician Benjamin Banneker, but he had not considered revisiting his infamous "suspicion" that blacks were inferior beings. Though it wasn't in his nature, Martin could rest easy; he had fulfilled his "sacred trust."[45]

While this three-year battle generated pages of affidavits, testimony, and correspondence about it—research that shed significant light on what happened on the Ohio in the spring of 1774—none of it had anything to do with what Martin called "the real Logan of nature," or the persistent whisper of trauma and horror that was the original context for and cause of his lament. Both Martin and Jefferson severed the Mingo Chief from this context, from the Shickellamy family history which produced it. Martin had justly accused Jefferson of inventing a fictitious Logan, but so had he. Both appropriated him for their own purposes, to influence audiences either in faraway European salons or closer by in family parlors. Jefferson conscripted Logan to refute the speculative theories of the Comte du Buffon, while Martin denied that any Native person could think in such lofty ways. Even when they asked people to submit testimony about what happened in 1774, none of them did so on Logan's terms. Jefferson's and Martin's investigations were to settle very different scores than what Logan intended when he wept under the elm tree, mourning the loss of his murdered family, the scorched lands of his people, and the lives he took in retribution. This wasn't about Logan at all. It was about them.

Going forward into the nineteenth century, the generation that followed Jefferson and Martin continued to ignore, efface, and eliminate what Logan actually intended under the elm tree. But soon that hijacking would enter into a very different, even more destructive phase.

Jefferson had sought to establish Native voices as deserving of respect, as noble savages that proved New World superiority and American identity. The next generation was one of Indian Removal. It added a different reading of the haunting final line of Logan's Lament. For this new generation of settlers, the lament was not evidence of sublime eloquence, but rather served as a call to action and a celebration of victory. Perhaps no one *should* be left to mourn Logan and his people.

Although Luther Martin's pugnacity left him with few friends at the end of his life, his hatred for Thomas Jefferson made him the champion of anyone who opposed the man. He defended Samuel Chase when President Jefferson tried to have him impeached from the Supreme Court, and followed that up by representing Aaron Burr in his 1807 treason trial. During Burr's trial, Jefferson finally offered his opinion about the Marylander who had long been a thorn in his side, calling Martin an "unprincipled and impudent federal bull-dog." Martin and Burr's connection as fellow haters of Jefferson made them fast friends. Late in his life, Martin became a derelict. Alcoholism and a severe stroke left him on the streets of Baltimore in the early 1820s, often wandering into the courthouse and interrupting trials. In 1823, Burr took Martin into his home in New York City, where he died six days after his nemesis Thomas Jefferson, on July 10, 1826. As fate would have it, Luther Martin would be laid to rest in the same city as the father-in-law he scarcely met but defended so vigorously.[46]

Yet, unlike Michael Cresap, whom the blaze of Revolution had made a hero in New York City, there was no public mourning or citywide funeral procession for Luther Martin. His participation at the Constitutional Convention and service during the Revolution did not matter. No one paid for Martin to be buried next to his vaunted father-in-law, but instead Burr sent his body to the St. John's Burying Ground, a mile and a half up Greenwich Street, which was part of the Trinity parish. No marker was ever purchased. Martin had spat upon the notion that Logan could have possibly turned the despondency he felt about the prospect of dying without anyone to mourn him into the eloquent words Jefferson had attributed to him. When this precise thing happened to Luther Martin, he left no such lasting, moving remark. All of his words simply faded into obscurity.[47]

Logan's certainly did not. In fact, by the time Martin and Jefferson died in 1826, the lament was everywhere. In the 1820s, more and more school texts kept appearing with Jefferson and Logan in them. Some of them used Jefferson's original language from *Notes* to introduce Logan's speech; some used his 1800 revision. When William McGuffey incorporated the speech into one of his *Eclectic Readers* in 1837, however, it meant a whole new order of saturation among young Americans.[48]

In the 1820s, McGuffey—who was born not far from Yellow Creek a few months after Jefferson published his appendix—was a professor at Miami University in Oxford, Ohio (founded 1809), and an associate of several important reformers, including the influential Reverend Lyman Beecher, his daughters Catherine and Harriet, and Harriet's husband Oliver Stowe. When a Cincinnati publisher approached Catherine Beecher to put together a series of pedagogical readers to help instruct American schoolchildren how to be pious, patriotic, hard-working citizens, she recommended McGuffey. In 1836–37, McGuffey brought out the first four readers, soon called *McGuffey's Eclectic Readers*. The fourth volume featured Logan's Lament, complete with Jefferson's revised introduction.

The lament's original inclusion in *Notes* and Bingham's *American Preceptor* initially established Logan's fame. McGuffey made his popularity explode. Hundreds of thousands of American children had encountered Logan's speech in all the various editions of textbooks since 1787, but with its inclusion in *McGuffey's Fourth Eclectic Reader*, millions would. At least 120 million *McGuffey Readers* sold before 1960, and millions more had access to them either in their classrooms or by passing them around at home. At 250 words (twenty less than the Gettysburg Address), Logan's Lament was a perfect school exercise, and students stood at their desks and delivered it all throughout the nineteenth century, especially in the Midwest. Because of the *McGuffey Readers*, by the 1880s, newspaper articles could make off-hand claims that Michael Cresap has been "charged in several million school-boy declamations," or that "half the school boys in the country" have recited Logan's Lament.[49]

Its placement in American schoolbooks was not the only way in which Logan's speech became a cultural phenomenon. Logan and Cresap provided material for a host of artists. There was fiction: John Neal's 1822 novel *Logan: A Family History* and Joseph Doddridge's stage play *Logan: The Last of the Race of Shikellemus*. There were songs: "The Blackbird, or Logan's Lament," was a folksong handed down through multiple generations in Ohio and recorded in 1957. And there were poems.[50]

There were many more books of nonfiction as well. In the middle of the nineteenth century, white Americans published lots of volumes about

Native culture and history. Washington Irving used the opening sentence from the lament to frame his 1820 essay "Traits of Indian Character" defending Natives from the "double wrongs" of the violence of settlers and the aspersions of scribblers who excused their acts. Samuel Drake included Logan among the profiles he compiled for his *Indian Biography* (1832), and, after the "very favorable reception" of that work, turned it into a larger edition called the *Book of Indians of North America* (1833), which was also a commercial success, going through more than a dozen editions over the next half century.[51]

As Logan and his speech bobbed along the surface of American culture in the mid-1800s, others took up Luther Martin's quest to clear the Cresap name. Infuriated by Logan's rising celebrity, John Jeremiah Jacob decided he should write up what he knew about Michael Cresap. We've met Jacob a few times before: as a youth he worked in Cresap's store in Redstone, and he was the one Thomas sent in 1775 to find Michael and bring him to Oldtown to take command of his new company, and who Michael confessed to that he thought he was not going to return from Massachusetts. When Cresap's rifles tramped off, Jacob stayed behind to manage Michael's property. He responded to Congress's emergency call for troops in the fall of 1776 and later served as an officer with a Maryland regiment in five military campaigns in the southern theater of the Revolutionary War.[52]

In 1781, Captain Jacob returned to Oldtown to find Mary Cresap widowed for a second time. Jacob, now twenty-four, proposed to Mary, now thirty-six, and the two were quickly married. Jacob had all but grown up in the house Michael had built in Oldtown, and he soon began building an addition on the side. Jacob left his military career behind and became a Methodist minister. Mary herself professed being born again in 1785. They would live together in that house for forty years, until at the age of seventy-six, Mary Whitehead Cresap Rogers Jacob died at Oldtown on January 27, 1821.

In the 1790s, Jacob had also planned to set Jefferson straight, but happily deferred to Luther Martin, helping him assemble the materials for his assault on the then vice president. Thinking Martin had done what he could, Jacob let the matter drop for nearly a quarter century until a book insinuating that Cresap was *the* cause of "the destructive war of 1774" had "lately fallen into my hands." The author's wish that Yellow Creek could be "blotted from the annals of our country" enraged Jacob. "The old sore is irritated and laid open again," he wrote, and, having possession of all Michael's "papers, books, and memorandum," set out to renew the fight. In 1826, a printer in Cumberland, Maryland, published the result, *A Biographical Sketch of the Life of the Late Captain Michael Cresap.*[53]

Jacob retraced Martin's steps, offering extensive details on the Cresap family, Michael's life up to 1774, and his actions during Dunmore's War. He included an extended version of the interview with Benjamin Tomlinson that Luther Martin had first cited in 1798, the main source that denied Logan was the true author of the lament. Readers of Jacob's book would find the Cresaps being kind and generous to all and settlers in general acting strictly on the defensive. They would also find the first reference to Pennsylvanians calling Thomas Cresap a "monster" nearly a century before.[54]

Unfortunately for Jacob, readers were few and far between. But his volume did contribute to a growing movement to collect facts about the early history of the Upper Ohio Valley. In the 1830s–40s, as the generation that first "settled" Ohio was dying out, there was an intense effort to preserve oral and written histories detailing all that had happened there since 1750. Antiquarians interviewed elderly settlers, interested citizens established historical societies and pooled funds to publish their findings in monthly journals, and travelers scoured the countryside hunting for documents.

Founding historical societies was all the rage around the fiftieth anniversary of American Independence. The Historical Society of Pennsylvania was established in 1824, Virginia's in 1831. This trend to secure and preserve the colonial past was especially strong west of the Appalachians. Cincinnati founded one the same year that Richmond did, and a few years later, the Kentucky Historical Society began operating out of a law office in Louisville.[55]

On July 28, 1841, "an assemblage of pioneers and citizens from different parts of the Scioto Valley" gathered near Logan's elm tree to listen to another speech, this one by a local magistrate named George Corwin. Judge Corwin had a proposal, not a lament. The crowd, he said, should "resolve ourselves into a society, determined to perpetuate those principles for which Logan suffered the sneers of his red brethren, by the erection of a monument to his memory, and by the careful collection, safe keeping, and lasting preservation, for the use of posterity, the many scattered but interesting fragments of the history of the early settlements of the western country." Right there, they founded the Logan Historical Society, whose aim was to "secure from oblivion, and preserve for posterity, the unpublished history of our early and successive western settlements . . . which is fast fading from the memories of our early settlers or sinking into the grave with those who had an active part in a series of hardships, privations, and improvements which have no parallel." They pledged money, and promised to start a journal, which appeared the following year, called *The American Pioneer*.[56]

It's clear from a cursory perusal of the more than one hundred articles published in the first year of the *American Pioneer* that the central goal of the Logan Historical Society was to celebrate the terrible ordeals that early colonists had endured. The *Pioneer*'s pages were filled with descriptions of forts, battles, and accounts about settlers who were taken captive by Natives. They weren't out to document stories of settlers killing Natives, but rather sought to redirect history, establishing themselves as victims and thereby deserving of all the Ohio country's vast rewards. The society had promised in their founding by-laws that they were would "collect and safely keep all that is or can be well authenticated of aboriginal history," but the pessimism of that statement suggests they didn't hold out hope of finding much. Natives (especially in league with the British) featured primarily as the villains of their story, the source of their "hardships and privations."[57]

That outlook did not, however, apply to Logan. He was different. As

Judge Corwin's keynote address indicated, the proposed Logan Historical Society believed that its namesake's kindly statements about white
people had incurred sneers from his own people, implying that Logan
was some sort of race traitor. Although there was no evidence that his
lament had engendered any discord among his people, it does shed some
light on why these Ohioans revered Logan. Not only did they name their
organization after him, but they also promised to undertake a search to
find his remains and then reinter them under the elm tree. They also
pledged to pool funds for the monument to Logan, on which they would
inscribe his speech.

The details for that monument, however, underscore how the settlers
refused to hear the persistent whisper of past trauma all around them. In
the base of the monument that they sought to erect to Logan, they were
"to deposit" a copy of Jefferson's *Notes*, the Declaration of Independence,
and the US Constitution. They didn't—or wouldn't—realize how those
documents contributed to the continued suffering of Logan's people. The
last of the Shawnees had been forced to leave western Ohio a decade
before as part of the US government's effort to remove all Natives from
the east. Since there really were none left in Ohio to mourn Logan, it
was now safe to turn him into a relic, a symbol for white Americans to
co-opt. The *American Pioneer* featured a decorative title page with Logan
sitting under the elm dictating his speech to Gibson. It is a rustic scene:
a dove sits on a tree limb and a creek runs tranquilly past a small group
of Native teepees. This is an imagined Ohio, a fantasy far removed from
the pain, suffering, and ghastly violence of 1774. The *American Pioneer*
claimed on its masthead that it was "devoted to the truth and justice of
history," but the scene rendered on its front page was neither true, nor
just, history. It was pioneer history, an extension of Jefferson's veneration
of God's chosen people in *Notes*.

The *American Pioneer* lasted for two years. Its editor continually
bemoaned its financial struggles, which persisted and meant the Logan
Historical Society supporters would never fulfill their promise to build
their monument under the elm. But the small magazine did attract
attention and inspired others.[58]

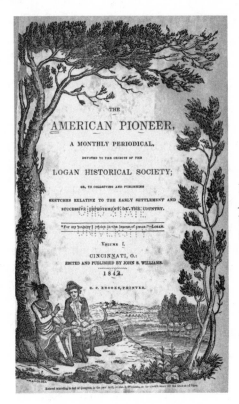

Figure 32. The title page of the
American Pioneer, published
by the Logan Historical
Society, 1842–43.

One of the contributors to *American Pioneer* was Lyman Copeland Draper, who in the early 1840s was a young man about to embark on an extensive mission to collect as many documents, stories, and testimonies as he could find about the history of Ohio from 1750 to 1800. Draper claimed he had travelled sixty thousand miles throughout the region tracking down personal papers from early colonial settlers. By the end of 1845 he had amassed ten thousand pages of materials: half of them were original manuscripts and the other half notes he had compiled from transcribing documents that he couldn't take with him and records of the hundreds of interviews he conducted, including Michael Cresap Jr., now a sixty-year-old man living at "Cresap's Bottom" on the Ohio. Draper was especially enamored with Michael Cresap's friend and associate George Rogers Clark, and many of his investigations surrounded the causes and consequences of Dunmore's War. He planned on writing a dozen books on frontier history.[59]

Draper also shared his expertise with anyone who might benefit from it. He was born a generation before Frederick Jackson Turner, but his labor recording and archiving sources would be essential for that later historian to form his thesis in 1893. In fact, he deposited his entire massive frontier archive at the newly founded State Historical Society of Wisconsin in Madison (1846), an institution he directed from the 1850s until his retirement in 1886, a mere four years before Turner became professor of history across the street at the University of Wisconsin. Starting in the 1840s, Draper would make copies of pertinent papers and send them around to interested scholars, including Francis Parkman and Jared Sparks, two of the most prominent historians of the era.

In 1850, Draper heard that Brantz Mayer was working on the Logan-Cresap affair. Mayer, the prime mover behind the establishment of the Maryland Historical Society in Baltimore, had written several books on the history, people, and architecture of Mexico after he had returned from holding a diplomatic post there in 1842–43. Mayer then turned his attention to a topic more proximate to his audience. As he explained in a letter to James Fenimore Cooper, Mayer set out to "make a case in favor of the traduced but meritorious Marylander" Michael Cresap: "I have taken pains to discover all the now acceptable authorities, and I hope I have not failed to cleanse his memory from some of the blood with which history has debaubed it."[60]

The "authorities" Mayer mentioned included significant help from Lyman Draper. Draper had only just completed a trip to western New York in 1850 and had visited with some people of the Seneca nation. One of the people he met with was a Seneca (whom Draper judged to be 108 years old) named Captain John Decker. According to Draper, Decker, who was also known as Dahganondo, "was the best Indian Chronicler I have met with." Decker's stories were "generally sustained by other evidence," Draper told Mayer, "and never seem confused or improbable." Although Decker said that he had gotten his information from Tod-kah-dos himself, Draper's confidence was at least partially ill-advised, most of all because it was from this interview that the misleading name "Tah-gah-jute" emerged, which has caused significant confusion ever since. Decker told Draper, who told Mayer, that "Logan's name was 'Tah-Gah-Jute,' or Short Dress, and added that 'he was a very bad Indian.'"[61]

On May 9, 1851, at the sixth anniversary of the Maryland Historical Society, Mayer delivered an address that took Decker's name for Logan as its title: "Tah-Gah-Jute: Or Logan and Captain Michael Cresap." Mayer was very interested in names. This address is the origin (with sentences plagiarized directly from John Jeremiah Jacob) of what would become the renowned nickname for Thomas, the "Maryland Monster." But Mayer's main focus was to promote Logan's "real" Indian name. His concentration on Logan's name gave Mayer's talk the appearance that he was presenting fresh material from the Native perspective. He also sprinkled references throughout to documents and information provided by "his friend" Lyman Draper, as part of what was new about his entry into this now half-century-old fight to restore the reputation of the Cresap family. It is, in fact, from Mayer's 1851 talk that we know that Tod-kah-dos had died in 1844 on the Cornplanter Reservation.[62]

But Mayer's purpose was not to understand Logan. It was, as Luther Martin's had been, to bury him and his people. In order to "reverse the decree of history," as Mayer put it on the dedication page of the published version of his address, and refute Jefferson's slanders on the Cresap family, he had to attack the Mingo—and he did with gusto.

In Mayer's hands, Yellow Creek, while despicable, was justified because it was defensive. The Mingos, Mayer said emphatically, were *"all naked, painted, and completely armed for war."* The attack at Baker's Bottom was a "desperate and bloody measure," but it was "in *anticipation* of an Indian attack." Afterward, Logan and his party took a horrific revenge: "Men, women, and children—and even cattle—were all indiscriminately scalped and butchered. The females were stripped and shamefully outraged."[63]

Mayer reached his peak, however, when he thoroughly dismissed

Logan's speech, saying it was merely "a reported conversation with, or message from, a cruel and blood-stained savage; excited perhaps when he delivered it as well by the cruelties he had committed as by liquor." Mayer ended his 1851 talk with these words:

> Imagination transformed the savage into a romantic myth; yet it has been my task not only to reduce this myth to a man, but to paint him degraded by cruelties and intemperance even beneath the scale of an aboriginal birth-right. Indian instincts, rekindled by wrongs and the flame of the "fire-water," blighted a nature which at its dawn promised a noble and generous career. In his intercourse with white men LOGAN lost nothing but the virtues of a savage, while unfortunately he gained from civilization naught but its destructive vices.

Mayer's disgraceful portrayal of Logan, like Martin's, won some converts. The Maryland historian sent the published version of his lecture around to several antebellum political luminaries. Charles Sumner, the senator from Massachusetts, was taken with it, and responded that "thus one after another are images toppled down. In our boyhood we have all looked up to Logan . . . on the pedestal erected by Jefferson. You show him to be a brutal, drunken savage."[64]

Like the publishers of the *American Pioneer*, Mayer argued that his investigation of the Logan-Cresap affair was really about exposing the American people to "the danger of considering as always unquestionable what are called the *facts* of history." But his, too, was another exercise in the establishment of pioneer history. Just as he invoked century-old tropes of "anti-Indian sublime" that first emerged in the 1750s, Mayer's vindication of Michael Cresap via denouncing Logan and Jefferson deepened the growing American adoration for the pioneer that had been revolutionized in 1775–76. In this rendering, men like Michael Cresap were "liberal and hospitable" folk who empathized with those around them and were "prompt to ameliorate the condition of all who ventured beyond the Alleghanies." For Mayer, Michael Cresap was "a picturesque being, as he was beheld descending the slopes of the mountains or relieved against the blue sky or the dark shadows of the forest."[65]

Mayer's defense of Cresap was steeped in the eighteenth century, but it also anticipated by forty years some of the process arguments inherent in Frederick Jackson Turner's famous frontier thesis. "The Pioneer," Mayer wrote, "may be said to bait the forest like a trap, for the Trader. . . . The Farmer, at length, plants himself on the land that the Ranger wrests from the Indian." When all their work is done and the land is tamed and saved from Native wastage, American farmers could go to their rest, which, "wildly won is quietly and permanently enjoyed." Mayer didn't have to do this: his defense of Michael Cresap's reputation did not depend on a lavish evocation of how American pioneer farmers were the only proper custodians of North America. But the rewriting of "the facts of history"—which meant the fabrication of mythological versions of both Logan and Cresap—was part of the final phase of the settler colonialism project. Although Turner thought he had discovered these "facts" in 1893 when he wrote "The Significance of the Frontier to American History," the idea that pioneers created civilization through their taming of the wilderness had been in the works for more than a century—ever since the first days of the Revolutionary War.[66]

Logan's speech—especially its celebrated final line—had become ubiquitous by the middle of the nineteenth century. In 1853, a cemetery commission in Auburn, New York, raised a fifty-foot limestone obelisk to Logan, with a plaque presenting the lament's last line.

By then, however, Logan's words had lost a good deal of their power. They now appeared in advice books for girls and tourist guides to entertain passengers looking out the windows of new railroad cars. "In America," the author of the *Ohio Railroad Guide, Illustrated* said, "who has not heard of Logan?" The lament's final line had become a banality, an adage drained of all meaning that was available for anyone to use as they saw fit. When a new political party, the Whigs, seemed on the ascendent in

Figure 33. The fifty-foot-tall
obelisk monument to Logan
in the Fort Hill Cemetery,
Auburn, New York. The white
plaque reads: "Who is there to
mourn for LOGAN."

the presidential election of 1840, newspapers said the famous Democrat
Martin Van Buren was going to be returned to his home and "no one
would mourn for Logan." When a similar thing happened in 1859 for the
renowned Illinois senator Stephen Douglas—when it became clear that
his political relevance was fading—a Chicago paper said "who was there
to mourn for Logan. Not one." When the former Civil War general and
later Illinois senator John A. Logan had any political setback (and there
were several), the pithy retort that no one would mourn for this Logan was
always ready. Finally, when the Democrats defeated James G. Blaine and
John Logan for the presidency in 1884, an Indiana newspaper rejoiced:

> Who is there to mourn for Logan?
> Oh, who will weep for Blaine?
> We'll paint the town Indian red,
> From Mexico to Maine.[67]

Almost as soon as John Gibson had recorded Logan's words, they became just another piece of stolen property taken by settler colonists. White Americans used them to settle scores in transatlantic philosophical debates. Republicans and Federalists conscripted them in their party conflicts in the 1790s, and, for decades, they continued to be embraced as a way to stir up controversy and scandal. When members of the Cresap clan wanted to prove they were part of a proud, deserving republican family, they belittled Logan's words as mere sounds made by a worthless savage. Most of all, future generations of white Americans memorized and performed them, but not in a fashion that honored or revered what the speaker had endured, but as a way to show through proper republican education that they were deserving of American citizenship and all its legal, political, and economic benefits. Eventually, they became so careless and callous with Logan's words that they turned them into a joke. These acts of violence, conducted with ink and paper rather than

"WHO WILL MOURN FOR LOGAN NOW?"

Figure 34. Whenever Senator John A. Logan failed in his political career, satirists easily made the reference to Logan's Lament. *Harper's Weekly*, 9 May 1874.

rifle and club, were the essential second phase of the double dispossession. They were how the conquest of Ohio was to be, as Mayer put it, "permanently enjoyed."[68]

＝

The final transformation of Logan's Lament was made possible by one fact: by the middle decades of the nineteenth century, the threat of actual violence from Native peoples in Ohio had vanished. Finally, after six decades of terrible bloodshed, failed invasions, and seemingly endless conflict, the actual war to control Ohio had reached a decisive conclusion. While Thomas Jefferson had initially made Logan famous, it wasn't until the 1830s, as his speech was included in dozens of school readers and was part of the virtual war to control Ohio, that Logan became a household name. It was not a coincidence that this also happened to be the era of Indian Removal.

In their constant recitation of Logan's speech, white Americans "learned resignation, having now largely resolved [their] ambivalence over Indian suffering," as one historian has put it. That resignation allowed for the United States to "move ahead" without Native peoples. In the 1820s, "moving ahead" came to mean the expulsion of all Indians east of the Mississippi River. Thus, the uses to which white Americans put Logan's words did not float above the ground as literary or textual exercises alone. They helped anchor the political and military campaign known as Indian Removal.[69]

To illustrate the overlap between the cultural appropriation of Logan in the antebellum years and the actual elimination of Native peoples from the eastern United States, it is necessary to discuss one last nephew: John Gibson's nephew, George Gibson Jr.

As we have seen, John Gibson's younger brother, George, led a party of vigilantes into Pittsburgh to force the release of John Connolly after Pennsylvanians had taken him prisoner in 1775. The show of force worked, and a grateful Connolly mistakenly thought Gibson was his friend and therefore shared his plans to instigate Native hostility against the patriot cause, much to his regret. The Gibson brothers, John and

George, would serve as officers in the Continental Army throughout the Revolution, each commanding a regiment of troops. The Virginia government trusted Captain George Gibson enough to send him to New Orleans to procure a secret shipment of gunpowder in 1776–77, the very gunpowder that made Mary Cresap a widow for a second time. His luck would run out in 1791: now-Lt. Col. George Gibson had the misfortune of being attached to Arthur St. Clair's troops when Little Turtle's Natives all but wiped them out at the Wabash River. He was mortally wounded and died hours after the battle.

His son, George Jr., was born a few months after the 1775 ride into Pittsburgh. George Jr., sixteen when his father never returned from Ohio, soon followed family tradition and joined the army. He fought in the War of 1812 and the First Seminole War under Andrew Jackson. In 1818, he became the commissary general of the US Army, a post he would hold for four decades, until his death in 1861. Gibson's job meant that he was to be in charge of the logistics of Indian Removal.

Acting on an understanding from the Six Nations, the nephew of Logan took his life. The nephew of the man to whom Logan dictated his speech would, also on orders, be responsible for arranging the expulsion and deportation of thousands of Logan's people. All of the bills and invoices regarding food, transport, shelter, and medical care for the removal of thousands of Native peoples came to Colonel George Gibson's office. It was his job to sort through the receipts of dispossession. "It is not an exaggeration to say," one historian has recently written, that, throughout the 1830s, "Gibson and his clerks made life-and-death decisions," weighing what was best for Native families *against* what was in the "public interest" of the United States.[70]

Many of the groups with whom Logan had associated ceded nearly five hundred square miles of land in Ohio not long before the establishment of the Logan Historical Society: the Delawares (1829), Shawnees (1831), and Wyandots (1832, 1836). Thirty-five hundred of them would be forced across the Mississippi. One of the early efforts of deportation that Gibson oversaw was the ejection of 630 Delaware and Seneca

Figure 35. Colonel George Gibson Jr., born a few months after his father freed John Connolly from a Westmoreland County jail. In addition to Koonay being his aunt, and the lone survivor of Yellow Creek being his cousin, Gibson had a second mixed-race cousin, John Gibson Jr. The main US Army installation tasked with keeping relations with deported Native peoples in Indian Territory (Oklahoma) would be named Fort Gibson, in honor of the man who oversaw the logistics of Removal.

people from Sandusky, Ohio, the place where Tod-kah-dos had killed his uncle. They split into two parties, one going overland through Illinois, the other taking steamboats to St. Louis. It was another episode of bewilderment for them—and for the underprepared and poor planners in George Gibson's army office who arranged their ejection. After eight months of travel, which included a brutal winter and a measles outbreak in Missouri, they finally reached Indian Territory (what is today Oklahoma). Nearly 10 percent of the group that went overland didn't survive the trip. The lessons Gibson drew from this catastrophe was that the group had taken far too much personal property with them from Ohio. Gibson and his colleagues decided in the future they would be much more "systematic" in their future "plan of operations." They never questioned the idea that "civilization" demanded Native peoples could not be a part of the republican experiment.[71]

The child that was spared at Yellow Creek, the baby of Koonay and John Gibson, was Colonel George Gibson's cousin, and only a little bit older than he. Her name might have been Polly Gibson, and she may have been baptized by the Presbyterian minister of the Redstone parish in 1787, but we can't be sure. It is all we know of her. That Colonel Gibson had kin among the people he arranged to deport isn't surprising. It is part of the entanglements of the tragic American story of removal, of how relationships of love and blood intermingled in Ohio. But that history, the real context of Yellow Creek, had been all but eliminated by the time Colonel Gibson was given the job of deporting his own extended family across the Mississippi. It had been replaced by mythology and republican expectations.[72]

The deportation "plan of operations" George Gibson developed and refined could not exist without fictional creations like the formerly fearsome but now vanishing Indians. Now that Natives like Logan—or King Philip, Pontiac, and Tecumseh—were a spent force, it was safe to turn them into legends. In the 1760s, boys in the east like Archibald Loudon quaked with fear when Native men visited them in their cabins. Americans in the era of Indian Removal could celebrate and even empathize with the weeping, tragic figure of Logan under the elm tree because they no longer dreaded the terrifying, violent Mingo lurking near Muddy or Sinking Creek about to murder their children.[73]

The American Revolution played a crucial role in this transformation. It had given rise to a new regime in North America, one that valorized frontiersmen as the epitome of American patriotism. A hero worship of pioneers lay near the center of the new constructions of American national identity. Even if those thousands of American schoolchildren specifically referred to Michael Cresap as "a man infamous," they certainly didn't condemn pioneers or the American pioneering spirit. Every lesson in the McGuffey readers made sure of that. Those enormously influential texts were ethics readers that celebrated the Protestant republic and its intrepid pioneer-citizens. The Cresaps and their defenders hardly needed to have been so prickly: even if Logan incorrectly and unfairly named them, the larger universe of American culture stood solidly on their side. They, not Logan's people, were the beneficiaries of the republic's vast political, legal, economic, and cultural power. Thomas Jefferson had referred to the yeoman farmers of America as God's chosen people. All of the people who touched the Logan-Cresap story after 1787—Caleb Bingham, Luther Martin, William McGuffey, Lyman Draper, Brantz Mayer, and many others—did not doubt that Jefferson's vision of republican civilization was anything but beneficent for North America.

These Americans told stories about the hardships and privations that pioneers endured to tame the wilderness and bring peace to America. They repeated these things to make themselves feel comfortable, to distract from, hide from, or turn away from confronting the horrors that had taken place at Yellow Creek, Muddy Creek, and Sinking Creek—or Patterson's, or Penn's, or Conestoga Creeks before them—or at Gnadenhutten after. These reassuring tales drowned out the persistent whisper of colonialism and dispossession that was all around them. They replaced the uncertainty, bewilderment, and horror of eighteenth-century Ohio with bland, accepted inevitabilities, a confident logic collected in a singular notion of a benevolent American empire and civilization advancing westward, a destiny manifest in curated explanations of the recent past. That rewriting of history helped to secure Ohio for future generations of American settlers. For their own purposes, white Americans erased Soyechtowa, his brothers, his father, his sister, his mother, his nephew, and his people. They replaced them with an empty, mythological figure steeped in the dictates of an American racism born out of the colonial past and perfected by the American Revolution: "Logan the Mingo Chief."

DARKNESS WAS HERE YESTERDAY

"We live in the flicker—may it last as the old earth keeps rolling!
But darkness was here yesterday."

—*Heart of Darkness*

As the twentieth century approached, in the face of rapid, distressing change—intensive industrialization, massive immigration, and social unrest—many descendants of early settlers redoubled their efforts to underscore their connection to American history, defending and justifying how their families had "tamed" the continent since the early 1600s. Between roughly 1875 and 1925, groups all over the United States pooled funds to erect statues, build monuments, and dedicate public spaces. They did so especially to commemorate the Civil War and the American Revolution, but this reflective mood also brought renewed attention to pioneer and frontier history. With the decades-long wars against Native peoples throughout North America drawing to a close, they celebrated "civilization's" triumph over "savagery."

In 1909, West Virginians dedicated a granite monument on the Point Pleasant battlefield more than eighty feet tall, complete with a plaque that stated "that day there was fought the most important battle ever waged between the forces of civilization and barbarism in America." At the monument's base there was an eight-foot-tall colonial soldier dressed in a hunting shirt and holding a rifle. The myth of America's powerful pioneers depended on desperate battles to fight, hardships to overcome, and mythical Indians to vanquish. "Logan, the famous Mingo Chief" exactly fit the bill.[1]

Three years later, on October 2, 1912, a crowd gathered around Logan's elm tree. Worried about the tree's health and to preserve the land around it, a group of local women in Circleville, Ohio, had successfully lobbied for the area to be designated a state park. According to one witness, more than five thousand people crowded the roads all around the elm and trampled the neighboring fields for the dedication of Logan Elm State Memorial. Special trains from Cincinnati and Chillicothe weren't enough to satisfy the demand. A brass band played on the "balmy and fine day," and speakers regaled the crowd with Logan's history. Ten Native people were in attendance, along with "all of Pickaway County."[2]

A number of speakers stood on a raised platform made of hay and adorned with American flags to entertain the crowd on that warm October afternoon. Mary McMillen Jones, president of the Pickaway County

Figure 36. Celebration of the dedication of Logan Elm State Memorial, October 1912.

Historical Society, proclaimed that Logan's speech "is known by every school-boy and school-girl throughout the land. It is a message filled with fervor, kindness, and love, yet it bristles with righteous anger and fearless revenge . . . and ends in a sentence which is masterful in depicting the extreme sorrow of a great mind." Charles E. Daganett (Peoria), the highest ranking Native in the US Bureau of Indian Affairs, delivered a speech to the collected throng solemnizing Logan. But, aside from five acres surrounding the tree being made a state park, nothing permanent commemorating Logan, the tree, or the lament materialized on the Pickaway Plains. In the years that followed, the elm played host to "all-day pioneer meetings," with songs and ice cream, but still no marker commemorating Logan appeared.[3]

Members of the Cresap family noticed all the attention being paid to Logan's tree, however. The Cresaps had neither forgiven nor forgotten, and they still could not allow Logan to have the last word. A few dozen members of the family decided that they needed to write the Cresaps' history into stone. There was already one historical marker close by the elm tree, a pillar placed in the 1880s by the son of John Boggs to celebrate his father's feat as "the first settler on the Pickaway Plains," and the Cresaps intended to follow his lead. They made plans to place a memorial near the tree honoring their family's connection to this piece of ground.

Four Octobers after the park's dedication, a few dozen members of the Cresap family conducted their own gathering around a stone boulder emerging from a square stone pedestal, displaying two tablets. This was what the Cresaps' had purchased to commemorate their ancestor. One side read, "IN MEMORIUM Captain MICHAEL CRESAP," and described him as "a Colonial and Revolutionary Hero of Ohio, Virginia, and Maryland, whose military services assisted in Gaining the 'Dunmore Treaty.'" It also fixed in stone and metal what Jefferson had done in his paper appendix: "Captain Michael Cresap's Companions in Arms, Ebenezer Zane, General George Rogers Clark, Colonel Benjamin Wilson, Benjamin Robinson, and Others, Corrected Logan's Mistake in Associating Captain Cresap with the Yellow Creek Affair." On the other side of the boulder, the second tablet listed the twenty Virginia

Figure 37. Monument to
Michael Cresap erected
at Logan Elm State
Memorial, 1916.

militia officers who signed the "Dunmore Treaty." The Cresaps thought
they had finally, permanently, corrected Logan and Jefferson's slander.

They were mistaken. After the Cresaps placed their rather crude
monument, Logan Elm State Memorial became, quite literally, the final
battleground of the Logan-Cresap controversy. Ironically, the Cresaps'
monument initiated a movement to erect a permanent marker to Logan.
Within weeks of the Cresaps' act, an article entitled "A Plea for Some
Memorial to Logan," appeared in a local newspaper. Howard Jones,
husband of the lead organizer of the 1912 event, Mary McMillen Jones,
criticized the Cresaps for making the site about them and asked Ohio state
officials to remove the memorial "so inappropriately placed in this park."
Two local farmers started a subscription fund and asked contributors to
send between $1 and $25 to pay for a memorial to Logan. Within two
years they had collected the $1,200 a local monument company required
to erect a ten-foot-tall gray granite monument. On October 10, 1919, the
one hundred and forty-fifth anniversary of the battle of Point Pleasant,
what the Cresaps had feared (but had in reality provoked) came true, as

Figure 38. Logan monument erected at Logan Elm State Memorial, 1919.

a monument to Logan and his speech went up a few dozen yards across from—and facing—the Cresap rebuttal.[4]

On one side of the impressive monument was a plaque illustrating the impressive tree with the text of Logan's Lament engraved underneath. On the other was another plaque with a profile of Logan's (imagined) face with an engraved explanation below. "Beside the spring then flowing beneath this majestic elm," it read, "Logan, the chief of the Mingoes and friend of the whites, here delivered his oration . . . unequalled for eloquence, lofty sentiment, solemn truth, and poignant sorrow." The engraving, a gift of well-meaning Pickaway farmers, concluded with a remark that nevertheless showed the scars of the double dispossession: "The descendants of the pioneers of this community" placed it as "a tribute from civilization to a noble man of a savage race."

The members of the Cresap family were not among those "descendants of the pioneers" who felt magnanimous toward Logan. The Cresaps who had gathered at Logan Elm State Memorial in 1916 reconvened later that evening at the Chittenden Hotel in Columbus to form the Cresap Society. While Pickaway County residents sent their spare dollars to contribute to the Logan monument fund, the Cresap Society convened annually in Ohio, holding larger and larger gatherings, and making ever more elaborate plans.

The Cresap Society was part of a growing national trend. Like their grandparents who had founded historical societies during the era of Indian Removal and gathered primary sources to establish "pioneer history," white Americans in the late nineteenth century founded a host of lineage and genealogical societies so they could prove that their families had made the United States: Sons and Daughters of the American Revolution (1889–90), Colonial Dames of America (1891), Society for Colonial Wars (1893), Order of the Founders and Patriots of America (1896), Mayflower Society (1897), and Order of the First Families of Virginia (1912), to name just a few. Individual families were also caught up in this trend. The descendants of Captain John Underhill, the military leader who led the 1637 Puritan raid on Mystic Fort during the Pequot War, founded the Underhill Society in 1892. The Winthrop Society followed not long after.

After their initial success at Logan Elm in 1916, the Cresap Society made plans to place more memorials to their heroic ancestors. In June 1919, they met in Cumberland, Maryland, to erect a second monument, this one to Thomas. The Society unveiled a large, rough-hewn stone column facing the Potomac near where Wills Creek joined it, the site of the original Ohio Company storehouse and from which Thomas set off to blaze a trail to Redstone in the 1740s. Around the base they placed a few dozen stones, which they said came from the ruins of Cresap's house at Oldtown. On the Potomac side, the family placed a plaque with a depiction of Cresap's original log cabin from 1740. On the other was a long tablet that listed his accomplishments and the names of his sons and grandsons (no daughters, legitimate or otherwise). All of this appeared under the announcement: "IN MEMORY OF COL. THOMAS CRESAP, PATHFINDER—PIONEER—PATRIOT." Just as the Revolutionaries had done in 1775 when they merged Michael's capacity to fight the British and Native peoples into a single, powerful idea, the Cresap Society reinforced the notion that pioneering and pathfinding were synonymous with American patriotism.[5]

Americans dedicated several memorials celebrating the accomplishments of pioneers and pathbreakers in the first quarter of the twentieth century. In Louisville, Kentucky, at the turn of the century a statue of Daniel Boone clutching his rifle greeted visitors as they entered to a new city park (Cherokee Park). In Charlottesville, the University of Virginia erected a statue to Lewis and Clark in 1919 and followed it in 1921 with a majestic statue celebrating Michael Cresap's friend George Rogers Clark—the "Conqueror of the Northwest," according to the large engraving on the pedestal. Three years later, the Pennsylvania Historical Commission erected a second stone memorial to Thomas Cresap, this one documenting the 1736 border war, and placed it near his former Pleasant Garden estate. Later on, the Cresap Society would put up another monument, complete with the same tablets, in a field halfway between Michael's and Thomas's houses in Oldtown.

At the same time that they erected monuments to pioneer-patriots, white Americans also commemorated invented versions of Native leaders. Legends about the heralded Natives these pioneers encountered flooded American culture. During the same time that memorials went up to Cresap and Clark, newspapers all over the United States ran features called "Stories of Great Indians," "Tales of the Chiefs," "True Stories of Some Bad Indians," and "American Indian Day." All of them included Logan.[6]

In 1915, three years after Ohioans gathered to venerate Logan and his elm tree, the city of Sunbury, Pennsylvania (formerly Shamokin), made preparations to venerate his father, Shickellamy. The local chapter of the Daughters of the American Revolution and the Pennsylvania Historical Commission co-sponsored another stone monument, five feet tall and three feet square. In June they put it up on the bank of the Susquehanna River near where Fort Augusta formerly stood, and announced there would be an official dedication ceremony in October to lay a plaque that referred to the Oneida leader as a "diplomat and stateman and a firm friend of the province of Pennsylvania."

A week before that ceremony was to take place, "a number of historians" took a train to Pittsburgh and then traveled to a remote Native reservation in the northwest sector of the state. They went to talk to a very elderly man who was thought to be Shickellamy's great-grandson.[7]

His name was Jesse Logan, and he still lived on the Cornplanter Reservation along the Alleghany River, near where John Adlum had interviewed his father in 1794. Because it was "a kind of mountain fortress, a shabby Shangra-la hidden from alien eyes in the forests of the Alleghany Mountains," Cornplanter's Tract survived the nineteenth century. At one point, not long after Adlum's visit, about four hundred Iroquois people lived there in houses clustered near the river. In his seventies, Tachnedorus joined them, with Tod-kah-dos, his wife Annie, and their five children nearby. The youngest of these was Jesse Logan.[8]

Jesse claimed he was 106 years old in 1915 when he suddenly became a popular attraction. Over the summer, as preparations for Shickellamy's monument were finalized, a newspaper reporter from Buffalo came to interview him. The reporter, Jeannette Sherman, talked with the "old old man." She found him "a large, well-built man, straight for his years." He was at first skeptical of her motives, but warmed as they talked and he agreed to pose for a photograph. A few months later, when those historians descended on his house and barraged him with questions about his family in connection with the monument to his great-grandfather, he was more prepared and gave them a lengthy statement about his family heritage.[9]

Jesse told them he remembered his grandfather Tachnedorus (John Logan) well. He taught me to hunt, Jesse said, and pointed to his grave over near Cornplanter's. According to Jesse, Tachnedorus had died about 1820. Although Jesse never met Soyechtowa, he and his wife Susan (a Seneca woman) had named their only child James, to honor "my great-uncle, the immortal Cayuga orator." Jesse expressed regret that the monument committee had not "invited him to attend the unveiling of my great-grandfather's monument in Sunbury next week, but I guess

JESSE LOGAN, GRANDSON OF CORNPLANTER.
With Charley Gordon, a nephew of Jesse Logan, and Josephine Miller
and Charley Miller, daughter and grandson of Charley Gordon. All are
descendants of the great Seneca chief Cornplanter.

Figure 39. Jesse Logan, seated. *Buffalo Morning Express*, 29
August 1915.

the world has forgotten Logan." He was planning, he said, to visit the
mountains of the Juniata Valley where Tod-kah-dos had lived in the 1760s,
and "view the scenes that my father loved to talk about." Unfortunately,
before he could do so, Jesse died the following February, a few months
before the Cresaps laid their monument at Logan Elm State Memorial.[10]

Jesse was wrong about one thing: the world had not forgotten Logan.
For decades after Jesse died, Americans continued to recite his words
and commemorate Shickellamy and his son. In the second half of the
twentieth century, Pennsylvania would create Shickellamy State Park
high above Sunbury, Pennsylvania, and West Virginia set aside Chief
Logan State Park in Logan, West Virginia.

Logan's place in American culture turned out to be far more secure
than his celebrated elm tree. In 1950, an ice storm tore down many
of the tree's long limbs. Then, in 1961, newspapers from Chicago to
Alamogordo, New Mexico, reported how a vicious thunderstorm had

Figure 40. Logan Statue,
Chief Logan State Park,
Logan, West Virginia.

Figure 41. The Logan Elm after being crippled in a 1961
summer storm. This photograph ran in the *Cincinnati Enquirer*
with the headline "Raging Storm Claims Famed 'Logan Elm',"
11 June 1961.

swept across the Pickaway Plains and ripped the famous tree apart. This storm didn't kill Logan's elm, but it did cripple it. Three years later, the surgeons couldn't save it any longer, and the Logan Elm was no more.[11]

In *Heart of Darkness*, Joseph Conrad invokes the effect of a lightning flash across the horizon as a way to suggest that humans have a need to comfort themselves against the terrifying darkness. We do that by creating artificial devices so that we can feel safe, secure, adjusted, and at peace. "We live in the flicker—may it last as long as the old earth keeps rolling!" Conrad's narrator says.[12]

In this American story, we have seen human beings use all sorts of devices to try to comfort themselves against the bewildering darkness. To project organization and control, they created empires, borderlines, maps, treaties, colonial charters, land companies, and speculation schemes; to foster belonging and community, they created nations, adoption ceremonies, republicanism, confederacies, citizenship, and patriotism; to craft and shape stories, they created historical societies, monuments, statues, memorials, books, and newspapers; and to justify their actions, they created concepts like "civilization," "savagery," "progress," "exceptionalism," and "race." These are all things human beings have constructed to make sense of the confounding darkness and to resolve bewilderment in their favor. They are the flicker of light in a frightening nighttime thunderstorm, an effort to prolong and "live in" that feeling of safety and orientation.

One of the most important and enduring flashes of lightning was Frederick Jackson Turner's "frontier thesis." Turner's interpretation of American history has captured the attention of both the historical community and the public at large since 1893. But Turner's thesis was not an original intervention. Pioneer historians like Lyman Draper and Brantz Mayer had been collecting and telling these stories for decades before Turner's famous lecture at the Columbian Exposition. Moreover, Turner constructed his thesis in a context of white Americans forming lineage societies and dedicating monuments to men like Thomas Cresap for

being a "Pathfinder—Pioneer—Patriot." The frontier thesis was more of
a capstone to a centuries-long settler colonialism project than a sudden,
disruptive interpretation—yet another attempt at prolonging the flicker.
Turner's interpretation has always been Cresap's frontier thesis, born in
revolution time not industrial America.

Unfortunately, the devices we construct to reassure, justify, and orient
ourselves cannot eliminate the darkness. When Conrad's narrator tells
us we live in the flicker, he ends by saying, "but darkness was here yesterday." We think we are safe when we use hoary legends to illuminate
the night sky; the light cast from myths of "civility," of "progress," and
of "exceptionalism" make us feel secure, maybe even invulnerable. But
this is fantasy; darkness continues to surround us and it always has.[13]

This is especially true because the human devices we construct to live
in the flicker rarely apply to everyone. In the case of Conrad's Congo,
imperialism wreaked havoc on the land and peoples of central Africa.
Europeans made colorful maps to organize their occupation, built railroads, steamships, and trading stations in the name of "progress," and
totted up account books to track their profits. All of this came at the
expense of the Congolese people. Imperial authorities labelled them
"criminals," "enemies," and "rebels," so that they could work them to
death with clear consciences. Those flickers did not eradicate the darkness. Rather, they produced bewildering, absurd, and tragic groves of
death in the interior of Africa.

As we've seen, the flickers of empire also served to intensify the
darkness and destruction for Native peoples in Ohio. Since its founding,
settler colonialism lay at the heart of the United States. The location of
Michael Cresap's grave—at the corner of Broadway and Wall Street—
captures this perfectly. By the twenty-first century, the intersection of
those Manhattan streets had become synonymous with American culture, commerce, and global influence. Since 1775, the church building
at that intersection, Trinity, has had to be rebuilt twice. The Great Fire
of 1776 destroyed the original building erected at the end of the seven-

teenth century, and disrepair forced the second version to be demolished in 1839. Michael Cresap's gravestone, despite being one of the closest markers to the church, survived all this upheaval. The original stone laid in 1775 stood there through the Civil War, but just before its one hundredth birthday, church authorities decided it was too valuable to lose and sent it to the New-York Historical Society for safekeeping in 1867. Unwilling to have the grave vanish forever, the Trinity churchwardens arranged to have a replica made, thereby redoubling New Yorkers' peculiar investment. As patriot leaders had done in 1775, New Yorkers again made arrangements to honor the memory of a stranger. Michael Cresap's gravestone has thus been an unbroken, constant presence at the corner of Broadway and Wall Streets. It was there before American independence, and it remains, even through the damage the current Trinity edifice and surrounding graveyard suffered when the World Trade Center towers collapsed nearby on September 11, 2001.

The persistence of Michael Cresap's grave at this intersection is another instance of Americans commemorating their pathfinders, pio-

Figure 42. A replica of Michael Cresap's headstone in Trinity Churchyard, New York City. The original, in the permanent care of the New-York Historical Society, is currently on loan to the Museum of the American Revolution in Philadelphia.

neers, and patriots. It is also a memorial to the double dispossession, the settler colonial impulse to not only take land from Natives but eliminate their history and culture. *How* that elimination came about, as we have seen, was not the product of a confident logic or teleology, but the result of almost countless human choices and moments of continency.

Take, for instance, a counterfact. If Michael would have died just a few days earlier, at the Peacock Tavern, the army hospital outside the Cambridge camp, his death would probably have earned a notice in one of the patriot newspapers still printing around Boston, especially given his new celebrity status. However, it is doubtful that General Washington—even though he'd known the Cresap family since he was sixteen—would've taken the time to organize the lavish funeral procession and extensive commentary that patriots in Manhattan assumed. The particular political situation in that place at that moment dictated how New Yorkers mourned this individual. The political necessities of union demanded that many Americans far from New York City would also hear prodigious details about his funeral procession. Had he died at the Peacock, Michael would've been just another promising officer cut down by camp disease, and Revolutionary leaders would have been unable to use his death as a way to generate support for the "common cause," and to further their project of nationalism, patriotism, race-making, and nation-making. Instead of being a grave marker that has kept a silent vigil at one of the world's most renowned intersections for almost 250 years, Michael Cresap might've been buried in a forgotten grave somewhere on the outskirts of Boston, and he wouldn't have aided in the cultural construction of the American pioneer-citizen hero. In the same way, if, in his raids on the Clinch River in September 1774, Logan would've come upon a few Virginia militiamen and killed their officer, the legend of Daniel Boone would have been drastically altered. Daniel Boone and Michael Cresap would have still contributed something to how Native peoples were doubly dispossessed of their lands and their culture, but that darkness would not have surrounded us in exactly the same way.

Even though it did happen that the United States became a republic created of, by, and for settler colonists, how this came to be is a matter historians must continue to investigate. Rather than leaning on confident logic that the dispossession of Native peoples, their culture, and their history was something that was bound to occur—either to create "civilization" or to destroy it—we must go back and look at all these moments of choice, contingency, and biography. Then we might be able to better "see" how the modern world actually came to be.

For the persistence of Michael Cresap's grave in the heart of New York City is also a reminder that it is impossible to detach America's place in the contemporary world from its colonial conquest of North America. What the Cresaps and their fellow settler colonists did along the Susquehanna, Potomac, and Ohio Rivers in the eighteenth century made it possible for American cultural and commercial power to dominate the globe in the twentieth.

After 1776, they had an even greater force at their back spurring them forward across the continent: American patriotism. All of the resources these heroic pioneers accumulated in their dispossession of Native peoples were now the benefits of American citizenship. Logan's Lament served to highlight their power; his lament was a realization, a surrender to the mighty wave of settler colonialism. His family labored to channel that wave in the middle of the eighteenth century through negotiation and compromise. They failed. Shickellamy's way was replaced by the horror of Yellow Creek.

Not only the land but the history of Shickellamy, his family, and his people became the property of settler colonists, especially after they became United States pioneer-citizens. While they recited Logan's words, gathered under his elm tree, founded organizations in his name, and even erected granite memorials to him, they did so falsely. Despite all of the attempts to destroy the darkness by couching their actions in heroic terms—"the dreams of men, the seeds of commonwealths, the germs of empires"—the Cresaps and their fellow pioneer-citizens produced bewildering, absurd, and tragic groves of death in the interior of North America.[14]

In the nineteenth century, citizens of the United States cherished their creation, "Logan, the famous Mingo chief." This mythological figure had nothing to do with Soyechtowa (James Logan Shickellamy). They empathized with the final, touching line of Logan's Lament, but only once the real danger had passed, severing his words from the man, his history, and his family's struggles. They memorized Logan's words while they deported Native peoples, went to war with them for a century, and forced them onto reservations.

———

Jesse Logan's father-in-law, Cornplanter, was one of the first to experience life on a reservation. Pennsylvania established Cornplanter's Tract just after it ratified the Constitution, and it would last until the United States Corps of Engineers started building the Kinzua Dam in 1961, the year that Logan's Elm was nearly destroyed. When the Dam opened in 1965, Cornplanter's Tract formed the bottom of the Alleghany Reservoir, and the graves of Tachnedorus, Tod-kah-dos, and many of Shickellamy's descendants were washed away to provide flood control and electricity for Pittsburgh, the modern industrial powerhouse that George Croghan, John Connolly, Arthur St. Clair, Lord Dunmore, William Crawford, George Washington, and Thomas and Michael Cresap helped to build. Who protected their burial places, or raised money to create replicas of their gravestones? Not one.

We could end this story with that final silencing, a moment of drama that pays tribute to Logan's anguish for his people. But that would be too dark altogether. Instead, let us end in the autumn of 1915, and fall in behind that group of historians walking up the road near the Alleghany River—just as John Adlum did in his moccasins in 1794—to find out that Shickellamy's family had not been extinguished at Yellow Creek after all, and listen as Jesse recounts his memories of Shickellamy's son teaching him how to hunt, of Shickellamy's grandson talking about his days in the Pennsylvania mountains, and how he carried on family tradition by naming his son after his immortal grand-uncle. One of the main reasons Soyechtowa became "Logan, the famous Mingo chief" was because he claimed he was the last of his family. But, despite the bewilderment and horror that Shickellamy's family experienced, he wasn't.

APPENDIX

THE LOGAN PROBLEM

It goes almost without saying, but the historical record has left next to nothing about the Native women at the heart of this story. In reality, given the matrilineal nature of Iroquoian society, Neanoma should be the focal point of any retelling of the Shickellamy family. She was the center, but colonial archives have left scarcely any mention of her. The same goes for Shickellamy's two daughters, Cajadis and Koonay. We can't be sure which of the two daughters took refuge with the Conestogas in the 1750s, or how long she remained among them. Even of Koonay, who became the subject of frontier legend after her death at Yellow Creek and was married to the renowned John Gibson, we know very little. Historians of American women (especially Native women) would find none of this at all surprising. That I cannot flesh out more of the story around what Neanoma, Koonay, and Cajadis did, thought, and said in this book is an all too typical consequence of the structures of inequality that revolve around race and gender, they would rightly argue. The same silences often don't usually apply to men—even Native ones when they were as prominent and featured in landmark colonial events as Shickellamy's sons were. But yet, even here, fundamental mysteries abide.

Because both Tachnedorus and Soyechtowa carried the name Logan, a controversy has raged since the eighteenth century about which brother became "the famous Mingo chief." Scholarly articles addressing this question appear about once a generation. The insidious effects of settler colonialism—the double dispossession—cloud their conclusions. It is inconceivable that we might be unsure as to which of Thomas Cresap's clan we were referring to. Their marriage records, deeds, and letters are preserved and protected in historical societies, courthouses, and repositories throughout the United States; the Shickellamys left far fewer records, even though they were one of the most prominent Native families of their time and place.

Not only are we unsure which brother is which, significant questions remain about what they looked like. Contemporary observers were often maddeningly vague about Logan's physical appearance. Someone who met him in 1772 said he was "the most martial of Indians I had ever seen." Another said he was "the best specimen of humanity I ever met with, either *white* or *red*." In 1811, Archibald Loudon published his reminiscence about encountering Logan in his parents' cabin fifty years earlier. Loudon remembered him as a "remarkable tall man, considerably over six feet high," which was likely accurate. To this he added words that only fit the description of a "famous Mingo chief," which by then Logan had already "become": "strong and well proportioned, of a brave, open, manly countenance, as straight as an arrow; and to appearance, would not be afraid to meet any man."[1]

Loudon fixed the image of Logan for everyone who followed. Every description of Logan afterward copied him nearly verbatim. Brantz Mayer added some flair to Loudon's memory, but the original is still quite evident. Mayer said Logan was "several inches more than six feet in height, was straight as an arrow; lithe, athletic, and symmetrical in figure; firm, resolute, and commanding in feature; but the brave, open, and manly countenance he possessed in his earlier years was now changed for one of savage ferocity." Lyman Draper said that Logan was "above six feet in height, strong and well-proportioned . . . a brave, open, manly countenance . . . straight as an arrow." Theodore Roosevelt, in his 1889 *The Winning of the West*, also plagiarized Loudon. Logan, Roosevelt wrote, "was a man of splendid appearance, over six feet high, straight as a spear shaft, with a countenance as open as it was brave and manly. . . . of commanding dignity." Another early twentieth-century writer took these embellishments of Loudon to even more romantic heights. For him, Logan was "a fine specimen of robust manhood with a commanding presence, dignified in bearing and brave as the bravest of the brave. He was built in the style of the primeval forest, six feet two or more, broad shouldered, lithe of limb and alert and as soft of tread as a tiger; he was self-reliant and straight as an arrow." These plagiarized accounts of Loudon also reflect—and reinforce—expectations, drawn from the colonial past, of what "noble savages" *ought* to look like.[2]

But: a decade before young Archie Loudon's encounter, Tachnedorus referred to his younger brother as "the lame one" when he went out of his way to reassure angry Pennsylvania leaders that he couldn't possibly go to war against them. He wasn't physically able, Tachnedorus testified. Had Logan's fame and emerging tropes about "noble savages" clouded Loudon's memory? Have they prevented us from grasping that Logan might not have been statuesque but instead perhaps had a disability? Was Logan's difficulty in walking permanent or temporary? We don't know. This mystery has, in fact, been part of the controversy about which brother—John Logan (Tachnedorus) or James Logan (Soyechtowa)—was actually "Logan the Mingo Chief."[3]

JAMES? JOHN? TACHNEDORUS? TAHGAHJUTE? SOYECHTOWA?: THE MYSTERY OF LOGAN'S IDENTITY

The Moravian minister John Heckewelder, who knew Logan, gave testimony to Jefferson in 1799 that Logan was "the second son of Shickellemus," thus meaning Soyechtowa (James Logan). For Reverend Heckewelder there was no mystery: Logan was James. Case closed.[4]

This consensus held for much of the nineteenth century. Even though white Americans like Luther Martin, John Jeremiah Jacob, and others cast doubt on Logan's ability to construct and deliver the lament, there was little disagreement about which brother was which. Lyman Draper's 1850 interview with the elderly Seneca man named "Captain Decker" began to complicate matters. "Decker" told Draper that Logan's real Native name was actually "Tah-gah-jute," and it meant "short dress." Draper thought this man was a reliable source, especially since he (Decker) said he received his information from Tod-kah-dos himself.

When Draper heard that Brantz Mayer was working on the Logan-Cresap affair, he forwarded notes from this interview to the Baltimore historian. Mayer featured Draper's interview in his 1851 talk that took this Native name for its title. Mayer arranged for the publication of his lecture and in 1867 it was subsequently enlarged under the title *Tah-Gah-Jute: or Logan and Captain Michael Cresap.* Mayer, following Draper's endorsement of Decker, said that Logan was James, and that his Native name was "Tah-gah-jute," which meant "short dress." For the next generation, most writers followed Mayer's (and Draper's) lead. "Tah-gah-jute" became synonymous with Logan and the name Soyechtowa disappeared.[5]

Soon enough, however, there would be controversy about every aspect of that identification. To begin, not all agreed with Draper's Native source about what that name meant. In his 1901 work *The Wilderness Trail*, a compendium of primary sources and stories from the eighteenth-century Ohio country, Charles Hanna still referred to Logan as Tah-gah-jute, but he said that name did not mean "short dress," but rather "short foot." In 1908, the editor of the *Handbook of Tribal Names of Pennsylvania* offered a third definition, contending that Tah-gah-jute meant "his eyelashes stick out and above." A 1921 book entitled *Logan the Mingo* endorsed both the name and this meaning, as did a second published in 1932 and a third in 1958.[6]

One article, published in 1916, did not take issue with the famous Mingo being James, but rejected Tah-gah-jute as his Native name. In response to the reference made of Logan being Tah-gah-jute in previous volumes of the *Annual Report of the American Scenic and Historical Preservation Society*, William Martin Beauchamp wrote in to protest. Beauchamp had published several books on Iroquois ethnology and had recently retired as archaeologist of the New York State Museum after twenty-five years. The Society asked Beauchamp, "the learned authority on Indian subjects," to submit a formal paper giving his reasons why Tah-gah-jute was not Logan's correct name. In his response, he recounted the source material from the 1750s and 60s from both Moravian and Pennsylvania colonial documents that recorded James's name as Soyechtowa or Soyeghtowa. The name Tah-gah-jute, he argued with obvious frustration, had appeared merely because "Brantz Mayer had a letter from Lyman Draper." Beauchamp searched his records of "over a thousand Senecas" and could not find anyone with the name "Captain Decker" with whom Draper had conversed. Logan was indeed Shickellamy's second son James, Beauchamp believed, but his name wasn't Tah-gah-jute; it was Soyechtowa.[7]

There was only one dissenting voice that doubted Logan was James, and its provenance casts doubt on Beauchamp's snide remark. In 1911, the Ohio Historical Society published a draft of a manuscript that Lyman Copeland Draper, then dead for twenty years, had written back in the 1870s. Apparently the renowned collector-historian had experienced a change of heart about

Logan's identity since sending his letter to Mayer. In a lengthy piece entitled "Logan—the Mingo Chief," Draper asserted that Logan was not James but John. John's Native name was Tachnedorus, which meant "the branching oak of the forest." Draper didn't offer any proof or argument as to why he—the originator of the notion that Logan was James/Tah-gah-jute—now thought Logan was John, but he proceeded to tell the story with the assumption that the famous Mingo was Shickellamy's first born son.[8]

Until the 1960s, however, there remained a general consensus that the famous Logan was James and his name was Tah-gah-jute. Some historians ducked the issue by not offering a name or simply referring to him as "Chief Logan," "the famous Mingo chief Logan," or the "celebrated chief and orator, Logan," but there seemed to be relatively little disagreement for nearly a century since Brantz Mayer's book.[9]

Then Paul Wallace stepped into the fray. Wallace was a specialist in the history, anthropology, and ethnography of the Native peoples of the mid-Atlantic. He had published, among other books, a biography on Conrad Weiser and an important work mapping all the Native footpaths through Pennsylvania. In 1962, he published a short note in *Pennsylvania Archaeologist* entitled "Logan the Mingo: A Problem of Identification." In it, he rejected the received wisdom and affirmed Draper's second thoughts: Logan was John, not his younger brother James.[10]

Wallace's claim rested on two important pieces of evidence: Robinson's note left at the Roberts farm that was signed "Captain John Logan," and Tachnedorus's 1756 claim that Soyechtowa walked with a limp. Regarding the first, Wallace said, we know that Tachnedorus was made a captain in a military unit formed to defend Shamokin in 1755. Thus, when Tachnedorus began being called "Captain John Logan" in the 1760s, the name and rank fit. Why, Wallace wondered, would James say his name was Captain John Logan? The second was just as difficult to understand. Tachnedorus said during the Seven Years' War that his younger brother was unable to undertake any military action because he was lame. As cited above, Tachnedorus told Conrad Weiser in 1756, "My two Brothers went with the Delawares to fetch provisions. The lame one [Soyechtowa], whom you know very well, could not perform the Journey." From this evidence, Wallace assumed Soyechtowa could not undertake all the traveling we know Logan to have done over the following decades. He did not speculate whether this might have been a temporary injury, but conflated the notion that Soyechtowa had a "short foot" and deemed him permanently disabled. This statement from his older brother convinced Wallace that the "famous Mingo chief" had to be John.[11]

WHAT DO WE THINK NOW?

There have been twenty-five books published since 1990 that discuss Logan. Three camps have developed about Logan's identity. The first group, which comprises seven of the twenty-five works and includes some of the most influential books written on the Ohio Valley in the Revolutionary era, takes no stance and follows a lengthy tradition of not wading into these treacherous waters.[12]

The second camp is Team James. Eight of the twenty-five studies declare that Logan is James—but they do not accept the name Tah-gah-jute. In 1999, the prolific, iconoclastic historian Francis Jennings wrote the entry for James Logan in the *American National Biography*. In it, he dismantled the name Tah-gah-jute and its proponents. He called Brantz Mayer's book "probably the most cited, and certainly the least reliable, study" on Logan, and rightly judged it to be "erroneous from the first word of the title and crafted as anti-Indian propaganda." After Jennings' criticism, only a very few scholars have referred to James as Tah-gah-jute. Instead, those who believe James is the "famous Mingo chief" follow William Beauchamp's lead and call him Soyechtowa.[13]

The largest camp, by a small margin, is Team John. Ten of the twenty-five books, which include works by recent prominent scholars, have followed Paul Wallace's lead. Though there is no controversy over his name (Tachnedorus), or what it means ("Spreading Oak"), this third of the scholarly community is convinced that Captain John Logan is who he said he was.[14]

In other words, after centuries of investigation, there is still no scholarly consensus on which of Shickellamy's sons is which. This should be a bracing reminder about how much we really do know about America's past. Logan is one of the most important Native figures and is from one of the most prominent families of eighteenth-century North America—and yet no one really knows who he is.

NATIVE EVIDENCE

There is one piece of evidence that must be weighed against all others, however: Jesse Logan's testimony. Of course, it too has its weaknesses, not the least of which was the alleged age of the testifier. When Jesse was interviewed in 1915, the newspaper reporter figured Jesse was 106 years old. Before we hurry to reject the memory of someone this elderly, though, it should be remembered that nearly all of the evidence in the Logan-Cresap affair were supplied many decades after the fact—sometimes a quarter century later, sometimes sixty years on. With such a large gap between event and documentation, many things could have intervened to transform everyone's memories. The effort to dispossess Natives of their history as well as their land mediates nearly all of what we think we know about Logan's physical stature, his personality, his alcohol intake, his manner of speaking, his relationship with whites, and even his gait.

I can't explain why Soyechtowa (James Logan) would sign that note "Captain John Logan." Did the captured colonist write it down wrong? Did Robinson actually think James's name was Captain John? If Logan indeed had a disability, why did no one apart from apart from Tachnedorus comment on it? I haven't settled these questions myself.

Having said that, while I have my qualms about the aged memory of Jesse Logan, that skepticism is not sufficient to throw out this important piece of Native knowledge. Concluding that Native family tradition would be mistaken about so fundamental a fact perpetuates those subtle influences of settler colonialism. It seems more reasonable to question why on that July day in 1774 the wrong name was scrawled hastily on a scrap of paper rather than to reject all of Shickellamy family history.

In the light of this, despite my doubts, I choose to believe Jesse. His statement that he named his son James "for my great-uncle, the immortal Cayuga orator" settles the issue for me. Jesse's recitation of his family history—that he was the son of Tod-kah-dos, the grandson of Tachnedorus, and the grandnephew of Soyechtowa—is the best piece of evidence for resolving this controversy. With all these contradictions, qualifications, and hesitations in mind, the best solution to the Logan problem is that he is Soyechtowa, James Logan, the second son of Shickellamy.[15]

ACKNOWLEDGMENTS

I have been thinking about Logan and the Cresaps for a long time. More than twenty years ago, sitting in front of a microfilm reader at Alderman Library, I came upon an unusual graphic illustration of a funeral procession in a newspaper and I began to wonder who was in the casket. That person must've been pretty important to merit this kind of treatment, I thought. So I began to explore the funeral, the deceased, and what was going on in New York City in the fall of 1775 that would produce such an event. That research put my dissertation on hold for a good part of 2003 and culminated in "From Indian Killer to Worthy Citizen: The Revolutionary Transformation of Michael Cresap," in the January 2006 issue of the *William & Mary Quarterly*, material that proved to be a very early draft of chapter nine of this book. My thanks to the Omohundro Institute of Early American History and Culture for permission to include that work.

A few months before that article came out, I began my first teaching position at Shepherd University, in Shepherdstown, West Virginia. Every semester I had to teach multiple sections of contemporary world history since 1789. I developed a rotation of books in that course as the years went by, but I found myself continually assigning Joseph Conrad's *Heart of Darkness*. Every time I discussed that book with my students I would leave the classroom with a nagging feeling that the world Conrad was depicting was not one that was foreign to early America. It felt to me like a familiar story.

I set Logan and Cresap aside to work on other projects, but they remained with me, as did that pesky feeling of the American-ness of Conrad's Congo. After my first book came out in 2016, my daughters were starting high school and I needed something to work on that did not necessitate extended visits to archives. I decided to turn back to the story of Yellow Creek and the Logan-Cresap controversy as a writing project that I anticipated could be completed in a year or two. (Ha!) I also began to think seriously about what it would be like to consider Conrad's novella as a frame for this very American story.

As I fumbled around figuring out what I was trying to say, I had a few boosters who were very helpful in pushing me to stick to my guns. Honor Sachs, in her capacity as an organizer of SHEAR's extraordinary Second Book Writers' Workshop (which I attended in 2018), and as a good friend, was an early adopter of this project, encouraging me to keep exploring the Conrad framing. Nadine Zimmerli, now editor at the University of Virginia Press, was another supporter, reading through early drafts of the introduction, pointing out pitfalls, and trying to help me strategize for publication. I had other fantastic cheerleaders in my corner, especially Molly Warsh, Brett Rushforth, Brian Murphy, and Brad Jones.

As they are so perfect at doing, Peter Onuf and Annette Gordon-Reed stepped in at exactly the right moment to workshop drafts of a proposal in my efforts to land a contract with their publisher, Liveright. They, along with some well-needed backing from editor Dan Gerstle, helped accomplish that goal. Peter, Annette, and Dan were considerably helpful in getting me to think about what *Heart of Darkness* was doing for this interpretation and how to get the fuel mixture right of using a novella about Africa from 1902 to help explain America in the middle of the eighteenth century. I continue to be so, so appreciative of Peter and Annette's generosity, consideration, and encouragement. Dan, who has now moved on to become editor-in-chief for W. W. Norton, was kind enough to bring this project with him and I am excited to be among the first of many authors he'll publish in that position. Dan saw promise in this unusual project where others did not, and I am very grateful for his enthusiastic support and sharp, smart editor's eye. At Norton, Zeba Arora and Anna Oler were incredibly helpful, answering all my many questions. Anna helped me find Michael Borop, who drew the maps. Many thanks, Zeba, Anna, and Michael, for helping me get across the finish line.

The first three chapters I wrote as the 2018–2019 Patrick Henry Writing Fellow at the Starr Center for the Study of the American Experience at Washington College, in Chestertown, Maryland. Adam Goodheart and Ken Miller were excellent hosts, and I thoroughly enjoyed my thinking, reading, and writing time on the Eastern Shore. I workshopped an early version of the first chapter for the Washington Area Early American Seminar at Mount Vernon in 2017. My thanks to Rick Bell, Holly Brewer, and Doug Bradburn for the opportunity to share a very rough draft.

Writing this book has been an exercise in bewilderment for me, as well. The layers of mythology, legend, misunderstandings, and mysteries spread in so many directions that it was difficult to get a handle on what parts of this story were needed and what weren't. Luckily, I had the good sense to engage the phenomenal editorial services of Moon and Company. Thomas LeBien and Amanda Moon went over bulky chapters with a scalpel and did tremendous work slicing and paring. Thomas's experience with many fantastic early American books was indispensable in helping me hone this interpretation. The dean's office of Harpur College at Binghamton University helped defray the cost of Moon and Company's services with a much-appreciated subvention grant. With Thomas and Amanda's help, this book is a far superior product. I cannot recommend them highly enough.

As the book neared completion, Charlene Boyer Lewis, James Lewis, and Brett Rushforth were kind enough to read the manuscript. They helped save me from several errors, pushed and prodded, and overall greatly helped improve this manuscript. At Binghamton University, colleagues Diane Miller Sommerville and Steve Ortiz have been stellar supporters and great friends. My superb PhD student Zachary Deibel helped collect as many references to Logan and Cresap as he could find in the nineteenth century. A faculty fellowship from BU's Institute for Advanced Study in the Humanities (IASH) in 2020 aided in the book's progress, as did a sabbatical leave in 2021. My thanks to chairs of the History Department Kent Schull and Nate Andrade for their support.

It is a huge shame that I am not able to share this book with my late father. One of the attractions of this story to me is how close it is to homes past and present. My father was born in what used to be Catfish Camp, and my mother was raised near Mingo Creek, Pennsylvania. When I was teaching in Shepherdstown, a walk of ten minutes could take me to two cemeteries where, in the first, one of the perpetrators of the Yellow Creek massacre was buried and, in the second, one of the witnesses to Michael Cresap's stormy skirmish in Boston lay. Dad especially loved hearing about the Pittsburgh parts of this story, and I hope he would've enjoyed the final product.

This book traces the history of two families. Although both the Shickellamys' and the Cresaps' lives revolved around a tremendous amount of violence, pain, and suffering, I tried to look for moments in their lives where they experienced happiness and love. That impulse to find familial joy comes from the women who surround me. As might be suspected, being as they were in high school and college while it was written, my daughters Abby and Carly were largely oblivious to this book's creation. It is a marvel to watch them build their own lives and endure the trials of going to college during a global pandemic. Abby helped by generously letting me borrow her snazzy camera, giving photography tips, and taking the author's photo, while Carly kept me entertained by feeding me music and movie recommendations for when I couldn't write anymore. They were excited to hear when I was making progress, but didn't want to know too much about the details. The same largely goes for the other wonderful women in my life: my sister Susan, nieces Katie and Amelia, and mother Jane. My twin stepdaughters, Evelyn and Mileur, especially loved hearing about the West Virginia parts of this story, and were very interested in the struggle over what to call it.

Julia Sandy, on the other hand, has had to put up with a considerable amount of nonsense with the writing of this book. She's listened to horrific stories, accompanied me to some fairly sketchy places along the Ohio and Potomac Rivers, crawled through fences, kept lookout while her husband did some mild trespassing, and, most of all, read draft after draft after draft after draft. So many times I would appear on the stairs, interrupting her work, to say, can you look at this? As hard as I tried, I could not shake her faith in this book or its author. Julia's steadfast belief in it and me is a beautiful gift, one I can never fully repay. Her boundless encouragement and galactic-sized heart has brought this book to life. This one is absolutely for her.

NOTES

LIST OF ABBREVIATIONS IN NOTES

4 Am. Archives: Peter Force, ed., *American Archives* 4th series, *Containing a Documentary History of the English Colonies in North America . . .,* 6 vols. (Washington, DC, 1837–1846).

DGW: Donald Jackson and Dorothy Twohig, eds., *The Diaries of George Washington* (Charlottesville, VA, 1976–79).

DHDW: Reuben Gold Thwaites and Louis Phelps Kellogg, eds., *Documentary History of Dunmore's War* (Madison, WI, 1905).

DRCNY: E. B. O'Callaghan and B. Fernow, eds., *Documents Relative to the Colonial History of the State of New York . . .,* 15 vols. (Albany, NY, 1856–1887).

GC: Clarence Edwin Carter, ed., *The Correspondence of Thomas Gage*, 2 vols. (New Haven, CT, 1931–33).

HSP: Historical Society of Pennsylvania, Philadelphia.

JCC: Worthington C. Ford et al., eds., *Journals of the Continental Congress, 1774–1789* (Washington, DC, 1904–1937).

LDC: Paul H. Smith et al., eds., *Letters of Delegates to Congress, 1774–1789*, 26 vols. (Washington, DC, 1976–2000).

MdA: William Hand Browne et al., eds., *Archives of Maryland*, 72 vols. (Baltimore, 1883–).

MDG: *Maryland Gazette* (Annapolis).

MPCP: *Minutes of the Provincial Council of Pennsylvania, from the Organization to the Termination of the Proprietary Government,* 10 vols., Colonial Records of Pennsylvania (Harrisburg, 1851–52).

Notes: William Peden, ed. *Notes on the State of Virginia* (Chapel Hill, NC, 1982 [1954]).

NYG: *New York Gazette & Weekly Mercury* (New York City).

NYPL: New York Public Library.

PA: *Pennsylvania Archives* 1st series, 12 vols., ed. Samuel Hazard (Philadelphia, 1852–1856).

PBF: Leonard W. Labaree et al., eds, *Papers of Benjamin Franklin* (New Haven, CT, 1959–).

PFF: George Reese, ed., *The Official Papers of Francis Fauquier, Lieutenant Governor of Virginia, 1758–1768,* 3 vols. (Charlottesville, VA, 1980–83).

PGW:C: W. W. Abbot et al., eds., *Papers of George Washington: Colonial Series* (Charlottesville, VA, 1983–1995).

PGW:RW: W. W. Abbot et al., eds., *Papers of George Washington: Revolutionary War Series* (Charlottesville, VA, 1985–).

PHB: S. K. Stevens et al., eds., *Papers of Henry Bouquet,* 6 vols. (Harrisburg, PA, 1972–1994).

PMHB: Pennsylvania Magazine of History & Biography.

PSWJ: James Sullivan et al., eds., *The Papers of Sir William Johnson,* 14 vols. (Albany, NY, 1921–1965).

PTJ: Julian P. Boyd et al., eds., *Papers of Thomas Jefferson* (Princeton, NJ, 1950–).

PAG: Pennsylvania Gazette (Philadelphia).

PAJ: Pennsylvania Journal (Philadelphia).

Rev. Va.: Robert L. Scribner et al., eds., *Revolutionary Virginia: The Road to Independence; A Documentary Record,* 7 vols. (Charlottesville, VA, 1973–1983).

RNYG: Rivington's New York Gazetteer (New York City).

St.CP: William Henry Smith, ed., *The St. Clair Papers: The Life and Public Services of Arthur St. Clair* (Cincinnati, IN, 1882).

VAG: Virginia Gazette (Williamsburg).

VMHB: Virginia Magazine of History & Biography.

WMQ: William & Mary Quarterly 3rd series.

INTRODUCTION:
IN THE MIDST OF THE INCOMPREHENSIBLE

1. Mary Beth Norton, *1774: The Long Year of Revolution* (New York, 2020), 78.
2. John Mack Faragher, *Rereading Frederick Jackson Turner: "The Significance of the Frontier in American History" and Other Essays* (New York, 1994), 1.
3. Turner, "Significance of the Frontier to American History," in Faragher, *Rereading Turner,* 32, 59, 248.
4. The sharpest critique of Turner is Patricia Nelson Limerick, *A Legacy of Conquest: The Unbroken Past of the American West* (New York, 1987). Key texts on Native-colonial encounter featuring regional differences include David J. Weber, *The Spanish Frontier in North America* (New Haven, CT, 1982); Richard White, *The Middle Ground: Indians, Empires, and Republics in the Great Lakes Region, 1650–1815* (Cambridge, MA, 1991); Jeremy Adelman and Stephen Aron, "From Borderlands to Borders: Empires, Nation-States, and Peoples in Between in North American History," *American Historical Review* 104 (June 1999): 814–41; Andrés Reséndez, *Changing Identities at the Frontier: Texas and New Mexico, 1800–1850* (Cambridge, MA, 2004); Kathleen DuVal, *The Native Ground: Indians and Colonists in the Heart of the Continent* (Philadelphia, 2006).
5. Key texts include Patrick Wolfe, "Settler Colonialism and the Elimination of the Native," *Journal of Genocide Research* 8 (December 2006): 387–409; Lorenzo Veracini, *Settler Colonialism: A Theoretical Overview* (New York, 2010). For a history of settler colonialism as a concept, see Lorenzo Veracini, "'Settler Colonialism': Career of a Concept," *Journal of Imperial and Commonwealth History* 41 (June 2013): 313–33.

6. Patrick Wolfe called attention to the similarities of his theories to Turner in a 2013 essay: "the land hungry, the diggers of gold, the extractors of oil, the scalpers, the doggers, the sex workers, the pastoralists, the railroad men and the farmers—Turner's whole litany of types—arrive at the boundaries [of places] to which Natives have been removed, and the process starts all over again." Wolfe, "Recuperating Binarism: A Heretical Introduction," *Settler Colonial Studies* 3 (2013): 257–79, quote on 258. Samuel Truett pointed out some of the harmonies in the process arguments of both settler colonialism and Turner in "Settler Colonialism and the Borderlands of Early America," *WMQ* 76 (July 2019): 435–37. This is, however, not to suggest that there is a "line" of settlement that sweeps over everything and everyone evenly. Wolfe is careful to point out that "settler colonialism is not a monolith. It manifests unevenly and regionally." Wolfe, "The Settler Complex: An Introduction," *American Indian Culture and Research Journal* 37 (2013): 1–22, quote on 16. "Invasion": Wolfe, "Elimination of the Native," 388; "pursues": Veracini, "Introducing Settler Colonial Studies," *Settler Colonial Studies* 1 (2011): 1–12, quote on 3.

7. Michael John Witgen, *Seeing Red: Indigenous Land, American Expansion, and the Political Economy of Plunder in North America* (Chapel Hill, NC, 2022), 28. Following the lead of Anishinaabe theorist Gerald Vizenor, many scholars of Indigenous peoples in North America reject the idea that the settler colonialism project actually eliminated Native people and culture. Vizenor coined the term "survivance" to connote how Native peoples not only survived settler colonial efforts to eliminate them but also developed and enhanced their own cultures and identities in those efforts of resistance. "Survivance stories," he writes, "are renunciations of dominance, detractions, obtrusions, the unbearable sentiment of tragedy, and the legacy of victimry." in Gerald Vizenor, ed., *Survivance: Narratives of Native Presence* (Lincoln, NE, 2008), 1. Scholars of Indigenous peoples in America also take issue with how the quasi-Turnerian logic of process removes contingency, the idea that things might have turned out differently. As we will see, contingency is essential to trying to understand the problem of imperial encounter in North America, especially in the decades before and during the American Revolution. For a survey of historians' insights about settler colonialism theory, see Jeffrey Ostler and Nancy Shoemaker, eds., "Forum: Settler Colonialism in Early American History," *WMQ* 76 (July 2019): 361–450.

8. This description was provided several decades later by someone who knew him at the end of the 1880s. See Frederick R. Karl, *Joseph Conrad: The Three Lives* (New York, 1979), 255–56.

9. Joseph Conrad, *Heart of Darkness* (Penguin, 1999 [1902]), 8.

10. Greg Grandin, *The End of the Myth: From the Frontier to the Border Wall in the Mind of America* (New York, 2019), 3, 168.

11. Armstrong further argues that "Marlow's journey to the dark heart of the Congo is similarly an escalating series of disorientations that challenge his sense of identity and unsettle his convictions about the world." Paul B. Armstrong, *The Challenge of Bewilderment: Understanding and Representation in James, Conrad, and Ford* (Ithaca, NY, 1987), 109.

12. Charles Johnson, *The Way of the Writer: Reflections on the Art and Craft of Storytelling* (New York, 2016), 200.

13. Conrad, *Heart of Darkness*, 4, 5, 6–7.

14. Conrad, *Heart of Darkness*, 7.

15. Chinua Achebe, "An Image of Africa," *Massachusetts Review* 18 (Winter 1977): 782–94, quotes on 788, 792. For more see Peter Edgerly Firchow, *Envisioning Africa: Racism and Imperialism in Conrad's Heart of Darkness* (Lexington, KY, 2000), and Sven Lindqvist, *"Exterminate All the Brutes": One Man's Odyssey into the Heart of Darkness and the Origins of European Genocide*, trans. by Joan Tate (New York, 1996 [1992]). "Partnership": Conrad, *Heart of Darkness*, 93. "Kinship": ibid, 94. "Acute angles": ibid, 28–29.

16. William Cronon, George Miles, and Jay Gitlin, "Becoming West: Toward a New Meaning for Western History," Cronon, Miles, and Gitlin, eds., *Under an Open Sky: Rethinking America's Western Past* (New York, 1992), 3–27, esp. 6–7.

17. Conrad, *Heart of Darkness*, 9.

CHAPTER 1. A SCRAMBLE FOR OHIO, 1730–1753

1. This is in sharp contrast to the Lower Ohio Valley, farther downriver, where, as Susan Sleeper-Smith has shown, Native women maintained vital agricultural worlds throughout this period. See *Indigenous Prosperity and American Conquest: Indian Women of the Ohio River Valley, 1690–1792* (Chapel Hill, NC, 2018). Laura Keenan Spero also locates significant early Shawnee settlements before their seventeenth-century diaspora on regions even farther from the Forks, on the Tennessee and Cumberland Rivers. See Spero, "'Stout, Bold, Cunning, and the Greatest Travellers in America': The Colonial Shawnee Diaspora" (University of Pennsylvania diss., 2010), 55–57. For more on how the recent migration of bison to the tallgrass Illinois prairies west of the Ohio Valley attracted Natives there throughout the 1600s, see Robert Michael Morrissey, *People of the Ecotone: Environment and Indigenous Power at the Center of Early America* (Seattle, 2022), esp. 101–115.

2. Stephen Warren, *The World the Shawnees Made: Migration and Violence in Early America* (Chapel Hill, NC, 2014), 12–13, 76; Francis Jennings, *The Ambiguous Iroquois Empire: The Covenant Chain Confederation of Indian Tribes with English Colonies* (New York, 1984), 195–97.

3. Spero, "Colonial Shawnee Diaspora," 204–12.

4. Warren, *World the Shawnees Made*, 173. Spero claims that in 1711 Opessa "removed to Ohio," but he hadn't yet; there was an intermediate stop on the Potomac before his later migration farther west. See Spero, "Colonial Shawnee Diaspora," 245.

5. Council Minutes, 20 May 1725, *MdA*, 25:443.

6. Michael N. McConnell, *A Country Between: The Upper Ohio Valley and its Peoples, 1724–1774* (Lincoln, NE, 1992), 22; Spero, "Colonial Shawnee Diaspora," 248, 255.

7. James H. Merrell, "Shickellamy, 'A Person of Consequence,'" in *Northeastern Indian Lives, 1632–1816*, ed. Robert S. Grumet (Amherst, MA, 1996), 227–57, esp. 228–29.

8. Lyman C. Draper, "Logan—The Mingo Chief, 1710–1780," *Journal of the Ohio Archaeological and Historical Society* 20 (April 1911): 137–75. When the baby died in infancy, the Pennsylvania government sent an official note of condolence. See Governor Gordon to Shickellamy, 18 August 1729, *PA*, 1:241–43.

9. Jennings, *Ambiguous Iroquois Empire*, 312. On the details of the Walking Purchase, see pp. 334–46; Amy C. Schutt, *Peoples of the River Valleys: The Odyssey of the Delaware Indians* (Philadelphia, 2007), 86-88.

10. Cresap family researchers have found marriage records from Leeds, eighteen miles from Skipton, which show that Thomas Crissop of Headrow married Sarah Cromble-Holme of New Chappell on 16 April 1691 and that Thomas Cryssop of Ye Lower Headrow was buried on 21 May 1700, so it seems most likely that Thomas was born sometime in the mid- to late-1690s, perhaps as late as early 1701. See Joseph Ord Cresap and Bernarr Cresap, *The History of the Cresaps*, rev. ed. (Gallatin, TN, 1987), 14; Kenneth P. Bailey, *Thomas Cresap: Maryland Frontiersman* (Boston, 1944), 28–29.

11. Baltimore County Land Patent, volume 8, folio 106. Currently, much of what was Pleasant Garden is part of Pennsylvania's Susquehanna Heritage Park. For Cresap's War, see Paul Doutrich, "Cresap's War: Expansion and Conflict in the Susquehanna Valley," *Pennsylvania History* 53 (April 1986): 89–104, and Patrick Spero, *Frontier Country: The Politics of War in Early Pennsylvania* (Philadelphia, 2016), 74–107.

12. Cresap's deposition, *PA*, 1:311–12.

13. Spero, *Frontier Country*, 77–78, 84.

14. *PAG* 3 February 1736/7.

15. *PAG* 3 February 1736/7.

16. The nickname "Maryland Monster," which has become synonymous with Thomas Cresap, doesn't seem to originate in the 1730s, or even the eighteenth century. There is no direct evidence that Pennsylvanians called TC this at the time. The first reference to Philadelphians using the word "monster" when Cresap rode through town is in 1826 when John Jeremiah Jacob described how "the streets, windows, and doors were crowded with spectators, to view such a

monster of a man." See John Jeremiah Jacob, *A Biographical Sketch of the Life of the Late Captain Michael Cresap* (Cumberland, MD, 1826), 26. But Jacob did not coin the name in this book. That honor goes to Brantz Mayer, who wrote in 1851 that "the streets, windows, and doors were crowded with spectators to see the Maryland monster." It is possible that Thomas may have told family members (including John Jacob) that Philadelphians called him "monster," but it is highly unlikely that anyone called Cresap the "Maryland Monster" in the eighteenth century. Even though nearly all historians, biographers, and writers of the Cresaps adopt it, that name seems to have (like other things, as we'll see) emerged from the mind of Brantz Mayer more than one hundred years after the fact. See Mayer, *Tah-Gah-Jute: Logan and Captain Michael Cresap* (Baltimore, 1851), 17.

17. Deposition of George Aston, 3 December 1736, *PA*, 1:510.

18. Spero, *Frontier Country*, 100. See also, Edward G. Gray, *Mason-Dixon: Crucible of a Nation* (Cambridge, MA, 2023), 61–84.

19. Spero, *Frontier Country*, 96.

20. Aubrey C. Land, *Colonial Maryland: A History* (Millwood, NY: 1981), 199–200.

21. Bailey, *Thomas Cresap*, 59.

22. Bailey, *Thomas Cresap*, 60–61.

23. Indian Seat/Fields: William B. Marye, " 'Potomeck Above Ye Inhabitants': A Commentary on the Subject of an Old Map," part 4: "The Several Indian 'Old Towns' on the Upper Potomac River," *Maryland Historical Magazine* 34 (Winter 1939): 325–32. Description of Oldtown: Charles Lewis journal, 1755, quoted in Bailey, *Thomas Cresap*, 65.

24. Michael Witgen, *An Infinity of Nations: How the Native New World Shaped Early America* (Philadelphia, 2012), 293; Brett Rushforth, *Bonds of Alliance: Indigenous & Atlantic Slaveries in New France* (Chapel Hill, NC, 2012); Morrissey, *People of the Ecotone*, 171–96.

25. Richard White, *The Middle Ground: Indians, Empires, and Republics in the Great Lakes Region, 1650–1815* (Cambridge, MA, 1991), 187.

26. Fred Anderson, *Crucible of War: The Seven Years' War and the Fate of Empire in British North America, 1754–1766* (New York, 2000), 18–20.

27. Merrell, "Shickellamy," *Northeastern Indian Lives*, 228–29.

28. Alfred P. James, *The Ohio Company: Its Inner History* (Pittsburgh, 1959), 7–8.

29. House: Conrad Weiser to James Logan, 29 September 1744, *PA*, 1:661. Tachnedorus mission: *MPCP*, 4:643. Soyechtowa: *MPCP*, 4:646; Merrell, "Shickellamy," *Northeastern Indian Lives*, 243.

30. Lawrence Henry Gipson, *The British Empire before the American Revolution*, vol. 4: *Zones of International Friction: North America, South of the Great Lakes Region, 1748–1754* (New York, 1939), 173; Michael A. McDonnell, *Masters of Empire: Great Lakes Indians and the Making of America* (New York, 2015), 135.

31. George Croghan to Richard Peters, 26 May 1747, *PA*, 1:742; Erik Hinderaker, *Elusive Empires: Constructing Colonialism in the Ohio Valley, 1673–1800* (Cambridge, MA, 1997), 42. "Twightwees": *MDG* 27 September 1749.

32. James H. Merrell, *Into the American Woods: Negotiators on the Pennsylvania Frontier* (New York, 1999); Thomas A. Lewis, *For King and Country: The Maturing of George Washington, 1748–1760* (New York, 1987), 47–72.

33. The list of original partners is in *George Mercer Papers relating to the Ohio Company of Virginia*, Lois Mulkearn, ed. (Pittsburgh, 1954), 2.

34. Cresap filing petition: Thomas P. Abernathy, *Western Lands and the American Revolution* (Charlottesville, VA, 1937), 5. Ohio Company grant: James, *Ohio Company*, 10.

35. On 30 December 1745, Elizabeth Mauduit Lamy, then eighteen, witnessed a purchase memorandum on Thomas Cresap's behalf. This is the first evidence that they had at least met. Memo in Frederick County MD, Ended Causes, Box 5, August 1746 File no. 2, in W. H. Rice, ed., *Colonial Records of the Upper Potomac, vol. 2: The Peaceful Years, 1744–1748* (Parsons, WV, 2012), 97–98. Cohabitation suit: Millard Milburn Rice, ed., *This Was the Life: Excerpts from the Judgment Records of Frederick County, Maryland, 1748–1765* (Redwood City, CA, 1979), 76. Rachael

Guest has gone through the extant evidence about Elizabeth Lamy at https://polychromes
.blogspot.com/2018/11/hidden-history-elizabeth-lamy.html?m=1. Accessed 4 August 2022.

36. Matthew C. Ward, *Breaking the Backcountry: The Seven Years' War in Virginia and Pennsylvania, 1754–1765* (Pittsburgh, 2003), 27–30; Hinderaker, *Elusive Empires*, 40–43.

37. "Unknown to me": Thomas Bladen to George Thomas, Annapolis, 2 August 1746, *PA*, 1:692. "vile fellow": Richard Peters to Thomas Penn, 28 July 1748, Peters Letter Book, HSP, 4:143. Very early into his activities with the Ohio Company, however, it is clear that Cresap saw a chance to square his old grudges with Pennsylvania as one of the benefits of his burgeoning trade with the Indians. In 1750, George Croghan reported back to the Pennsylvania Council that Cresap had been sending messages to Native peoples that he was selling goods "much cheaper than the Pennsylvania traders sold them." Moreover, they should not trust Pennsylvanians, "for they constantly cheated them in all their dealings, which he Col. Cresap was very well acquainted with." *MPCP*, 5:440.

38. Eliga H. Gould, *The Persistence of Empire: British Political Culture in the Age of the American Revolution* (Chapel Hill, NC, 2000), 35–71; David Armitage, *Ideological Origins of the British Empire* (Cambridge, MA, 2000), 170–98.

39. W. J. Eccles, *The French in North America, 1500–1783*, rev. ed. (East Lansing, MI, 1998), 184, 191. According to historicalstatistics.org, with conversion to current (2015) US dollars, this sum would be $5.11 quintillion. https://www.historicalstatistics.org/Currencyconverter.html (accessed 3 August 2022).

40. Paul W. Mapp, *The Elusive West and the Contest for Empire, 1713–1763* (Chapel Hill, NC, 2011), 308.

41. Matthew L. Rhoades, *Long Knives and the Longhouse: Anglo-Iroquois Politics and the Expansion of Colonial Virginia* (Lanham, MD, 2011), 77–129, and L. Scott Philyaw, *Virginia's Western Visions: Political and Cultural Expansion on an Early American Frontier* (Knoxville, TN, 2004), 37–64; Jane T. Merritt, *At the Crossroads: Indians & Empires on a Mid-Atlantic Frontier, 1700–1763* (Chapel Hill, NC, 2003), 77–79.

42. Natives visiting Oldtown: Bailey, *Thomas Cresap*, 71–73. "Worst road": *DGW*, 1:12. "Thirty odd" and dancing: *DGW*, 1:13.

43. *DGW*, 1:15.

44. *DGW*, 1:18.

45. James, *Ohio Company*, 16.

46. Shamokin Diary, Nov. 2–3, 1745, *Records of the Moravian Mission among the Indians of North America* (New Haven, CT, 1978), from original materials at the Archives of the Moravian Church, Bethlehem PA, microfilm, 40 reels, reel 28, box 217, folder 12B, item 1. See James H. Merrell, "Shamokin, 'the very seat of the Prince of Darkness': Unsettling the Early American Frontier," *Contact Points: American Frontiers from the Mohawk Valley to the Mississippi, 1750–1830* Andrew R.L. Cayton and Fredrika J. Teute, eds. (Chapel Hill, NC, 1998), 16–59, esp. 16–29.

47. Smallpox: Merrell, "Shickellamy," *Northeastern Indian Lives*, 248. "extremely poor": Weiser to Council, 15 October 1747, *MPCP*, 5:138. Gifts to Shickellamy: *MPCP*, 5:138. Weiser: Merrell, "Shickellamy," 249.

48. Baptism: Merrell, "Shickellamy," 250–51. Boat capsized: *New York Gazette & Weekly Post-Boy* 5 December 1748.

49. James, *Ohio Company*, 23–24.

50. Rumors: George Croghan to Richard Peters, 3 July 1749, *PA*, 2:31. "Vile fellow": Peters Letterbooks, HSP, 4:143. Croghan land: James, *Ohio Company*, 28.

51. Henry Read McIlwaine, ed., *Executive Journals, Council of Colonial Virginia*, 2nd ed. (Richmond, 1967), 5:295–97.

52. Anderson, *Crucible of War*, 26; Eccles, *France in North America*, 200.

53. The other witness was Jarvis Hougham of Oldtown, which meant that Elizabeth Lamy was nearby. Contract between Ohio Company and Neal Ogullion, 9 February 1750/51, Frederick County, MD Land Records, Liber B, Folios 347–48.

54. Lee deaths: Paul C. Nagel, *The Lees of Virginia: Seven Generations of an American Family* (New

York, 1990), 46. Dinwiddie share: James, *Ohio Company*, 46. "hear frequently": Dinwiddie to TC, 25 January 1752, reproduced in Bailey, *Thomas Cresap*, 193–94, quote on 194.

55. James, *Ohio Company*, 44, 49.
56. James, *Ohio Company*, 94–95.
57. "heaped": Anderson, *Crucible of War*, 28. Tanaghrisson: Colin G. Calloway, *The Indian World of George Washington: The First President, the First Americans, and the Birth of the Nation* (New York, 2018), 59.
58. Alfred Goodman, ed., *Journal of Captain William Trent, from Logstown to Pickawillany, 1752* (Cincinnati, OH, 1871), 85–90. News of the raid in *VAG* (Hunter) 20 October 1752; *MDG* 9 November and 7 December 1752; McDonnell, *Masters of Empire*, 152–59.
59. R. E. Banta, *The Ohio* (New York, 1949), 8.
60. Anderson, *Crucible of War*, 32.
61. Bailey, *Thomas Cresap*, 95.
62. Scarouady: *DGW*, 1:133. French deserters: *DGW*, 1:135.
63. St. Pierre's letter translated in *DGW*, 1:151. "much anxiety": *DGW*, 1:152.
64. *DGW*, 1:155.
65. *DGW*, 1:177. Jumonville Glen: Anderson, *Crucible of War*, 5–7.

CHAPTER 2. STRAIGHTFORWARD FACTS, 1754–1759

1. GW to Robert Hunter Morris, Winchester, 9 April 1756, *PGW:C*, 2:345.
2. *DGW*, 1:157.
3. Fred Anderson, *Crucible of War: The Seven Years' War and the Fate of Empire in British North America, 1754–1766* (New York, 2000), 46–47; Thomas A. Lewis, *For King and Country: The Maturing of George Washington, 1748–1760* (Edison, NJ, 1993), 132–35.
4. David Preston, *Braddock's Defeat: The Battle of the Monongahela and the Road to Revolution* (New York, 2015), 31–34.
5. *PSWJ*, 2:465–6.
6. Braddock march: Charles Hamilton, ed., *Braddock's Defeat: The Journal of Captain Robert Cholmley's Batman* (Norman, OK, 1959), 14. "Damned rascal": "Extracts of a Journal of the Proceedings of the Seaman (a detachment), ordered by Commodore Keppel to assist on a late expedition to the Ohio . . .," in Winthrop Sargent, ed., *A History of an Expedition against Fort Duquesne in 1755, under Major General Edward Braddock* (New York, 1971 [1855]), 372. "nam'd Crisop": Fairfax Harrison, ed., "With Braddock's Army: Mrs. Browne's Diary in Virginia and Maryland," *VMHB* 32 (October 1924): 315–20, quote on 316.
7. The Expedition of Major General Braddock to Virginia with the Two Regiments of Hacket and Dunbar: Being Extracts of Letters from an Officer in One of Those Regiments to His Friend in London, Describing the March and Engagement in the Woods. Printed for H. Carpenter, 1755. Indigenous Peoples: North America, http://tinyurl.galegroup.com/tinyurl/92Vo39, Letter 3, page 14. Accessed 6 February 2019.
8. Supplies to Ft. Cumberland: Captain Robert Orme's journal, in Sargent, *History of an Expedition*, 308, spoiled beef: 313. "Pennsylvania Flower": Edward Braddock to Robert Hunter Morris, Fort Cumberland, 24 May 1755, *MPCP*, 6:400.
9. "Damned rascal": "Extracts of a Journal of the Proceedings of the Seaman (a detachment), ordered by Commodore Keppel to assist on a late expedition to the Ohio . . .," in Sargent, *History of an Expedition*, 372–73. Frontier man: J. A. Leo Lemay, "The Frontiersman from Lout to Hero: Notes on the Significance of the Comparative Method and the Stage Theory in Early American Literature and Culture," *Proceedings of the American Antiquarian Society* 88 (1978): 187–223, esp. 189–90. Whether or not the British officers knew it, "rattlesnake colonel" did have a specific meaning in America. One Maryland colonist, traveling in New York a decade before Braddock's march, noted the term in his diary. After nearly stepping on a snake, he opined "had it been a rattlesnake I should have been entitled to a colonel's commission, for it is a common saying here that a man has no title to that dignity until he

has killed a rattlesnake." Dr. Alexander Hamilton, *Itinerarium* (New York, 1971 [1744]), 94. A scholarly exchange about this phrase occurred in the *New England Quarterly* in the mid-twentieth century, for which see Albert Matthews, "Rattlesnake Colonel," *New England Quarterly* 10 (June 1937): 341–45.

10. *PSWJ*, 2:475–76.

11. Diagram of Ft. Pitt: Anderson, *Crucible of War*, 95. Braddock response: Beverly W. Bond Jr., "The Captivity of Charles Stuart, 1755–1757," *Mississippi Valley Historical Review* 13 (June 1926): 58–81, quote on 63. "Very much enraged": ibid., 64.

12. Flight: *MDG* 10 July 1755. Thomas Cresap deed to Elizabeth Lamy, Frederick County, Maryland Land Records, Liber E, Folios 667–68. The deed was recorded on 18 March 1755 and stipulated she had lifetime use of all the buildings, houses, improvements currently on the land provided she actually reside there.

13. Scarouady to Robert Hunter Morris, Shamokin, 11 September 1755, *MPCP*, 6:615. On Shickellamy's sons as diplomatic couriers in 1755, see Conrad Weiser to Robert Hunter Morris, Heidelberg in Berks County, 4 October 1755, *MPCP*, 6:640–41.

14. "Cut off": Adam Stephen to GW, Winchester, 4 October 1755, *PGW:C*, 2:72. "Barbarians": *MDG* 9 October 1755; *PAG* 16 October 1755; *PAJ* 16 October 1755; *New York Mercury* 20 October 1755; *Boston Gazette* 27 October 1755; *Boston News-Letter* 30 October 1755; *South Carolina Gazette* 13 November 1755.

15. James H. Merrell, *Into the American Woods: Negotiators on the Pennsylvania Frontier* (New York, 1999), 227–28.

16. "Now stir": Conrad Weiser to Richard Peters, Heidelberg, 2 May 1754, quoted in Paul A. W. Wallace, *Conrad Weiser: Friend of Colonist and Mohawk* (Philadelphia, 1945), 355. Albany Purchase: Jane T. Merritt, *At the Crossroads: Indians and Empires on a Mid-Atlantic Frontier* (Chapel Hill, NC, 2003), 173; Merrell, *Into the American Woods*, 231–32; Timothy J. Shannon, *Indians and Colonists at the Crossroads of Empire: The Albany Congress of 1754* (Ithaca, NY, 2000), 108–9. For details of the Albany Purchase, see *MPCP*, 6: 110–20.

17. John Harris to Robert Hunter Morris, Paxton, 28 October 1755, *MPCP*, 6:654; Wallace, *Conrad Weiser*, 397.

18. "Terrible Mountains": William Parsons to Richard Peters, Stonykiln, 31 October 1755, *PA*, 2:444. "Thirty miles of Baltimore": *MDG* 6 November 1755; *PAG* 13 November 1755; *South Carolina Gazette* 25 December 1755. Earthquake: *MDG* 13 November 1755. The Cape Ann earthquake was centered off the coast of Massachusetts. It has been estimated at a strength of 6.0–6.3 on the modern earthquake scale. According to contemporary colonial newspapers, residents as far south as Maryland's eastern shore reported feeling its effects. *MDG* 20 November 1755. "Frightful charm": *Boston Evening Post* 1 December 1755; *PAG* 11 December 1755.

19. BF to Peter Collinson, 25 October 1755, *PBF*, 6:229.

20. Instructions to Conrad Weiser, 19 January 1756, *PA*, 2:550. "Apprehensive": *MPCP*, 7:47.

21. *MPCP*, 7:51.

22. *MPCP*, 7:52. The question of Soyechtowa's physical disability is addressed in the appendix.

23. *MPCP*, 7:54.

24. *MPCP*, 7:65.

25. "Fearful, ignorant": Edward Shippen to Robert Hunter Morris, Lancaster, 19 April 1756, *PA*, 2:634. Scalp bounty in *MPCP*, 7:88–90; printed in *PAG* 15 April 1755. "Conistogo": Thomas McKee to Edward Shippen, Hunter's Mill, 5 April 1756, *PA*, 2:616. We don't know which of Shickellamy's two daughters, Cajadis or Koonay, was the one sent to Conestoga.

26. "Confusion and distress": William Parsons to Richard Peters, 31 October 1755, *PA*, 2:444. "Poor families": Thomas Gage to GW, Albany, 23 November 1755, *PGW:C*, 2:179.

27. "Tied to trees": *PAG* 1 April 1756; young girls: *PAG* 8 April 1756; Body on road: Horatio Sharpe to Calvert, 5 May 1756, *MdA*, 6:409.

28. "Cruel robberies": Robert Dinwiddie to Robert Hunter Morris, 30 April 1756, *MPCP*, 7:133. "Dressed and painted": *MDG* 29 April 1756; *PAG* 6 May 1756; *New York Mercury* 10 May 1756; *Boston Gazette* 17 May 1756; *Boston News-Letter* 20 May 1756.

29. "One gun": *PAG* 27 May 1756. "Privately as they could": *MDG* 6 May 1756.

30. "Death is lamented": *MDG* 6 May 1756; *Boston News-Letter* 4 June 1756. The reference to two children is inaccurate; they only had one young daughter, Charity. There was more coverage the week following, for which see *MDG* 13 May 1756 and *PAG* 13 and 27 May 1756. "Very great loss": *PAG* 27 May 1756. Motion: *MdA*, 52:436.

31. *PAG* 13 November 1755; *South Carolina Gazette* 25 December 1755.

32. *PAG* 13 November 1755; *South Carolina Gazette* 25 December 1755.

33. Cresap expedition: *PAG* 13 May 1756; *PAJ* 13 May 1756; *New York Mercury* 17 May 1756; *South Carolina Gazette* 1 July 1756. Letter from Col. Thomas Cresap, 6 June 1756, *PAG* 17 June 1756. Also in *New York Mercury* 21 June 1756.

34. "Not able to distinguish": *MDG* 10 June 1756. Accounts of Gist/Cresap engagement also in *PAG* 24 June 1756; *New York Mercury* 28 June 1756; *Boston Gazette* 5 July 1756; *Boston Evening Post* 5 July 1756; *Boston News-Leader* 8 July 1756. Return to Cumberland: *PAG* 24 June 1756; *MDG* 1 July 1756.

35. Letter from Col. Cresap, 1 July, *MDG* 8 July 1756; *PAG* 15 July 1756; *PAJ* 15 July 1756; *New York Mercury* 19 July 1756; *Connecticut Gazette* 24 July 1756; *Boston News-Letter* 5 August 1756.

36. *MDG* 29 July 1756; *PAG* 12 August 1756; *New York Mercury* 16 August 1756; *Boston News-Letter* 2 September.

37. For Cresap leading parties out of Fort Frederick (near the Conococheague), see *MDG* 2 September 1756, *PAG* 16 September 1756. From 1755 to 1757, Michael occasionally attended the Free School (est. 1746) run by Reverend Thomas Craddock out of the Trentham Mansion in what is today Owings Mills, Maryland.

38. *MDG* 9 March 1758.

39. "Lost ourselves": Conversation between Conrad Weiser and Shekellamy, 18 September 1756, *PA*, 2:776. "Almost perished": *PA*, 2:777–78. "Constant friend": *PA*, 2:778. "Large assortment": Quoted in Wallace, *Conrad Weiser*, 456.

40. Michael A. McDonnell, *Masters of Empire: The Great Lakes Indians and the Making of America* (New York, 2015).

41. Paul Kelton, "The British and Indian War: Cherokee Power and the Fate of Empire in North America," *WMQ* 69 (October 2012): 763–92.

42. Anderson, *Crucible of War*, 275.

43. *MPCP*, 8:204.

44. *MDG* 7 and 14 December 1758.

45. Adam Stephen to Henry Bouquet, Bedford, 27 May 1759, *PHB*, 3:329.

46. "Emblem of empire": Anderson, *Crucible of War*, 329; Daniel P. Barr, *A Colony Sprung from Hell: Pittsburgh and the Struggle for Authority on the Western Pennsylvania Frontier, 1744–1794* (Kent, OH, 2014), 93; Ward, *Breaking the Backcountry*, 202.

47. Francis Fauquier to Board of Trade, Williamsburg, 1 December 1759, *PFF*, 1:276.

CHAPTER 3. GROVES OF DEATH, 1760–1763

1. Levi Trump to Conrad Weiser, Fort Augusta, 28 January 1760, and Conrad Weiser to Levi Trump, Reading, 3 February 1760, *PA*, 3:698–99.

2. Colonel Burd Diary, 17 February 1760, quoted in Paul A. W. Wallace, *Conrad Weiser: Friend of Colonist and Mohawk* (New York, 1971 [1945]), 564. "Great service": Richard Peters to Conrad Weiser, Philadelphia, 21 February 1760, quoted in Wallace, *Conrad Weiser*, 565; Colonel Hugh Mercer to Lieutenant Graydon, Harris's Ferry, 3 May 1760, *PA*, 3:728.

3. "Journal of John Hays, 1760," *PA*, 3:735–41, quote on 739.

4. Thomas Cresap to Henry Bouquet, Oldtown, 24 July 1760, *PHB*, 4:656.

5. "No settlement will be permitted": Henry Bouquet to Thomas Cresap, Presque Isle, 12 September 1760, *PHB*, 5:32. Cresap to repair warehouse: Lois Mulkearn, ed., *George Mercer Papers: Relating to the Ohio Company of Virginia* (Pittsburgh, 1954), 180. Request for militia: *MdA*, 56:478.

6. Election: Thomas Cresap to Henry Bouquet, Oldtown, 27 May 1761, *PHB*, 5:510. In 1760, Bouquet bought from Daniel Dulany a four thousand-acre plot called Long Meadow Enlarged, adjacent to Cresap's five hundred-acre Long Meadow tract north of Hagerstown. See *PHB*, 4:503. Decline: Henry Bouquet to Thomas Cresap, Fort Pitt, 9 June 1761, *PHB*, 5:535.

7. Mingo problems: Henry Bouquet to General Robert Monckton, Fort Pitt, 4 May 1761, *PHB*, 5:459; Bouquet to Monckton, 15 May 1761, *PHB*, 5:482; Lt. Townshend Guy to Bouquet, Fort LaBoeuf, 1 June 1761, *PHB*, 5:521. Seneca unrest: Captain Donald Campbell to Bouquet, Detroit, 16 June 1761, *PHB*, 5:555–56; Bouquet to Campbell, 30 June 1761, *PHB*, 5:596.

8. "Such crowds": McDonald to Bouquet, Fort Burd, 25 October 1761, *PHB*, 5:840. Bouquet Proclamation, 30 October 1761, *PHB*, 5:844.

9. "Some uneasiness": Fauquier to Bouquet, Williamsburg, 17 January 1762, *PHB*, 6:39. "Ten new Huts": Bouquet to Fauquier, Fort Pitt, 8 February 1762, *PHB*, 6:44–45, quotes on 44 and 45. "Set on fire over them": George Croghan and Nicholas B. Wainwright, eds. "George Croghan's Journal, April 3, 1759 to April [30], 1763," *PMHB* 71 (October 1947): 423. "Frighted the people": McDonald to Bouquet, Fort Burd, 8 April 1762, *PHB*, 6:74. See also Croghan to SWJ, Fort Pitt, 10 May 1762, *PSWJ*, 3:732–734.

10. Bouquet to Amherst, Fort Pitt, 1 April 1762, *PHB*, 6:72.

11. "By force or otherwise": Thomas Cresap to Horatio Sharpe, Oldtown, 11 June 1762, *MdA*, 32:39. Resentment: Sharpe to Amherst, Annapolis, 26 June 1762, *MdA*, 14:62.

12. "Extracts of Minutes–Treaty of Lancaster," *PSWJ*, 10:498–99 and *MPCP*, 8:723–70. "Without molestation": *MPCP*, 8:754. Pennsylvania governor Hamilton agreed that he would send their request to Maryland governor Sharpe, for which see *MPCP*, 8:769. Trade station established: Sharpe to SWJ, Annapolis, 25 November 1762, *PSWJ*, 10:573–74; *MdA*, 14:80–81; Sharpe to TC and the Six Nations, 28 March 1763, *MdA*, 32:58.

13. TC to Sharpe, 5 May 1763, *MdA*, 32:57.

14. HB to Croghan, Fort Bedford, 16 August 1759, *PHB*, 3:569; HB to Colonel George Mercer, Fort Bedford, 16 August 1759, *PHB*, 3:571. "Villain": Mercer to HB, Pittsburgh, 20 August 1759, *PHB*, 3:591. Rumor: Entry for 6 July 1761, James Kenny and John W. Jordan, "Journal of James Kenny, 1761–1763" Part 1 *PMHB* 37 (1913): 10. Challenge: Entry for 15 July 1762, James Kenny and John W. Jordan, "Journal of James Kenny, 1761–1763" Part 2 *PMHB* 37 (1913): 162.

15. Entry for 20 December 1762, Kenny and Jordan, "Journal of James Kenny," 176.

16. Gregory Evans Dowd, *War Under Heaven: Pontiac, the Indian Nations, and the British Empire* (Baltimore, 2002), 143, 150.

17. Croghan pass: *MdA*, 32:57. Their dissatisfaction is in the form of a letter from the Six Nations to Sharpe, dated Oldtown, 15 May 1763. Three Iroquois leaders signed the letter, which said, "We find nothing but what said Cresap has given us on his own Account, viz. some victuals, a few Knives, and some Tobacco. Therefore We desire our request may be complied with, which will prevent our taking anything from the Poor Inhabitants." *MdA*, 32:57–58.

18. Forbes road: Lt. Ourry to Amherst, Fort Bedford, 10 June 1763, *PHB*, 6:248. Shamokin Daniel: Dowd, *War Under Heaven*, 140–42.

19. "Starving": Ourry to Amherst, Fort Bedford, 10 June 1763, *PHB*, 6:246. "Melancholy sight": *PAG* 30 June 1763. "Panic more general": *MDG* 21 July 1763.

20. Rains "greater and frequenter than can be remembered" and wheat rust, *MDG* 30 June 1763.

21. James Livingston to HB, Cumberland, 1 o'clock in the morning, 16 July 1763, *PHB*, 6:317–18.

22. TC to Sharpe, 15 July 1763, *MdA*, 14:104. Cresap also dashed off a letter to Major James Livingston at Fort Cumberland at the same time. It reached Cumberland late that night using many of the same phrases as the one to Sharpe. Livingston recounted the battle in a letter he hurried to Bouquet at 1 a.m. on July 16. One of Livingston's other informants about what happened around Cresap's was a Tomlinson, one son of the hunter killed at Redstone the year before. See James Livingston to HB, Cumberland, 1 o'clock in the morning, 16 July 1763, *PHB*, 6:317–18.

23. TC to Sharpe, 15 July 1763, *MdA*, 14:104.

24. "Repeated reports": *MDG* 14 July 1763; *PAG* 28 July 1763; *PAJ* 28 July 1763; *Newport Mercury* 1 August 1763; *New York Mercury* 1 August 1763; *New-London Summary* 5 August 1763; *Boston*

Evening Post 8 August 1763; *Boston Post-Boy* 8 August 1763; *New Hampshire Gazette* 12 August 1763; *Georgia Gazette* 8 September 1763. Retraction: *MDG* 21 July 1763; *PAG* 28 July 1763; *NYG* 1 August 1763; *New York Mercury* 8 August 1763. "A proper check": *MDG* 28 July 1763; *PAG* 11 August 1763; *NYG* 8 August 1763; *Newport Mercury* 15 August 1763; *Boston News-Letter* 18 August 1763; *Boston Post-Boy* 22 August 1763; *New-London Summary* 26 August 1763.

25. In total, thirty-one people had been killed or taken captive in the area around Oldtown from May to July. See Lt. Ourry's return, *PHB*, 6:410. Settlers returning: *MDG* 18 August 1763.

26. Lt. Ourry to HB, Fort Bedford, 27 August 1763, *PHB*, 6:372.

27. Kevin Kenny, *Peaceful Kingdom Lost: The Paxton Boys and the Destruction of William Penn's Holy Experiment* (New York, 2009), 125–26; Merrell, *Into the American Woods*, 285.

28. Conestoga discontent: Kenny, *Peaceable Kingdom Lost*, 12–13. The Conestoga pledge was at the 23 January 1756 conference at Lancaster, for which see *MPCP*, 7:7–8. Rangers plans to march: Kenny, *Peaceable Kingdom Lost*, 134–35.

29. Benjamin Franklin, "A Narrative of the Late Massacres in Lancaster County," *PBF*, 11:42–69, quote on 50.

30. "Baskets, Brooms, and Bowls": Franklin, "Narrative of the Late Massacres," 50. Workhouse: John Hay to Governor Hamilton, Lancaster, 27 December 1763, *MPCP*, 9:102–4. Two of the women survivors provided Sheriff Hay with the list of names of those killed at Conestoga and those still alive in Lancaster.

31. Hay to Governor Hamilton, Lancaster, 27 December 1763 p.m., *MPCP*, 9:103. Because two Conestoga women provided them to Sheriff Hay at Lancaster just before they too were murdered, we know the names of all twenty victims of the Paxton Boys' rampage.

32. "Kin at Conestoga": *DHDW*, 246.

33. Franklin, "Observations on the Increase of Mankind," (1751), *PBF*, 4:225–34; all quotes on 234.

34. See the appendix in Peter Silver, *Our Savage Neighbors: How Indian War Transformed Early America* (New York, 2008), 303–5. Silver examined all references to white people in the *Pennsylvania Gazette*, seeing a massive spike in 1755–56 and then again in 1763. "White people": GW to John Stanwix, 30 July 1757, *PGW:C*, 4:353. In a search of Readex's "America's Historical Newspapers" database, the term "white people" got 216 hits from 1720 to the end of 1763, with 75 percent of them coming after 1754. Search done 24 April 2019. For suffering, see Silver, *Our Savage Neighbors*, xxi.

35. "Unhappy perpetrators": Franklin, "Narrative of Late Massacres, *PBF*, 11:66–67. "Noise and Hubbub": "The Conduct of the Paxton Men, Impartially Represented," in John R. Dunbar, ed., *The Paxton Papers* (The Hague, 1957), 269–98, quote on 282. "RIOTERS, REBELS": ibid., 274.

CHAPTER 4. MESSENGERS OF THE MIGHT, 1764-1768

1. *MDG* 23 February 1764.

2. *PAG* 14 June 1764; *PAJ* 14 June 1764.

3. Archibald Loudon, *A Selection of the Most Interesting Narratives of Outrages Committed by the Indians in their Wars with the White People*, 2 vols. (Carlisle, 1811), 2:214. For more on Loudon and this publication, see Judith Ridner, "Archibald Loudon and the Politics of Print and Indian-Hating in the Early Republic," *Early American Studies* 19 (Summer 2021): 528–67.

4. Loudon, *A Selection*, 2:214–215. In 1811, Loudon swore he had met the "famous Mingo chief Logan," but whether he had actually met Tachnedorus or Soyechtowa is not verifiable. For more on the controversy over which brother was Logan, see the appendix.

5. R. P. Maclay account reprinted in Sherman Day, *Historical Collections of the State of Pennsylvania* (Philadelphia, 1843), 467–68. McClay does not make any comment if Soyechtowa had difficulty walking.

6. Stuart Banner, *How The Indians Lost Their Land: Law and Power on the Frontier* (Cambridge, MA, 2005), 92–93. For the larger and longer imperial effort to establish a "boundary" with Natives, see S. Max Edelson, *The New Map of Empire: How Britain Imagined America before Independence* (Cambridge, MA, 2017), 144–73.

7. Fred Anderson, *Crucible of War: The Seven Years' War and the Fate of Empire in British North America, 1754–1766* (New York, 2000), 645.

8. *MDG*, 29 August 1765. "Certain unwelcome officer": *MDG*, 5 September 1765. Hood in NY: Ronald Hoffman, *A Spirit of Dissension: Economics, Politics and the Revolution in Maryland* (Baltimore, 1973), 51; Anderson, *Crucible of War*, 674, Paul H. Giddens, "Maryland and the Stamp Act Controversy," *Maryland Historical Magazine* 27 (June 1932): 79–98.

9. "Writing": Proceedings of the Council of Maryland, 1761–1769, David Ross testimony, 11 December 1765, *MdA*, 32:113.

10. *MdA*, 32:113.

11. J. Thomas Scharf, *History of Western Maryland*, 2 vols. (Philadelphia, 1882), 1:122; *MDG* 10 December 1765. "Repudiation Day" is still observed in the city of Frederick, with banks being closed for a half-day every 23 November.

12. *MDG* 10 December 1765.

13. Cresap's request for leave: *MdA*, 59:168. Michael and Mary Whitehead were wed on 6 August 1764. St. Paul's Church marriage records, page 14, *Historic Pennsylvania Church and Town Records*, HSP, microfilm reel 240.

14. *MdA*, 32:172–73.

15. *MdA*, 32:110.

16. *MdA*, 32:111.

17. Sharpe to Cecil Calvert, 21 December 1765, *MdA*, 14:253.

18. Patrick Spero, *Frontier Rebels: The Fight for Independence in the American West, 1765–1776* (New York, 2018), 15.

19. For Washington's concerns about how Forbes Road was going to be to Virginia's disadvantage, see GW to Francis Fauquier, Fort Cumberland, 2 September 1758, *PGW:C*, 5:441.

20. Spero, *Frontier Rebels*, 20–21.

21. Thomas Perkins Abernathy, *Western Lands and the American Revolution* (Charlottesville, VA, 1937), 29.

22. George E. Lewis, *The Indiana Company, 1763–1798: A Study in Eighteenth Century Frontier Land Speculation and Business Venture* (Glendale, CA, 1941), 38–39, 43.

23. Lewis, *Indiana Company*, 45–46.

24. King's Instructions to John Penn, 24 October 1765, *MPCP*, 9:321. "Lawless ruffians": Gage forwarded SWJ's remarks to Conway, 5 May 1766, *GC*, 1:91. "Cursed villains": Gage to SWJ, NY, 19 May 1766, *PSWJ*, 12:92. "General war": Croghan to Gage, Fort Pitt, 26 May 1766, *MPCP*, 9:323.

25. "Drove away": Gage to SWJ, NY, 22 June 1766, *PSWJ*, 12:111–12. "Ridstone": Shelburne to Gage, Whitehall, 13 September 1766, *GC*, 2:45; Shelburne to SWJ, Whitehall, 13 September 1766, *PSWJ*, 5:375.

26. Penn Proclamation, 23 September 1766, *MPCP*, 9:327–28; Gage to Shelburne, 11 November 1766, *GC*, 1:112. For the Virginia and Pennsylvania governors conversing about this, see John Penn to Francis Fauquier, 15 November 1766, *PFF*, 3:1191–92, Fauquier to Penn, 11 December 1766, *PFF*, 3:1406, and Fauquier to Shelburne, 18 December 1766, *PFF*, 3:1411.

27. Baynton, Wharton, and Morgan to SWJ, 28 December 1766, *PSWJ*, 12:236–37.

28. SWJ to Lords of Trade, 15 January 1767, *DRCNY*, 7:891.

29. Bernard Bailyn, *Voyagers to the West: A Passage in the Peopling of America on the Eve of the Revolution* (New York, 1986), 26.

30. Benjamin Franklin to William Franklin, 12 September 1766, *PBF*, 13:414-15.

31. Richard White, *The Middle Ground: Indians, Empires, and Republics in the Great Lakes Region, 1650–1815* (Cambridge, MA, 1991), 340.

32. Baynton, Wharton, and Morgan to SWJ, 14 March 1767, *PSWJ*, 12:277–78. SWJ's answer of 1 April is *PSWJ*, 12:291–92.

33. SWJ to Gage, 18 April 1767, in O'Callahan, *Documentary History of the State of New York* 2:848–50, quote on 849. See also Gage to Shelburne, 7 April 1767, which mentions Gage

having received Ft. Pitt commander Capt. William Murray's letter of 27 February 1767 that documents the slaying. See *GC*, 1:133.

34. "first aggressor": Gage to SWJ, 28 June 1767, *PSWJ*, 5:574; "usurped": Gage to SWJ, 5 April 1767, *PSWJ*, 12:296. Curb alcohol: Rob Harper, *Unsettling the West: Violence and State Building in the Ohio Valley* (Philadelphia, 2018), 24.

35. "Conduct": Francis Fauquier to Capt. William Murray, Williamsburg, 12 April 1767, *PFF*, 3:1438. Parcel of refugees": Horatio Sharpe to Hugh Hamersley, 11 February 1768, *MdA*, 14:468. Ejection orders: Gage to SWJ, NYC, 4 May 1767, *PSWJ*, 12:308.

36. "Most": Gage to SWJ, 11 May 1767, *PSWJ*, 5:548. "Still remain": Gage to Shelburne, NYC, 13 June 1767, *GC*, 1:142. "Double the number": George Croghan to SWJ, Ft. Pitt, 18 October 1767, *PSWJ*, 12:374. "Daily Increase": SWJ to Shelburne, Johnson Hall, 3 December 1767, *DRCNY*, 7:998.

37. "Curiosity": Entry for 10 January 1765, in A. Hughlett Mason, ed., *The Journal of Charles Mason and Jeremiah Dixon* (Philadelphia, 1969), 66. "Open War": Entry for 17 January 1765, Mason, *Journal of Mason and Dixon*, 67. "Beautiful Estate": Mason, *Journal of Mason and Dixon*, 178. They stayed at Oldtown 7–8 July 1767, noting "this is the same Gentleman mentioned in Journal of the 17th of January 1765."

38. "Open rupture": Gage to SWJ, NYC, 28 June 1767, *PSWJ*, 5:574. "Talk from Northern Indians," Oldtown, 10 September 1767, *PFF*, 3:1497–98. Fauquier reacted to Cresap's private move to negotiate peace as "officious interfering in a business with which he had nothing to do." *PFF*, 3:1509.

39. Entry for 9 October 1767, Mason, *Journal of Mason and Dixon*, 187. For more, see Edward G. Gray, *Mason-Dixon: Crucible of a Nation* (Cambridge, MA, 2023), 135– 63.

40. GW to William Crawford, 17 September 1767, *PGW:C*, 8:28–29.

41. "Boundary line": Shelburne to SWJ, Whitehall, 19 December 1767, *PSWJ*, 6:22–23. "Loss of time": Shelburne to SWJ, 5 January 1768, *DRCNY*, 8:2; Peter Marshall, "Sir William Johnson and the Treaty of Fort Stanwix, 1768," *Journal of American Studies* 1 (October 1967): 149–79, esp. 149–52; Edelson, *New Map of Empire*, 173–77.

42. Earl P. Olmstead, *Blackcoats among the Delaware: David Zeisberger on the Ohio Frontier* (Kent, OH, 1991), 11; Marshall, "Johnson and the Treaty of Fort Stanwix," 169–73; Alan Taylor, *The Divided Ground: Indians, Settlers, and the Northern Borderland of the American Revolution* (New York, 2006), 42–45.

43. Taylor, *Divided Ground*, 44.

44. The treaty is printed in *DRCNY*, 8:111–34. Croghan moves: Wainwright, *Wilderness Diplomat*, 254–57.

45. SWJ to Gov. Henry Moore, Ft. Stanwix, 28 September 1768, *PSWJ*, 6:411.

46. SWJ to Hillsborough, 18 November 1768, in O'Callaghan, *Documentary History of State of New York*, 2:917–19. Hillsborough's strategy in Jack M. Sosin, *Whitehall and the Wilderness: The Middle West in American Colonial Policy, 1760–1775* (Lincoln, NE, 1961), 166–67.

47. For Johnson's detailed instructions from the Board of Trade about the line and what it was to mean, see *DRCNY*, 8:19–31. For Hillsborough's reaction see Abernathy, *Western Lands and American Revolution*, 43–44. Orders to Johnson: Hillsborough to SWJ, Whitehall, 13 May 1769, *DRCNY*, 8:165–66.

48. McConnell, *A Country Between*, 255–56.

CHAPTER 5. FEELING VERY SMALL, VERY LOST, 1769–1770

1. *DGW*, 2:284.

2. *MDG* 19 March 1767.

3. My inference that Cresap used this method of crossing the Atlantic comes from the fact that there were no direct ships to London from Philadelphia in August 1769. Four years earlier, when Benjamin Franklin went to London, he went first to New York and then caught the

regular packet service that went between those cities weekly as a function of Manhattan being the central mail depot for the mainland American colonies. There were three ships listed in the Customs House records as outwards from Philadelphia to New York in the time period Cresap was in town, but the *Endeavour* makes the most sense given that we know he left around August 5–6. See *PAG* 10 August 1769.

4. Thomas Wharton to SWJ, Philadelphia, 16 August 1769, *PSWJ* 7:97.

5. Thomas P. Abernathy, *Western Lands and the American Revolution* (Charlottesville, VA, 1937), 44.

6. The articles drawn up in June 1769 are in *PBF*, 16:163–69.

7. Benjamin Franklin to William Franklin, 14 July 1773, *PBF*, 20:300–314. https://founders .archives.gov/documents/Franklin/01-20-02-0165.

8. "Petition to the Treasury from Franklin and others for a Grant of Land, 4 January 1770," *PBF*, 17: 8–11.

9. The old Ohio Company partners received (collectively) two shares in the Grand Ohio Company. See *PBF*, 17:135–36. Kingdom: *VAG* (Rind) 25 March 1773.

10. "Full and perfect": GW to Botetourt, 8 December 1769, *PGW:C*, 8:272. "Petition to Botetourt," [15 December 1769], *PGW:C*, 8:277–79; Washington paid for the advertisement to run in Rind's *VAG* for 22 weeks, from 21 December 1769 to 14 June 1770. See *PGW:C*, 8:280. "Foot of land": GW to Charles Washington, Mount Vernon, 31 January 1770, *PGW:C*, 8:301.

11. "Profound secret": GW to William Crawford, 17 September 1767, *PGW:C*, 8:28–29. "King's Part": Crawford to GW, 29 September 1767, *PGW:C*, 8:39. Crawford wrote this ten days before Mason and Dixon would be prevented from drawing their line any farther west.

12. Jonathan Boucher to GW, Annapolis, 18 August 1770, *PGW:C*, 8:367.

13. GW to Botetourt, Mount Vernon, 9 September 1770, *PGW:C*, 8:378–80. "Well-grounded hopes": GW to Botetourt, Mount Vernon, 5 October 1770, *PGW:C*, 8:388.

14. *DGW*, 2:287.

15. For the weather on October 8–9, *DGW*, 2:284.

16. GW to George Mercer, Mount Vernon, 22 November 1771, *PGW:C*, 8:555.

17. Dinner: *DGW*, 2:292. "Brothers of Virginia": *DGW*, 2:293.

18. *DGW*, 2:293. Washington later learned from Iroquois farther downriver that by "Virginians," Natives "mean all the People settled upon Redstone." *DGW*, 2:297.

19. *DGW*, 2:295.

20. *DGW*, 2:295.

21. *DGW*, 2:295.

22. *DGW*, 2:296.

23. Mingo Town: *DGW*, 2:296. "Cuttawbas": *DGW*, 2:297.

24. *DGW*, 2:297.

25. *DGW*, 2:304.

26. *DGW*, 2:304.

27. *DGW*, 2:307, 308.

28. Guyasuta: *DGW*, 2:310. Violent current: *DGW*, 2:313.

29. *DGW*, 2:318–19.

30. *DGW*, 2:316.

31. "Intelligent Man": *DGW*, 2:322. For doubts on Connolly as Croghan's nephew see Nicholas B. Wainwright, *George Croghan: Wilderness Diplomat* (Chapel Hill, NC, 1959), 287; and the editors of the Papers of George Washington, *DGW*, 2:323.

32. *DGW*, 2:323. Perhaps Lee did earn one thing from being along for this trip after all: at some point in 1771 Washington stopped referring to him as "Billy" and instead would now refer to his twenty-year-old enslaved valet as William or Will.

33. Memorandum to William Crawford, 24 November 1770, *PGW:C*, 8:402–3; GW to George Croghan, Stewart's Crossing, Pa., 24 November 1770, *PGW:C*, 8:403–4. Within two weeks Crawford headed back to Pittsburgh to complete Washington's survey. See William Crawford to GW, 6 December 1770, *PGW:C*, 8:405–6.

34. GW to Croghan, Stewart's Crossing, Pa., 24 November 1770, *PGW:C*, 8:404.
35. GW to William Crawford, Mount Vernon, 6 December 1770, *PGW:C*, 8:566.

CHAPTER 6. BACKBITING AND INTRIGUING, 1771–1773

1. Dunmore to Hillsborough, New York, 9 March 1771, in Dunmore Family Papers, Rockefeller Library, Colonial Williamsburg Foundation, vol. 3, no. 41; Dunmore to Lord Hillsborough, New York, 2 July 1771, CO 5/154, f. 20. Replacement ploy: William Tryon to Hillsborough, New York, 31 August 1771, CO 5/154 f. 25. Arrival: James Corbett David, *Dunmore's New World: The Extraordinary Life of a Royal Governor in Revolutionary America* (Charlottesville, VA, 2013), 39–43.
2. Dunmore to Hillsborough, Williamsburg, March 1772, CO 5/154, ff. 35–36.
3. Dunmore's instructions, 1771, in Aspinwall Papers, 2:655–56, in George Chalmers Collection, NYPL.
4. Purchases: William Crawford to GW, Spring Garden, Pa., 15 April 1771, *PGW:C*, 8:445. Croghan survey: William Crawford to GW, 20 April 1771, *PGW:C*, 8:449–50 and William Crawford to GW, Stewart Crossing, Pa., 2 August 1771, *PGW:C*, 8:513. "Minutes of the Meeting of the Officers of the Virginia Regiment of 1754," Winchester, 5 March 1771, *PGW:C*, 8:439–41. Young men: Hooper to SWJ, 9 February 1771, *PSWJ*, 7:1132. "Cup and the Lip": Benjamin Franklin to William Franklin, London, 20 April 1771, *PBF*, 18:76.
5. "Full of people": Hooper to SWJ, 9 February 1771, *PSWJ*, 7:1132. "Dreadful battle": John J. Jacob, *A Biographical Sketch of the Life of the Late Captain Michael Cresap* (New York, 1971 [1826]), 48.
6. Keith Frye, "The Fairfax Stone," *Banisteria: The Journal of the Virginia Natural History Society* 5 (1995): 36–38.
7. Jonathan Boucher to GW, Annapolis, 4 July 1771, *PGW:C*, 8:493–94.
8. "Secrecy": [Samuel Wharton and William Trent] to [George Croghan and Michael? Cresap], London, 21 July 1771, George Croghan Papers, Cadwallader Collection, Box 203, folder 35, HSP. The letter has been mistakenly attributed to Michael, but it is clear by the repeated references to "Col. Cresap" that Wharton meant Thomas. "Cheerfully disposed": Samuel Wharton to George Croghan, London, 21 July 1771, London, 21 July 1771, George Croghan Papers, Cadwallader Collection, Box 203, folder 31, HSP.
9. Petition plan: [Samuel Wharton and William Trent] to [George Croghan and Thomas Cresap], London, 21 July 1771, George Croghan Papers, Cadwallader Collection, Box 203, folder 35, HSP. "God only knows": Samuel Wharton to George Croghan, London, 4 September 1770, George Croghan Papers, Cadwallader Collection, Box 203, folder 31, HSP.
10. Thomas Cresap to Thomas Wharton, Skipton, 15 November 1771, reprinted in Kenneth P. Bailey, *Thomas Cresap: Maryland Frontiersman* (Boston, 1944), 212–13.
11. Robert Callendar to John Penn, 21 April 1771, *PA*, 4:411–12.
12. Killbuck to Philadelphia: Robert Callendar to Joseph Shippen Jr., 22 April 1771, *PA*, 4:413. Council fire: *MPCP*, 9:738. The Pennsylvania council met with Killbuck on 7, 8, and 13 May 1771, *MPCP*, 9:735–41; Gage to Hillsborough, New York, 7 May 1771, *GC*, 1:298. Imminent war: *PAG* 9 May 1771. "Not our friends": SWJ to Gage, Johnson Hall, 9 August 1771, *PSWJ*, 8:220; SWJ to Gage, Johnson Hall, 19 September 1771, *PSWJ*, 8:261.
13. *MPCP*, 9:730.
14. *St.CP*, 1:2–9.
15. *MDG* 5 June 1771; *PAG* 27 June 1771.
16. William Crawford to James Tilghman, Stewart's Crossing, Pa., 9 August 1771, *PA*, 4:424–25.
17. "Depend on suffering": Deposition of Thomas Woods, sheriff, sworn to Arthur St. Clair, 19 September 1771, *PA*, 4:435. "Impossible to collect": St. Clair to Joseph Shippen, Bedford, 24 September 1771, *PA*, 4:437.
18. Boston: Merrill Jensen, *The Founding of a Nation: A History of the American Revolution, 1763–1776* (New York, 1968), 370, 411. Virginia floods and boycotts: Bruce A. Ragsdale, *A Planter's*

Republic: The Search for Economic Independence in Revolutionary Virginia (Madison, WI, 1996), 102. Thomas was still making demands on the Maryland Assembly for repayment for Seven Years' War/Pontiac's War defense expenses in the summer of 1771, applying to Gage to secure Royal Treasury funds. See Gage to Grey Cooper, New York, 6 May 1771. Gage held a board of inquiry on 15 May and found Cresap's claims invalid, for which see Gage to Grey Cooper, 3 June 1771. Both in *GC*, 2:576, 578–79.

19. David, *Dunmore's New World*, 49–50.

20. Dunmore illness: David, *Dunmore's New World*, 65. "prime mover": St. Clair to Joseph Shippen, Jr., Bedford, 18 July 1772, *St.CP*, 1:265; "chiefly abetted": St. Clair to Joseph Shippen, Jr., Bedford, n.d., written shortly after 18 July 1772, *St.CP*, 1:267. "put to death": *St. CP*, 1:268. "Deep laid scheme": St. Clair to Shippen, Bedford, 18 July 1772, *PA*, 4:546.

21. Sosin, *Whitehall and the Wilderness*, 202–4. "Spirits": Samuel Wharton to Croghan, 3 February 1773, George Croghan Papers, Cadwalader Collection, Box 203, folder 31, HSP.

22. Gage to Barrington, NYC, 4 March 1772, *GC*, 2:601.

23. Dexter, *Diary of Reverend David McClure*, 19 October 1772, ("surprise and grief"), 101; 9 October 1772, ("frightfully painted"), 100.

24. Entry for 15 September 1772, Dexter, *Diary of David McClure*, 57.

25. Dexter, *Diary of David McClure*, 57. It is highly likely that Logan's later fame and reputation colored McClure's memory. The editor of his diary said that McClure had only made "fitful" notes in 1772 and then in 1805 went back and wrote them into fuller entries. By then the troubled man he had talked with in the woods had become a legend. For "fitful," see Dexter, *Diary of David McClure*, iii.

26. Gage to Captain Charles Edmundstone, 17 December 1772, Gage papers, Clements Library; Croghan to Gage, 27 November 1772, ibid.

27. "Dangerous situation": Richard Penn to Pa. Assembly, 29 January 1773, *MPCP*, 10:68–69. In 1771, Governor John Penn, who had been Pennsylvania's governor since 1763, returned to England after the death of his father. John's brother Richard Penn Jr. became governor of Pennsylvania in his absence, from 1771 to 1773, until John returned. John Penn then resumed the position from the fall of 1773 through American independence. This reference to "Governor Penn" is Richard. "Unspeakable sufferings": Richard Penn to Assembly, 5 February 1773, *MPCP*, 10:71.

28. "Some kingdoms": *VAG* (Rind) 25 March 1773, exchanged from a 4 January 1773 Charleston, South Carolina newspaper, which is not extant. Notice was also in *South Carolina Gazette* 7 January 1773; *South Carolina Gazette & Country Journal* 12 January 1773; *PAG* 24 February 1773; *VAG* (Purdie and Dixon) 18 March 1773; *VAG* (Rind) 18 March 1773.

29. 7 March 1773, *DGW*, 3:165. Travel arrangements: GW to Dunmore, Mount Vernon, 13 April 1773, *PGW:C*, 9:217–18.

30. Bernhard Knollenberg, *George Washington: The Virginia Period, 1732–1775* (Durham, NC, 1964), 94–95. Daniel P. Barr, *A Colony Sprung from Hell: Pittsburgh and the Struggle for Authority on the Western Pennsylvania Frontier, 1744–1794* (Kent, OH, 2014), 146. News that the new colony was imminent and was going to be named Pittsylvania, not Vandalia, in *VAG* (Purdie and Dixon) 27 May 1773; *PAG* 9 June 1773; 25,000 migrants: *VAG* (Purdie and Dixon) 10 June 1773.

31. Dunmore to GW, Williamsburg, 3 July 1773, *PGW:C*, 9:258–59.

32. Dunmore to Lord Dartmouth, Williamsburg, 18 March 1774, CO 5/1352 ff. 16–20.

33. John Connolly to GW, Pittsburgh, 18 September 1772, *PGW:C*, 9:95–99; Connolly to GW, Pittsburgh, 29 June 1773, *PGW:C*, 9:245–51.

34. John Connolly to GW, Pittsburgh, 29 August 1773, *PGW:C*, 9:314. Since Connolly was a British army veteran, Dunmore thought he could finesse this grant through the authority of the 1763 Royal Proclamation, which allowed provisions for soldier bounties. See David, *Dunmore's New World*, 67. Dunmore also cultivated Croghan's support, promising to ratify his shaky land claims near Fort Pitt. See Nicholas B. Wainwright, *George Croghan: Wilderness Diplomat* (Chapel Hill, NC, 1959), 286.

35. "Paragraph from a Correspondent," *Maryland Journal & Baltimore Advertiser* 9 September 1773; *RNYG* 16 September 1773; *VAG* (Rind) 7 October 1773; *South Carolina Gazette & Country Journal* 12 October 1773.

36. Benjamin Hillman, ed., *Executive Journals of Virginia Council*, vol. 6 (Richmond, 1966), 6:543.

37. Dexter, *Diary of David McClure*, 49, 53

38. John Connolly to GW, Fredericksburg, 23 December 1773, *PGW:C*, 9:414.

39. Connolly advertisement, *MPCP*, 10:141–42.

40. "loose people": Croghan to General Frederick Haldimand, 4 October 1773, Croghan Papers, folder 6, HSP; "very alarming jealousy": *RNYG* 26 August 1773; *Pennsylvania Packet* 30 August 1773; *Connecticut Courant* 31 August 1773; *MDG* 16 September 1773; *VAG* (Purdie and Dixon) 16 September 1773; *South Carolina Gazette & Country Journal* 21 September 1773. "Some mischief": Croghan to Haldimand, 4 October 1773, Croghan Papers, HSP. Guyasuta related Croghan's message in his 5–15 January 1774 conference at Johnson Hall, for which see *PSWJ*, 12:1047. "Stopped up ears": Journal of Alexander McKee, October 1773, *PSWJ*, 12:1032–33. "Plunder canoes": Rev. David Jones, "A Journal of Two Visits Made to Some Nations of Indians on the West Side of the River Ohio, in the Years 1772 and 1773 (Burlington, NJ, 1774), 14. "Beyond all doubt": *PSWJ*, 12:1057.

41. *PSWJ*, 12:1051–52.

42. Indian Conference, 9 October 1773, *PSWJ*, 12:1034–6.

43. Mary Beth Norton, *1774: The Long Year of Revolution* (New York, 2020).

CHAPTER 7. APPROACH CAUTIOUSLY, 1774

1. St. Clair to Penn, Ligonier, 2 February 1774, *PA*, 4:477. At the end of 1773, John Penn returned to Pennsylvania and took over the office of Pennsylvania governor from his brother Richard. From 1774 to 1776, references to "Governor Penn" mean John.

2. "Statement from the Pennsylvania j.p.s," enclosed in St. Clair to Penn, 2 February 1774, *PA*, 4:478–80.

3. "Assuming powers": Penn to St. Clair, Philadelphia, 20 January 1774, *St.CP*, 1:276. St. Clair did not have the Riot Act in his hands when he arrested Connolly on 24 January; Penn's letter did not arrive until 28 January. Penn's letter had told St. Clair to arrest Connolly *after* the muster, but he had already done so beforehand. See St. Clair to Penn, 2 February 1774, *PA*, 4: 476–78. Penn to Dunmore, 31 January 1774, *MPCP*, 10:149–51.

4. Connolly to GW, Westmoreland county jail, 1 February 1774, *PGW:C*, 9:464–66. St. Clair to Penn, 2 February 1774, *PA*, 4:477. Mackay to Penn, Pittsburg[h], 4 April 1774, *4 Am. Archives*, 1:269.

5. "very loose society": Marc Bloch, "Reflections of a Historian on the False News of War," trans. James P. Holoka, *Michigan War Studies Review* (July 2013 [1921]): 1–11, quote on 10. See also Gregory Evans Dowd, *Groundless: Rumors, Legends, and Hoaxes on the Early American Frontier* (Baltimore, 2015), 3–8 and passim.

6. "General applause": Entry for 24 January 1774, *Journal and Letters of Philip Vickers Fithian: Plantation Tutor of the Old Dominion, 1773–1774*, Hunter Dickinson Farish, ed., (Charlottesville, VA, 1957), 59. Doubts about tea party: Benjamin Franklin to Massachusetts Assembly Committee of Correspondence, 2 February 1774, *PBF*, 21:76; GW to George William Fairfax, Williamsburg, 10–[15] June 1774, *PGW:C*, 10:96.

7. Joseph Spear to St. Clair, Pittsburgh, 23 February 1774, *PA*, 4:481. "Men without character": William Crawford to John Penn, 8 April 1774, *4 Am. Archives*, 1:262.

8. "Open and avowed": St. Clair to Joseph Shippen Jr., Ligonier, 25 February 1774, *PA*, 4:482. "At his peril": Spear to St. Clair, 23 February 1774, *PA*, 4:481. "Croghan's Emissaries": St. Clair to Shippen, 25 February 1774, *PA*, 4:482.

9. Va. Council meeting 28 February 1774, *Executive Journals of Va. Council* 6:554–55. Dunmore to Penn, 3 March 1774, *MPCP*, 10:156–57.

10. Dunmore to Dartmouth, Williamsburg, 18 March 1774, in K. G. Davies, ed., *Documents of the American Revolution, 1770–1783 (Colonial Office Series)*, vol. 8 (Dublin, 1975) 8:65–67, quote on 67.

11. Penn to LD, Philadelphia, 31 March 1774, *MPCP*, 10:157–62, quote on 162.

12. Aeneas Mackay to Penn, 4 April 1774, 4 *Am. Archives*, 1:270.

13. Aeneas Mackay to Penn, 4 April 1774, 4 *Am. Archives*, 1:270. For Crawford's understanding that Connolly had gotten Augusta County warrants for St. Clair and others, see Crawford to Penn, 8 April 1774, 4 *Am. Archives*, 1:262. "Constant pursuit": Mackay to Penn, 4 April 1774, 4 *Am. Archives*, 1:270.

14. Croghan to Dunmore, 9 April 1774, in Nicholas Wainwright, "Turmoil at Pittsburgh: Diary of Augustine Prevost, 1774," *PMHB* 85 (April 1961): 144–46, quote on 145. Sheila L. Skemp, *The Making of a Patriot: Benjamin Franklin at the Cockpit* (New York, 2013); Thomas P. Abernathy, *Western Lands and the American Revolution* (Charlottesville, VA, 1937), 54–58.

15. Crawford to Penn, 8 April 1774, 4 *Am. Archives*, 1:263; "Remarks on the Proceedings of Doctor Connolly, 1774," Pittsburgh, 25 June 1774, *PA*, 4:528.

16. "Swords drawn": Thomas Smith to Joseph Shippen, Westmoreland County, 8 April 1774, 4 *Am. Archives*, 1:271. Guards: Deposition of George Wilson, 6 April 1774, *PA*, 4:492–93. "Clamour and confusion": Smith to Shippen, 4 *Am. Archives*, 1:272.

17. Mackay and Smith to Penn, 9 April 1774, *MPCP*, 10:169–70; McFarlane to Penn, 9 April 1774, *PA*, 4:487–88.

18. Deposition of Ephraim Hunter, taken on 25 April 1774, *PA*, 4:491–92.

19. "Remarks on the Proceedings of Doctor Connolly," 1774, *PA*, 4:529.

20. "Patrolling our streets": Aeneas Mackay to Penn, Pittsburgh, 4 April 1774, 4 *Am. Archives*, 1:270–71. Sawmill Run: Devereaux Smith to Dr. William Smith, Pittsburgh, 10 June 1774, *PA*, 4:511–12.

21. "Waylaid" and "made off": Smith to Smith, 10 June 1774, *PA*, 4:512. Interview with Benjamin Tomlinson, 14 April 1797, in John J. Jacob, *A Biographical Sketch of the Life of the Late Captain Michael Cresap* (New York, 1971 [1826]), 134. See also Glenn F. Williams, *Dunmore's War: The Last Conflict of America's Colonial Era* (Yardley, PA, 2017), 56.

22. John Connolly, "Journal of My Proceedings, etc., Commencing from the Late Disturbances with the Cherokees upon the Ohio," 14–15 April 1774, mss., Chalmers Collection, NYPL, p. 1.

23. Entry for 16 April 1774, Journal of Alexander McKee, 16 April–5 May 1774, *PSWJ*, 12:1087–90.

24. Va. Council meeting, 20 and 25 April 1774, in *Exec. Journal. Va. Council* 6:556–58. Commissioners: Pa. Council minutes for 22 April 1774, *MPCP* 10:171–72. Penn also sent word to the three imprisoned Westmoreland magistrates offering his support. "Repel any Insult": Dunmore proclamation, 25 April 1774, *PA*, 4:490–91.

25. McKee messages: 17 April 1774 entry in McKee Journal, *PSWJ*, 12:1090. Guyasuta: *PSWJ*, 12:1091–94. "Insulted and abused": 20 April 1774 entry in Connolly journal, 1.

26. 20 April 1774 entry for Connolly journal, 1–2.

27. 27 April 1774 entry, McKee journal, *PSWJ*, 12:1095. McKee had just the day before gotten information that a group of Cayuga Natives—Shickellamy's people—intended to "plant this year at the mouth of Big Beaver Creek," and requested ammunition. See ibid., 1094.

28. GW to MC, Mount Vernon, 26 September 1773, *PGW:C*, 9:334–35. Cresap hires: Jacob, *Biographical Sketch of Michael Cresap*, 49–50. See also Cameron B. Strang, "Michael Cresap and the Promulgation of Settler Land-Claiming Methods in the Backcountry, 1765–1774," *VMHB* 118 (2010): 122–24.

29. John Mack Faragher, *Daniel Boone: The Life and Legend of an American Pioneer* (New York, 1992), 92–94.

30. Thomas Hanson's journal, *DHDW*, 114–15.

31. Hanson's journal said 26, Clark in 1798 said "80 or 90" men were there at Point Pleasant. "The question" and "settling a plantation": George Rogers Clark to Samuel Brown, 17 June 1798, James Alton James, ed., *Collections of the Illinois State Historical Library*, vol. 8: *George Rogers Clark Papers, 1771–1781* (Springfield, IL, 1912), 5–6.

32. "Dissuaded": James, *Clark Papers*, 8:6. Hanson's scouting party did not go with them to Wheeling, but went farther down into Kentucky, scouting lands for Patrick Henry and others into early August. See Hanson's journal, *DHDW*, 116–33.
33. Clark to Brown, 17 June 1798, in James, *Clark Papers*, 8:6–7.
34. James, *Clark Papers*, 8:7.
35. James, *Clark Papers*, 8:7.
36. "Solemn manner": James, *Clark Papers*, 8:7. War post: Williams, *Dunmore's War*, 65.
37. Ebenezer Zane to John Brown, 4 February 1800, *Notes*, 235.
38. "Weeds": Zane to Brown in *Notes*, 235. "Threatening language": Entry for 1 May 1774, McKee journal, *PSWJ*, 12:1095.
39. It appeared as "intelligence from Pittsburgh," but is almost verbatim from McKee's journal. *Pennsylvania Packet* 23 May 1774, *PAG* 25 May 1774; *NYG* 30 May 1774; *VAG* (Purdie & Dixon) 2 June 1774, *Massachusetts Gazette & Boston Weekly News-Letter* 2 June 1774, *Connecticut Journal* 3 June 1774, *Norwich Packet* 16 June 1774, *New Hampshire Gazette* 17 June 1774, *South Carolina & American General Gazette* 15 July 1774.
40. Pitched battle: Entry for 1 May 1774, McKee journal, *PSWJ*, 12:1096; Crawford to GW, 8 May 1774, *PGW:C*, 10:54. "Warlike stores": Clark to Brown, James, *Clark Papers* 8:7; Zane to Brown, *Notes*, 235.
41. Clark to Brown, 17 June 1798, in James, *Clark Papers,* 8:7–8.
42. James, *Clark Papers*, 8:8.
43. Testimony of John Gibson, taken 4 April 1800, *Notes*, 233.
44. Gibson testimony, *Notes*, 234.

CHAPTER 8. THE HORROR, 1774

1. "Recollections of Capt. Michael Myers, Newburgh, Ohio, given to Dr. Draper, 25–26 February 1850," *DHDW*, 17–19, quote on 19.
2. "Painted black: "Information given to Dr. Draper by Michael Cresap, Jr. in the autumn of 1845," *DHDW*, 15. Koonay's warning: Declaration of John Sappington, 13 February 1800, *Notes,* 255. Lucy told Greathouse: "Recollections of George Edgington of West Liberty, Pa., related to Dr. Draper in 1845," *DHDW*, 16. 21 people: Sappington declaration, *Notes*, 255. Muster: Testimony of Charles Polke, *Notes*, 241.
3. "Drink with them": Testimony of John Anderson, 30 June 1798, *Notes*, 238. "Decoyed": 3 May 1774 entry, McKee journal, *PSWJ*, 12:1097. "Intimate companion": Deposition of James Chambers, 20 April 1798, *Notes*, 239. "Hostile intention": Jolly reminiscence, *DHDW*, 14.
4. Sappington declaration, *Notes*, 255.
5. Contest: Jolly recollection, *DHDW*, 10. Redcoat: "Testimony of Bazaleel Wells, related to Dr. Draper in 1845," *DHDW*, 16; for a list of who was in the front room, see Cresap Jr. testimony, *DHDW*, 15. "Strut about": Sappington declaration, *Notes*, 256.
6. Cresap Jr. testimony, *DHDW*, 15.
7. Wells testimony, *DHDW*, 16.
8. Deer: Edgington recollection, *DHDW*, 17. Forehead: 3 May 1774 entry, McKee journal, *PSWJ*, 12:1097–98. "Inhuman manner": *PSWJ*, 1097–98. "Big with child": Declaration of William Robinson, 28 February 1800, *Notes*, 243. The false story of Koonay's baby being ripped out of her still appears in scholarship today, even among careful historians of Native America. See Michael A. Lafaro, *Daniel Boone: An American Life* (Lexington, KY, 2003), 45; Colin G. Calloway, *The Indian World of George Washington: The First President, the First Americans, and the Birth of the Nation* (New York, 2018), 208.
9. "Ranged themselves": Sappington declaration, *Notes*, 256. Canoes crossing and "melancholy cry": 3 May 1774 entry, McKee journal, *PSWJ*, 12:1097.
10. 3 May 1774 entry, McKee journal, *PSWJ*, 12:1097.
11. "Babe": Jolly reminiscence, *DHDW*, 10. Baby's return: Crawford to GW, 8 May 1774, *PGW:C*, 10:54.

12. "One thousand people": Valentine Crawford to GW, Jacob's Creek, Pa., 7 May 1774, *PGW:C*, 10:52. "Whole country": William Crawford to GW, 8 May 1774, *PGW:C*, 10:54.

13. 3 May 1774 entry in John Connolly journal, Chalmers Collection, NYPL, p. 3. *VAG* (Rind) 21 July 1774.

14. For an explanation of "emotion work" and how "emotional regimes" can help explain how both Natives and colonists reacted in similar moments of crisis, see Matthew Kruer, "Bloody Minds and Peoples Undone: Emotion, Family, and Political Order in the Susquehannock-Virginia War," *WMQ* 74 (July 2017): 401–36. Stay calm: George Croghan to John Connolly and Alexander McKee, 4 May 1774, in Cadwallader Family Papers, series 4: Croghan papers, box 201, folder 33, HSP; "Journal of Mission on Muskingum," *PA*, 4:496; Arthur St. Clair to the Six Nations and Delawares, May 1774, *PA*, 4:500; "Speech of Shawnees to Alex. McKee," 20 May 1774, *PA*, 4:497–98. Stop firing guns: 7 May 1774 entry, Connolly journal, 7.

15. "39 Ohio Indians": *RNYG* 19 May 1774. This article was reprinted in *Boston News-Letter* 26 May 1774, *New Hampshire Gazette* 3 June 1774. "Put to death": *Pennsylvania Packet* 23 May 1774; *PAG* 25 May 1774; *PAJ* 25 May 1774; *NYG* 30 May 1774; *VAG* (Purdie and Dixon) 2 June 1774; *Boston News-Letter* 2 June 1774; *Connecticut Journal* 5 June 1774; *Norwich Packet* 15 June 1774; *New Hampshire Gazette* 15 June 1774; *South Carolina & American General Gazette* 15 July 1774. Cresap's fault: 8 May 1774 entry, Connolly journal, 10.

16. MC return to Oldtown: Devereux Smith to Dr. William Smith, Pittsburgh, 10 June 1774, *PA*, 4:512; John J. Jacob, *A Biographical Sketch of the Life of the Late Captain Michael Cresap* (New York, 1971 [1826]), 67–68. "Fall upon": 16 May 1774 entry, Connolly journal, 12. White Eyes threatened: Entry for 11 May 1774, in Connolly journal, 11.

17. Entry for 19 May 1774, in Connolly journal, 12.

18. Entry for 21 May 1774, in Connolly journal, 14.

19. Entry for 21 May 1774, in Connolly journal, 15.

20. Entry for 21 May 1774, in Connolly journal, 15–16.

21. Entry for 24 May 1774, Connolly journal, 16. "Fight it out": Jacob, *Life of Captain Michael Cresap*, 68.

22. Gekelemuckepuck: Entry for 8 May 1774 in "Extract of a Journal of the United Brethren's Mission on the Muskingum," *PA*, 4:495–96. "Very angry": Entry for 15 May 1774, *PA*, 4:496.

23. "Arthur St. Clair to John Penn, Ligonier, 29 May 1774, *PA*, 4:503–4.

24. John Connolly to George Croghan, 3 June 1774, in Cadwalader Family Papers, Series 4: Croghan papers, box 201, folder 17, HSP.

25. "Indian Intelligence," 5 June 1774, *PA*, 4:508.

26. "Cannot yet judge": St. Clair to Penn, Ligonier, 8 June 1774, *PA*, 4:510. First account with no details of the family name: *VAG* (Purdie and Dixon) 23 June 1774; *RNYG* 7 July 1774; *Boston News-Letter* 13 July 1774; *Essex Gazette* (Salem, MA) 19 July 1774. Benjamin Spier: *PAG* 22 June 1774; *Connecticut Gazette* 1 July 1774; *Connecticut Journal* 1 July 1774; *Connecticut Courant* 9 August 1774. "Consternation and distress": *VAG* (Rind) 16 June 1774; *NYG* 27 June 1774; *PAG* 29 June 1774; *PAJ* 29 June 1774; *MDG* 30 June 1774; *Pennsylvania Packet* 4 July 1774; *Maryland Journal & Baltimore Advertiser* 9 July; *Connecticut Courant* 19 July 1774; *Norwich Packet* 21 July 1774.

27. Peter Silver, *Our Savage Neighbors: How Indian War Transformed Early America* (New York, 2008), xx–xxii, 85–88.

28. Disappearance: Valentine Crawford to GW, Jacob's Creek, Pa., 8 June 1774, (2nd letter of that date), *PGW:C*, 10:91; William Crawford to GW, Spring Garden, Pa., 8 June 1774, *PGW:C*, 10:93. Jenkins' Fort: *PAG* 22 June 1774; Williams, *Dunmore's War*, 97.

29. Aeneas Mackay to John Penn, Pittsburgh, 14 June 1774, *PA*, 4:517; St. Clair to Penn, Ligonier, 16 June 1774, *St.CP*, 1:308–9; *PAG* 29 June 1774; Williams, *Dunmore's War*, 98; Sipe, *Indian Wars of Pennsylvania*, 495.

30. "Dangerous Consequence": SWJ to Haldimand, Johnson Hall, 9 June 1774, *PSWJ*, 8:1164. "Nothing to prevent it": Haldimand to SWJ, NYC, 15 June 1774, *PSWJ*, 8:1167. "Trophy of

his Valor": Hugh Wallace to SWJ, NYC, 27 June 1774, *PSWJ*, 8:1178–79. "Murdered near 30": SWJ to Gage, Johnson Hall, 4 July 1774, *PSWJ*, 8:1114–15.

31. "Instrumental": Dartmouth to Gage, 6 July 1774, *GC*, 2:170. "Very great trouble": SWJ to William Franklin, Johnson Hall, 27 June 1774, *PSWJ*, 8:1177.

32. *RNYG* 16 June 1774; *NYG* 20 June 1774; *Connecticut Gazette* 24 June 1774; *VAG* (Rind) 7 July 1774.

33. "Inevitable": *Pennsylvania Packet,* 20 June 1774; *RNYG*, 22 June 1774; *New York Journal* 23 June 1774; *Essex Journal* (Salem, MA) 29 June 1774; *Boston News-Letter* 30 June 1774; *Providence Gazette* 2 July 1774; *VAG* (Purdie and Dixon) 7 July 1774; *VAG* (Rind) 7 July 1774; *Virginia Gazette & Norfolk Intelligencer* 7 July 1774; *New Hampshire Gazette* 8 and 22 July 1774; *South Carolina & American General Gazette* 15 July 1774; *Essex Gazette* (Salem, MA) 19 July 1774. "Barbarous murder": *PAJ* 29 June 1774; *VAG* (Rind) 14 July 1774; *MDG* 14 July 1774; *Massachusetts Spy* 15 July 1774. "Letter of thanks": *PAG* 13 July 1774; *PAJ* 13 July 1774; *Norwich Packet* 21 July 1774; *Providence Gazette* 23 July 1774; *Boston News-Letter* 28 July 1774; *South Carolina & American General Gazette* 5 August 1774; *South Carolina & Country Journal* 16 August 1774. Some printers did not include all of this letter, and did not reprint the paragraph about Cresap. See *NYG* 18 July 1774, and *Connecticut Journal* 22 July 1774.

34. "Worse savages": *PAG* 6 July 1774; *PAJ* 6 July 1774; *Pennsylvania Packet* 11 July 1774; *New York Journal* 14 July 1774; *Connecticut Courant* 26 July 1774; *South Carolina & American General Gazette* 29 July 1774. "Lord North": *Newport Mercury* 11 July 1774; *Boston Gazette* 18 July 1774; *Essex Gazette* (Salem, MA) 19 July 1774; *Boston News-Letter* 21 July 1774; *Massachusetts Spy* 21 July 1774; *Essex Journal* (Salem, MA) 27 July 1774; *South Carolina & Country Journal* 23 August 1774.

35. Dunmore to Gage, Williamsburg, 11 June 1774, Thomas Gage Papers, Clements Library. "Hopes of pacification": Dunmore circular letter, Williamsburg, 10 June 1774, *DHDW*, 33–35.

36. "Sit still": John Montgomery to John Penn, Carlisle, 30 June 1774, *PA*, 4:533–34. "Listen to the chiefs": St. Clair to John Penn, Ligonier, 22 June 1774, *St.CP*, 1:316.

37. *DRCNY*, 8:477–78.

38. *RNYG* 21 July 1774; *NYG* 25 July 1774; *PAG* 27 July 1774; *New York Journal* 28 July 1774; *Connecticut Gazette* 29 July 1774; *Providence Gazette* 30 July 1774; *Boston Post-Boy* 1 August 1774; *MDG* 4 August 1774; *Massachusetts Spy* 4 August 1774; *Essex Gazette* (Salem, MA) 9 August 1774; *Boston News-Letter* 11 August 1774.

39. *DHDW*, 246; Williams, *Dunmore's War*, 163–64.

40. Deposition of William Robinson, 28 February 1800, *Notes*, 242.

41. Robinson deposition, *Notes*, 242–43.

42. Logan's letter printed in *DHDW*, 246. More about the confusion over Logan's identity is covered in the appendix.

43. Robinson deposition, *Notes*, 243–44.

44. Dunmore to Col. Andrew Lewis, Winchester, 24 July 1774, *DHDW*, 97–98.

45. "Letter from Redstone," n.d., *MDG* 15 September 1774; *VAG* (Purdie and Dixon) 13 October 1774.

46. Sketch by Abraham Thomas, quoted in "Unveiling of the Cresap Tablet, 1916," *Ohio Archaeological and Historical Quarterly* 26 (January 1917): 134.

47. "Quantity of blood" and "every other thing": *MDG* 15 September 1774. Casualties: MacDonald to Connolly, 9 August 1774, *DHDW*, 151–54.

48. An abridged version of MacDonald's letter to Connolly appeared in *VAG* (Purdie and Dixon) 18 August 1774; *VAG* (Rind) 18 August 1774; *PAG* 31 August 1774; *PAJ* 31 August 1774; *NYG* 5 September 1774; *Maryland Journal & Baltimore Advertiser* 7 September 1774; *Boston News-Letter* 8 September 1774; *Connecticut Gazette* 9 September 1774; *Connecticut Journal* 9 September 1774; *Boston Post-Boy* 12 September 1774; *Newport Mercury* 12 September 1774; *South Carolina & American General Gazette* 16 September 1774; *South Carolina & Country Journal* 20 September 1774; *New Hampshire Gazette* 23 September 1774.

49. James Robertson to Col. William Preston, Culberson's Bottom, 11 August 1774, *DHDW*, 139.

50. Williams, *Dunmore's War*, 201.

51. John Lybrook interview, 1836, Lyman Draper notes, Draper Series S, 31: 425–26.

52. This narrative of the Sinking Creek attacks is gathered from Arthur Campbell to Daniel Smith, Royal-Oak, 9 August 1774, *DHDW*, 134; Campbell to William Preston, 9 August 1774, ibid., 135–36; James Robertson to William Preston, Culberson's Bottom, 12 August 1774, ibid., 140–42; William Preston to GW, Smithfield, 15 August 1774, *PGW:C*, 10:151–52; and Williams, *Dunmore's War*, 200–203.

53. John Lybrook interview, 1836, Lyman Draper notes, Draper Series S, Historical Society of Wisconsin, 31:425–26.

54. Robertson to Preston, 12 August 1774, *DHDW*, 140.

55. Council of War, Bottetourt County, 12 August 1774, Bullitt family papers, Filson Historical Society, Louisville, Kentucky.

56. *VAG* (Purdie and Dixon) 25 August 1774; *PAG* 7 September 1774; *RNYG* 8 September 1774; *Norwich Packet* 15 September 1774; *Boston News-Letter* 15 September 1774; *Providence Gazette* 17 September 1774; *Maryland Journal & Baltimore Advertiser* 21 September 1774; *New Hampshire Gazette* 23 September 1774.

57. Adam Stephen to Richard Henry Lee, Winchester, 27 August 1774, Richard H. Lee, ed., *Memoirs of the Life of Richard Henry Lee and his Correspondence*, 2 vols. (Philadelphia, 1825), 1:207–8.

58. The incidents at Mackay's house happened on 27 May and 7 June 1774, for which Arthur St. Clair gathered depositions on 22 August, *PA*, 4:560–61, 565–66, 568.

59. Guy Johnson to Thomas Gage, Guy Park, 19 August 1774, *PSWJ*, 13:669–71, quote on 670.

60. Nicholas B. Wainwright et al., "Turmoil at Pittsburgh: Diary of Augustine Prevost, 1774," *WMQ* 85 (April 1961): 111–62.

61. Wainwright, "Turmoil at Pittsburgh," 124–25.

62. Wainwright, "Turmoil at Pittsburgh," 127. See also Arthur St. Clair to John Penn, Ligonier, 25 August 1774, *PA*, 4:573; Aeneas Mackay to St. Clair, 4 September 1774, *St.CP*, 1:343.

63. Wainwright, "Turmoil at Pittsburgh," 128.

64. Wainwright, "Turmoil at Pittsburgh," 128, 129, 130.

65. Wainwright, "Turmoil at Pittsburgh," 131.

66. Wainwright, "Turmoil at Pittsburgh," 130.

67. Mary Beth Norton, *1774: The Long Year of Revolution* (New York, 2020), 180–81.

68. He did have the strength to take a stroll along the Alleghany River with Prevost, though. See Wainwright, "Turmoil at Pittsburgh," 138. "Council between Dunmore and the Indians," 4 *Am. Archives*, 1:871–78; Williams, *Dunmore's War*, 240–41.

69. Wainwright, "Turmoil at Pittsburgh," 138.

70. Wainwright, "Turmoil at Pittsburgh," 140.

71. *DHDW*, 85 and note; Williams, *Dunmore's War*, 250. Gauntlet: Major Arthur Campbell to Col. William Preston, 26 September 1774, *DHDW*, 209–10.

72. Fractured skull: Arthur Campbell to William Preston, 3 October 1774, *DHDW*, 218n. "Mammy": Arthur Campbell to William Preston, 6 October 1774, *DHDW*, 233.

73. "Extract of a Letter from Colonel William Preston, dated Fincastle, 28 September 1774," 4 *Am. Archives*, 1:808; Arthur Campbell to Preston, Royal-Oak, 29 September 1774, *DHDW*, 218–19.

74. Campbell to Preston, 12 October 1774, *DHDW*, 246–47. Memento: Judge Harry Innes to Thomas Jefferson, 2 March 1799, *Notes*, 232. Innes later misremembered that the note arrived in July, not October, a misconception surely reinforced by the fact that the note was dated July 21.

75. Campbell to Preston, 1 October 1774, *DHDW*, 219.

76. *DHDW*, 302n; Williams, *Dunmore's War*, 267–68.

77. "Very hard day": Isaac Shelby to John Shelby, Point Pleasant, 16 October 1774, *DHDW*, 276. The Virginians only found about twenty bodies on the field, but witnesses saw Natives removing corpses and throwing them into the river so they could not be scalped or used as trophies. There were multiple sources of information about the battle that then were exchanged throughout colonial newspapers. With the exception of the *Essex Gazette* (Salem, MA), *Pennsylvania Packet*, and two of three prints in South Carolina, every newspaper in the colonies published news of

the battle, including casualty numbers. General details/casualty numbers: *VAG* (Pinkney) 10 November; *VAG* (Purdie and Dixon) 10 and 17 November; *MDG* 10 and 24 November and 1 December; *PAG* 16 November; *PAJ* 16 November; *Maryland Journal & Baltimore Advertiser* 16 November; *New York Journal* 17 and 24 November; *RNYG* 17 November; *NYG* 21 November; *Connecticut Courant* 21 November; *Norwich Packet* 24 November; *Providence Gazette* 24 November; *Boston News-Letter* 24 November; *Massachusetts Spy* 24 November; *Connecticut Journal* 25 November; *Boston Gazette* 28 November; *Boston Post-Boy* 28 November; *Essex Journal* (Salem, MA) 30 November; *New Hampshire Gazette* 2 December; *Connecticut Gazette* 2 December; *Newport Mercury* 5 December; *South Carolina & American General Gazette* 9 December 1774. "Such a battle": *PAG* 16 November 1774; *New York Journal* 24 November 1774; *Providence Gazette* 26 November 1774; *Newport Mercury* 1 December 1774; *South Carolina & American General Gazette* 9 December 1774.

78. "Hideous cries": Shelby to Shelby, *DHDW*, 276. "Cries of our wounded": Col. William Christian to Preston, Point Pleasant, 15 October 1774, *DHDW*, 262.

79. John Gibson deposition, 4 April 1800, *Notes*, 234.

80. Archibald Loudon, *A Selection of the Most Interesting Narratives of Outrages Committed by the Indians in their Wars with the White People*, 2 vols. (Carlisle, PA, 1811), 2:214. Matthew 25:35–36, King James Version. The whole speech—with its rhetorical questions and embrace of vengeance—also shows the influence of the "Song of Moses" in Deuteronomy 32.

81. Text of the lament: *Notes*, 62–63.

82. *Notes*, 63.

83. Lament recited in camp: John Jeremiah Jacob, *Life of Captain Michael Cresap* (New York, 1971 [1826]), 95. "Tomahawk Greathouse": George Rogers Clark to Dr. Samuel Brown, 17 June 1798, in James Alton James, ed., *Collections of the Illinois Historical Library*, vol. 8: *George Rogers Clark Papers, 1771–1781* (Springfield, IL, 1912), 8.

84. Jacob, *Life of Captain Michael Cresap*, 94.

85. What became of the seventh captive, Thomas Hallen, is unknown.

86. Recollection of Lewis to Arthur Campbell, *DHDW*, 303.

87. St. Clair to John Penn, Ligonier, 4 December 1774, *PA*, 4:587. James Corbett David makes this point in *Dunmore's New World*, 90.

88. "Meeting of the Officers under Earl of Dunmore," Fort Gower, 5 November 1774, 4 *Am. Archives*, 1:962–63. Lewis's men, back at Point Pleasant, had received copies of them within a week, for which see Capt. William Russell to Preston, Fort Blair [Point Pleasant] 12 November 1774, *DHDW*, 311.

89. Baby announcement: *VAG* (Purdie and Dixon) 8 December 1774; *VAG* (Pinkney) 8 December 1774; *PAJ* 21 December 1774; *RNYG* 22 December 1774; *South Carolina & American General Gazette* 20 January 1775. "Fatiguing service": *VAG* (Purdie and Dixon) 8 December 1774; *VAG* (Pinkney) 8 December 1774.

90. *VAG* (Purdie and Dixon) 22 December 1774; *Massachusetts Spy* 19 January 1775; *Essex Journal* (Salem, MA) 19 January 1775; *Essex Gazette* (Salem, MA) 24 January 1775; *South Carolina & Country Journal* 7 March 1775. The Fort Gower Resolves did get Dunmore in trouble at home. Debate in Parliament raged in the spring about American resistance, and people wondered publicly how Dunmore could be unaware of these resolutions written by people who had associated themselves in his name. For which see the excerpt in *PAG* 10 May 1775.

91. Dartmouth to Dunmore, Whitehall, 8 September 1774, Davies, *Documents of the American Revolution*, 8:195.

92. Dunmore to Dartmouth, 24 December 1774, Davies, *Documents of the American Revolution*, 8:252–70, quote on 253.

93. Davies, *Documents of the American Revolution*, 8:258.

94. Manuscripts and Archives Division, NYPL. "Thomas Cresap to [Lord Dunmore]" NYPL Digital Collections. https://digitalcollections.nypl.org/items/3f882160-3ca6-0134-9a75-00505686a51c. Accessed February 28, 2022.

95. Dunmore to Dartmouth, 24 December 1774, Davies, *Documents of the American Revolution*, 8:264.

96. "Morsel of eloquence": TJ to John Henry, Philadelphia, 31 December 1797, *PTJ*, 29:601. TJ's copying down the speech in James A. Bear and Lucia Stanton, eds., *Jefferson's Memorandum Books: Accounts with Legal Records and Miscellany, 1767–1826*, 2 vols. (Princeton, NJ, 1997), 1:385–86.

97. Madison election: Orange County Committee election, *Rev. Va.*, 2:207. "Specimen of Indian Eloquence": James Madison to William Bradford, Orange County, Va., 20 January 1775, William T. Hutchinson and William M. E. Rachal, eds., *Papers of James Madison* (Chicago, 1962), 1:136–37. "Pathetic and expressive": William Bradford to James Madison, 3–6? March 1775, *Papers of James Madison*, 1:138.

98. *PAJ* 1 February 1775; *VAG* (Dixon and Hunter) 4 February 1775; *Pennsylvania Evening Post* 2 February 1775; *Pennsylvania Ledger* 11 February 1775; *RNYG* 16 February 1775; *NYG* 20 February 1775; *Connecticut Courant* 20 February 1775; *Connecticut Journal* 22 February 1775; *Norwich Packet* 23 February 1775; *Newport Mercury* 23 February 1775; *Massachusetts Spy* 9 March 1775. "Flew thro'": Jefferson to Henry, 31 December 1797, *PTJ*, 29:601.

99. John Heckewelder declaration, *Notes*, 248.

CHAPTER 9. ON THE THRESHOLD OF GREAT THINGS, 1775–1776

1. "Indian war": *RNYG* 19 May 1774; *NYG* 20 June 1774. "Worthy and esteemed": *NYG* 23 October 1775; *New York Journal* 26 October 1775. "Happy country": *RNYG* 19 October 1775; *New York Constitutional Gazette* 21 October 1775.

2. David Brion Davis, *The Problem of Slavery in the Age of Revolution, 1770–1823* (Ithaca, NY, 1975), 308.

3. Francis Bailey, *Philadelphia; April 25th 1775; An Express arrived at Five o'Clock This Evening, by which we Have the Following Advices* [Lancaster, Pa.] Charles Evans, ed., *Early American Imprints, Series 1: 1639–1800* (New York, 1983 [1903]), no. 14026.

4. Boyd Crumrine, ed., *History of Washington County, Pennsylvania* (Philadelphia, 1882), 179, 639.

5. Pa. Council meeting, 25 January 1775, *MPCP*, 10:227–28; Depositions of attack on Westmoreland jail, 7 February 1775, *Pennsylvania Archives* 4th series (Harrisburg, 1900), 4:608–12. "Extreme": Pa. Council meeting 25 February 1775, *MPCP*, 10:234. JC's recall: John Connolly to GW, Winchester, 9 February 1775, *PGW:C*, 10:259–60.

6. "Paradise": John Brown to William Preston, 5 May 1775, Reuben Gold Thwaites and Louise Phelps Kellogg., eds., *The Revolution on the Upper Ohio, 1775–1777* (Madison, WI, 1908), 10. five hundred people: William Preston to Dunmore, 10 March 1775, ibid., 2.

7. Lincoln Macveagh, ed., *The Journal of Nicholas Cresswell, 1774–1777* (New York, 1924), 44, 57.

8. Macveagh, *Journal of Cresswell*, 65, 69–70.

9. Brown to Preston, 5 May 1775, Thwaites and Kellogg, *Revolution on the Upper Ohio*, 11. Macveagh, *Journal of Cresswell*, 72, 73.

10. Macveagh, *Journal of Cresswell*, 75, 77, 78.

11. Macveagh, *Journal of Cresswell*, 78.

12. Macveagh, *Journal of Cresswell*, 82, 87.

13. Macveagh, *Journal of Cresswell*, 93–94.

14. Creation of riflemen: *JCC*, 2:88. "Exquisite marksmen": John Adams to Elbridge Gerry, Philadelphia, 18 June 1775, Robert Taylor, ed., *Papers of John Adams* (Cambridge, MA, 1977), 3:25. Company officers: Frederick County Committee, 21 June 1775, 4 *Am. Archives*, 2:1044–45.

15. Horatio Gates to GW, Travellers-Rest, 22 June 1775, *PGW:RW*, 1:23.

16. John Jeremiah Jacob, *Life of Captain Michael Cresap* (New York, 1971 [1826]), 120.

17. "Depressed": Jacob, *Life of Captain Michael Cresap*, 120. "Brave old": Silas Deane to Elizabeth Deane, Philadelphia, 29 June 1775, *LDC*, 1:557.

18. Macveigh, *Journal of Cresswell*, 97.

19. Woody Holton, *Forced Founders: Indians, Debtors, Slaves, and the Making of the American Revolution in Virginia* (Chapel Hill, NC, 1999), 140–48; John E. Selby, *The Revolution in Virginia*,

1775–1783 (Charlottesville, VA, 1988), 1–7. "Ashes": Deposition of Dr. William Pasteur, in regard to the Removal of Powder from the Williamsburg Magazine, 1775," *VMHB* 13 (1905): 49.

20. Virginia Convention, 25 March 1775, 4 *Am. Archives*, 2:170. That resolution was causing big problems for Virginia patriots in Congress. Richard Henry Lee wrote that "nothing has given more concern and disgust to these northern Colonies than our unhappy vote of that sort in last Convention. Yesterday one of the first Men on the Continent for wisdom, sound judgment, good information and integrity, said to me 'I was much grieved and concerned for the good sense of Virginia, when I saw that ill-founded, ill-judged Compliment.'" Richard Henry Lee to Francis Lightfoot Lee, Philadelphia, 21 May 1775, *LDC*, 1:366.

21. St. Clair to Penn, Ligonier, 25 May 1775, *St.CP*, 1:355.

22. "A Narrative of the Transactions, Imprisonment, and Sufferings of John Connolly, An American Loyalist and Lt. Col. In his Majesty's Service," *PMHB* pt. 1, vol. 12 (1888): 310–24, quotes on 316, 317.

23. Connolly, "Narrative of the Transactions," 316–17.

24. Connolly, "Narrative of the Transactions," 317, 318.

25. Valentine Crawford to GW, 24 June 1775, *PGW:RW*, 1:29.

26. Daniel P. Barr, *A Colony Sprung from Hell: Pittsburgh and the Struggle for Authority on the Western Pennsylvania Frontier, 1744–1794* (Kent, OH, 2014), 177. Connolly, "Narrative of the Transactions," 321; "Thanks to Brave and Spirited Captain, with Qualification," West Augusta Committee Proceedings, 26 June 1775, *Rev. Va.*, 3:229.

27. Danske Dandridge, *Historic Shepherdstown* (Charlottesville, VA, 1910), 79.

28. Robert Greenhalgh Albion and Leonidas Dodson, eds., *Philip Vickers Fithian: Journal, 1775–1776, Written on the Virginia-Pennsylvania Frontier and in the Army around New York* (Princeton, NJ, 1934), 21, 24.

29. Albion and Dodson, *Fithian Journal*, 31–32.

30. George Bancroft, *History of the United States from the Discovery of the American Continent* 4th ed. (Boston, 1860), 7:312.

31. *Rev. Va.*, 3:238–40, 246–49, 257–61, 262–66.

32. "Answer of the Mohawks to the Speech of the Magistrates, etc. of Albany and Schenectady," Guy Park, 25 May 1775, 4 *Am. Archives*, 2:843. New York Provincial Congress to New York Delegates of Continental Congress, 7 June 1775, ibid., 2:1281.

33. John Stuart to Thomas Gage, St. Augustine, 9 July 1775, in Thomas Gage Papers, vol. 131, Clements Library.

34. For use of the word "tampering" see South Carolina Governor Lord William Campbell to Dartmouth, Charleston, 2 July 1775, in K. G. Davies, ed., *Documents of the American Revolution 1770–1783* (Dublin, 1976), 11:34. Johnson retired: *New York Journal* 22 June 1775; *Connecticut Journal* 28 June 1775; *New England Chronicle* 29 June 1775; *Essex Journal* (Salem, MA) 30 June 1775; *New Hampshire Gazette* 4 July 1775. Canadian (Caughnawaga) Indians take up hatchet: *PAJ* 28 June 1775; *Pennsylvania Mercury* 30 June 1775; *Boston Gazette* 10 July 1775; *Georgia Gazette* 12 July 1775; *New Hampshire Gazette* 18 July 1775; *Pennsylvania Evening Post* 22 July 1775; *MDG* 27 July 1775. "Alarming nature": Philip Schuyler to Congress, New York, 28 June 1775, read in Congress on 3 July, 4 *Am. Archives*, 2:1123.

35. "Declaration of the Causes and Necessity of Taking Up Arms," *JCC*, 2:152; see also *PTJ*, 1:187–219. "World stands": Benjamin Franklin to Jonathan Shipley, Philadelphia, 7 July 1775, *PBF*, 22:97. "It is certain": Joseph Hewes to James Iredell, Philadelphia, 8 July 1775, *LDC*, 1:611; "Let loose": Hewes to Samuel Johnston, Philadelphia, 8 July 1775, *LDC*, 1:613.

36. *Rev. Va.*, 3:270.

37. James Wood journal, Thwaites and Kellogg, *Revolution on the Upper Ohio*, 38.

38. Thwaites and Kellogg, *Revolution on the Upper Ohio*, 50–51.

39. Thwaites and Kellogg, *Revolution on the Upper Ohio*, 49.

40. Thwaites and Kellogg, *Revolution on the Upper Ohio*, 49.

41. Thwaites and Kellogg, *Revolution on the Upper Ohio*, 49.

42. Thwaites and Kellogg, *Revolution on the Upper Ohio*, 57. James Wood to Virginia Convention, 20 September 1775, *Revolution on the Upper Ohio*, 66.

43. · Thwaites and Kellogg, *Revolution on the Upper Ohio*, 66.

44. Virginia and Pennsylvania Delegates to the Inhabitants West of the Laurel Hill," Philadelphia, 25 July 1775, *LDC*, 1:665.

45. Albion and Dodson, *Fithian Journal*, 61. Butternuts: *NYG* 31 July 1775; *Connecticut Journal* 2 and 9 August 1775; *New York Journal* 3 August 1775; *Connecticut Gazette* 4 August 1775; *Norwich Packet* 7 August 1775; *Massachusetts Spy* 16 August 1775; *New Hampshire Gazette* 22 August 1775.

46. Henry J. Young, "The Spirit of 1775: A Letter of Robert Magaw, Major of the Continental Riflemen, to the Gentlemen of the Committee of Correspondence in the Town of Carlisle, Dated at Cambridge, 13 August 1775," *John and Mary's Journal* 1 (March 1975): 22. There was a $24.50 claim filed in 1776 for the rifles, for which see 4 *Am. Archives*, 6:1679. Greathouse: Louis Alexander Burgess, *Virginia Soldiers of 1776*, vol. 1 (Richmond, 1927), 1242.

47. Nose: *Pennsylvania Evening Post* 11 July 1775; *Newport Mercury* 31 July 1775; *Massachusetts Spy* 2 August 1775; *Providence Gazette* 5 August 1775. For more analysis on Cresap's unit and the march to Boston see James McIntyre, "Separating Myth from History: The Maryland Riflemen in the War of Independence," *Maryland Historical Magazine* 104 (2009): 101–19.

48. *PAG* 6 July 1774.

49. *PAG* 16 August 1775.

50. *PAG* 16 August 1775.

51. *PAG* 16 August 1775.

52. The above letter exchanged from the *PAG* in *Pennsylvania Mercury* 18 August 1775; *VAG* (Dixon and Hunter) 19 August 1775; *NYG* 21 August 1775; *New York Journal* 24 August 1775; *Connecticut Journal* 30 August 1775; *Virginia Gazette & Norfolk Intelligencer* 6 September 1775; *VAG* (Pinkney) 7 September 1775; *North Carolina Gazette* 6 October 1775; *South Carolina & American General Gazette* 13 October 1775.

53. In his 1900 book, Julian Hawthorne (Nathaniel's son) said Daniel Morgan was "a superb giant, nearly seven feet tall" and called one of the Pennsylvania rifle captains "another Agamemnon." *History of the United States from the Landing of Columbus to the Signing of the Peace Protocol with Spain* 3 vols. (New York, 1900), 2:439. "Bullet holes": *Pennsylvania Packet* 28 August 1775 [Postscript].

54. *Pennsylvania Packet* 28 August 1775.

55. *Pennsylvania Packet* 28 August 1775.

56. Shirts: Kate Haulman, "Fashion and the Culture Wars of Revolutionary Philadelphia," *WMQ* 62 (October 2005): 645. Lice: Charles Royster, *A Revolutionary People at War: The Continental Army and American Character, 1775–1783* (Chapel Hill, NC, 1979), 34.

57. Thomas A. Foster, *Sex and the Eighteenth-Century Man: Massachusetts and the History of Sexuality in America* (Boston, 2006), 120–27.

58. Lester C. Olson, *Emblems of American Community in the Revolutionary Era* (Washington, DC, 1991), 75, 78–79; Philip J. Deloria, *Playing Indian* (New Haven, CT, 1998), 28–29. "England became": Deloria, *Playing Indian*, 22.

59. Deloria, *Playing Indian*, 1–3, 28–32.

60. John Grenier, *The First Way of War: American War Making on the Frontier* (Cambridge, MA, 2005).

61. "£40,000": *Virginia Gazette & Norfolk Intelligencer* 6 September 1775; *VAG* (Purdie) 8 September 1775; *New York Journal* 21 September 1775; *Connecticut Courant* 25 September 1775; *Connecticut Journal* 27 September 1775; *MDG* 28 September 1775; *New England Chronicle* 28 September 1775; *Massachusetts Spy* 29 September 1775; *Connecticut Gazette* 29 September 1775; *Newport Mercury* 2 October 1775; *New Hampshire Gazette* 10 October 1775. Trent took obvious offense to this vicious report, and an account exonerating him appeared in *PAJ* 29 November 1775 and *Pennsylvania Evening Post* 30 November. Note the disparity in the coverage between the accusation and the retraction. Trent: *Maryland Journal & Baltimore Advertiser* 29 August 1775; *NYG* 4 September 1775; *PAG* 6 September 1775; *PAJ* 6 September 1775; *Connecticut*

Journal 6 and 13 September 1775; *RNYG* 7 September 1775; *New York Journal* 7 September 1775; *Pennsylvania Evening Post* 8 September 1775; *Pennsylvania Ledger* 9 September 1775; *Pennsylvania Mercury* 9 September 1775; *Pennsylvania Packet* 11 September 1775; *New England Chronicle* 14 September 1775; *Connecticut Gazette* 15 September 1775; *VAG* (Dixon & Hunter) 16 September 1775; *New Hampshire Gazette* 19 September 1775; *Massachusetts Spy* 20 September 1775; *Essex Journal* (Salem, MA) 22 September 1775; *Providence Gazette* 30 September 1775.

62. Albion and Dodson, *Fithian Journal*, 112.

63. Dunmore to White Eyes and Connolly to Gibson, 9 August 1775, Thwaites and Kellogg, *Revolution on the Upper Ohio*, 72–74.

64. *Arundell*: *VAG* (Dixon and Hunter) 26 August 1775. Cresap arrival: *Boston Gazette* 28 August 1775; *Massachusetts Spy* 30 August 1775; *Connecticut Gazette* 1 September 1775; *Pennsylvania Evening Post* 5 September 1775; *PAJ* 6 September 1775; *Virginia Gazette & Norfolk Intelligencer* 20 September 1775.

65. "200 of the Regulars": Daniel McCurtin, "Journal of the Times at the Siege of Boston," in Thomas Balch, ed., *Papers Relating Chiefly to the Maryland Line During the Revolution* (Philadelphia, 1857), 15. McCurtin noted the thunderstorm in his journal entry. "Lost his gun": Henry Bedinger journal, published in Dandridge, *Historic Shepherdstown*, 108.

66. "Journals of Lt.-Col. Stephen Kemble," *Collections of the New-York Historical Society: For the Year 1883* 16 (New York, 1883), 50, 55–57, quote on 57.

67. "Checked the spirits": "Journals of Lt.-Col. Stephen Kemble," 58. "Disgrace we are all in": "Boston in 1775: A Letter, from John Lukens to John Shaw, Jr.," *Historical Manuscripts in the Public Library of the City of Boston* no. 1 (1900): 24. "Do not boast": Artemas Ward to John Adams, 30 October 1775, Taylor, *Papers of John Adams*, 3:236.

68. "Lies here sick": "Boston in 1775," 28. Camp diseases: Elizabeth A. Fenn, *Pox Americana: The Great Smallpox Epidemic of 1775–1782* (New York, 2001), 49.

69. "Strain every nerve": Gage to Carleton, 5 September 1775, Gage Papers, vol. 135, Clements Library. Connolly notification: Gage to Dunmore, 10 September 1775; to Capt. Lernoult, Detroit, 10 September 1775, to Carleton, 10 September 1775; to Guy Johnson, 11 September 1775; to Capt. Lord, Illinois, 12 September 1775; to Alexander McKee, 12 September 1775; to John Stuart 12 September 1775, all in ibid., vol. 135.

70. "Deposition of William Cowley," 12 October 1775, 4 *Am. Archives*, 3:1047–48.

71. William Cowley to GW, 30 September 1775, *PGW:RW*, 2:67–69.

72. "The Intelligencer" [Hugh Hughes] to John Adams, NYC, 18–19 October 1775, Taylor, *Papers of John Adams*, 3:210.

73. GW to John Hancock, Cambridge, 12 October 1775, *PGW:RW*, 2:148. George Mason to Maryland Committee of Safety, Robert Rutland, ed., *Papers of George Mason* (Chapel Hill, NC, 1970), 1:258–59. Washington wrote to Lund Washington on 15 October in which it is assumed he informed him of Connolly's plot, even though the letter has not survived. Lund noted that he had received a letter from GW dated 15 October.

74. "Nursery of loyalty": Edwin G. Burrows and Mike Wallace, *Gotham: A History of New York City to 1898* (New York, 1999), 219. British "common cause": Brad A. Jones, *Resisting Independence: Popular Loyalism in the Revolutionary British Atlantic* (Ithaca, NY, 2020), 104–37.

75. Seize control: Ruma Chopra, *Unnatural Rebellion: Loyalists in New York City during the Revolution* (Charlottesville, VA, 2011), 35. "Indistinguishable": Paul A. Gilje, *The Road to Mobocracy: Popular Disorder in New York City, 1763–1834* (Chapel Hill, NC, 1987), 62.

76. *RNYG* 19 October 1775.

77. Cresap's funeral covered in *New York Constitutional Gazette* 21 October 1775; *NYG* 23 October 1775; *New York Journal* 26 October 1775; *RNYG* 26 October 1775.

78. For Johnson's casket, see *NYG* 1 August 1774. See figure 19.

79. John Adams to James Warren, Philadelphia, 23 October 1775, *LDC*, 2:232.

80. *Pennsylvania Evening Post* 21 October 1775; *Pennsylvania Packet* 23 October 1775; *Connecticut Journal* 25 October 1775; *PAG* 25 October 1775; *PAJ* 25 October 1775; *MDG* 26 October 1775; *New England Chronicle* 26 October 1775; *Connecticut Gazette* 27 October 1775; *Pennsylvania*

Ledger 28 October 1775; *Providence Gazette* 28 October 1775; *Boston Gazette* 30 October 1775; *Connecticut Courant* 30 October 1775; *Maryland Journal & Baltimore Advertiser* 1 November 1775; *VAG* (Purdie) 3 November 1775; *VAG* (Pinkney) 9 November 1775; *VAG* (Dixon and Hunter) 11 November 1775; *South Carolina & American General Gazette* 24 November 1775; *Georgia Gazette* 6 December 1775.

81. Cameron: *New York Constitutional Gazette* 7 October 1775; *NYG* 9 October 1775; *Pennsylvania Evening Post* 10 October 1775; *PAG* 11 October 1775; *PAJ* 11 October 1775; *Connecticut Journal* 11 October 1775; *New York Journal* 12 October 1775; *Pennsylvania Mercury* 13 October 1775; *Connecticut Gazette* 13 October 1775; *Boston Gazette* 16 October 1775; *Newport Mercury* 16 October 1775; *Pennsylvania Packet* 16 October 1775; *MDG* 19 October 1775; *New England Chronicle* 19 October 1775; *Massachusetts Spy* 20 October 1775; *VAG* (Dixon and Hunter) 28 October 1775. Guy Fawkes: *Connecticut Courant* 6 November 1775; *New England Chronicle* 9 November 1775; *Essex Journal* (Salem, MA) 10 November 1775; *Newport Mercury* 13 November 1775; *Pennsylvania Packet* 13 November 1775; *Georgia Gazette* 27 December 1775.

82. *New York Journal* 12 October 1775; *New England Chronicle* 19 October 1775; *Connecticut Gazette* 20 October 1775; *Massachusetts Spy* 20 October 1775; *Boston Gazette* 23 October 1775; *Connecticut Courant* 26 October 1775; *VAG* (Purdie) 26 October 1775; *Newport Mercury* 30 October 1775.

83. Macveigh, *Journal of Cresswell*, 114, 115.

84. *JCC*, 3:280. Va. Delegates to Congress to Va. Committee of Safety, Philadelphia, 23 October 1775, *Rev. Va.*, 4:262.

85. John E. Selby, *The Revolution in Virginia, 1775–1783* (Charlottesville, VA, 1988), 56–58, 63–66.

86. Given the notoriety of Alexander Cameron at that moment in 1775—he was John Stuart's deputy as superintendent of Indian affairs for the Southern Department—many people at the time and since have confused or conflated Connolly's associate Allen with Alexander. Travel route: Connolly, "Narrative," pt. 2, *PMHB* 12 (1888):411–12.

87. Connolly, "Narrative," pt. 2, 412, 413.

88. Connolly, "Narrative," pt. 2, 413.

89. *Maryland Journal & Baltimore Advertiser* 15 November 1775.

90. "Clamourous rabble": Connolly, "Narrative," pt. 2, 414. "Abused us": John Frederick Dalziel Smyth, *A Tour in the United States of America* (London, 1784), 2:252–53.

91. "Soiled and besmeared": Connolly, "Narrative," pt. 2, 414–15. Connolly, "Proposals for Raising An Army to the Westward, and for effectually obstructing a communication between the Southern and Northern Governments," 4 *Am. Archives*, 3:1661. "Decidedly prisoners": Connolly, "Narrative," pt. 2, 415.

92. Order for Philadelphia jail: *JCC*, 3:415. News: *VAG* (Pinkney) 23 November and 16 December 1775; *VAG* (Purdie) 1 December 1775; *Pennsylvania Mercury* 1 December 1775; *Pennsylvania Evening Post* 2, 12, and 23 December 1775; *Pennsylvania Ledger* 2 December 1775; *Pennsylvania Packet* 4 and 25 December 1775; *PAG* 6 and 27 December 1775; *New York Constitutional Gazette* 6 and 30 December 1775; *MDG* 7 December 1775; *New York Journal* 14 December 1775; *Essex Journal* (Salem, MA) 15 December 1775; *Massachusetts Spy* 15 December 1775; *VAG* (Dixon and Hunter) 16 December 1775; *Connecticut Journal* 20 December 1775; *Maryland Journal & Baltimore Advertiser* 20 December 1775; *Newport Mercury* 25 December 1775; *PAJ* 27 December 1775; *NYG* 1 January 1776; *South Carolina & American General Gazette* 5 January 1776; *Norwich Packet* 8 January 1776. "Rogue's March": Connolly, "Narrative," pt. 2, 418. Connolly would be among the prisoners held longest in close confinement during the Revolution. Despite several appeals to Congress by both he and his wife, Connolly would not be released until 1781.

93. *Pennsylvania Evening Post* 26 December 1775; *PAG* 27 December 1775; *PAJ* 27 December 1775; *Pennsylvania Ledger* 30 December 1775; *New York Constitutional Gazette* 30 December 1775; *Pennsylvania Packet* 1 January 1776; *NYG* 1 January 1776; *Maryland Journal & Baltimore Advertiser* 3 January 1776; *MDG* 4 January 1776; *New York Journal* 4 January 1776; *VAG* (Purdie) 5 January 1776; *Norwich Packet* 8 January 1776; *New England Chronicle* 11 January 1776; *Massachusetts Spy* 12 January 1776; *Connecticut Gazette* 12 January 1776; *Providence Gazette* 13

January 1776; *Boston Gazette* 15 January 1776. Four of these issues had both the "feast" story and Connolly's letters on the same page. See Robert G. Parkinson, *The Common Cause: Creating Race and Nation in the American Revolution* (Chapel Hill, NC, 2016), 182. Congress's order: Richard Smith's diary, 22 December 1775, *LDC*, 2:513; *JCC*, 3:445, 456.

94. *VAG* (Purdie) 5 January 1776; *PAJ* 17 January 1776; *New York Constitutional Gazette* 24 January 1776; *New York Journal* 25 January 1776; *Norwich Packet* 29 January 1776; *New England Chronicle* 1 February 1776; *Providence Gazette* 10 February 1776.

95. Parkinson, *Common Cause*, 254–55.

CHAPTER 10. WHATEVER HE WAS, HE WAS NOT COMMON, 1776–1794

1. Donald H. Kent and Merle H. Deardorff, eds., "John Adlum on the Allegheny: Memoirs for the Year 1794: Part 2," *PMHB* 84 (October 1960): 470.

2. Donald H. Kent and Merle H. Deardorff, eds., "John Adlum on the Allegheny: Memoirs for the Year 1794: Part 1," *PMHB* 84 (July 1960): 273.

3. Kent and Deardorff, "Adlum on the Allegheny: Part 2," 471.

4. Kent and Deardorff, "Adlum on the Allegheny: Part 2," 471–72.

5. Kent and Deardorff, "Adlum on the Allegheny: Part 2," 472.

6. Kent and Deardorff, "Adlum on the Allegheny: Part 2," 472.

7. The final manuscript was written at the end of Adlum's life, sometime in the 1840s, but the editors of his 1794 narrative insist it "stands up very well when compared with contemporary sources," as he had taken copious notes at the time. Kent and Deardorff, "Adlum on the Allegheny: Part 1," 279–80. For Logan as a drunk see the memory of Major Charles Cracraft as related by his son to Brantz Mayer in 1853 in appendix 3 of Brantz Mayer, *Tah-Gah-Jute; or Logan and Cresap, an Historical Essay* (Albany, 1867), 185–86.

8. Rob Harper, *Unsettling the West: Violence and State Building in the Ohio Valley* (Philadelphia, 2018), 73, 76.

9. Randolph C. Downes, *Council Fires on the Upper Ohio* (Pittsburgh, 1940), 194.

10. Indian Commissioners to Congress, 31 August 1776, in George Morgan Letterbook, 1:28, mss., Carnegie Library, Pittsburgh.

11. Downes, *Council Fires on the Upper Ohio*, 203.

12. Robert G. Parkinson, *The Common Cause: Creating Race and Nation in the American Revolution* (Chapel Hill, NC, 2016), 383. Gregory P. Dowd, *A Spirited Resistance: The North American Indian Struggle for Unity, 1745–1815* (Baltimore, 1991), 72.

13. John D. Barnhart, ed., *Henry Hamilton and George Rogers Clark in the American Revolution; with the Unpublished Journal of Lieut. Gov. Henry Hamilton* (Crawfordsville, IN, 1951), 73–75, 182–83; Bernard W. Sheehan, " 'The Famous Hair Buyer General': Henry Hamilton, George Rogers Clark, and the American Indian," *Indiana Magazine of History* 74 (1983): 1–28.

14. Washington's Instructions to Sullivan, 31 May 1779, Otis G. Hammond, ed., *Letters and Papers of Major-General John Sullivan, Continental Army* (Concord, NH, 1939), 3:48–49. Alan Taylor, *The Divided Ground: Indians, Settlers, and the Northern Borderlands of the American Revolution* (New York, 2006), 98. Colin G. Calloway, *The American Revolution in Indian Country: Crisis and Diversity in Native American Communities* (Cambridge, MA, 1995), 137.

15. Fort Pitt commander Edward Hand, for example, wrote his wife on 9 November 1777 that he was sure "the prosperity of our affairs to the Northward will have a happy influence on the Western Indians." Within two weeks Cornstalk was dead and he wrote, "if we had anything to expect from [the Shawnee] it is now vanished." Edward Hand to Catherine Hand, Ft. Pitt, 9 November 1777, Reuben Gold Thwaites and Louise Phelps Kellogg, eds., *Frontier Defense on the Upper Ohio, 1777–778* (Madison, WI, 1912), 156; Hand to Jasper Yeates, Ft. Pitt, 24 November 1777, Edward Hand Papers, Thomas Addis Emmet Collection, NYPL.

16. "Two souls": Reminiscence of Jonathan S. Williams, 1842, *American Pioneer* 1 (October 1842): 359. "Torment": John Heckewelder declaration, *Notes*, 250.

17. Heckewelder to John Gibson, Coshocking, 19 March 1779, Louise Phelps Kellogg, ed., *Frontier Advance on the Upper Ohio, 1778–1779* (Madison, WI, 1916), 259.

18. John McDonald, *Biographical Sketches of General Nathaniel Massie, General Duncan McArthur, Captain William Wells, and General Simon Kenton: Who Were Early Settlers in the Western Country* (Dayton, OH, 1852), 231; Mayer, *Tah-Gah-Jute*, 136.

19. For more on McComb, see Tiya Miles, *The Dawn of Detroit: A Chronicle of Slavery and Freedom in the City of the Straits* (New York, 2017), 73–76; Cracraft's recollection supplied by Draper in Mayer, *Tah-Gah-Jute*, 183.

20. John Sugden, *Blue Jacket: Warrior of the Shawnees* (Lincoln, NE, 2000), 61.

21. Miles, *Dawn of Detroit*, 83, 87.

22. Capt. Henry Bird to Major Arnet S. De Peyster, Ohio River, 11 June 1780, "The Haldimand Papers," *Michigan Pioneer & Historical Collections*, 19:534.

23. Brett Rushforth, *Bonds of Alliance: Indigenous and Atlantic Slaveries in New France* (Chapel Hill, NC, 2012), 35–51.

24. Cracraft's recollection supplied by Draper in Mayer, *Tah-Gah-Jute*, 184–85. When he supplied Cracraft's recollection to Brantz Mayer, Lyman Draper commented that he "saw no reason to doubt its correctness." ibid., 186.

25. Heckewelder testimony, *Notes*, 250. In late January, a Kentucky militia officer informed Virginia governor Thomas Jefferson that Logan was dead. John Todd to TJ, Lexington, KY, 24 January 1781, *PTJ*, 1:441–43.

26. Franklin B. Sawvel, *Logan: The Mingo* (Boston, 1921), 100. This rendering of Logan's death is repeated verbatim in Harry E. Swanger, "The Logans, Sons of Shickellamy," (Sunbury, PA, 1996), 29, rpt. from *Proceedings of the Northumberland County Historical Society* 17 (1949): 1–39.

27. Patrick Griffin, *American Leviathan: Empire, Nation, and Revolutionary Frontier* (New York, 2007), 172.

28. Griffin, *American Leviathan*, 167–75; Peter Silver, *Our Savage Neighbors: How Indian War Transformed Early America* (New York, 2008), 265–74; Parkinson, *Common Cause*, 534–38; Harper, *Unsettling the West*, 136–42.

29. *Pennsylvania Packet* 22 December 1781; *New Jersey Gazette* 2 January 1782; *Connecticut Courant* 8 January 1782; *Norwich Packet* 10 January 1782; *Boston Evening Post* 12 January 1782; *Providence Gazette* 12 January 1782; *Boston Gazette* 14 January 1782; *Independent Ledger* (Boston) 14 January 1782; *Connecticut Journal* 17 January 1782; *Salem Gazette* 17 January 1782; *Connecticut Gazette* 18 January 1782. A second, different report about the Wyandot ultimatum to the Delaware appeared in *Freeman's Journal* (Philadelphia) 26 December 1781; *Pennsylvania Evening Post* 28 December 1781; *Independent Chronicle* (Boston) 17 January 1782; *New Hampshire Gazette* 19 January 1782. "So alarmed the people": *Pennsylvania Packet* 16 April 1782; *Pennsylvania Evening Post* 16 April 1782; *PAG* 17 April 1782; *PAJ* 17 April 1782; *New Jersey Journal* 24 April 1782; *Connecticut Courant* 30 April 1782; *Continental Journal* (Boston) 2 May 1782; *Connecticut Journal* 2 May 1782; *Salem Gazette* 2 May 1782; *Boston Evening Post* 4 May 1782; *Providence Gazette* 4 May 1782; *Independent Ledger* (Boston) 6 May 1782; *Connecticut Gazette* 10 May 1782.

	Another account that mentioned Gnadenhutten simply said, in its entirety: "Advice has been received of fifty savages being put to the sword at the Moravian Town." *Maryland Journal & Baltimore Advertiser* 9 April 1782; *Pennsylvania Packet* 16 April 1782; *VAG* (Hayes) 20 April 1782; *New Jersey Journal* 24 April 1782; *Salem Gazette* 2 May 1782; *Newport Mercury* 4 May 1782. "Innate barbarity": *PAJ* 18 May 1782.

30. "Supplement to the Boston Independent Chronicle," *PBF*, 37:184–96, quotes on 187, 190, 193.

31. "Substance is truth": BF to John Adams, Passy, 22 April 1782, *PBF*, 37:196–97; BF to John Jay 24 April 1782; ibid., 205–7; BF to Dumas, 3 May 1782, ibid., 268–69; BF to Richard Price, 13 June 1782, ibid., 472–73. Publication in Britain: *Parker's General Advertiser and Morning Intelligencer* 29 June 1782; *Public Advertiser* (London) 27 September 1782; *The Remembrancer; or Impartial Repository of Public Events* part 2 (1782), 135–36. In America: *New Jersey Gazette* 18 December 1782; *Pennsylvania Packet* 26 December 1782; *Connecticut Courant* 14 January 1783; *New York Packet* 16 January 1783; *Providence Gazette* 18 January 1783; *Massachusetts Spy*

23 January 1783; *Continental Journal* (Boston) 23 January 1783; *New York Gazetteer* (Albany) 27 January 1783.

32. BF to James Hutton, Passy, 7 July 1782, *PBF*, 37:586–87. "Behavior": Griffin, *American Leviathan*, 154.

33. Captain William Caldwell to Major A. S. DePeyster, Sandusky, 13 June 1782, in Frederick Haldimand: Unpublished Papers and Correspondence, 1758–1784, reels 43, item no. 21762, 80, British Library, London.

34. "Frontier legend": Griffin, *American Leviathan*, 169. Dr. Knight and John Slover's narratives of Crawford's torture in [Hugh Henry Breckenridge], *Narratives of a Late Expedition against the Indians; with an Account of the Barbarous Execution of Col. Crawford* (Philadelphia, 1783), Evans, *Early American Imprints* no. 17993. "Indian allies of Britain" and "fierce and cruel": [Hugh Henry Breckenridge], *Narratives of a Late Expedition against the Indians*, preface. Knight and Slover's narratives also appeared in several newspapers: *Freeman's Journal* (Philadelphia) 30 April, 7, 14, 21, and 28 May 1783; *Boston Evening Post* 24 and 31 May 1783; *Massachusetts Spy* 2 October 1783; *Connecticut Gazette* 17 and 24 October 1783; *Connecticut Courant* 11 November 1783; *Connecticut Journal* 19 and 26 November 1783.

35. Parkinson, *Common Cause*, 549–50. "Fruitless": *VAG* (Hayes) 28 December 1782.

36. William Hogeland, *Autumn of the Black Snake: George Washington, Mad Anthony Wayne, and the Invasion That Opened the West* (New York, 2017), 16, 20. This alliance has gone by several names, including the Western Confederacy and the Miami Confederacy. At their founding meeting in 1792, Native federationists referred to themselves as the United Indian Nations, which is a compelling reason to employ this term. See Samantha Seeley, *Race, Removal, and the Right to Remain: Migration and the Making of the United States* (Chapel Hill, NC, 2021), 61, 100–128.

37. Joel Achenbach, *The Grand Idea: George Washington's Potomac and the Race to the West* (New York, 2004), 7–8 and passim.

38. GW to William Crawford, Mount Vernon, 25 September 1773, *PGW:C*, 9:330; GW to Michael Cresap, Mount Vernon, 26 September 1773, *PGW:C*, 9:334–35.

39. Sale of four hundred acres on 8 December 1779, Clara McCormack Sage and Laura Sage Jones, *Early Records of Hampshire County, Virginia* (Delavan, WI, 1939), 12.

40. Sketch of David Rogers in Louise Phelps Kellogg, ed., *Frontier Retreat on the Upper Ohio, 1779–1781* (Madison, WI, 1917), 82.

41. Luther Martin, *Modern Gratitude, in Five Numbers: Addressed to Richard Raynal Keene, Esq., Concerning a Family Marriage* (Baltimore, 1802), 148.

42. Paul S. Clarkson and R. Samuel Jett, *Luther Martin of Maryland* (Baltimore, 1970), 57. "Happy husband": Martin, *Modern Gratitude*, 148.

43. Marriage notice: *Maryland Journal* (Baltimore) 16 January 1784; Will of Thomas Cresap, 17 January 1784. Cresap's living with newlyweds: Luther Martin, "To the Honorable Thomas Jefferson, Esq., Vice-President of the United States," 8 January 1798, *Porcupine's Gazette* 13 January 1798.

44. "More than one hundred": Catharine Van Cortlandt Mathews, *Andrew Ellicott: His Life and Letters* (New York, 1908), 34. "Peevishness" and "blind and deaf": *Porcupine's Gazette* 13 January 1798.

45. *DGW*, 4:12.

46. Thomas Cresap corresponded with GW in 1775 about a controversy over his brother Lawrence's lands on the North Branch of the Potomac, for which see TC to GW, Oldtown, 21 March 1775, *PGW:C*, 10:306.

47. Cook, *Washington's Western Lands*, 93; *DGW*, 4:17-18.

48. Gregory Evans Dowd, *A Spirited Resistance: The North American Indian Struggle for Unity, 1745–1815* (Baltimore, 1992), 103–9; Sugden, *Blue Jacket*, 128–41.

49. Legion: Colin G. Calloway, *The Indian World of George Washington: The First President, the First Americans, and the Birth of the Nation* (New York, 2018), 433–35. Wayne: Hogeland, *Autumn of the Black Snake*, 185–202. "Nothing more": Jefferson, "Memorandum of Consultation on Indian Affairs, 9 March 1792, *PTJ*, 23:242.

50. War post: Kent and Deardorff, "Adlum on the Allegheny: Part 2," 450–51. Cornplanter and other Seneca Chiefs to GW, 1 December 1790, Jack Warren, ed., *Papers of George Washington: Presidential Series* (Charlottesville, VA, 1998), 7:7. Cornplanter at Stanwix: Taylor, *Divided Ground*, 246–48; Calloway, *Indian World of George Washington*, 400–404. "Town Destroyer": Thomas S. Abler, ed., *Chainbreaker: The Revolutionary War Memoirs of Governor Blacksnake* (Lincoln, NE, 1989), 250–55.

51. Kent and Deardorff, "Adlum on the Allegheny: Part 2," 452.

52. Kent and Deardorff, "Adlum on the Allegheny: Part 2," 469, 470.

53. Kent and Deardorff, "Adlum on the Allegheny: Part 2," 470, 471.

CHAPTER 11. THE PERSISTENT WHISPER

1. Robert H. Berkhofer Jr., *The White Man's Indian: Images of the American Indian from Columbus to the Present* (New York, 1978); Brian W. Dippie, *The Vanishing American: White Attitudes and U.S. Indian Policy* (Middletown, CT, 1982); Roy Harvey Pearce, *Savagism and Civilization: A Study of the Indian and the American Mind* (Berkeley, 1989); Jill Lepore, *The Name of War: King Philip's War and the Origins of American Identity* (New York, 1998); Philip J. Deloria, *Playing Indian* (New Haven, 1998); Gordon M. Sayre, *The Indian Chief as Tragic Hero: Native Resistance and the Literatures of America from Moctezuma to Tecumseh* (Chapel Hill, NC, 2005).

2. Henry Nash Smith, *Virgin Land: The American West as Symbol and Myth* (Cambridge, MA, 1950); Roderick Nash, *Wilderness and the American Mind* (New Haven, CT, 1967); Richard Slotkin, *Regeneration through Violence: The Mythology of the American Frontier, 1600–1860* (Middletown, CT, 1973); John Mack Faragher, *Daniel Boone: The Life and Legend of an American Pioneer* (New York, 1992).

3. Michael Kranish, *Flight from Monticello: Thomas Jefferson at War* (New York, 2010), 297.

4. *Notes*, xi.

5. *Notes*, 10.

6. Thomas Jefferson, *Notes on the State of Virginia*, David Waldstreicher, ed. (Boston, 2002), 25.

7. "Natural republicans": Peter S. Onuf, *Jefferson's Empire: The Language of American Nationhood* (Charlottesville, VA, 2000), 19. "Eminence in oratory": *Notes*, 62. James A. Bear Jr. and Lucia C. Stanton, eds., *Jefferson's Memorandum Books: Accounts, with Legal Records and Miscellany, 1767–1826* (Princeton, NJ, 1997), 1: 1385–86.

8. Text of lament and TJ's introduction: *Notes*, 62–63. "Before we condemn": Thomas Jefferson, *Notes on the State of Virginia* (London, 1787), 104–6.

9. TJ to John Henry, Philadelphia, 31 December 1797, *PTJ*, 29: 600–601.

10. Annette Gordon-Reed and Peter S. Onuf, *"Most Blessed of the Patriarchs": Thomas Jefferson and the Empire of the Imagination* (New York, 2016), 83–92.

11. "Levelled up": Gordon-Reed and Onuf, *"Most Blessed,"* 85. "Labor in the Earth": *Notes*, 164–65.

12. Douglas L. Wilson, "The Evolution of Jefferson's *Notes on the State of Virginia*," *VMHB* 112 (2004): 98–133. Logan's speech and Jefferson's introduction from *Notes* appeared in the *Vermont Journal* (Windsor) on 7 June 1785, very soon after Jefferson had sent his first printed copies from France. Publication history: Dorothy Medlin, "Thomas Jefferson, André Morellet, and the French Version of *Notes on the State of Virginia*," *WMQ* 35 (January 1978): 85–99.

13. TJ to John Stockdale, Paris, 1 February 1787, *PTJ*, 8:107. Barlow to TJ, Hartford, 15 June 1787, *PTJ*, 11:473. Starting in late April 1787, printers Josiah Meigs and Eleutheros Dana began publishing excerpts of the *Notes* (they claimed when they began it was "a work never yet published") in their *New-Haven Gazette and Connecticut Magazine*. Logan's Lament ran on 3 May 1787. *The Annual Register, or a View of the History, Politics, and Literature for the Year 1787* (London, 1789), 151. *Universal Magazine of Knowledge and Pleasure* (London, 1788), 181–82; *English Review*, vol. 11 (London, 1788), 133–34; *Historical Magazine* (London, 1789), 422–23; *Encyclopedia Britannica*, Dublin edition (1791) 1:561, Edinburgh edition (1797) 1:561. It continued into the 4th edition (1810) 2:24 and 5th edition (1817) 2:24. Noah Webster, "Elo-

quence of the Natives of This Country," *American Magazine* no. 2 (January 1788): 106–8. John Lendrum, *A Concise and Impartial History of the American Revolution* (Boston, 1795), 75–76.

14. Jedidiah Morse, *The American Geography; Or a View of the Present Situation of the United States of America* (Elizabethtown, NJ, 1789), 18–19; William Guthrie and John Knox, *A New System of Modern Geography, Or a Geographical, Historical, and Commercial Grammar; and Present State of Several Nations of the World* (Philadelphia, 1795), 220; William Winterbotham, *An Historical, Geographical, Commercial, and Philosophical View of the United States of America . . .* (New York, 1795), 132–34.

15. David Blight, introduction to *The Columbian Orator*, bicentennial ed. (New York, 1998), xvii; sales statistics from Lillian O. Rosenfield, "Caleb Bingham, 1757–1817," unpublished paper written at the Library science School, Simmons College, January 1854, p. 18, copy in American Antiquarian Society, Worcester, MA. Caleb Bingham, *The American Preceptor* (New York: Isaiah Thomas and E. T. Andrews, 1795), 35–36. Later editions: *American Preceptor* 32nd ed. (Boston, 1807), 63; *American Preceptor*, 42nd ed. (Boston, 1811), 35–36; *American Preceptor Improved*, 11th New York ed. (New York, 1820), 35–36; *American Preceptor Improved* 66th (Sixth Improved) ed. (Rochester, 1826), 35–36.

16. For more on Cresap's grave marker, see Francis Zumbrun, "The Colonel Thomas Cresap Standing Stone Project," *Mid-Maryland: A Crossroads of History*, Michael A. Powell and Bruce A. Thompson, eds. (Charleston, SC, 2005), 145–52.

17. Thomas Cresap will in Joseph Ord Cresap and Bernard Cresap, *History of the Cresaps*, rev. ed. (Gallatin, TN, 1987), 117.

18. Martin at Constitutional Convention and after: Pauline Maier, *Ratification: The People Debate the Constitution, 1787–1788* (New York, 2010), 90–1; 430–32. "Monarchical nature": Luther Martin, "The Genuine Information II," *Maryland Gazette* (Baltimore), 1 January 1788.

19. *Porcupine's Gazette* 3 April 1797.

20. The family details (i.e., the birth order of the girls and their ages) are not completely clear. For the best estimate, see Clarkson and Jett, *Luther Martin of Maryland*, 57, and Charlene Boyer Lewis, "Modern Gratitude: Patriarchy, Romance, and Recrimination in the Early Republic," *Journal of the Early Republic* 39 (Spring 2019): 35.

21. *Philadelphia Inquirer* 1 March 1797.

22. Luther Martin, "To the Editor of the Porcupine Gazette," 30 March 1797, *Porcupine's Gazette*, 3 April 1797.

23. *Porcupine's Gazette* 3 April 1797. By "Caffree of Africa," Martin meant "kaffir," a word in the 18th century to describe someone indigenous to southern Africa, but one that has become a derogatory and offensive slang term since. See "Kaffir, n. and adj." *OED Online*. Oxford University Press. Accessed 27 June 2022.

24. James Fennell, "To the Editor of Porcupine's Gazette," 3 April 1797, *Porcupine's Gazette*, 5 April 1797.

25. Cobbett: Richard N. Rosenfeld, *American Aurora: A Democratic-Republican Returns: The Suppressed History of our Nation's Beginnings and the Heroic Newspaper that Tried to Report It* (New York, 1997), 23–25. Jefferson later explained that he saw it "in the Baltimore paper," which was *Federal Gazette & Baltimore Daily Advertiser*, 10 April 1797; TJ to John Henry, Philadelphia, 31 December 1797, *PTJ*, 29:600–04. "Drunkenness": Peregrine Fitzhugh to TJ, Washington County, Md., 20 June 1797, *PTJ*, 29:444. Bothered him: TJ to Peregrine Fitzhugh, Philadelphia, 4 June 1797, *PTJ*, 29:417.

26. TJ to John Gibson, Philadelphia, 31 May 1797, *PTJ*, 29:408–10. Jefferson and Gibson exchanged several letters after the first: Gibson to TJ, Pittsburgh, 17 June 1797, *PTJ*, 29:440–41; TJ to Gibson, Philadelphia, 24 June 1797, *PTJ*, 29:451; TJ to Gibson, Philadelphia, 31 December 1797, *PTJ*, 29:599–600.

27. Luther Martin, "To the honorable Thomas Jefferson, Esq., Vice President of the United States," Baltimore, 24 June 1797, *Porcupine's Gazette* 17 July 1797. Also in *Federal Gazette & Baltimore Daily Advertiser*, 22 July 1797, *Federal Gazette & Daily Advertiser* (Boston) 19 January 1798.

28. Luther Martin, "To the Hon. Thomas Jefferson," Baltimore, 11 December 1797, *Porcupine's Gazette* 14 December 1797. Also in *Salem Gazette* 29 December 1797.

29. TJ to Henry, *PTJ*, 29:600–604.

30. TJ to John Page, Philadelphia, 1 January 1798, *PTJ*, 30:7. The following day Jefferson wrote to John's brother Mann Page asking him the same thing. TJ to Mann Page, Philadelphia, 2 January 1798, *PTJ*, 30:83.

31. Luther Martin, "To the Honorable Thomas Jefferson, Esq., Vice President of the United States," 1 January 1798, *Porcupine's Gazette* 4 January 1798.

32. Luther Martin, "To the Honorable Thomas Jefferson, Esq., Vice-President of the United States," Baltimore, 14 January 1798, *Porcupine's Gazette*, 20 January 1798. The three letters defending TC were: *Porcupine's Gazette* 4, 13, and 20 January 1798. Michael's son James was a likely conduit of information for Martin. James had attended Princeton in the early 1790s (a departure for the Cresaps that probably stemmed from their connection to Martin, a heralded alumnus), but had barely graduated. He had gotten into fights, got caught being drunken and disorderly, and was once briefly expelled. After graduating he stayed in close contact with Martin even after his sister Maria's death, a connection that almost landed him in a duel in 1802 over a different family dispute that Martin made public. See "James Cresap," J. Jefferson Looney and Ruth L. Woodward, *Princetonians, 1791–1794: A Biographical Dictionary* (Princeton, 1991), 352–55; Lewis, "Modern Gratitude," 27–56. Michael's former clerk John Jeremiah Jacob later said he helped provide Martin with evidence.

33. Luther Martin, "To the Honorable Thomas Jefferson, Esq., Vice-President of the United States," Baltimore, 3 February 1798, *Porcupine's Gazette* 8 February 1798.

34. Luther Martin, "To the Honorable Thomas Jefferson, Esq., Vice-President of the United States," Baltimore, 14 February 1798, *Porcupine's Gazette* 20 February 1798.

35. Luther Martin, "To the Honorable Thomas Jefferson, Esq., Vice-President of the United States," Baltimore, 26 February 1798, *Porcupine's Gazette* 3 March 1798.

36. *Porcupine's Gazette* 3 March 1798. Pause was the operative word, for Martin did not stop trying to clear his in-laws' name, as evidenced by John Gibson reporting to TJ in March 1800 that he had received a letter from LM with a list of queries. Gibson thought Martin was "fully convinced he is actuated by party Spirit," and did not reply, forwarding a copy of the letter on to TJ. John Gibson to TJ, Pittsburgh, 14 March 1800, *PTJ*, 31:435.

37. *Porcupine's Gazette* 10 March 1798.

38. David Redick to TJ, Washington, Pa., 19 April 1798, *PTJ*, 30:285–86; David Redick to John Fenno, Philadelphia, 29 March 1798, *PTJ*, 30:286. TJ to John Page, Philadelphia, 6 June 1798, *PTJ*, 30:392.

39. Stevens Thomson Mason's copy of Logan's speech, 20 January 1798, *PTJ*, 30:38; Notes on a Conversation with Uriah Springer, 20 January 1798, *PTJ*, 30:39; Mann Page to TJ, Mansfield, Va., 13 February 1798, containing a statement from John Anderson and Hugh Mercer's copy of Logan's speech, *PTJ*, 30:101–3. TJ to John Heckewelder, Philadelphia, 11 April 1798, *PTJ*, 30:264–65. For Madison's role in the Logan episode, see Irving Brant, *James Madison: The Virginia Revolutionist* (Indianapolis, 1941), 281–91.

40. Thomas Jefferson, *An Appendix to the Notes on Virginia: Relative to the Murder of Logan's Family* (Philadelphia, 1800). Eventually the appendix would get a bit longer. One final testimony, a statement from John Sappington, one of the actual perpetrators of the Yellow Creek massacre, arrived just after Jefferson posted the manuscript to Smith. Jefferson thought it too important not to include it so, in all future printings, Sappington's testimony was tacked to the end as a fifteenth document. "Recipients of Appendix to the Notes on the State of Virginia," [c. April 1800], *PTJ*, 31:551–54.

41. On Michael firing on canoes: Statement of Ebenezer Zane, *Notes*, 235–36. On the trap at Baker's Bottom see the testimony provided by Anderson, Chambers, Innes, Polke, and Sappington, *Notes*, 238–42, 255–58. On Koonay: Statement of William Robinson, *Notes*, 242–44.

42. Declaration of John Heckewelder, *Notes*, 246–50, quote on 248.

43. *Notes*, 249, 250.

44. Jefferson summary, *Notes*, 250–54, quotes on 253. Revised text: *Notes*, 62.

45. Bingham's *Preceptors* did revise the introduction to reflect Jefferson's changes. The 4th (1802) and 5th (1805) editions of Jedidiah Morse's *American Universal Geography* still maintained the original language, as did a new edition of Noah Webster, *An American Selection of Lessons in Reading and Speaking . . . A New Edition* (New Haven, CT, 1804), 63. Benjamin Banneker to TJ, 19 August 1791, *PTJ*, 22:49–54.

46. TJ to George Hay, Washington, 19 June 1807, *Founders Online,* National Archives, https://founders.archives.gov/documents/Jefferson/99-01-02-5779. End of Martin's life: Clarkson and Jett, *Luther Martin of Maryland*, 302.

47. In the late 1800s, the city turned the St. John Burying Ground into a park, known today as James J. Walker Park in Greenwich Village.

48. Readers that used original *Notes*: Albert Picket, *The Juvenile Mentor No. 3* (New York, 1813), 85, also in 1818 and 1826 editions; John J. Harrod, *The Academical Reader* (Baltimore, 1831), 140; Noah Webster, *Instructive and Entertaining Lessons for Youth* (New Haven, CT, 1835), 87–88. Readers that used the post-1800 language in *Notes*: John Pierpont, *The National Reader* (Boston, 1827), 35–36, also in 1829 and 1832 editions; George B. Cheever, *American Common-Place Book of Prose* (Boston, 1832), 74–75; Lyman Cobb, *Cobb's New Sequel to the Juvenile Readers* (New York, 1843), 194–99; *The Southern Reader and Speaker* (Charleston, SC, 1850), 254–55; and Charles Northend, *The American Speaker* (New York, 1852), 109–10. Two books that didn't use Jefferson were Increase Cooke, *Introduction to The American Orator* (New Haven, CT, 1812), 241, and Charles D. Cleveland, *The National Orator* (New York, 1832), 245.

49. For more on the impact and importance of the McGuffey readers, see Elliott J. Gorn's introduction in *The McGuffey Readers: Selections from the 1879 Edition* (New York, 1998), 1–36; Johann N. Neem, "The Strange Afterlife of William McGuffey and His Readers," *Hedgehog Review* (Summer 2018); Jess McHugh, *Americanon: An Unexpected U.S. History in Thirteen Bestselling Books* (New York, 2021), 114–44. Logan's speech first appeared in *McGuffey's Eclectic Fourth Reader* (Cincinnati, 1838), 82–83, and continued to be in editions in 1844, 1848, and 1853. It was also in *McGuffey's Fifth Eclectic Reader* (New York, 1866), 121–22; and *McGuffey's New Juvenile Speaker* (New York, 1866), 324 (the speech only without Jefferson). On the centennial anniversary of the original publication, Henry Ford—who was a huge fan of the *Readers* and even paid for the western Pennsylvania cabin McGuffey was born in to be transported and rebuilt at Ford's Greenfield Village—sponsored a collection of 150 "greatest hits" from the series, which included Logan's Lament. See Harvey Minnich, ed., *Old Favorites from the McGuffey Readers* (New York, 1936), 340–41. "Millions of declamations": *Butler Weekly Times* (Butler, MS) 31 January 1883; *Indianapolis Journal* 10 February 1886.

50. Novels: John Neal, *Logan: A Family History* 2 vols. (Philadelphia, 1822). For analysis of this novel, see Dana D. Nelson, *National Manhood: Capitalist Citizenship and the Imagined Fraternity of White Men* (Durham, NC, 1998), 88–101, and Sayre, *Indian Chief as Tragic Hero*, 197–202. Plays: John Doddridge, *Logan: The Last of the Race of Shickellemus, a Dramatic Piece* (Cincinnati, 1868). For background on Doddridge see Samuel J. Richards, "The East-West Divide and Frontier Efforts of the Reverend Dr. Joseph Doddridge," *Pennsylvania History* 85 (Autumn 2018): 460–87. Songs: Mary O. Eddy, ed., *Ballads and Songs from Ohio* (Hatboro, PA, 1964 [1939]), 254–56; Anne Grimes, "Logan's Lament," *Ohio State Ballads*, Folkways Records, 1957, FH 5217. Poems: "Logan, the Indian," *The Plough Boy, and Journal of the Board of Agriculture*, vol. 4, no. 4 (Albany, 1822): 32; "Logan's Lament," *The New Jersey Monthly Magazine* (April 1825): 31; "Logan's Lament," *The Ladies' Literary Portfolio*, vol. 1, no. 24 (Philadelphia, 1829): 191; Adam Kidd, *The Huron Chief, and Other Poems* (Montreal, 1830); Jane Locke, "Logan," *Atkinson's Casket*, vol. 7 (Philadelphia, 1832), 172–73; "The Last of a Race," *Ladies Repository, and Gatherings of the West*, vol. 1 (Cincinnati, 1841): 244.

51. Washington Irving, "Traits of Indian Character," James W. Tuttleton, ed., *Washington Irving: History, Tales, and Sketches* (New York, 1983), 1002–12, quotes on 1002. Samuel G. Drake, *Indian Biography: Containing the Lives of More than Two Hundred Indian Chiefs . . .* (Boston, 1832), 160–64; Samuel G. Drake, *The Book of the Indians of North America . . .* (Boston, 1833), "very

favorable reception": preface; Logan material: book 5, pp. 26–28. Sayre, *Indian Chief as Tragic Hero*, 11–13. Others would try to profit from this expanding market, publishing more books on Native history that always included Logan, which were often very closely lifted from one another, for which see James Wimer, *Events in Indian History* (Lancaster, PA, 1841), 301–11.

52. Jacob, *Biographical Sketch of Captain Michael Cresap*, 12. John Jeremiah Jacob, in "Biographical Dictionary of Maryland Legislators, 1635–1789," *MdA*, 426:480–81.

53. "Lately fallen" and "memorandum": Jacob, *Life of Michael Cresap*, 8. "Blotted": Joseph Doddridge, *Notes on the Settlement and Indian Wars of the Western Parts of Virginia and Pennsylvania from the year 1763 to the year 1783* (Wellsburg, VA, 1824), 225.

54. Jacob, *Life of Michael Cresap*, 133–44. "Monster": ibid., 26.

55. William B. Hesseltine, *Pioneer's Mission: The Story of Lyman C. Draper* (Madison, WI, 1954), 53.

56. Jonathan S. Williams, "The Logan Historical Society," *American Pioneer* (Chillicothe, OH, 1842), 1:5–6.

57. Williams, "Logan Historical Society," 1:5.

58. See John Williams, "Editorial Finale," *American Pioneer*, vol. 1 no. 12 (December 1842): 439–40.

59. Rueben Gold Thwaites, *Lyman Copeland Draper: A Memoir* (Madison, WI, 1892), 5. Reprinted from *Wisconsin Historical Collections*, vol. 12; Hesseltine, *Pioneer's Mission*, 53.

60. Jerry E. Patterson, "Brantz Mayer, Man of Letters," *Maryland Historical Magazine* 52 (December 1957): 275–89. Brantz Mayer to James Fenimore Cooper, Baltimore, 2 July 1851, quoted in ibid., 284–85.

61. Draper's letter to Mayer cited in Brantz Mayer, *Tah-Gah-Jute; Or Logan and Captain Michael Cresap*, (Baltimore, 1851), 68n. "Very bad Indian": ibid., 32n.

62. Mayer, *Tah-Gah-Jute*, 67–68n.

63. Mayer, *Tah-Gah-Jute*, 52, 53, 55.

64. Mayer, *Tah-Gah-Jute*, 61, 69. Charles Sumner to Brantz Mayer, Boston, 9 July 1851, in Joseph Ord Cresap and Bernard Cresap, *History of the Cresaps*, rev. ed. (Gallatin, TN, 1987), 124–25.

65. Brantz Mayer, *Tah-Gah-Jute; Or Logan and Cresap, an Historical Essay* (Albany, 1867), v, 12.

66. Mayer, *Tah-Gah-Jute*, 10.

67. Lydia Howard Huntley Sigourney, *Letters to Young Ladies* (New York, 1840), 35; William Bromwell, *Locomotive Sketches, with Pen and Pencil, or, Hints and Suggestions to the Tourist Over the Great Central Route from Philadelphia to Pittsburgh* (Philadelphia, 1854), 94–97. Edward Deering Mansfield, *The Ohio Railroad Guide, Illustrated* (Columbus, 1854), 46–51, quote on 46. Van Buren: *Southern Banner* (Athens, GA) 10 May 1839. Douglass: "North Side of Douglasism," *Chicago Press & Tribune*, 16 December 1859. "Weep for Blaine": *The Daily Evening Democrat* (Shelbyville, IN) 21 November 1884.

68. Mayer, *Tah-Gah-Jute*, 10.

69. Carolyn Eastman, *A Nation of Speechifiers: Making an American Public after the Revolution* (Chicago, 2009), 109.

70. Claudio Saunt, *Unworthy Republic: The Dispossession of Native Americans and the Road to Indian Territory* (New York, 2020), 110–24, quote on 118.

71. Saunt, *Unworthy Republic*, 91, 136–40; "plan of operations": 141. Samantha Seeley, *Race, Removal and the Right to Remain: Migration and the Making of the United States* (Chapel Hill, NC, 2021), 289.

72. *Minutes of the Presbytery of Redstone of the Presbyterian Church of the USA, 1781–1831* (Cincinnati, OH, 1878), 53. For more on Gibson's mixed-race relations, see Gary S. Williams, *"No Man Knows This Country Better": The Frontier Life of John Gibson* (Akron, OH, 2022), 77.

73. For this phenomenon in relation to the changing attitudes toward King Philip (Metacom), see Lepore, *The Name of War*, 191–226. See also Sayre, *Indian Chief as Tragic Hero*, passim.

CONCLUSION. DARKNESS WAS HERE YESTERDAY

1. The monument is depicted in figure 21.

2. May Lowe, "Dedication of the Logan Elm," *Ohio History* 22 (1912): 267–307, quote on 284.

3. Lowe, "Dedication of the Logan Elm," 288, 289. "Pioneer meetings": "Under the Spreading, Defiant Logan Elm: An All Day Pioneer Meeting on Historic Grounds, September 13, 1917," *Chillicothe Gazette* 1 September 1917, p. 8.

4. "A Plea for Some Memorial to Logan, Mingo Chief," *Chillicothe Gazette* 22 November 1916, p. 2. "Logan Elm Park and the Cresap Monument," *Circleville Daily Herald* 31 January 1919. "Dedication of Monument to Indian Chief Logan, Oct. 10th," *Chillicothe Gazette* 3 October 1919, p. 10.

5. *The Cresap Society Meeting at Cumberland, Maryland, June 24, 1919* (Columbus, OH, 1919).

6. Run via the "Western Newspaper Union," the "Stories of Great Indians" series by author Elmo Scott Watson ran throughout the early 1920s. For an example, see Logan's story in *Pocahontas Record* (Pocahontas, IO) 6 April 1922 and *Osceola Record* (Osceola, NE) 6 April 1922. "Tales of the Chiefs," by Edith L. Watson; Logan in *Shiner Gazette* 15 September 1932. "True Stories of Some Bad Indians," *Baltimore Sun* 18 April 1909; "American Indian Day" series featured Logan on 15 September 1932 all over the United States, from Utah to New Jersey. For an example, see *Anita Tribune* (Anita, IO) 15 September 1932.

7. "A number of historians" in "Smallest School in State is on Indian Reservation," *Altoona Tribune* (Altoona, PA) 29 November 1921.

8. Anthony F.C. Wallace, *The Death and Rebirth of the Seneca* (New York, 1970), 184–85.

9. Jeannette E. Sherman, "A Visit to Cornplanter's Grave," *Buffalo Morning Express and Illustrated Buffalo Express* 29 August 1915, p. 9. "A number of historians": "Smallest School in State is on Indian Reservation," *Altoona Tribune* 29 November 1921.

10. "Statement of Jesse Logan, Aged 106 Years," in Henry W. Shoemaker, *Captain Logan: Blair County's Indian Chief* (Altoona, 1915), 39, 40. Jesse Logan obituary, *Altoona Tribune*, 23 February 1916, p. 12. Many years later, another newspaper reporter checked up on Jesse's facts, and asked an authority from the Seneca Reservation to double-check his memory. That person believed Jesse was not born in 1809 but rather in 1827. In a census taken in 1916, his age listed at death was recorded at 89. This, therefore, shakes a bit of his story: if Tachnedorus died in 1820, then Jesse did not meet him, let alone learn to hunt from him. "Mystery solved," *The Daily Item* (Sunbury, PA), 25 September 1982, p. 5.

11. "Logan Elm Falls: High Wind Hit Recreation Center; Damage is Heavy," *Circleville Herald* 16 May 1961; "Who Laments Logan?" *Chicago Tribune* 20 May 1961; "Historic Tree Injured," *Alamogordo Daily News* (Alamogordo, NM) 5 June 1961.

12. Joseph Conrad, *Heart of Darkness* (New York, 1999 [1902]), 6.

13. Conrad, *Heart of Darkness*, 6.

14. Conrad, *Heart of Darkness*, 4.

APPENDIX. THE LOGAN PROBLEM

1. Franklin Dexter, ed., *Diary of David McClure: Doctor of Divinity, 1748–1820* (New York, 1899), 57. "Most martial": *Pittsburg Daily American* 17 and 21 March 1842, reprinted in Sherman Day, *Historical Collections of the State of Pennsylvania* (Philadelphia, 1843), 467. Italics in original. "Remarkable tall man": Archibald Loudon, *A Selection of the Most Interesting Narratives of Outrages Committed by the Indians in their Wars with the White People* 2 vols (Carlisle, PA, 1811), 2:214–15.

2. Brant Mayer, *Tah-Gah-Jute: Or, Logan and Cresap* (Albany, 1867), 59. Lyman Draper, "Logan—the Mingo Chief," *Ohio History Journal* 20 (April 1911): 137–75, quote on 167. Theodore Roosevelt, *The Winning of the West* (New York, 1889), 1:203–4. Franklin B. Sawvel, *Logan the Mingo* (Boston, 1921), 67.

3. *MPCP*, 7:52.

4. Reverend John Heckewelder statement, *Notes*, 249.

5. Brantz Mayer, *Tah-Gah-Jute: Or Logan and Captain Michael Cresap, a Discourse by Brantz Mayer* (Baltimore, 1851), 3, 32n., 59n1. *Appleton's Encyclopedia* (1887), 4:4–5, says Tah-gah-jute.

6. Charles Hanna, *The Wilderness Trail* (1901), 1:381n3. Thomas K. Donnalley, ed., *Hand Book of Tribal Names of Pennsylvania, Together with the Signification of Indian Words* (Philadelphia, 1908),

10. Donnalley says that "Taghneghdoarus" means "a small stream," and is one of Shickellamy's sons. No mention of his individuality can be found." P. 41. Shoemaker, *Captain Logan*, 8–9; Sawvel, *Logan the Mingo*, 14; C. Hale Sipe, *Fort Ligonier and its Times* (Harrisburg, PA, 1932), 288; Harry E. Swanger, "The Logans, Sons of Shickellamy," *Proceedings of the Northumberland County Historical Society* 17 (1949): 1–39; Grace Stevenson Haber, *With Pipe and Tomahawk: The Story of Logan, the Mingo Chief* (New York, 1958), 10. All four said Shickellamy's second son and "his eyelashes stick out."

7. *Twenty-First Annual Report of the American Scenic and Historic Preservation Society, 1916* (Albany, 1916), 415. W[illiam] M[artin] Beauchamp, "Shikellamy and His Son Logan," *Twenty-First Annual Report of the American Scenic and Historic Preservation Society, 1916* (Albany, 1916), 601–11, quote on 610.

8. Draper, "Logan—the Mingo Chief," quote on 138–39. Draper identified James Logan as Soyechtowa (calling him Say-ugh-towa) and not Tah-gah-jute. "Logan—the Mingo Chief" was chapter twelve of a book Draper wrote in collaboration with Conrad Butterfield but never published, titled "Border Forays and Adventures." The original mss. of the chapter is in the Draper Manuscripts 2D-72-127, Historical Society of Wisconsin. Draper's naming of John/Tachnedorus is on 2D-75.

9. "Chief Logan": Thomas Perkins Abernathy, *Western Lands and the American Revolution* (Charlottesville, VA, 1937), 106; "famous Mingo Chief Logan": Albert T. Volwiler, *George Croghan and the Westward Movement, 1741–1826* (Cleveland, OH, 1926), 303; "celebrated chief and orator": Randolph C. Downes, *Council Fires on the Upper Ohio: A Narrative of Indian Affairs in the Upper Ohio Valley until 1795* (Pittsburgh, 1940), 162.

10. Paul A. Wallace, "Logan the Mingo: A Problem of Identification," *Pennsylvania Archaeologist* 32 (1962): 91–96.

11. *MPCP*, 7:52.

12. Richard White, *The Middle Ground: Indians, Empires, and Republics in the Great Lakes Region, 1650–1815* (Cambridge, 1991), 314; R. Douglas Hurt, *The Ohio Frontier: Crucible of the Old Northwest, 1720–1830* (Bloomington, IN, 1996), 57–59; Eric Hinderaker, *Elusive Empires: Constructing Colonialism in the Ohio Valley, 1673–1800* (Cambridge, 1997), 191; Gordon M. Sayre, *The Indian Chief as Tragic Hero: Native Resistance and the Literature of America, From Moctezuma to Tecumseh* (Chapel Hill, NC, 2005), 182; Patrick Griffin, *American Leviathan: Empire, Nation, and Revolutionary Frontier* (New York, 2007), 109; Michael McDonnell, *Masters of Empire: Great Lakes Indians and the Making of America* (New York, 2015), 274; Rob Harper, *Unsettling the West: Violence and State Building in the Ohio Valley* (Philadelphia, 2018), 55.

13. Francis Jennings, "James Logan," in John A. Garraty and Marc C. Carnes, eds. *American National Biography*, vol. 13 (New York, 1999), 836–37. Only the recent Daniel Boone biographers have used the name Tah-gah-jute. See John Mack Faragher, *Daniel Boone: The Life and Legend of an American Pioneer* (New York, 1992), 103; Michael A. Lofaro, *Daniel Boone: An American Life* (Lexington, KY, 2003), 45; Meredith Mason Brown, *Frontiersman: Daniel Boone and the Making of America* (Baton Rouge, 2008), 58. Soyechtowa James H. Merrell, *Into the American Woods: Negotiators on the Pennsylvania Frontier* (New York, 1999), 314; Edward G. Gray, "The Making of Logan, the Mingo Orator," in Edward G. Gray and Norman Fiering, eds., *The Language Encounter in the Americas, 1492–1800* (New York, 2000), 256–278; John Corbett David, *Dunmore's New World: The Extraordinary Life of a Royal Governor in Revolutionary America* (Charlottesville, VA, 2013), 77; Ian K. Steele, *Setting All the Captives Free: Capture, Adjustment, and Recollection in Allegheny County* (Montreal, 2013), 377; Glenn F. Williams, *Dunmore's War: The Last Conflict of America's Colonial Era* (Yardley, PA, 2017), 70; the editors of *PTJ*, 29:409n.

14. Michael N. McConnell, *A Country Between: The Upper Ohio Valley and its Peoples, 1724–1774* (Lincoln, NE, 1992), 275; Anthony F. C. Wallace, *Jefferson and the Indians: The Tragic Fate of the First Americans* (Cambridge, MA, 1999), 5; Larry L. Nelson, *A Man of Distinction: Alexander McKee and the Ohio Country Frontier, 1754–1799* (Kent, OH, 1999), 78; Woody Holton, *Forced Founders: Indians, Debtors, Slaves, and the Making of the American Revolution in Virginia*

(Chapel Hill, NC, 1999), 33; John Sugden, *Blue Jacket: Warrior of the Shawnees* (Lincoln, NE, 2000), 40; Daniel K. Richter, *Facing East from Indian Country: A Native History of Early America* (Cambridge, MA, 2001), 213; Gary B. Nash, *The Unknown American Revolution: The Unruly Birth of Democracy and the Struggle to Create America* (New York, 2005), 167; Daniel Barr, *A Colony Sprung from Hell* (Kent, OH., 2014), 158; Colin G. Calloway, *The Indian World of George Washington: The First President, the First Americans, and the Birth of the Nation* (New York, 2018), 207; Judith Ridner, "Archibald Loudon and the Politics of Indian-Hating," *Early American Studies* 19 (Summer 2021): 561. In his most recent book, Woody Holton has it both ways, referring to Logan as John but identifying him as "Tahgahjute or Tachnedorus" in *Liberty Is Sweet: A Hidden History of the American Revolution* (New York, 2021), 134. In this book, too, Holton continues to circulate the mistake he made in *Forced Founders* that Logan was half-French, which has influenced other writers (Nash) into perpetuating the error.

15. "Statement of Jesse Logan, Aged 106 Years," Shoemaker, *Captain Logan*, 38.

CREDITS

INDEX

Page numbers after 388 refer to notes.